By

William D. Black, M. D.

Published in the United States of America
By
The Tennessee Publishing House
Belle Arden Run
496 Mountain View Drive
Mosheim, Tennessee 37818-3524
Third Edition, May 2017

Cover Design by Kellie J. Warren

Disclaimer

This document is an original work of the author. It may include reference to information commonly known or freely available to the general public. Any resemblance to other published information is purely coincidental. The author has in no way attempted to use material not of his own origin unless such information has been cited, documented or given some other properly recognized written form of credit for such work. The Tennessee Publishing House disclaims any association with or responsibility for the ideas, opinions, or facts as expressed by the author of this book.

Any biblical scriptures used have been taken from the New Internal Version, copyright 1984, or sources listed in the Bibliography of this book with permission wherein necessary.

Printed in the United States of America
Cataloging-in-Publication
ISBN: 978-1-58275-327-0   Paperback Edition
Copyright January 2016 by William D. Black

Table of Contents

Dedication

This book is dedicated to my lovely wife, Kay, who stood by me during the malpractice suit and was with me in the courtroom throughout the trial experience. Her love and support were invaluable.

Introduction

As of this writing, I am a 73 year-old physician who practiced Nephrology in my hometown of Knoxville, TN for 32 years before retiring in 2010. I thought it was appropriate to give a little explanation about my experiences that have led to the writing of this book, about my anger and spiritual lessons learned through an encounter with America's legal system.

Several years ago, I had a patient who died shortly after arriving home from an outpatient hemodialysis procedure. She had been switched from peritoneal dialysis (PD) to hemodialysis a few weeks prior because of acute peritonitis related to an infection from her PD catheter. Because of the infection, her PD catheter had to be removed. When she was brought to the emergency room at another hospital, her serum potassium was low. The cardiologist who saw her told her husband that the low serum potassium was the cause of an arrhythmia and her sudden demise. A year later a lawsuit was filed, charging me with a wrongful death due to wrongly prescribed hemodialysis, dialysis without enough potassium in the dialysate.

The last time I had seen the patient was several days before her death. I had recommended hospitalization for the chronic peritonitis that was not getting any better. The patient was unable to eat, and her nutritional status was poor, which had contributed to her general decline in health. She looked me straight in the eye and said with great determination, "I'll be all right." I've heard that remark before. What it means is this: "I'll probably die, and I'm content with that.

3

I'm tired of life the way it is. I'd rather die than do as you recommend."

When the patient was taken to the other hospital her serum Albumin was very low and her serum phosphorus was less than 1 mg/dL, both signs of severe malnutrition, a much greater risk for death in dialysis patients than hypokalemia. Her blood urea nitrogen level was normal, a value that goes up in patients with kidney failure and when normal in dialysis patients, also a sign of severe malnutrition. For hypokalemia to be a risk factor for dialysis-induced arrhythmias, the rate of drop in serum potassium is as important as the actual level. After dialysis, the potassium is coming back out of the cells and the serum potassium is coming back up. Dialysis induced arrhythmias do not occur hours after the procedure.

My attorney knew about the conversation we had the last time I had seen the patient, but he didn't ask me about it while I was on the witness stand. There were a lot of other things he should have done but didn't. The plaintiff attorney spoke about some things I should have done for the patient. In retrospect, perhaps it would have been a good idea to do some of them, but not doing them was no violation of the standard of care. He also gave incorrect information about me. After the trial, I complained to my attorney about all the lies that were told. His response was something like this: "That's just what we do." In the courtroom, the attorneys are not under oath and do not have to tell the truth.

After the judgment went against me and the trial was over, I continued to be upset about the way I was treated. The insurance company was pleased about the relatively low dollar value of the settlement and thought it was too risky to file an appeal. For me, I was not happy. Certain thoughts or words would ignite rage. I say rage, because at times, my reaction was uncontrollable. The worst scenario would be if I tried to talk with someone about the case. I would spew out venom, and it would keep on coming. There were times when I couldn't control my mouth. I resolved to forgive the

4

individuals involved, but when certain events would come to mind, the rage returned. My mind would go first to one person or situation and then another. I knew it was harmful for me to be this way, but I didn't know how to handle it.

Finally, I decided to begin a more thorough study of what the Bible has to say about the issues. When I came to the subject of testing God, I realized that continued anger about something that was over and done with and couldn't be changed was rebellion against God. The idea of rebelling against God put fear in my heart, and I felt my spirit begin to submit. The door to my healing began to crack open.

Chapter One
Testing God

P eople have different responses when they face difficult circumstances; some are positive, but some are detrimental. We are told in Romans 14:23b that, "Everything that does not come from faith is sin." As we go through our own struggles, we should not put the Lord our God to the test the way the Israelites did in the desert (Deuteronomy 6:16). Moses led the children of Israel out of Egypt, but over the next two years, while they were sojourning in the desert, the Israelites tested God no fewer than ten times (Numbers 14:22). William MacDonald lists the ten occurrences in his *The Believer's Bible Commentary - Old Testament.* **(1)** The Hebrew word *nasa* means to test or try or tempt. In his *Theological Wordbook of the Old* Testament, Harris writes that when it comes to testing God the way the Israelites did in the desert, the word *nasa* carries the idea of having a defiant attitude. **(2)** If we look at what the Bible says about those ten incidents, we can get a better idea of what it means to test God.

1. After the Israelites initially left Egypt, they were camped by the Red Sea. When they realized the Egyptian army was approaching, they became frightened and began complaining (Exodus 14:10–12).

2. At Marah, the Israelites grumbled about the bitter water (Exodus 15:22–24). The word *marah* actually means "bitter."

3. In the Desert of Sin, they grumbled because they were hungry (Exodus 16:1–3).

4. When God sent manna, some of the Israelites disobeyed and kept it, during the week, overnight (Exodus 16:19, 20).

5. Some of the Israelites tried to gather manna on the Sabbath (Exodus 16:22–27).

6. At Rephidim, the Israelites quarreled with Moses because they were thirsty. They tested the Lord saying, "Is the Lord among us or not?" Moses called the place Massah which means "testing" and Meribah, which means "quarreling" (Exodus 17:1–7).

7. At Horeb, their impatience led to idolatry; God referred to them as a stiff-necked people. Aaron let them get out of control, and they were running wild (Exodus 32:1–35).

8. At Taberah, the Israelites complained because of hardship (Numbers 11:1–3).

9. At Kibroth Hattaavah, the Israelites complained because they were not satisfied with God's provision. They craved other food besides manna. They wanted meat. They rejected the Lord (Numbers 11:4–34).

10. At Kadesh, they grumbled. They lacked faith regarding God's ability to help them conquer the land of Canaan (Numbers 13, 14).

Many of these occurrences were first mentioned in the historical record, but they were also cited again, later in the Bible. There are references in books such as Exodus and Numbers but also in Psalms, Ezekiel, and in the New Testament. All these passages teach us the significance of the different ways the Israelites tested God. We are given examples of what we should not do.

These ten occurrences are highlighted in the Bible, but according to Psalms 95:7-11, Acts 13:18, and Hebrews 3:7-11, the Israelites tested God the whole forty years in the desert.

The ways the Israelites tested God during their wilderness wanderings.

1. The Israelites did not remember the great things the Lord had already done for them.

7

We have sinned, even as our fathers did; we have done wrong and acted wickedly. When our fathers were in Egypt, they gave no thought to your miracles; they did not remember your many kindnesses, and they rebelled by the sea, the Red Sea. Yet he saved them for his name's sake, to make his mighty power known. He rebuked the Red Sea, and it dried up; he led them through the depths as through a desert. He saved them from the hand of the foe; from the hand of the enemy he redeemed them. The waters covered their adversaries; not one of them survived. Then they believed his promises and sang his praise. But they soon forgot what he had done and did not wait for his counsel. In the desert they gave in to their craving; in the wasteland they put God to the test. So he gave them what they asked for, but sent a wasting disease upon them (Psalm 106:6-15).

2. The Israelites were not satisfied with the Lord's provision.

But they continued to sin against him, rebelling in the desert against the Most High. They willfully put God to the test by demanding the food they craved. They spoke against God, saying, "Can God spread a table in the desert? When he struck the rock, water gushed out, and streams flowed abundantly. But can he also give us food? Can he supply meat for his people?" When the Lord heard them, he was very angry; his fire broke out against Jacob, and his wrath rose against Israel, for they did not believe in God or trust in his deliverance. Yet he gave a command to the skies above and opened the doors of the heavens; he rained down manna for the people to eat, he gave them the grain of heaven. Men ate the bread of angels; he sent them all the food they could eat. He let loose the east wind from the heavens and led forth the south wind by his power. He rained meat down on them like dust, flying birds like sand on the seashore. He made them come down inside the camp, all around their tents. They ate till they had more than enough, for he had given them what they craved. But before they turned from the food they craved, even while it was still in their mouths, God's anger rose against them; he put to death the sturdiest among them, cutting down the young men of Israel (Psalm 78:17-31).

3. The Israelites lacked faith in God.

But they put God to the test and rebelled against the Most High; they did not keep his statutes. Like their fathers they were disloyal and faithless, as unreliable as a faulty bow (Psalm 78:56, 57).

4. The Israelites became impatient.

At Horeb: "When the people saw that Moses was so long in coming down from the mountain, they gathered around Aaron and said, 'Come, make us gods who will go before us. As for this fellow Moses who brought us up out of Egypt, we don't know what has happened to him'" (Exodus 32:1).

8

5. The Israelites demanded what they wanted.

They willfully put God to the test by demanding the food they craved (Psalm 78:18).

6. The Israelites spoke out against God.

They spoke against God, saying, "Can God spread a table in the desert?" (Psalm 78:19)

7. The Israelites grumbled and were disobedient.

Then they despised the pleasant land; they did not believe his promise. They grumbled in their tents and did not obey the Lord. So he swore to them with uplifted hand that he would make them fall in the desert, make their descendants fall among the nations and scatter them throughout the lands (Psalm 106:24-27).

The Hebrew word for murmur or grumble is *lun* or *lin*. Strong's Concordance says the verb means to stop (usually overnight) or by implication to stay permanently, (hence in a bad sense) to be obstinate. **(3)** According to R. Laird Harris in *Theological Wordbook of the Old Testament*, the word is used with the preposition 'al meaning against. The object of their [the Israelites'] verbal assaults is usually Moses and Aaron. At other times the Lord himself is the object of their abuse. "In the final analysis their murmuring was always against God who commissioned the leaders of the people. The murmuring, of course, was not without reason, namely, hunger or thirst in the desert, or an apparently unattainable goal. But they sinned because they doubted God and cast aspersion on his justice, goodness, and power...the verb means to express resentment, dissatisfaction, anger, and complaint by grumbling in half-muted tones of hostile opposition to God's leaders and the authority, which he has invested in them. The true nature of this murmuring is seen in the fact that it is an open act of rebellion against the Lord...and a stubborn refusal to believe God's word and God's miraculous works...Thus the right attitude in real difficulty is unconditional acceptance and obedience. God's own must never stand in judgment upon him." **(4)**

I note in Psalm 106:26, 27 that part of the reason for the eventual dispersion of the Israelites was because they tested God while they were in the desert.

8. The Israelites quarreled with Moses.

The whole Israelite community set out from the desert of Sin, traveling from place to place as the Lord commanded. They camped at Rephidim, but there was no water for the people to drink. So they quarreled with Moses and said, "Give us water to drink." Moses replied, "Why do you quarrel with me? Why do you put the Lord to the test?" (Exodus 17:1, 2)

9. The Israelites treated God with contempt.

The Lord replied [to Moses], "I have forgiven them, as you asked. Nevertheless, as surely as I live and as surely as the glory of the Lord fills the whole earth, not one of the men who saw my glory and the miraculous signs I performed in Egypt and in the desert but who disobeyed me and tested me ten times - not one of them will ever see the land I promised on oath to their forefathers. No one who has ever treated me with contempt will ever see it (Numbers 14:20-23).

10. The Israelites were stiff-necked.

"I have seen these people," the Lord said to Moses, "and they are a stiff-necked people. Now leave me alone so that my anger may burn against them and that I may destroy them" (Exodus 32:9,10a).

The English word stiff-necked is translated from two Hebrew words *qasha* and *orep*, used together. According to R. Laird Harris in *Theological Wordbook of the Old Testament*, the word *qasha* arose from an agricultural milieu. "It emphasizes, first, the subjective effect exerted by an overly heavy yoke, which is hard to bear, and secondarily, the rebellious resistance of oxen to the yoke...A frequent use of the word relates to the stubborn (stiff-necked) subjects of the Lord. Like rebellious oxen, calf-worshiping Israel quickly turned aside from the Lord's service...The spirit of Israel remained (for the most part) stubborn, intractable, and non-responsive to the guiding of their God." **(5)** We must remember,

10

however, that Christ's yoke is easy (Matthew 11:29, 30), although it does require submission and discipline.

Regarding *orep* he writes, "This anatomical term is often used metaphorically." It has been related to an Akkadian word meaning "neck" and an Arabian word meaning "mane of a horse, crest of a cock." "One can see the possible semantic development of "neck" to "stiffness, arrogance, recalcitrance, refractoriness." "Arrogance on the part of the vassal to the suzerain is a form of rebellion and treason." **(6)**

11. The Israelites rejected the Lord.

Tell the people: "Consecrate yourselves in preparation for tomorrow, when you will eat meat. The Lord heard you when you wailed, "If only we had meat to eat! We were better off in Egypt!" Now the Lord will give you meat, and you will eat it. You will not eat it for just one day, or two days, or five, ten or twenty days, but for a whole month - until it comes out of your nostrils and you loathe it - because you have rejected the Lord, who is among you, and have wailed before him, saying, "Why did we ever leave Egypt?" (Numbers 11:18-20)

12. The Israelites let their behavior get out of control.

At Horeb: "Moses saw that the people were running wild and that Aaron had let them get out of control and so become a laughingstock to their enemies." (Exodus 32:25)

13. The Israelites rebelled against the Lord.

But they [the Israelites] put God to the test and rebelled against the most high; they did not keep his statutes. (Psalm 78:56)

14. The Israelites were guilty of idolatry.

At Horeb they made a calf and worshipped an idol cast from metal. They exchanged their Glory for an image of a bull, which eats grass. They forgot the God who saved them, who had done great things in Egypt, miracles in the land of Ham and awesome deeds by the Red Sea. So he said he would destroy them - had

not Moses, his chosen one, stood in the breach before him to keep his wrath from destroying them. (Psalm 106:19-23)

All of these acts could be considered as various forms of rebellion. We are rebelling when we refuse to put our trust in and obey God, our Creator and Redeemer. Consider these words from the New Testament:

Now these things occurred as examples to keep us from setting our hearts on evil things as they did. Do not be idolaters as some of them were; as it is written: "The people sat down to eat and drink and got up to indulge in pagan revelry." We should not commit sexual immorality, as some of them did—and in one day twenty-three thousand of them died. We should not test the Lord, as some of them did—and were killed by snakes. And do not grumble, as some of them did—and were killed by the destroying angel. These things happened to them as examples and were written down as warnings for us, on whom the fulfillment of the ages has come. (1 Corinthians 10:6–11)

We must not rebel against the Lord as the Israelites did in the desert. When we rebel against God, there are consequences. One major consequence is that rebellion leads to lack of understanding (Ezekiel 12:2). Rebellion impairs our ability to comprehend God's truth.

After my study on the subject of testing God, the next thing that began to bother me was realization that Satan had established a stronghold in my life. I didn't like the idea and resolved to do something about it. During my study on satanic strongholds, I dusted off some old notes about Job.

Chapter Two
Satanic Strongholds

S atan is a formidable adversary. We need to be aware of the devil's schemes.

Put on the full armor of God so that you can take your stand against the devil's schemes. For our struggle is not against flesh and blood, but against the rulers, against the authorities, against the powers of this dark world and against the spiritual forces of evil in the heavenly realms. (Ephesians 6:11, 12)

We also know that the power of God is greater than the power of the evil one.

…the one who is in you is greater than the one who is in the world. (I John 4:4b)

The Greek word for stronghold is *ochuroma*. According to Bauer, Arndt, and Gingrich's *A Greek-English Lexicon of the New Testament*, the word means stronghold or fortress or prison. **(1)**

For though we live in the world, we do not wage war as the world does. The weapons we fight with are not weapons of the world. On the contrary, they have divine power to demolish strongholds. We demolish arguments and every pretension that sets itself up against the knowledge of God, and we take captive every thought to make it obedient to Christ. (II Corinthians 10:3-5)

As I read II Corinthians 10:3-5, it appears to me that satanic strongholds are rooted in incorrect ideas and wayward thoughts.

Ephesians 4:27b carries the same idea, but is phrased somewhat differently.

…do not give the devil a foothold. (Ephesians 4:27b)

The Greek word *topos* means space or place or opportunity. An alternate translation would be, "Do not give the devil a chance to exert his influence." **(2)**

The meanings of a couple of other Greek words are worth mentioning here. The Greek word for arguments is *logismos* and is translated *imaginations* in the KJV. According to Bauer, Arndt, and Gingrich, the word means calculation, reasoning, reflection or thought. In the plural it can mean thoughts or sentiments. It can mean the (prejudiced) thoughts that occupy a person's mind or the designs of the heathen. It has to do with reasoning power. **(3)** The word has been translated sophistries. **(4)** A sophistry is a subtly deceptive reasoning or argumentation. **(5)** It seems to me that the idea of "political correctness" is right in line with the concept of sophistries.

The Greek word for pretension is *hupsoma*. According to Bauer, Arndt, and Gingrich, the word means height or exaltation. It consists of "everything that rises up, all pride (every proud obstacle...)" that rises up against it [that sets itself up against the knowledge of God]. **(6)** It appears to me these subtly deceptive ideas are rooted in pride. Setting something up against the knowledge of God is rebellion.

According to II Corinthians 10:4, 5, we are to demolish arguments that set themselves up against the knowledge of God, destroy every pretension that sets itself up against the knowledge of God, and take captive every thought and make it obedient to Christ. The way to combat false ideas is to study the Scriptures so we'll know the truth. Truth comes from God, not from within ourselves.

Consider this passage in Ephesians 4:

It was he [Christ] who gave some to be apostles, some to be prophets, some to be evangelists, and some to be pastors and teachers, to prepare God's people for works of service, so that the body of Christ may be built up until we all reach unity in the faith and in the knowledge of the Son of God and become mature, attaining to the whole measure of the fullness of Christ. Then we will no longer be infants, tossed back and forth by the waves, and blown here and there by every wind of teaching and by the cunning and craftiness of men in their deceitful scheming. Instead, speaking the truth in love, we will in all things grow up into him who is the Head, that is, Christ. (Ephesians 4:11-15)

Ephesians 4:11-15 tells me that we are supposed to use our spiritual gifts to build each other up in the faith. We depend on each other to help us understand what Scripture really means and to help us be spiritually mature.

I've heard it said that the first three chapters of Ephesians teach us what we have and who we are in Christ; the last three chapters tell us how we are to respond to the realities mentioned in the first three chapters. The word *finally* in Ephesians 6:10 suggests to me that the subsequent passage about putting on the full armor of God is a continuation of ideas previously set forth and include practice of a godly lifestyle. It seems to me these last three chapters give us some guidelines about how we are to deal with the forces of Satan in our lives, both in preventing him from gaining a foothold, and should that foothold develop, wresting it from him. As I read Ephesians 4-6, the following exhortations are apparent to me.

Things we are to do according to Ephesians 4-6.

1. Understand our identity in Christ.
2. Study the Scriptures.
3. Live a life worthy of our calling and be cooperative with God about our sanctification.
4. Love one another.
5. Be humble, gentle, patient, and kind, bearing with and forgiving one another.
6. Live in unity with fellow believers and be at peace with them.
7. Use individual spiritual gifts for service to others and build up one another in the faith.
8. Control our temper and our tongue.
9. In our hearts make music to the Lord, giving thanks for everything.
10. Submit to one another out of reverence for Christ.
11. Husbands love our wives, and wives submit to and respect their husbands.
12. Children obey their parents in the Lord.
13. Fathers bring up our children in the training and instruction of the Lord.

14. Obtain our strength from the Lord and His mighty power.
15. Take our stand against the devil with the weapons of truth, righteousness, and faith.
16. Be ready to defend our faith and to share it with others.
17. Be able to use the truth of God's word to combat error.
18. Be alert.
19. Pray in the Spirit on all occasions, and always keep on praying for all the saints.
20. Be active in sharing our faith.

I pray that you may be active in sharing your faith, so that you will have a full understanding of every good thing we have in Christ. (Philemon 6)

It's amazing to me what Satan can get us to do if he is able to plant wrong ideas in our heads. This deception has both personal and societal implications. For example, the world says that a woman has a right to do whatever she pleases with her own body (translation: kill her unborn child). The Bible says, "You shall not murder" (Exodus 20:13). The world tells us that people in same sex relationships have a right to happiness. The Bible says, "Do not lie with a man as one lies with a woman; that is detestable" (Leviticus 18:22). The world says that it's okay to practice sex outside of marriage if done "safely". The Bible says, "The body is not meant for sexual immorality..." (I Corinthians 6:13b). There is no safe sex outside of marriage. While the implications of many of these sophistries seem attractive to some people, the decline in our family structure is ripping apart the fabric of our society. Single parent families are the major cause of poverty in our country. Fatherless families often produce young men who are hostile and belligerent and a menace to society. Sexual promiscuity and neglect of children, especially by the fathers, are about to destroy us.

I believe the life of Job is an example of a man who was basically good, but who allowed Satan to establish a stronghold in his life.

Letters Addressed to Christians in Affliction was published in Glasgow, Scotland, in 1817. One of the letters was written by Mrs.

Isabella Graham of New York and speaks of Job:

Job was a holy man; his afflictions from God's own hand were very deep; the teasing unkindness and injustice of his friends made great part of the temptation, and he spoke unadvisedly with his lips…I believe he spoke truth when he said, "I delivered the poor that cried, the fatherless, and him that had none to help him. The blessing of him that was ready to perish, came upon me; and I caused the widow's heart to sing for joy. I was eyes to the blind, and feet to the lame. I was a father to the poor; and the cause that I knew not, I searched out." God allowed the weight of the trial to be upon his spirit, with the conviction of his presumption, till he brought him to his feet. "Behold I am vile, what shall I answer thee? I will lay my hand upon my mouth, &c [et cetera]. I abhor myself, and repent in dust and ashes." These things were written for our example and profit. (7)

In *Theological Wordbook of the Old Testament*, R. Laird Harris speaks of presumption as follows: "Because a person is proud he presumes too much in his favor, especially in the sense of authority. For instance, the false prophet was one who presumed to speak in the name of God, assuming authority to do so, without having been called." False prophets were to be put to death (Deuteronomy 18:20). Harris says that the other two aspects of pride are rebellion or disobedience and willful decision. (8)

A careful examination of the text of Job the book gives us evidence about the basis for such a charge of presumption against Job the man. Before Job's time of testing, the Bible describes him as a righteous man.

In the land of Uz, there lived a man whose name was Job. This man was blameless and upright; he feared God and shunned evil. (Job 1:1)

Based on this verse and other verses in the book of Job, some people have made the case for Job being sinless. The Hebrew word for blameless is the word *tamam* and means to be complete. The word is translated *perfect* in the KJV. According to R. Laird Harris in *Theological Wordbook of the Old Testament*, the word represents something less than sinless perfection. (9) Job was a good man, but he was still subject to error, as we all are.

Job even functioned as a priest for his family.

His sons took turns holding feasts in their homes, and they would invite their three sisters to eat and drink with them. When a period of feasting had run its course, Job would send and have them purified. Early in the morning he would sacrifice a burnt offering for each of them, thinking, "Perhaps my children have sinned and cursed God in their hearts." This was Job's regular custom. (Job 1:4, 5)

Job was a very wealthy, prosperous, and blessed man.

He [Job] had seven sons and three daughters, and he owned seven thousand sheep, three thousand camels, five hundred yoke of oxen and five hundred donkeys, and had a large number of servants. He was the greatest man among all the people of the East. (Job 1:2, 3)

Job did not trust in his wealth, as he knew such an attitude would be a sin.

If I have put my trust in gold or said to pure gold, "You are my security,"…if I have rejoiced over my great wealth, the fortune my hands had gained…then these also would be sins to be judged, for I would have been unfaithful to God on high. (Job 31: 24, 25, 28)

However, I do believe Job had become a little too cozy with his affluence.

Job did have some sense that his prosperity might not continue. During his initial address to his three friends he said,

What I feared has come upon me; what I dreaded has happened to me. (Job 3:25)

Job had concluded that sin would cause him to lose his blessings and that obedience to God was the way to continue to receive God's favor.

But this is what you [God] concealed in your heart, and I know that this was in your mind: If I sinned, you would be watching me and would not let my offense go unpunished. (Job: 10:13, 14)

If I have denied the desires of the poor or let the eyes of the widow grow weary, if I have kept my bread to myself, not sharing it with the fatherless - but from my youth I reared him as would a father, and from my birth I guided the widow - if I have seen anyone perishing for lack of clothing, or a needy man without a garment, and his heart did not bless me for warming him with the fleece from my sheep, if I have raised my hand against the fatherless, knowing that I had influence in court, then let my arm fall from the shoulder, let it be broken off at the joint. For I dreaded destruction from God, and for fear of his splendor I could not do such things. (Job 31:16-23)

Job had become proud; he was proud of his piety.

But he knows the way that I take; when he has tested me, I will come forth as gold. My feet have closely followed his steps; I have kept to his way without turning aside. I have not departed from the commands of his lips; I have treasured the words of his mouth more than my daily bread. (Job 23:10-12)

"Till I die, I will not deny my integrity. I will maintain my righteousness and never let go of it; my conscience will not reproach me as long as I live. (Job 27:5b, 6)

I am pure and without sin; I am clean and free from guilt. (Job 33:9)

Job was proud of his wisdom.

Men listened to me expectantly, waiting in silence for my counsel. After I had spoken, they spoke no more; my words fell gently on their ears. They waited for me as for showers and drank in my words as the spring rain. When I smiled at them they scarcely believed it; the light of my face was precious to them. I chose the way for them and sat as their chief; I dwelt as a king among his troops; (Job 29:21-25a)

Job was proud of his empathy for others.

I was like one who comforts mourners. (Job 29:25b)

Have I not wept for those in trouble? Has not my soul grieved for the poor? (Job 30:25)

Job was proud of his good works.

When I went to the gate of the city and took my seat in the public square, the young men saw me and stepped aside and the old men rose to their feet; the chief men refrained from speaking and covered their mouths with their hands; the voices of the nobles were hushed, and their tongues stuck to the roof of their mouths. Whoever heard me spoke well of me, and those who saw me commended me, because I rescued the poor who cried for help, and the fatherless who had none to assist him. The man who was dying blessed me; I made the widow's heart sing. I put on righteousness as my clothing; justice was my robe and my turban. I was eyes to the blind and feet to the lame. I was a father to the needy; I took up the case of the stranger. I broke the fangs of the wicked and snatched the victims from their teeth. (Job 29:7-17)

Job was actively looking for things to do to be helpful.

I was a father to the needy: And the cause of him that I knew not, I searched out. (Job 29:16-ASV)

Job was righteous in his own eyes.

So these three men stopped answering Job, because he was righteous in his own eyes. But Elihu son of Barakel the Buzite, of the family of Ram, became very angry with Job for justifying himself rather than God. (Job 32:1, 2)

Job had become presumptuous. Job thought God owed him something. He had developed a sense of entitlement. If Job had not thought God owed him something, he would have had no basis on which to charge God with injustice.

…know that God has wronged me [Job] and drawn his net around me. Though I cry, "I've been wronged!" I get no response; though I call for help, there is no justice. (Job 19:6, 7)

Job's initial response to his trials had been good. During the first set of trials, Satan was allowed to strike Job's possessions but could not touch his body (Job 1:11, 12). Note Job's response:

At this, Job got up and tore his robe and shaved his head. Then he fell to the ground in worship and said: "Naked I came from my mother's womb, and naked I will depart. The Lord gave and the Lord has taken away; may the name of the

Lord be praised." In all this, Job did not sin by charging God with wrongdoing. (Job 1:20-22).

When we hurt, it is a good thing to talk with God about our pain, but according to Job 1:22, charging God with wrongdoing is a sin. During the second set of trials, Satan was allowed to strike Job's flesh and bones, but he could not take his life (Job 2:5, 6). Consider Job's response to his second test:

His [Job's] wife said to him, "Are you still holding on to your integrity? Curse God and die!" He replied, "You are talking like a foolish woman. Shall we accept good from God and not trouble?" In all this, Job did not sin in what he said. (Job 2:9, 10)

Eventually, Job's attitude changed, and he became angry. Job thought he had been treated unfairly.

But I [Job] desire to speak to the Almighty and to argue my case with God. (Job 13:3)

I will surely defend my ways to his face. (Job13:15b)

Now that I have prepared my case, I know I will be vindicated. (Job 13:18)

How many wrongs and sins have I committed? Show me my offense and my sin. (Job 13:23)

…let God weigh me in honest scales and he will know that I am blameless. (Job 31:6)

I believe Job's anger toward God was rooted in a stronghold Satan had established in his life. I believe Satan had put false ideas in Job's head. Job thought God owed him. He thought God was unfair. Job said some terrible things about God.

What is man that you make so much of him, that you give him so much attention, that you examine him every morning and test him every moment? Will you never look away from me, or let me alone even for an instant? If I have sinned, what have I done to you, O watcher of men? Why have you made me your target? (Job 7:17-20)

Although I am blameless, I have no concern for myself; I despise my own life. It is all the same; that is why I say, "He [God] destroys both the blameless and the wicked." When a scourge brings sudden death, he mocks the despair of the innocent. (Job 9:21-23a)

Does it please you [God] to oppress me [Job], to spurn the work of your hands, while you smile on the schemes of the wicked? (Job 10:3)

Man's days are determined; you [God] have decreed the number of his months and have set limits he cannot exceed. So look away from him and let him alone, till he has put in his time like a hired man. (Job 14:5, 6)

But as a mountain erodes and crumbles and as a rock is moved from its place, as water wears away stones and torrents wash away the soil, so you [God] destroy man's hope. (Job 14:18, 19)

When God spoke to Job from the whirlwind, He answered Job's claims of injustice.

Will the one who contends with the Almighty correct him? Let him who accuses God answer him! (Job 40:1, 2)

Would you discredit my justice? Would you condemn me to justify yourself? Do you have an arm like God's, and can your voice thunder like his? Then adorn yourself with glory and splendor, and clothe yourself in honor and majesty. Unleash the fury of your wrath, look at every proud man and bring him low, look at every proud man and humble him, crush the wicked where they stand. Bury them all in the dust together; shroud their faces in the grave, Then I myself will admit to you that your own right hand can save you. (Job 40:8-14)

God also had a few words about Job's sense of entitlement:

...Who then is able to stand against me? Who has a claim against me that I must pay? Everything under heaven belongs to me. (Job 41:10b, 11)

Job had to learn that no man has any claim against God. God has a right to do anything He wants with what He has created. Note Job's contrition and repentance after God spoke to him:

Then Job replied to the Lord: "I know you can do all things; no plan of yours can be thwarted. You asked, 'Who is this that obscures my counsel without knowledge?' Surely I spoke of things I did not understand, things too wonderful

for me to know. You said, 'Listen now, and I will speak; I will question you, and you shall answer me.' My ears had heard of you but now my eyes have seen you. Therefore I despise myself and repent in dust and ashes." (Job 42:1-6)

In spite of Job's sin, he was still God's man. After the Lord spoke to Job, and Job gave evidence of his repentance, these words appear in the epilogue:

After the Lord had said these things to Job, he said to Eliphaz the Temanite, "I am angry with you and your two friends, because you have not spoken of me what is right, as my servant Job has. So now take seven bulls and seven rams and go to my servant Job and sacrifice a burnt offering for yourselves. My servant Job will pray for you, and I will accept his prayer and not deal with you according to your folly. You have not spoken of me what is right, as my servant Job has." So Eliphaz the Temanite, Bildad the Shuhite and Zophar the Naamathite did what the Lord told them; and the Lord accepted Job's prayer. (Job 42:7-9)

Perhaps Job was still God's man because he never lost his faith; he continued to persevere. Consider these words of Satan right before the first and then right before the second set of afflictions:

"Does Job fear God for nothing?" Satan replied, "Have you not put a hedge around him and his household and everything he has? You have blessed the work of his hands, so that his flocks and herds are spread throughout the land. But stretch out your hand and strike everything he has, and he will surely curse you to your face." (Job 1:9-11)

"Skin for skin!" Satan replied, "A man will give all he has for his own life. But stretch out your hand and strike his flesh and bones, and he will surely curse you to your face." (Job 2:4, 5)

I believe Satan was right about at least one of Job's motives for serving God; he was doing so in order to continue to receive God's favor. Satan was wrong in how he thought Job would respond, should his blessings be taken away. Job had hostile feelings toward God, but he was trying to work through them. He was still seeking the Lord.

He [God] is not a man like me that I might answer him, that we might confront each other in court. If only there were someone to arbitrate between us, to lay his hand upon us both, someone to remove God's rod from me, so that his terror would frighten me no more. Then I would speak up without fear of him, but as it now stands with me, I cannot. (Job 9:32-35)

Only grant me these two things, O God, and then I will not hide from you: Withdraw your hand far from me, and stop frightening me with your terrors. Then summon me and I will answer, or let me speak and you reply. How many wrongs and sins have I committed? Show me my offense and my sin. Why do you hide your face and consider me your enemy? (Job 13:20-24)

If only I knew where to find him [God]; if only I could go to his dwelling! I would

23

state my case before him and fill my mouth with arguments. I would find out what he would answer me, and consider what he would say…There an upright man could present his case before him, and I would be delivered forever from my judge. But if I go to the east, he is not there; if I go to the west, I do not find him. When he is at work in the north, I do not see him; when he turns to the south, I catch no glimpse of him. (Job 23:3-9)

Job did say, "It's not fair," but he never lost his faith. He never turned his back on God. Job continued to persevere despite his difficult situation. Consider James' words about Job's perseverance:

As you know, we consider blessed those who have persevered. You have heard of Job's perseverance and have seen what the Lord finally brought about. The Lord is full of compassion and mercy. (James 5:11)

According to Bauer, Arndt, and Gingrich, the Greek word *hupomonee* means "patience, endurance, fortitude, steadfastness, perseverance…especially as they are shown in the enduring of toil and suffering…the endurance that Christ showed… Christ-like fortitude…perseverance in doing what is right…steadfast endurance of sufferings…" **(10)**

In the middle of his affliction Job was able to say, "Though he slay me, yet will I hope in him" (Job 13:15a).

I [Job] know that my Redeemer lives, and that in the end he will stand upon the earth. After my skin has been destroyed, yet in my flesh I will see God. (Job 19:25, 26)

I believe the story of Job's life gives us lessons for today.

When we think we've been treated unfairly, there are things we are not to do, and there are things we are to do.

Don't	Be presumptuous with God.
	Have a sense of entitlement with God.
	Charge God with wrongdoing.
Do	Keep the faith.
	Humble yourself before the Lord.
	Examine your life and repent of any known sin.
	Seek the Lord.
	Remember God's character.
	Remember what God expects of you and what He has promised.
	Submit to the reality of the things you cannot change.
	Ask God for a right understanding of the issues involved.

When we understand God for who He really is and understand who we are in relation to Him, it should help make us more humble and straighten-out our attitudes.

What do we do when God seems distant, when we have lost our sense of the presence of the Lord and when we can't feel God's presence? We must continue to seek His face.

But if from there [in the land of captivity] you [Israelites] seek the Lord your God, you will find him if you look for him with all your heart and with all your soul. (Deuteronomy 4:29)

And you, my son Solomon, acknowledge the God of your father, and serve him with wholehearted devotion and with a willing mind, for the Lord searches every heart and understands every motive behind the thoughts. If you seek him, he will be found by you; but if you forsake him, he will reject you forever. (I Chronicles 28:9)

...if my [the Lord's] people, who are called by my name, will humble themselves and pray and seek my face and turn from their wicked ways, then I will hear from heaven and will forgive their sin and will heal their land. (II Chronicles 7:14)

The Lord is a refuge for the oppressed, a stronghold in times of trouble. Those who know your name will trust in you, for you, Lord, have never forsaken those who seek you. (Psalm 9:9, 10)

Who may ascend the hill of the Lord? Who may stand in his holy place? He who has clean hands and a pure heart, who does not lift up his soul to an idol or swear by what is false. He will receive blessing from the Lord and vindication from God his Savior. Such is the generation of those who seek him, who seek your face, O God of Jacob. (Psalm 24:3-6)

One thing I ask of the Lord, this is what I seek: that I may dwell in the house of the Lord all the days of my life, to gaze on the beauty of the Lord and to seek him in his temple. For in the day of trouble he will keep me safe in his dwelling; he will hide me in the shelter of his tabernacle and set me high upon a rock. (Psalm 27:4, 5)

O God, you are my God, earnestly I seek you; my soul thirsts for you, my body longs for you, in a dry and weary land where there is no water. I have seen you in the sanctuary and beheld your power and glory. Because your love is better than life, my lips will glorify you. (Psalm 63:1-3)

I [the Lord] love those who love me, and those who seek me find me. (Proverbs 8:17)

"For I know the plans I have for you," declares the Lord, "plans to prosper you and not to harm you, plans to give you hope and a future. Then you will call upon me and come and pray to me, and I will listen to you. You will seek me and find me when you seek me with all your heart. (Jeremiah 29:11-13)

Ask and it will be given to you; seek and you will find; knock and the door will be opened to you. For everyone who asks receives; he who seeks finds; and to him who knocks, the door will be opened. (Matthew 7:7, 8)

For some people, in order to overcome a satanic stronghold, it is necessary to have an accountability partner or be part of an accountability group.

Therefore confess your sins to each other and pray for each other so that you may be healed. The prayer of a righteous man is powerful and effective. (James 5:16)

I identified with Job in his presumption, his sense of entitlement, and his angry reaction to affliction. All three were sins I needed to overcome. I was sure there was some of God's truth that I did not perceive correctly. As I mentioned previously in this chapter, it seems to me satanic strongholds are rooted in incorrect ideas and wayward thoughts. I felt it necessary to study what the Bible has to say about spiritual blindness.

Chapter Three
Spiritual Blindness

To win the battle over anger and resentment, it is helpful to overcome any spiritual blindness we may be experiencing. Absolute truth is found in the Bible. It is only through the Holy Spirit that we can understand what we read in Scripture. If our response to certain stresses in life does not match up with what we see in the Bible as acceptable, we must find a way to triumph over our circumstances and live by what we know is true. The Greek word *elegcho* is used several times in the New Testament. According to Bauer, Arndt, and Gingrich, *elegcho* is defined as follows: "bring to light, expose, set forth . . . convict or convince someone of something . . . reprove, correct." **(1)** It is the Holy Spirit who turns on the light so we can see ourselves as we truly are.

I. For people without Christ, a veil covers their minds and hearts, preventing them from perceiving and understanding truth.

Jesus said to them [the Pharisees], "If God were your Father, you would love me, for I came from God and now am here. I have not come on my own; but he sent me. Why is my language not clear to you? Because you are unable to hear what I say. You belong to your father, the devil, and you want to carry out your father's desire. He was a murderer from the beginning, not holding to the truth, for there is no truth in him. When he lies he speaks his native language, for he is a liar and the father of lies. Yet because I tell you the truth, you do not believe me! Can any of you prove me guilty of sin? If I am telling the truth, why don't you believe me? He who belongs to God hears what God says. The reason that you do not hear is that you do not belong to God." (John 8:42-47)

And even if our gospel is veiled, it is veiled to those who are perishing. The god of this age has blinded the minds of unbelievers, so that they cannot see the light of the gospel of the glory of Christ, who is the image of God. (II Corinthians 4:3, 4)

II. Willful sin leads to spiritual blindness.

The wrath of God is being revealed from heaven against all the godlessness and wickedness of men who suppress the truth by their wickedness, since what may be known about God is plain to them, because God has made it plain to them. For since the creation of the world God's invisible qualities - his eternal power and divine nature - have been clearly seen, being understood from what has been made, so that men are without excuse. (Romans 1:18-20)

So I tell you this, and insist on it in the Lord, that you must no longer live as the Gentiles do, in the futility of their thinking. They are darkened in their understanding and separated from the life of God because of the ignorance that is in them due to the hardening of their hearts. Having lost all sensitivity, they have given themselves over to sensuality so as to indulge in every kind of impurity, with a continual lust for more. (Ephesians 4:17-19)

III. For an individual, spiritual blindness may be purposeful.

In his pride the wicked does not seek him; in all his thoughts there is no room for God. (Psalm 10:4)

The fear of the Lord is the beginning of knowledge, but fools despise wisdom and discipline. (Proverbs 1:7)

This is the verdict: Light has come into the world, but men loved darkness instead of light because their deeds were evil. Everyone who does evil hates the light, and will not come into the light for fear that his deeds will be exposed. But whoever lives by the truth comes into the light, so that it may be seen plainly that what he has done has been done through God. (John 3:19-21)

And the Father who sent me [Jesus] has himself testified concerning me. You [Jews] have never heard his voice nor seen his form, nor does his word dwell in you, for you do not believe the one he sent. You diligently study the Scriptures because you think that by them you possess eternal life. These are the Scriptures that testify about me, yet you refuse to come to me to have life. (John 5:37-40)

They [the leaders of the Jews in Rome] arranged to meet Paul on a certain day, and came in even larger numbers to the place where he was staying. From morning till evening he explained and declared to them the kingdom of God and tried to convince them about Jesus from the Law of Moses and from the Prophets. Some were convinced by what he said, but others would not believe. They disagreed among themselves and began to leave after Paul had made this final statement: "The Holy Spirit spoke the truth to your forefathers when he said through Isaiah the prophet: 'Go to this people and say, "You will be ever hearing but never understanding; you will be ever seeing but never perceiving." For this people's heart has become calloused; they hardly hear with their ears, and they have closed their eyes. Otherwise they might see with their eyes, hear with their ears, understand with their hearts and turn, and I would heal them.' Therefore I want you to know that God's salvation has been sent to the Gentiles, and they will listen!" (Acts 28:23-28)

IV. Spiritual blindness may be unintended.

An oracle is within my heart concerning the sinfulness of the wicked: There is no fear of God before his eyes. For in his own eyes he flatters himself too much to detect or hate his sin. (Psalm 36:1, 2)

Why do you look at the speck of sawdust in your brother's eye and pay no attention to the plank in your own eye? How can you say to your brother, "Brother let me take the speck out of your eye," when you yourself fail to see the plank in your own eye? (Luke 6:41, 42a)

We have much to say about this, but it is hard to explain because you are slow to learn. In fact, though by this time you ought to be teachers, you need someone to teach you the elementary truths of God's word all over again. You need milk, not solid food! Anyone who lives on milk, being still an infant, is not acquainted with the teaching about righteousness. But solid food is for the mature, who by constant use have trained themselves to distinguish good from evil. (Hebrews 5:11-14)

To the angel of the church in Sardis write: These are the words of him who holds the seven spirits of God and the seven stars. I know your deeds; you have a reputation of being alive, but you are dead. Wake up! Strengthen what remains and is about to die, for I have not found your deeds complete in the sight of my God. Remember, therefore, what you have received and heard; obey it, and repent. But if you do not wake up, I will come like a thief, and you will not know at what time I will come to you. (Revelation 3:1-3)

To the angel of the church in Laodicea write: These are the words of the Amen, the faithful and true witness, the ruler of God's creation. I know your deeds, that you are neither cold nor hot. I wish you were either one or the other! So, because you are lukewarm - neither hot nor cold - I am about to spit you out of my mouth. You say, "I am rich; I have acquired wealth and do not need a thing." But you do not realize that you are wretched, pitiful, poor, blind and naked. I counsel you to buy from me gold refined in the fire, so you can become rich; and white clothes to wear [white clothes signify a good character], so you can cover your shameful nakedness; and salve to put on your eyes, so you can see. (Revelation 3:14-18)

The deeds, of the people of the church in Laodicea, were neither hot nor cold and Jesus was going to spit them out of his mouth (verses

29

15 & 16). I once heard an illustration that their deeds were like lukewarm coffee and having them in His mouth was nauseating.

V. Spiritual blindness may be the result of multiple bad decisions and/or acts of carelessness, each one of more or less seriousness, having a cumulative effect over a period of time.

Wine is a mocker and beer a brawler; whoever is led astray by them is not wise. (Proverbs 20:1)

…my people are destroyed from lack of knowledge. (Hosea 4:6a)

Do not be misled: "Bad company corrupts good character." Come back to your senses as you ought, and stop sinning; for there are some who are ignorant of God - I say this to your shame. (I Corinthians 5:33-34)

Avoid godless chatter, because those who indulge in it will become more and more ungodly. (II Timothy 2:16)

We must pay more careful attention, therefore, to what we have heard, so that we do not drift away. (Hebrews 2:1)

Consider God's warning to Israel about a king and the subsequent downfall of Solomon:

When you enter the land the Lord your God is giving you and have taken possession of it and settled in it, and you say, "Let us set a king over us like all the nations around us," be sure to appoint over you the king the Lord your God chooses. He must be from among your own brothers. Do not place a foreigner over you, one who is not a brother Israelite. The king, moreover, must not acquire great numbers of horses for himself or make the people return to Egypt to get more of them, for the Lord has told you, "You are not to go back that way again." He must not take many wives, or his heart will be led astray. He must not accumulate large amounts of silver and gold. When he takes the throne of his kingdom, he is to write for himself on a scroll a copy of this law, taken from that of the priests, who are Levites. It is to be with him, and he is to read it all the days of his life so that he may learn to revere the Lord his God and follow carefully all the words of this law and these decrees and not consider himself better than his brothers and turn from the law to the right or to the left. Then he and his descendants will reign a long time over his kingdom in Israel. (Deuteronomy 17:14-20)

The king was to be the man of God's own choosing. He was to be an

Israelite. The king was not to acquire great numbers of horses, especially not from Egypt. Perhaps the reference to returning to Egypt had something to do with returning to the influence of earthly treasures or idolatry. The king was not to take many wives or accumulate large amounts of silver and gold. He was not to become prideful, not to consider himself better than his brothers. He was to make his own manuscript copy of the law, keep it with him, and read it every day. He was to follow carefully all the words of the law and not turn from the law to the right or the left. These admonitions were to keep his heart from being led astray.

In I Samuel 8, we read the story of Israel's request for a king.

So all the elders of Israel gathered together and came to Samuel at Ramah. They said to him, "You are old, and your sons do not walk in your ways; now appoint a king to lead us, such as all the other nations have." But when they said, "Give us a king to lead us," this displeased Samuel; so he prayed to the Lord. And the Lord told him: "Listen to all that the people are saying to you; it is not you they have rejected, but they have rejected me as their king. As they have done from the day I brought them up out of Egypt until this day, forsaking me and serving other gods, so they are doing to you. Now listen to them; but warn them solemnly and let them know what the king who will reign over them will do." Samuel told all the words of the Lord to the people who were asking him for a king. He said, "This is what the king who will reign over you will do: He will take your sons and make them serve with his chariots and horses, and they will run in front of his chariots. Some he will assign to be commanders of thousands and commanders of fifties, and others to plow his ground and reap his harvest, and still others to make weapons of war and equipment for his chariots. He will take your daughters to be perfumers and cooks and bakers. He will take the best of your fields and vineyards and olive groves and give them to his attendants. He will take a tenth of your grain and of your vintage and give it to his officials and attendants. Your menservants and maidservants and the best of your cattle and donkeys he will take for his own use. He will take a tenth of your flocks, and you yourselves will become his slaves. When that day comes, you will cry out for relief from the king you have chosen, and the Lord will not answer you in that day." But the people refused to listen to Samuel. "No!" they said. "We want a king over us. Then we will be like all the other nations, with a king to lead us and to go out before us and fight our battles." When Samuel heard all that the people said, he repeated it before the Lord. The Lord answered, "Listen to them and give them a king." (I Samuel 8:4-22a)

The first king was Saul. The second king was David. The third king was Solomon, David's son by his wife Bathsheba. God appeared to Solomon twice. It seems that Solomon was faithful to God until he was about 41 years old. He became king when he was 18 years old. During his initial three years as king, he established his rule; he had a good beginning. He then built the temple in Jerusalem over a period of about seven years. The making of the furnishings for the temple took another three years. He started building his palace as soon as the building of the temple was complete, at the same time he started making the temple furnishings. He built the palace over the next 13 years. He conscripted aliens to do the work: 70,000 men were assigned to be carriers, and 80,000 were assigned to be stonecutters in the hills with 3,600 foremen over them. (II Chronicles 2:1, 2)

Solomon created a large work force to build the temple and the palace. It seems to me that after those two buildings were completed, he kept that large work force and used it to fulfill his own personal desires. His general conduct was such that it was as if he had read in Deuteronomy 17 about what he was not supposed to do and then used that as a guide for what to do.

At the end of twenty years, during which Solomon built the temple of the Lord and his own palace, Solomon rebuilt the villages that Hiram had given him, and settled Israelites in them. Solomon then went to Hamath Zobah and captured it. He also built up Tadmor in the desert and all the store cities he had built in Hamath. He rebuilt Upper Beth Horon and Lower Beth Horon as fortified cities, with walls and with gates and bars, as well as Baalath and all his store cities, and all the cities for his chariots and for his horses - whatever he desired to build in Jerusalem, in Lebanon and throughout all the territory he ruled. All the people left from the Hittites, Amorites, Perizzites, Hivites and Jebusites (these peoples were not Israelites), that is, their descendants remaining in the land, whom the Israelites had not destroyed - these Solomon conscripted for his slave labor force, as it is to this day. But Solomon did not make slaves of the Israelites for his work; they were his fighting men, commanders of his captains, and commanders of his chariots and charioteers. They were also King Solomon's chief officials - two hundred and fifty officials supervising the men. Solomon brought Pharaoh's daughter up from the city of David to the palace he had built for her, for he said, "My wife must not live in the palace of David king of Israel, because the places the ark of the Lord has entered are holy." (II Chronicles 8:1-11)

32

The Israelites had been instructed to totally destroy the heathen from the land of Canaan (Deuteronomy 7:1-6; Deuteronomy 20:16-18), but they did not drive them out completely. There were times when they couldn't, and there were times when they wouldn't (Judges 1: 19-35). They kept them around to use them as slaves (Joshua 17:13). These aliens remained in the land and led the Israelites away from the Lord (Psalm 106:34-39).

Solomon had a lavish lifestyle.

When the queen of Sheba heard about the fame of Solomon and his relation to the name of the Lord, she came to test him with hard questions. Arriving at Jerusalem with a very great caravan - with camels carrying spices, large quantities of gold, and precious stones - she came to Solomon and talked with him about all that she had on her mind. Solomon answered all her questions; nothing was too hard for the king to explain to her. When the queen of Sheba saw all the wisdom of Solomon and the palace he had built, the food on his table, the seating of his officials, the attending servants in their robes, his cupbearers, and the burnt offerings he made at the temple of the Lord, she was overwhelmed. She said to the king, "The report I heard in my own country about your achievements and your wisdom is true. But I did not believe these things until I came and saw with my own eyes. Indeed, not even half was told me; in wisdom and wealth you have far exceeded the report I heard. How happy your men must be! How happy your officials, who continually stand before you and hear your wisdom! Praise be to the Lord your God, who has delighted in you and placed you on the throne of Israel. Because of the Lord's eternal love for Israel, he has made you king, to maintain justice and righteousness." (I Kings 10:1-9)

The weight of the gold that Solomon received yearly was 666 talents [about 25 tons], not including the revenues brought in by merchants and traders. Also all the kings of Arabia and the governors of the land brought gold and silver to Solomon. King Solomon made two hundred large shields of hammered gold; six hundred bekas [about 7 1/2 lb.] of hammered gold went into each shield. The king put them in the Palace of the Forest of Lebanon. Then the king made a great throne inlaid with ivory and overlaid with pure gold. The throne had six steps, and a footstool of gold was attached to it. On both sides of the seat were armrests, with a lion standing beside each of them. Twelve lions stood on the six steps, one at either end of each step. Nothing like it had ever been made for any other kingdom. All King Solomon's goblets were gold, and all the household articles in the Palace of the Forest of Lebanon were pure gold. Nothing was made of silver, because silver was considered of little value in Solomon's day. The king had a fleet of trading ships manned by Hiram's men. Once every three years it returned, carrying gold, silver and ivory, and apes and baboons. King Solomon was greater in riches and wisdom that all the other kings of the earth. All the kings of the earth sought audience with Solomon to hear the wisdom God had put in his heart. Year after year, everyone who came brought a gift - articles of silver and gold, and robes, weapons and spices, and horses and mules. Solomon had four thousand stalls for horses and chariots, and twelve thousand horses, which he kept in the chariot cities and also with him in Jerusalem. He ruled over all the kings from the river [Euphrates] to the land of the Philistines, as far as the border of Egypt. The king made silver as common in Jerusalem as stones, and cedar as plentiful as sycamore-fig trees in the foothills. Solomon's horses were imported from Egypt and from all other countries. (II Chronicles 9:13-28)

If you tour Israel today, guides will show you places where Solomon kept his horses.

I [Solomon] amassed silver and gold for myself, and the treasure of kings and provinces. I acquired men and women singers, and a harem as well - the delights of the heart of man. I became greater by far than anyone in Jerusalem before me...I denied myself nothing my eyes desired; I refused my heart no pleasure. (Ecclesiastes 2:8-10a)

King Solomon, however, loved many foreign women besides Pharaoh's daughter - Moabites, Ammonites, Edomites, Sidonians, and Hittites. They were from nations about which the Lord had told the Israelites, "You must not intermarry with them, because they will surely turn your hearts after their gods." Nevertheless, Solomon held fast to them in love. He had seven hundred wives of royal birth and three hundred concubines, and his wives led him astray. As Solomon grew old, his wives turned his heart after other gods, and his heart was not fully devoted to the Lord his God, as the heart of David his father had been. He followed Ashtoreth the goddess of the Sidonians, and Molech the detestable god of the Ammonites. So Solomon did evil in the eyes of the Lord; he did not follow the Lord completely, as David his father had done. On a hill east of Jerusalem, Solomon built a high place for Chemosh the detestable god of Moab, and for Molech the detestable god of the Ammonites. He did the same for all his foreign wives, who burned incense and offered sacrifices to their gods. The Lord became angry with Solomon because his heart had turned away from the Lord, the God of Israel who had appeared to him twice. Although he had forbidden Solomon to follow other gods, Solomon did not keep the Lord's command. So the Lord said to Solomon, "Since this is your attitude and you have not kept my covenant and my decrees, which I commanded you, I will most certainly tear the kingdom away from you and give it to one of your subordinates. Nevertheless, for the sake of David your father, I will not do it during your lifetime. I will tear it out of the hand of your son. Yet I will not tear the whole kingdom from him, but will give him one tribe for the sake of David my servant and for the sake of Jerusalem, which I have chosen. (I Kings 11:1-13)

There are certain temptations that go along with success in this life. I have heard it said that all medical doctors are prima donnas. So are a lot of other people. Of course, there are many variations. Most physicians I know, whether it's related to money, possessions, status, knowledge, wisdom, piety, kindness, good works, entrepreneurial skills, technical skills, or the amount of control they have over other people's lives feel they've accomplished something in life, and they have. However, we must not let our accomplishments get in the way of our relationship with the Lord. We must remain humble. Reviewing the life of Solomon should teach us not to be over-impressed by our own accomplishments. That attitude can be very destructive. It is dangerous to have too high a regard for anything about ourselves.

For successful people in this life, in some ways their temptations are similar to Solomon's. A list would include the following:

1. The temptation to worship false idols (e.g. power, prestige, or pleasure).
2. The temptation to accumulate excessive wealth.
3. The temptation to maintain the accouterments or the trappings of the wealthy.
4. The temptation to indulge in sexual sin.
5. The temptation to become over impressed with ourselves, leading to presumption, and at times, disobedience and willful decision.

Success can turn our heads. We must never depend on other things besides the Lord for our satisfaction or our significance in life. After the courtroom experience, it took me years to realize I was filled with rage because of my own presumption. I had made an idol of my own character, and *how dare anyone attack such a good man who does such good things!*

For an example of something that may turn our heads, consider how physicians are able to help others. It can be a heady thing to realize we have been used to save someone's life. In such a situation, I believe it's important to keep things in perspective. If I, as a physician, give the appropriate treatment that saves someone's life, for my part, it's only because God granted me the wisdom and/or the skill to do so. He also arranged the circumstances. For the patient's part, it means God wasn't ready to take him/her home yet. Actually, it was the Lord who saved them anyway, not me.

Another thing to consider is that anything I ever did medically for a patient was only temporary. If the Lord tarries, in the end, each person will still go to the grave. The only things I ever did for patients that were of eternal value, were when I was used to influence them spiritually. In the tenth chapter of Luke, Jesus appointed seventy-two others and sent them two by two ahead of Him to every town and place where He was about to go. The seventy-two returned with joy and said, "Lord, even the demons submit to us in your name." Jesus replied, "…do not rejoice that the spirits submit to you, but rejoice that your names are written in heaven." Our salvation and being in God's will are what are important. When we get over-inflated ideas about ourselves, it is spiritual blindness.

For Christians who are successful financially, money can distract them from their real purpose in life, which is to glorify God, to love God and love our neighbor. If money is our god, we'll never have enough. The Bible has some rather specific things to say about money and the love of money.

No one can serve two masters. Either he will hate the one and love the other, or he will be devoted to the one and despise the other. You cannot serve both God and Money [mammon]. (Matthew 6:24)

Provide purses for yourselves that will not wear out, a treasure in heaven that will not be exhausted, where no thief comes near and no moth destroys. (Luke 12:33b)

Whoever can be trusted with very little can also be trusted with much, and whoever

36

is dishonest with very little will also be dishonest with much. So if you have not been trustworthy in handling worldly wealth, who will trust you with true riches? (Luke 16:10, 11)

People who want to get rich fall into temptation and a trap and into many foolish and harmful desires that plunge men into ruin and destruction. For the love of money is a root of all kinds of evil. Some people, eager for money, have wandered from the faith and pierced themselves with many griefs. (I Timothy 6:9, 10)

Our accomplishments are not our gift to God; they are His gift to us.

Lord, you establish peace for us; all that we have accomplished you have done for us. (Isaiah 26:12)

For we are God's workmanship, created in Christ Jesus to do good works, which God prepared in advance for us to do. (Ephesians 4:10)

Recently I was pondering what it means to have child-like faith. I decided to go to the Bible to try to find answers.

People were also bringing babies to Jesus to have him touch them. When the disciples saw this, they rebuked them. But Jesus called the children to him and said, "Let the little children come to me, and do not hinder them, for the kingdom of God belongs to such as these. I tell you the truth, anyone who will not receive the kingdom of God like a little child will never enter it." (Luke 18:15-17)

Regarding Luke 18:17, in his *The MacArthur Study Bible*, John MacArthur writes, "See note on Matt. 18:3." (2) About Matthew 18:3 he writes,

18:3 become as little children. This is how Jesus characterized conversion. Like the Beatitudes, it pictures faith as the simple, helpless, trusting dependence of those who have no resources of their own. Like children, they have no achievements and no accomplishments to offer or commend themselves with. (3)

William MacDonald says that the message in Luke 18:15-17 is a reinforcement of the message in Luke 18:9-14. (4)

To some who were confident of their own righteousness and looked down on everybody else, Jesus told this parable: "Two men went up to the temple to pray, one a Pharisee and the other a tax collector. The Pharisee stood up and prayed about [or to] himself: 'God, I thank you that I am not like other men - robbers, evildoers, adulterers - or even like this tax collector. I fast twice a week and give a tenth of all I get.' But the tax collector stood at a distance. He would not even look up to heaven, but beat his breast and said, 'God have mercy on me, a sinner.' I tell you that this man, rather than the other, went home justified before God. For everyone who exalts himself will be humbled, and he who humbles himself will be exalted." (Luke 18:9-14)

It bothered me to realize I could ever be anything like that Pharisee. The Bible tells us to do nothing out of selfish ambition or vain conceit, but in humility consider others better than ourselves (Philippians 2:3). I believe the key here is to realize that all we have accomplished in life is by the grace and the gifts of God.

All of us need a dose of humility every now and then. We need to remember with Paul, "But by the grace of God I am what I am" (I Corinthians 15:10). Personally, all I can say about myself right now is that I am a sinner saved by grace. The only thing I deserve is hell.

Solomon's life should be an example for us to be careful about nurturing our relationship with the Lord. For those in a ministry, I'm reminded of the words of Howard Hendricks in a talk on *Finishing Well* that he delivered to a staff meeting of Campus Crusade for Christ, "Don't be so busy serving Christ that you lose Jesus in the process." If Solomon could fall, we can too.

VI. God wants to give us light so we can see and understand His truth and then share that truth with others.

The precepts of the Lord are right, giving joy to the heart. The commands of the Lord are radiant, giving light to the eyes. (Psalm 19:8)

Your [the Lord's] word is a lamp to my feet and a light for my path. (Psalm 119:105)

The unfolding of your [the Lord's] words gives light; it gives understanding to the simple. (Psalm 119:130)

My son, keep your father's commands and do not forsake your mother's teaching. Bind them upon your heart forever; fasten them around your neck. When you walk, they will guide you; when you sleep, they will watch over you; when you awake, they will speak to you. For these commands are a lamp, this teaching is a light, and the corrections of discipline are the way to life. (Proverbs 6:20-23)

You [disciples] are the light of the world. A city on a hill cannot be hidden. Neither do people light a lamp and put it under a bowl. Instead they put it on its stand, and it gives light to everyone in the house. In the same way, let your light shine before men, that they may see your good deeds and praise your Father in heaven. (Matthew 5:14-16)

When the time of their purification according to the Law of Moses had been completed, Joseph and Mary took him [the baby Jesus] to Jerusalem to present him to the Lord...Now there was a man in Jerusalem called Simeon, who was righteous and devout. He was waiting for the consolation of Israel, and the Holy Spirit was upon him. It had been revealed to him by the Holy Spirit that he would not die before he had seen the Lord's Christ...Simeon took him [the baby Jesus] in his arms and praised God saying: "Sovereign Lord, as you have promised, you now dismiss your servant in peace. For my eyes have seen your salvation, which you have prepared in the sight of all people, a light for revelation to the Gentiles and for glory to your people Israel." (Luke 2:22-32)

In the beginning was the Word [Jesus Christ], and the Word was with God, and the Word was God...In him was life, and that life was the light of men. The light shines in the darkness, but the darkness has not understood it. There came a man who was sent from God; his name was John [the Baptist]. He came as a witness to testify concerning that light, so that through him all men might believe. He himself was not the light; he came only as a witness to the light. The true light that gives light to every man was coming into the world. (John 1:1-9)

When Jesus spoke again to the people, he said, "I am the light of the world. Whoever follows me will never walk in darkness, but will have the light of life." (John 8:12)

On one of these journeys I [Paul] was going to Damascus with the authority and commission of the chief priests. About noon, O king [Herod Agrippa II], as I was on the road, I saw a light from heaven, brighter than the sun, blazing around me and my companions. We all fell to the ground, and I heard a voice saying to me in Aramaic, "Saul, Saul, why do you persecute me? It is hard for you to kick against the goads [promptings of the Holy Spirit and Paul's own conscience including his memory of Stephen's dying testimony]." Then I asked, "Who are you Lord?" "I am Jesus, whom you are persecuting," the Lord replied. "Now get up and stand on your feet. I have appeared to you to appoint you as a servant and as a witness of what you have seen of me and what I will show you. I will rescue you from your own people and from the Gentiles. I am sending you to them to open their eyes and turn them from darkness to light, and from the power of Satan to God, so that they may receive forgiveness of sins and a place among those who are sanctified by faith in me." (Acts 26:12-18)

For you were once darkness, but now you are light in the Lord. Live as children of light (for the fruit of the light consists in all goodness, righteousness and truth) and find out what pleases the Lord. Have nothing to do with the fruitless deeds of darkness, but rather expose them. For it is shameful even to mention what the disobedient do in secret. But everything exposed by the light becomes visible, for it is light that makes everything visible. This is why it is said: "Wake up, O sleeper, rise from the dead, and Christ will shine on you." (Ephesians 5:8-14)

VII. We must be careful to whom we pay attention and to what we allow to influence us.

Now the serpent [Satan – see Revelation 12:9; 20:2] was more crafty than any of the wild animals the Lord God had made. He said to the woman, "Did God really say, 'You must not eat from any tree in the garden'?" The woman said to the serpent, "We may eat fruit from the trees in the garden, but God did say, 'You must not eat fruit from the tree that is in the middle of the garden, and you must not touch it, or you will die.'" "You will not surely die," the serpent said to the woman. "For God knows that when you eat of it your eyes will be opened, and you will be like God, knowing good and evil." (Genesis 3:1-5)

Then the Lord said to me, "The prophets are prophesying lies in my name. I have not sent them or appointed them or spoken to them. They are prophesying to you false visions, divinations, idolatries, and delusions of their own minds." (Jeremiah 14:14)

Jesus answered: "Watch out that no one deceives you. For many will come in my name, claiming, 'I am the Christ,' and will deceive many." (Matthew 24:4, 5)

At that time [the end of the age] many will turn away from the faith and will betray and hate each other, and many false prophets will appear and deceive many people. (Matthew 24:10, 11)

At that time [the end of the age] if anyone says to you, "Look, here is the Christ!" or, "Look, there he is!" do not believe it. For false Christs and false prophets will appear and perform signs and miracles to deceive the elect - if that were possible. So be on your guard; I [Jesus] have told you everything ahead of time. (Mark 13:21-23)

Keep watch over yourselves and all the flock of which the Holy Spirit has made you overseers. Be shepherds of the church of God, which he bought with his own blood. I [Paul] know that after I leave, savage wolves will come in among you and will not spare the flock. Even from your own number men will arise and distort the truth in order to draw away disciples after them. So be on your guard! Remember that for three years I never stopped warning each of you night and day with tears. (Acts 20:28-31)

For such men [those who preach a different Jesus or a different gospel] are false apostles, deceitful workmen, masquerading as apostles of Christ. And no wonder, for Satan himself masquerades as an angel of light. (II Corinthians 11:13, 14)

But there were also false prophets among the people, just as there will be false teachers among you. They will secretly introduce destructive heresies, even denying the sovereign Lord who bought them - bringing swift destruction on themselves. Many will follow their shameful ways and will bring the way of truth into disrepute. In their greed these teachers will exploit you with stories they have made up. Their condemnation has long been hanging over them, and their destruction has not been sleeping. (II Peter 2:1-3)

Dear friends, do not believe every spirit, but test the spirits to see whether they are from God, because many false prophets have gone out into the world. This is how you can recognize the Spirit of God: Every spirit that acknowledges that Jesus Christ has come in the flesh is from God, but every spirit that does not acknowledge Jesus is not from God. This is the spirit of the Antichrist, which you have heard is coming and even now is already in the world. You, dear children, are from God and have overcome them, because the one who is in you is greater than the one who is in the world. They are from the world and therefore speak from the viewpoint of the world, and the world listens to them. We are from God, and whoever knows God listens to us; but whoever is not from God does not

listen to us. This is how we recognize the Spirit of truth and the spirit of falsehood. (I John 4:1-6)

Dear friends, although I was very eager to write to you about the salvation we share, I felt I had to write and urge you to contend for the faith that was once for all entrusted to the saints. For certain men whose condemnation was written about long ago have secretly slipped in among you. They are godless men, who change the grace of our God into a license for immorality and deny Jesus Christ our only Sovereign and Lord. (Jude 3, 4)

VIII. As we live our lives, and the more we cultivate our relationship with God, the better we understand His ways.

For comparison, let us consider the marriage relationship. In general, we come into the marriage relationship not knowing what we are getting into. None of life's other experiences can really prepare us for what happens after the wedding. Things often look differently before we are married and afterwards. James Dobson has said that it is a good idea to go into marriage with our eyes wide open and afterwards to shut them about halfway. My son says that during courtship, an individual tries to decide if the person he/she is dating is the right one for marriage. After the wedding, that person is the right one. He also says that after a person has been married a while, he realizes the person he married is just as selfish as he is. Another comment is that marriage is an intimate relationship between two sinners. After marriage, we really begin the work of building a relationship with our spouses. I Corinthians 7:28 contains the following words: "but those who marry will face many troubles in this life…" In marriage, there will be difficulties to overcome, but one of the reasons for those trials is for what they teach us about our existence here on earth. Marriage costs us everything, but, for many of us, it is still a bargain.

Becoming a Christian may look differently before and after we receive Christ. When people are witnessing to us, they often tell us that Christ paid the penalty for our sin, and all we need to do to be saved is accept the free gift that He offers. Salvation is by faith alone. We may be told it is easy. After salvation we begin to realize that being a Christ-follower is hard work. Each one of us is a new creation, and there are things we need to do to grow in our relationship with Christ. We must discipline ourselves if we are to become spiritually mature. We must spend time with the Lord in prayer and Bible study. We must seek to be obedient to the Lord in what we do. We must train our thought life and our appetites. We must fellowship with other believers for mutual edification.

We all have storms to weather in the Christian life. There are times of testing, but salvation from God and growing spiritually make it all worthwhile. Unless we grow in the grace and knowledge of our Lord Jesus Christ, we remain spiritual infants. Unless we grow in the grace and knowledge of our Lord Jesus Christ, we have reason to question our salvation. Part of learning to live the Christian life is learning to let go of resentment.

There are some additional things that we, as believers, need to remember about our knowledge of spiritual things. Knowledge, for the sake of itself, can be dangerous. We must maintain humility.

Knowledge puffs up, but love builds up. (I Corinthians 8:1b)

The important thing about knowledge is how we use the knowledge God has given us. Our knowledge of spiritual things may be increasing, but it is still far from complete. We are promised a more complete understanding when we reach heaven.

"For my thoughts are not your thoughts, neither are your ways my ways," declares the Lord. "As the heavens are higher than the earth, so are my ways higher than your ways and my thoughts than your thoughts." (Isaiah 55:8, 9)

In the same way, the Spirit helps us in our weakness. We do not know what we ought to pray for, but the Spirit himself intercedes for us with groans that words cannot express. And he who searches our hearts knows the mind of the Spirit, because the Spirit intercedes for the saints in accordance with God's will. (Romans 8:26, 27)

For we know in part and we prophesy in part, but when perfection comes, the imperfect disappears. When I was a child, I talked like a child, I thought like a child, I reasoned like a child. When I became a man, I put childish ways behind me. Now we see but a poor reflection as in a mirror; then we shall see face to face. Now I know in part; then I shall know fully, even as I am fully known. (I Corinthians 13:9-13)

For now, to grow in grace and in our knowledge of the Lord, we must study the Scriptures, do what they say, and filter all our experiences through the grid of a Christian worldview. We don't completely understand the truth, but we must live up to the amount of truth we do understand. If we do not, the level of understanding that we do have will be taken away. Becoming teachable requires humility. I can't be angry and truly humble at the same time. It's spiritual blindness for me to think I have a right to my resentment.

We must guard against doing things that lead us down the path of error. We must guard against doing things that blind us to God's truth and cause us to drift away from the Lord. We must guard against slipping into sins that affect our relationship with the Father.

Chapter Four
Having a Relationship with God

I've heard it said that any book written for a Christian audience should contain the plan of salvation. This chapter is about having a relationship with God, about salvation and about sanctification. It is about dealing with the sin problem that separates us from God and then growing in grace and in our relationship with the Lord.

Salvation

Salvation and initial sanctification (see below) come by grace through faith when we turn to God.

According to *Webster's New Collegiate Dictionary 150th Anniversary Edition*, grace is unmerited divine assistance given man for his regeneration or sanctification. **(1)**

In his *Introductory Lectures in Systematic Theology*, Henry Clarence Thiessen writes, "Conversion is that turning to God. It consists of two elements, repentance and faith...But [man] can of himself neither turn to God, nor repent, nor believe; the only thing prevenient [antecedent, anticipatory] grace enables him to do is to call upon God to turn him." **(2)**

But now a righteousness from God, apart from law, has been made known, to which the Law and the Prophets testify. This righteousness from God comes through faith in Jesus Christ to all who believe. There is no difference for all have sinned and fall short of the glory of God, and are justified freely by his grace through the redemption that came by Christ Jesus. God presented him as a sacrifice of atonement, through faith in his blood (Romans 3:21-25a).

For we maintain that a man is justified by faith apart from observing the law (Romans 3:28).

What does Scripture say? "Abraham believed God, and it was credited to him as righteousness." Now when a man works, his wages are not credited to him as a gift, but as an obligation. However, to the man who does not work but trusts God who justifies the wicked, his faith is credited as righteousness (Romans 4:3-5).

...that is, the word of faith we are proclaiming: That if you confess with your mouth, "Jesus is Lord," and believe in your heart that God raised him from the dead, you will be saved. For it is with your heart you believe and are justified, and it is with your mouth you confess and are saved (Romans 10:8b-10).

In him [Christ Jesus our Lord] and through faith in him we may approach God with freedom and confidence (Ephesians 3:12).

...faith is being sure of what we hope for and certain of what we do not see (Hebrews 11:1).

Let us consider some other passages describing what saving faith is, how it comes about, and what it accomplishes:

...Jesus declared, "I tell you the truth, no one can see the kingdom of God unless he is born again...I tell you the truth, no one can enter the kingdom of God unless he is born of water and the Spirit. Flesh gives birth to flesh, but the Spirit gives birth to spirit. You should not be surprised at my saying, 'You [plural] must be born again.' The wind blows wherever it pleases. You hear its sound, but you cannot tell where it comes from or where it is going. So it is with everyone born of the Spirit" (John 3:3-8).

Just as Moses lifted up the snake in the desert, so the Son of Man [Jesus] must be lifted up, that everyone who believes in him may have eternal life. For God so loved the world that he gave his one and only Son, that whoever believes in him shall not perish but have eternal life. For God did not send his Son into the world to condemn the world, but to save the world through him. Whoever believes in him is not condemned, but whoever does not believe stands condemned already because he has not believed in the name of God's one and only Son (John 3:14-18).

According to Vine, the verb *pisteuo* means to believe, also to be persuaded of, and hence, to place confidence in, to trust, signifies, in this sense of the word, reliance upon, not mere credence. **(3)**

Just as you used to offer the parts of your body in slavery to impurity and to ever-increasing wickedness, so now offer them in slavery to righteousness leading to holiness...What benefit did you reap at that time from the things you are now ashamed of? Those things result in death! But now that you have been set free from sin and have become slaves to God, the benefit you reap leads to holiness, and the result is eternal life. For the wages of sin is death, but the gift of God is eternal life in Christ Jesus our Lord (Romans 6:19b-23).

Now brothers, I [Paul] want to remind you of the gospel I preached to you, which you received and on which you have taken your stand. By this gospel you are saved, if you hold firmly to the word I preached to you. Otherwise, you have believed in vain. For what I received I passed on to you as of first importance: that Christ died for our sins according to the Scriptures, that he was buried, that he was raised on the third day according to the Scriptures, and that he appeared to Peter, and then to the Twelve. After that, he appeared to more that five hundred of the brothers at the same time, most of whom are still living, though some have fallen asleep. Then he appeared to James, then to all the apostles, and last of all he appeared to me also, as to one abnormally born. (I Corinthians 15:1-8)

According to Paul, in I Corinthians 15:1-8, there are four tenets of the gospel.

1. Christ died for our sins according to the Scriptures.
2. He was buried.
3. He was raised on the third day according to the Scriptures.
4. He was seen.

Therefore, if anyone is in Christ, he is a new creation; the old has gone, the new has come! All this is from God, who reconciled us to himself through Christ and gave us the ministry of reconciliation: that God was reconciling the world to himself in Christ, not counting men's sins against them. And he has committed to us the message of reconciliation. We are therefore Christ's ambassadors, as though God were making his appeal through us. We implore you on Christ's behalf: Be reconciled to God. God made him who had no sin to be sin for us, so that in him we might become the righteousness of God. (II Corinthians 5:17-21)

I [Paul] want you to know, brothers, that the gospel I preached is not something that man made up. I did not receive it from any man, nor was I taught it; rather, I received it by revelation from Jesus Christ. (Galatians 1:11, 12)

In him [Christ] we were also chosen, having been predestined according to the plan of him who works our everything in conformity with the purpose of his will, in order that we, who were the first to hope in Christ, might be for the praise of his glory. And you also were included in Christ when you heard the word of truth, the gospel of your salvation. Having believed, you were marked in him with a seal, the promised Holy Spirit, who is a deposit guaranteeing our inheritance until the redemption of those who are God's possession - to the praise of his glory. (Ephesians 1:11-14)

Ephesians 1:11-14 tells us how we are to respond to the message of the gospel.
1. We hear the word of truth, the gospel of our salvation.
2. We believe [*pisteuo*]. It's not just an awareness, but it's relying on Jesus to take care of us, to meet our needs, to save our souls.
3. We are marked in Him with the seal of the Holy Spirit.

If we claim to be without sin, we deceive ourselves and the truth is not in us. If we confess our sins, he [God] is faithful and just and will forgive our sins and purify us from all unrighteousness. (I John 1:8, 9)

> **After we have accepted Christ as Savior, when God looks at us, He imputes [attributes] Christ's righteousness to us. But we still have our sin nature. Dealing with our own sin requires us to exercise discipline. Acknowledging our sin, confessing our sin, seeking forgiveness, turning our back on the world, and worshipping God are things to do on a daily basis. We are also to study Scripture and fellowship with other believers.**

Assurance of Salvation

Let us also consider the fact that many people who think they are saved have never truly experienced Christ's transforming power.

Not everyone who says to me [Jesus], "Lord, Lord," will enter the kingdom of heaven, but only he who does the will of my Father who is in heaven. Many will say to me on that day, "Lord, Lord, did we not prophesy in your name, and in your name drive out demons and perform many miracles?" Then I will tell them plainly, "I never knew you. Away from me, you evildoers!" (Matthew 7:21-23)

Salvation is by grace alone, through faith, but after we become Christians, works do matter. If we truly receive Christ as Savior, people around us should be able to see evidence that each of us is a new creation. They should be able to see in each of us evidence of a changed life. There are some people who came forward at an altar call or signed a card and think they are Christians. But their lives lack evidence that they have been transformed. The Bible describes how true believers can set their hearts at rest about such issues.

Examine yourselves to see whether you are in the faith; test yourselves. Do you not realize that Christ Jesus is in you - unless, of course, you fail the test? And I trust that you will discover that we have not failed the test. (II Corinthians 13:5, 6)

If anyone has material possessions and sees his brother in need but has no pity on him, how can the love of God be in him? Dear children, let us not love with words or tongue but with actions and in truth. This then is how we know that we belong to the truth and how we set our hearts at rest in his presence whenever our hearts condemn us. For God is greater than our hearts, and he knows everything. Dear friends, if our hearts do not condemn us, we have confidence before God. (I John 3:17-21)

Consider those traits of the believer that accompany new life in Christ:

1. Believers confess that Jesus is Lord.

Whoever acknowledges [confesses] me [Jesus] before men, I will also acknowledge him before my Father in heaven. But whoever disowns me before men, I will disown him before my Father in heaven. (Matthew 10:32, 33)

2. Believers have God's Spirit in their hearts.

We know that we live in him and he in us, because he has given us his Spirit. (I John 4:13)

It's not that we have a certain feeling; it's that we see evidence of Him working in our lives. Talking about certain people who think they have to feel a certain way to know they are saved, a local evangelist named Homer Hammontree used to say, "I just don't feel like I feel like I ought to feel."

In his *Systematic Theology*, Wayne Grudem gives three things that are evidence of our salvation: a present trust in Christ for salvation, evidence of a regenerating work of the Holy Spirit in the heart, and a long term pattern of growth in the Christian life. **(4)**

3. Believers love our brothers.

Anyone who claims to be in the light but hates his brother is still in darkness. (I John 2:9)

49

We know that we have passed from death to life, because we love our brothers. Anyone who does not love remains in death. Anyone who hates his brother is a murderer, and you know that no murderer has eternal life in him. (I John 3:14, 15)

4. Believers turn from their sinful ways.

They [rebellious people] claim to know God, but by their actions they deny him. They are detestable, disobedient and unfit for doing anything good. (Titus 1:16)

No one who lives in him [Jesus] keeps on sinning. No one who continues to sin has either seen him or known him. (I John 3:6)

No one who is born of God will continue to sin, because God's seed remains in him; he cannot go on sinning, because he has been born of God. This is how we know who the children of God are and who the children of the devil are: Anyone who does not do what is right is not a child of God; nor is anyone who does not love his brother. (I John 3:9, 10)

5. Believers obey Jesus' commands.

Paul, a servant of Christ Jesus, called to be an apostle and set apart for the gospel of God - the gospel he promised beforehand through his prophets in the Holy Scriptures regarding his Son, who as to his human nature was a descendant of David, and who through the Spirit of holiness was declared with power to be the Son of God by his resurrection from the dead: Jesus Christ our Lord. Through him and for his name's sake, we received grace and apostleship to call people from among all the Gentiles to the obedience that comes from faith. (Romans 1:1-5)

We know that we have come to know him [Jesus Christ] if we obey his commands. The man who says, "I know him," but does not do what he commands is a liar, and the truth is not in him. But if anyone obeys his word, God's love is truly made complete in him. This is how we know we are in him: Whoever claims to live in him must walk as Jesus did. (I John 2:3-6)

6. Believers persevere during life's difficulties.

Luke chapter eight records Jesus' words as He told the parable of the sower.

A farmer went out to sow his seed. As he was scattering the seed, some fell along the path; it was trampled on, and the birds of the air ate it up. Some fell on rock, and when it came up, the plants withered because they had no moisture. Other seed fell among thorns, which grew up with it and choked the plants. Still other seed fell on good soil. It came up and yielded a crop, a hundred times more than was sown. (Luke 8:5-8a)

Consider Jesus' explanation of the parable.

"This is the meaning of the parable: The seed is the word of God. Those along the path are the ones who hear, and then the devil comes and takes away the word from their hearts, so they may not believe and be saved. Those on the rock are the ones who receive the word with joy when they hear it but they have no root. They believe for a while, but in the time of testing they fall away. The seed that fell among thorns stands for those who hear, but as they go on their way they are choked by life's worries, riches, and pleasures, and they do not mature. But the seed on good soil stands for those with a noble and good heart, who hear the word, retain it, and by persevering produce a crop." (Luke 8:11-15)

Notice that by persevering they produce a crop. They persevere in the faith in spite of the devil, life's worries, and the allure of sin. There are other passages about perseverance.

Remember those earlier days after you had received the light, when you stood your ground in a great contest in the face of suffering. Sometimes you were publicly exposed to insult and persecution; at other times you stood side by side with those who were so treated. You sympathized with those in prison and joyfully accepted the confiscation of your property, because you knew that you yourselves had better and lasting possessions. So do not throw away your confidence; it will be richly rewarded. You need to persevere so that when you have done the will of God, you will receive what he has promised. For in just a little while, "He who is coming will come and will not delay. But my righteous one will live by faith. And if he shrinks back, I will not be pleased with him." But we are not of those who shrink back and are destroyed, but of those who believe and are saved. (Hebrews 10:32-39)

Blessed is the man who perseveres under trial, because when he has stood the test, he will receive the crown of life that God has promised to those who love him. (James 1:12)

7. Believers minister to other people's needs.

Land that drinks in the rain often falling on it and that produces a crop useful to those for whom it is farmed receives the blessing of God. But land that produces thorns and thistles is worthless and is in danger of being cursed. In the end it will

51

be burned. Even though we speak like this, dear friends, we are confident of better things in your case - things that accompany salvation. (Hebrews 6:7-9)

If anyone does not provide for his relatives, and especially for his immediate family, he has denied the faith and is worse than an unbeliever. (I Timothy 5:8)

What good is it, my brothers, if a man claims to have faith but has no deeds? Can such faith save him? Suppose a brother or sister is without clothes and daily food. If one of you says to him, "Go I wish you well; keep warm and well fed," but does nothing about his physical needs, what good is it? In the same way, faith by itself, if not accompanied by action, is dead. (James 2:14-17)

One of the highest forms of service is to those who cannot repay.

Then Jesus said to his host, "When you give a luncheon or dinner, do not invite your friends, your brothers or relatives, or your rich neighbors; if you do, they may invite you back and so you will be repaid. But when you give a banquet, invite the poor, the crippled, the lame, the blind, and you will be blessed. Although they cannot repay you, you will be repaid at the resurrection of the righteous." (Luke 14:12-14)

In my mind, another form of service, high on the list, is to those who could repay, at least with gratitude, but will not do so. An example would be caregivers who unselfishly take care of family members but are still treated with contempt by the recipients of their care. In my opinion, no one can accuse them of seeking the praise of men.

Over the last twenty years, I've been on many mission trips. What I tell my fellow travelers going on these trips is that if they continue to go on them (or actively participate in any other ministry), God will show them things to do that if they weren't there, no one else would do them.

For example, in 1996, we went to Donetsk, Ukraine, to take chemotherapy drugs for children with cancer and to exchange ideas. I had purchased a brand new copy of the standard textbook of Nephrology, Brenner and Rector's *The Kidney* (5), to take along as a gift. When I presented the book to the hospital administrator, his eyes lit up in a way that greatly surprised me and thrilled my soul. It was a look of pure delight. I was later to be told that when most physicians give a medical book to a medical doctor in another country, they've just bought the new edition and are giving away the old one.

The experience in Ukraine gave me an idea. On my next trip to Central America, I purchased several Bible reference books, in Spanish, to give to the local pastors. Examples would include *Vine's Expository Dictionary of New Testament Words, Strong's Concordance,* and *Holman's Bible Dictionary.* I didn't even know that the Vine's was available in Spanish until the lady at the Christian bookstore said, "I have a Vine's. Do you want a Vine's?" I said, "Sure, throw it in." After I arrived in Central America I tried to assess the individual maturity of the pastors and pass out the books as seemed appropriate. The man who got the Vine's said he had been praying for a Vine's for two years. On each of my last three trips to Nicaragua, I have given the local hospital standard medical textbooks in Spanish for pediatrics, internal medicine, and emergency medicine.

Two years ago, a lady from our church went with us on a mission trip to Nicaragua. Unbeknown to me, in preparation for the trip, she rounded up several ladies in our congregation, and they all made dresses for the little girls. She arrived in Nicaragua with 50 or 60 dresses. The dresses were very well received. Making the dresses is something I would never have thought to do. On one mission trip to Guatemala, our departure for home was delayed by my medical assistant. She was concerned about the nutritional status of a newborn baby. The mother had just given birth to her tenth child and had no breast milk. We waited while my fellow traveler rounded up a two-month supply of infant formula.

The reason I'm telling these stories is to illustrate the fact that we all need to be actively searching for ways to be of service to others. We all have different things we identify with in others, knowledge about different things, and different gifts. If we are intentional about service, and if we abide in Christ, He will show us what we need to do to be of help to others.

8. Believers continue in the faith.

Wayne Grudem writes, "Only those who persevere to the end have been truly born again." **(6)**

All men will hate you because of me [Jesus], but he who stands firm to the end will be saved. (Matthew 10:22)

Dear children, this is the last hour; and as you have heard that the antichrist is coming, even now many antichrists have come…They [antichrists - men who deny that Jesus is the Christ] went out from us, but they did not really belong to us. For if they had belonged to us, they would have remained with us; but their going showed that none of them belonged to us. (I John 2:18, 19)

See that what you have heard from the beginning remains in you. If it does, you will also remain in the Son and in the Father. And this is what he [Jesus] promised us - even eternal life. And now, dear children, continue in him, so that when he appears we may be confident and unashamed before him at his coming. (I John 2:24, 25, 28)

When it comes to all the things believers are supposed to do, how do we accomplish such an impossible task? As I see it, it is only by the grace of God.

When I was twelve years old, a counselor at a Children's Bible Mission camp in Elizabethton, TN, asked me if I were going to heaven when I died. I replied that I thought so. He asked me if I had accepted Christ as my Savior. I told him I had done so when I was seven years old. He told me that if I had accepted Christ as my Savior, I could know for certain that I had eternal life. He pointed to I John 5:13: "I write these things to you who believe in the name of the Son of God so that you may know that you have eternal life." Regarding assurance of salvation, I thought that was all there was to it. However, many of the passages about assurance are from I John. I now realize that I John 5:13 is predicated on what has been written in the previous four and a half chapters of I John and that to have an assurance of salvation, our lives need to look like what has been written in those passages. Our salvation is a gift from God. After our salvation, as we begin and continue our walk with God, He gives us the will and power to do what we are supposed to do.

...for it is God who works in you to will and to act according to his good purpose. (Philippians 2:13)

We know that anyone born of God does not continue to sin; the one who was born of God [Jesus] keeps him safe, and the evil one cannot harm him. We know that we are children of God, and that the whole world is under the control of the evil one. We know also that the Son of God has come and has given us understanding, so that we may know him who is true. And we are in him who is true - even in his Son Jesus Christ. He is the true God and eternal life. (I John 5:18-20)

In dealing with resentment, I believe it is important for us as Christians to understand our true identity in Christ. We need to realize we have the power of the whole Godhead dwelling within us. We must study Scripture to understand what is going on and to find how to utilize the power that is already there.

I believe that people with a recurring uncontrolled anger problem have a right to question whether or not they have ever been truly saved.

Sanctification

Sanctification is the process of being made holy. Overcoming resentment is part of the sanctification process. Scripture mentions three aspects of our sanctification: the initial sanctification occurring at the time of our salvation, the gradual process of sanctification occurring as we live our lives as believers, and the final or complete sanctification, occurring simultaneously with our resurrection.

The righteousness we are granted at the time of our salvation is positional. It is an imputed righteousness. According to Bauer, Arndt, and Gingrich, the Greek verb for impute, *logizomai*, means to reckon or calculate. It can be an accounting word carrying the idea of "place to one's account" or to credit. **(7)** Regarding imputed righteousness, the *Holman Illustrated Bible Dictionary* reads as follows:

The imputation of righteousness lies at the heart of the biblical doctrine of salvation. This righteousness is seen in Christ who purchased redemption. God grants righteousness to those who have faith in Christ...This righteousness imputed or reckoned to believers is, strictly speaking, an alien righteousness. It is not the believer's own righteousness but God's righteousness imputed [credited] to the believer [to his account]. **(8)**

The Lord's gradual process of making us holy, here on earth, is the natural extension of the initial salvation He provides. As Wayne Grudem describes it in his *Systematic Theology*, it is a part of the application of redemption that is a progressive work and continues throughout our earthly lives. **(9)** It is also a work in which God and man cooperate, each playing distinct roles. **(10)** The process makes us more and more free from sin and more like Christ in our actual lives. Grudem says the gradual process of sanctification that occurs here on earth occurs best in community. **(11)** An important part of the process is believers fellowshipping with other believers for mutual edification. I believe that mentoring can do as much for the mentor as it does for the one being mentored.

The final sanctification, which will occur at believers' resurrection, will make our sanctification complete. To help understand sanctification, it was beneficial for me to consider the Greek words related to holiness or sanctification and to use a Greek Concordance to look up the pertinent passages. These words include *hagiadzoo* meaning to make holy, consecrate, sanctify, or purify, *hagiasmos* meaning holiness, consecration, or sanctification, and *hagios* meaning dedicated to God, holy, or sacred. **(12)** Let us take a look at some of the pertinent Scripture passages about sanctification. Some passages appear to be specific for one aspect of sanctification, whereas with others, there doesn't seem to be any clear distinction.

I. God the Father chooses believers for salvation and sanctification.

When the Gentiles heard this, they were glad and honored the word of the Lord; and all who were appointed for eternal life believed. (Acts 13:48)

For those God foreknew he also predestined to be conformed to the likeness of his Son, that he might be the firstborn among many brothers. And those he predestined, he also called; those he called, he also justified; those he justified, he also glorified. (Romans 8:29, 30)

Not only that, Rebekah's children had one and the same father, our father Isaac. Yet, before the twins were born or had done anything good or bad - in order that God's purpose in election might stand: not by works but by him who calls - she was told, "The older will serve the younger." Just as it is written: "Jacob I loved, but Esau I hated." What then shall we say? Is God unjust? Not at all! For he says to Moses, "I will have mercy on whom I have mercy, and I will have compassion on whom I have compassion." It does not, therefore, depend on man's desire or effort, but on God's mercy. For the Scripture says to Pharaoh: "I raised you up for this very purpose, that I might display my power in you and that my name might be proclaimed in all the earth." Therefore God has mercy on whom he wants to have mercy, and he hardens whom he wants to harden. (Romans 9:10-18)

But we ought always to thank God for you, brothers loved by the Lord, because from the beginning God chose you to be saved through the sanctifying work of the Spirit and through belief in the truth. (II Thessalonians 2:13)

But join with me [Paul] in suffering for the gospel, by the power of God, who saved us and called us to a holy life - not because of anything we have done but because of his own purpose and grace. This grace was given us in Christ Jesus before the beginning of time, (II Timothy 1:8b, 9)

II. Jesus Christ died on the cross to make provision for our sin debt. That payment was necessary for our justification, regeneration, and sanctification.

Husbands, love your wives, just as Christ loved the church and gave himself up for her to make her holy, cleansing her by the washing with water through the word, and to present her to himself as a radiant church, without stain or wrinkle or any other blemish, but holy and blameless. (Ephesians 5:25-27)

When Christ came as high priest of the good things that are already here, he went through the greater and more perfect tabernacle that is not man-made, that is to say, not part of this creation. He did not enter by means of the blood of goats and calves; but he entered the Most Holy Place once for all by his own blood, having obtained eternal redemption. The blood of goats and bulls and the ashes of a heifer sprinkled on those who are ceremonially unclean sanctify them so that they are outwardly clean. How much more, then, will the blood of Christ, who through the eternal Spirit offered himself unblemished to God, cleanse our consciences from acts that lead to death, so that we may serve the living God. (Hebrews 9:11-14)

But now he [Christ] has appeared once for all at the end of the ages to do away with sin by the sacrifice of himself. (Hebrews 9:26b)

First he [Christ] said, "Sacrifices and offerings, burnt offerings and sin offerings you [God] did not desire, nor were you pleased with them" (although the law required them to be made). Then he said, "Here I am, I have come to do your will." He sets aside the first to establish the second. And by that will, we have been made holy through the sacrifice of the body of Jesus Christ once for all. Day after day every priest stands and performs his religious duties; again and again he offers the same sacrifices, which can never take away sins. But when this priest had offered for all time one sacrifice for sins, he sat down at the right hand of God. Since that time he waits for his enemies to be made his footstool, because by one sacrifice he has made perfect forever those who are being made holy. (Hebrews 10:8-14)

The high priest carries the blood of animals into the Most Holy Place as a sin offering, but the bodies are burned outside the camp. And so Jesus also suffered outside the city gate to make the people holy through his own blood. (Hebrews 13:11, 12)

For anyone who may have doubts about Jesus being the only way to God, I offer some other pertinent scripture passages.

Whoever believes in him is not condemned, but whoever does not believe stands condemned already because he has not believed in the name of God's one and only [*monogenees*] Son [Jesus]. (John 3:18)

The Greek word *monogenes* is translated "only begotten" in the KJV. Speaking of Jesus, *monogenees* was used five times in the NT writings of John the Apostle (John 1:14, 18; John 3:16, 18; I John 4:9. **(13)** Liddell and Scott write that *monogenees* means "uniqueness, the only member of a kin or kind, or one and the same blood." **(14)** Bauer, Arndt, and Gingrich include the meaning of "the only example in its category." **(15)** Vine writes, "As the Son of God, [Jesus is] the sole representative of the Being and character of the Father who sent Him...the word "begotten" does not imply a beginning of His Sonship; it is an unoriginated relationship ...[Jesus] possesses every attribute of pure Godhood." Jesus' existence spans from eternity past to eternity future. He is an "absolute being." The Father and the Son have the deepest affection for each other. The Son and the Father have eternal union with each other in the Godhead **(16)** According to *Holman Illustrated Bible Dictionary*, "Being fully God and of the same nature as God the Father, Jesus the Son alone can

58

make God's glory known. (17) From these definitions I believe it is safe to say that *only begotten* means that the Father and the Son are of the same essence.

The Father loves the Son and has placed everything in his hands. Whoever believes in the Son has eternal life, but whoever rejects the Son will not see life, for God's wrath remains on him. (John 3:35, 36)

But he [Jesus] continued, "You [Pharisees] are from below; I am from above. You are of this world; I am not of this world. I told you that you would die in your sins; if you do not believe that I am the one I claim to be, you will indeed die in your sins." (John 8:23, 24)

In the *ASV* translation, John 8:24 reads as follows: "Except ye believe that I am he." *I am* is the translation of the Greek words *ego eimi.* The pronoun "he" is implied and is not in the original text.

Eimi means "I am." *Ego eimi* carries more emphasis and is a name for God. "*I myself am*" is the equivalent of the Hebrew Yahweh.

He who hates me [Jesus] hates my Father as well. (John 15:23)

"You are a king, then!" said Pilate. Jesus answered, "You are right in saying I am a king. In fact, for this reason I was born, and for this I came into the world, to testify to the truth. Everyone on the side of truth listens to me." (John 18:37)

For Moses said, "The Lord your God will raise up for you a prophet like me from among your own people; you must listen to everything he tells you. Anyone who does not listen to him will be completely cut off from among his people." (Acts 3:22, 23)

Acts 3:22, 23 is a quote from Deuteronomy 18:15, 18, 19. Christians believe that in this passage, Moses was talking about Jesus. I've always heard that the thing that made Jesus and Moses alike was that each of them was both a priest and a king.

Salvation is found in no one else [other than Jesus Christ of Nazareth], for there is no other name under heaven given to men by which we must be saved. (Acts 4:12)

For there is one God and one mediator between God and men, the man Christ Jesus, who gave himself as a ransom for all men - the testimony given in its proper time. (I Timothy 2:5, 6)

If we deliberately keep on sinning after we have received the knowledge of the truth, no sacrifice for sins is left, but only a fearful expectation of judgment and of raging fire that will consume the enemies of God. Anyone who rejected the Law of Moses died without mercy on the testimony of two or three witnesses. How much more severely do you think a man deserves to be punished who has trampled the Son of God underfoot, who has treated as an unholy thing the blood of the covenant that sanctified him, and who has insulted the Spirit of grace? (Hebrews 10:26-29)

Who is the liar? It is the man who denies that Jesus is the Christ. Such a man is the antichrist - he denies the Father and the Son. No one who denies the Son has the Father; whoever acknowledges the Son has the Father also. (I John 2:22, 23)

We accept man's testimony, but God's testimony is greater because it is the testimony of God, which he has given about his Son. Anyone who believes in the Son of God has this testimony in his heart. Anyone who does not believe God has made him out to be a liar, because he has not believed the testimony God has given about his Son. And this is the testimony: God has given us eternal life, and this life is in his Son. He who has the Son has life; he who does not have the Son of God does not have life. (I John 5:9-12)

III. Sanctification is a work implemented by the Holy Spirit.

Jesus: "When he [the Counselor, i.e. the Holy Spirit] comes he will convict the world of guilt in regard to sin and righteousness and judgment:" (John 16:8)

But when he, the Spirit of truth comes, he will guide you into all truth. He will not speak on his own; he will speak only what he hears, and he will tell you what is yet to come. He will bring glory to me [Jesus] by taking from what is mine and making it known to you. (John 16:13, 14)

For if you live according to the sinful nature, you will die; but if by the Spirit you put to death the misdeeds of the body, you will live, because those who are led by the Spirit of God are sons of God. (Romans 8:13, 14)

We do, however, speak a message of wisdom among the mature, but not the wisdom of this age or of the rulers of this age, who are coming to nothing. No, we speak of God's secret wisdom, a wisdom that has been hidden and that God destined for our glory before time began. None of the rulers of this age understood it, for if they had, they would not have crucified the Lord of glory. However, as it is written: "No eye has seen, no ear has heard, no mind has conceived what God has prepared for those who love him" - but God has revealed it to us by his Spirit. The Spirit searches all things, even the deep things of God. For who among men knows the thoughts of a man except the man's spirit within him? In the same way no one knows the thoughts of God except the Spirit of God. We have not received the spirit of the world but the Spirit who is from God, that we may understand what God has freely given us. This is what we speak, not in words taught us by human wisdom but in words taught by the Spirit, expressing spiritual truths in spiritual words. The man without the Spirit does not accept the things that come from the Spirit of God, for they are foolishness to him, and he cannot understand them, because they are spiritually discerned. (I Corinthians 2:6-14)

But you were washed, you were sanctified, you were justified in the name of the Lord Jesus Christ and by the Spirit of our God. (I Corinthians 6:11b)

Peter, an apostle of Jesus Christ, To God's elect, strangers in the world, scattered throughout Pontus, Galatia, Cappadocia, Asia and Bithynia, who have been chosen according to the foreknowledge of God the Father, through the sanctifying work of the Spirit, for obedience to Jesus Christ and sprinkling by his blood: Grace and peace be yours in abundance. (I Peter 1:1, 2)

Note that God's elect have been chosen for obedience to Jesus Christ.

IV. Believers are to be intentional about their sanctification.

Accepting Jesus Christ into our hearts is an act of obedience.

Dear friends, if our hearts do not condemn us, we have confidence before God and receive from him anything we ask, because we obey his commands and do what pleases him. And this is his command: to believe in the name of his Son, Jesus Christ, and to love one another as he commanded us. Those who obey his commands live in him, and he in them. (I John 3:21-24a)

Don't you know that when you offer yourselves to someone to obey him as slaves, you are slaves to the one whom you obey – whether you are slaves to sin, which leads to death, or to obedience which leads to righteousness? But thanks be to God that, though you used to be slaves to sin, you wholeheartedly obeyed the form of teaching to which you were entrusted. You have been set free from sin and have become slaves to righteousness. (Romans 6:16-18)

…when the Lord Jesus is revealed…He will punish those who do not know God and do not obey the gospel of our Lord Jesus. (II Thessalonians 1:7b, 8)

For in Scripture it says: "See I lay a stone in Zion, a chosen and precious

61

cornerstone [Jesus Christ], and the one who trusts in him will never be put to shame." Now to you who believe, this stone is precious. But to those who do not believe. "The stone the builders rejected has become the capstone," and, "A stone that causes men to stumble and a rock that makes them fall." They stumble because they disobey the message – which is also what they were destined for. (1 Peter 2:6-8)

For it is time for judgment to begin with the family of God; and if it begins with us, what will the outcome be for those who do not obey the gospel of God? (I Peter 4:17)

In order to maintain a close relationship with the Lord and for our sanctification here on earth to be progressive, we must cooperate

with the program. Some necessary acts of volition are underlined in the next few passages.

For we are the temple of the living God. As God has said: "I will live with them and walk among them, and I will be their God, and they will be my people." "Therefore come out from them and be separate, says the Lord. Touch no unclean thing, and I will receive you." "I will be a Father to you, and you will be my sons and daughters, says the Lord Almighty." Since we have these promises, dear friends, let us purify ourselves from everything that contaminates body and spirit, perfecting holiness out of reverence for God. (II Corinthians 6:16b-7:1)

Put to death, therefore, whatever belongs to your earthly nature: sexual immorality, impurity, lust, evil desires and greed, which is idolatry. Because of these, the wrath of God is coming. You used to walk in these ways, in the life you once lived. But now you must rid yourselves of all such things as these: anger, rage, malice, slander, and filthy language from your lips. Do not lie to each other, since you have taken off your old self with its practices and put on the new self, which is being renewed in knowledge in the image of its Creator. (Colossians 3:5-10)

For you know what instructions we gave you by the authority of the Lord Jesus. It is God's will that you should be sanctified: that you should avoid sexual immorality; that each of you should learn to control his own body in a way that is holy and honorable, not in passionate lust like the heathen, who do not know God; and that in this matter no one should wrong his brother or take advantage of him. The Lord will punish men for all such sins, as we have already told you and warned you. For God did not call us to be impure, but to live a holy life. Therefore, he who rejects this instruction does not reject man but God, who gives you his Holy Spirit. (I Thessalonians 4:2-8)

Do your best to present yourself to God as one approved, a workman who does not need to be ashamed and who correctly handles the word of truth [the Bible]. Avoid godless chatter, because those who indulge in it will become more and more ungodly...God's solid foundation stands firm, sealed with this inscription: "The Lord knows who are his," and, "Everyone who confesses the name of the Lord must turn away from wickedness." In a large house there are articles not only of gold and silver, but also of wood and clay; some are for noble purposes and some for ignoble. If a man cleanses himself from the latter, he will be an instrument for noble purposes, made holy, useful to the Master and prepared to do any good work...pursue righteousness, faith, love and peace, along with those who call on the Lord out of a pure heart. (II Timothy 2:15-22)

Make every effort to live in peace with all men and to be holy; without holiness no one will see the Lord. (Hebrews 12:14)

V. God uses believers to provide mutual edification for each other.

I [Paul] long to see you so that I may impart to you some spiritual gift to make you strong - that is, that you and I may be mutually encouraged by each other's faith. (Romans 1:11, 12)

Let us therefore make every effort to do what leads to peace and mutual edification. (Romans 14:19)

From him [Christ] the whole body, joined and held together by every supporting ligament, grows and builds itself up in love, as each part does its work. (Ephesians 4:16)

Therefore encourage one another and build each other up, just as in fact you are doing. (I Thessalonians 5:11)

Works of the flesh include many acts that destroy community.

The acts of the sinful nature are obvious: sexual immorality, impurity and debauchery; idolatry and witchcraft; hatred, discord, jealousy, fits of rage, selfish ambition, dissensions, factions and envy; drunkenness, orgies, and the like. I warn you as I did before, that those who live like this will not inherit the kingdom of God. (Galatians 5:19-21)

Fruits of the Spirit include many things that build community.

But the fruit of the Spirit is love, joy, peace, patience, kindness, goodness, faithfulness, gentleness and self-control. Against such things there is no law. (Galatians 5:22, 23)

The Greek word *alleelon* means "one another." **(18)** The word is used many times in the New Testament and frequently tells believers how they are supposed to treat each other and also our neighbors. Some of these passages have been very convicting for me personally.

Be devoted to one another in brotherly love. Honor one another above yourselves. (Romans 12:10)

Live in harmony with one another. (Romans 12:16a)

If you have any encouragement from being united with Christ, if any comfort from his love, if any fellowship with the Spirit, if any tenderness and compassion, then make my joy complete by being like-minded, having the same love, being one in spirit and purpose. Do nothing out of selfish ambition or vain conceit, but in humility consider others better than yourselves. Each of you should look not only to your own interests, but also to the interests of others. (Philippians 2:1-4)

And let us consider how we may spur one another on toward love and good deeds. Let us not give up meeting together, as some are in the habit of doing, but let us encourage one another - and all the more as you see the Day approaching. (Hebrews 10:24, 25)

Above all, love each other deeply, because love covers over a multitude of sins. Offer hospitality to one another without grumbling. Each one should use whatever gift he has received to serve others, faithfully administering God's grace in its various forms. If anyone speaks, he should do it as one speaking the very words of God. If anyone serves, he should do it with the strength God provides, so that in all things God may be praised through Jesus Christ. To him be the glory and the power for ever and ever. Amen. (I Peter 4:8-11)

VI. Progressive sanctification requires overcoming the world, the flesh (the sinful nature), and the devil.

Let us behave decently, as in the daytime, not in orgies and drunkenness, not in sexual immorality and debauchery, not in dissension and jealousy. Rather clothe yourselves with the Lord Jesus Christ, and do not think about how to gratify the desires of the sinful nature. (Romans 13:13, 14)

64

So I say, live by the Spirit, and you will not gratify the desires of the sinful nature. For the sinful nature desires what in contrary to the Spirit, and the Spirit what is contrary to the sinful nature. They are in conflict with each other, so that you do not do what you want. (Galatians 5:16, 17)

Religion that God our Father accepts as pure and faultless is this: to look after orphans and widows in their distress and to keep oneself from being polluted by the world. (James 1:27)

Submit yourselves, then, to God. Resist the devil, and he will flee from you. (James 4:7)

Be self-controlled and alert. Your enemy the devil prowls around like a roaring lion looking for someone to devour. Resist him standing firm in the faith, (I Peter 5:8. 9a)

Do not love the world or anything in the world. If anyone loves the world, the love of the Father is not in him. For everything in the world - the cravings of sinful man, the lust of his eyes and the boasting of what he has and does - comes not from the Father but from the world. The world and its desires pass away, but the man who does the will of God lives forever. (I John 2:15-17)

VII. God uses our difficult situations to discipline us, to instruct us, to draw us to Himself.

According to Bauer, Arndt, and Gingrich's *A Greek-English Lexicon of the New Testament*, the Greek noun *paideia* has to do with "upbringing, training, instruction, . . . As it is attained by discipline, correction...of the holy discipline of a fatherly God." God's discipline of believers is not something that is primarily punitive but for our spiritual growth. It's more about going to school than it is enduring the rod. The verb form is *paideuo*. **(19)**

When we are judged by the Lord, we are being disciplined [*paideuo*] so that we will not be condemned with the world. (I Corinthians 11:32)

And have you forgotten the word of encouragement that addresses you as sons: "My son, do not make light of the Lord's discipline, and do not lose heart when he rebukes you, because the Lord disciplines those he loves, and he punishes everyone he accepts as a son." Endure hardship as discipline; God is treating you as sons. For what son is not disciplined by his father? If you are not disciplined (and everyone undergoes discipline), then you are illegitimate children and not true sons. Moreover, we have all had human fathers who disciplined us and we respected them for it. How much more should we submit to the Father of our spirits and live! Our fathers disciplined us for a little while as they thought best; but God disciplines us for our good, that we may share in his holiness. No discipline [paideia] seems pleasant at the time, but painful. Later on, however, it produces a harvest of righteousness and peace for those who have been trained by it. (Hebrews 12:5-11)

Those whom I love, I rebuke and discipline [*paideuo*]. So be earnest, and repent. (Revelation 3:19)

The Greek word *sophronismos* is translated self-discipline in the NIV. Literally the word means "saving the mind." It is an "admonishing or calling to soundness of mind, or to self-control." **(20)** According to Bauer, Arndt, and Gingrich the word was used in secular Greek to denote "the teaching of morality, good judgment, or moderation; advice, improvement." It has to do with "moderation, self- discipline, prudence." **(21)**

For God did not give us a spirit of timidity, but a spirit of power, of love and of self-discipline [*sophronismos*]. (II Timothy 1:7)

The Hebrew word *yasar* is frequently used for discipline or chasten in the Old Testament. R. Laird Harris writes as follows:

The LXX [*Septuagint*] translates [the word] primarily as *paideuo*, which emphasizes the notion of education…From the usage and parallels in the OT, one must conclude that *yasar* and *musar* [a derivative of *yasar*] denote correction that results in education. The theological basis for discipline is grounded in the covenant relationship which Yahweh establishes with his people…God's corrective discipline seeks the reformation of the people…The discipline of Yahweh is not to be taken negatively, for the hardships in the wilderness were balanced by his miraculous provisions both designed to test "what was in your heart, whether or not you would keep his commands" (Deuteronomy 8:2). Hence by their hunger, as well as by the manna which he provided, they were to "understand that man does not live by bread alone, but…by everything that proceeds from the mouth of Yahweh" (Deuteronomy 8:3). **(22)**

Be careful to follow every command I [Moses] am giving you today, so that you may live and increase and may enter and possess the land that the Lord promised on oath to your forefathers. Remember how the Lord your God led you all the way in the desert these forty years, to humble you and to test you in order to know what was in your heart, whether or not you would keep his commands. He humbled you, causing you to hunger and then feeding you with manna, which neither you nor your fathers had known, to teach you that man does not live on bread alone but on every word that comes from the mouth of the Lord. Your clothes did not wear out and your feet did not swell during these forty years. Know then in your heart that as a man disciplines [yasar] his son, so the Lord your God disciplines you. (Deuteronomy 8:1-5)

Blessed is the man you discipline, O Lord, the man you teach from your law; you grant him relief from days of trouble. (Ps. 94:12, 13a)

> **If the Lord is using difficult words from another person or a nettlesome experience to discipline us, to help us grow spiritually, losing control of our temper clouds our judgment, and we are less likely to learn what He is trying to teach us.**

During Job's time of testing, the Sabeans carried off his oxen and donkeys and put his servants to the sword. Fire burned up the sheep and the servants caring for them. The Chaldeans carried off his camels and killed his servants. A mighty wind struck the house where his children were feasting and they all died. Satan afflicted Job with painful sores from the soles of his feet to the top of his head (Job chapters 1 & 2). I don't see anything in the text about Job being angry with the perpetrators. He took up his issues with God.

VIII. Sanctification requires spending time with the Lord in Bible study and prayer.

I have hidden your word in my heart that I might not sin against you [Lord]. (Psalm 119:11)

Oh, how I love your law! I meditate on it all day long. Your commands make me wiser than my enemies, for they are ever with me. I have more insight than all my teachers, for I meditate on your statutes. I have more understanding than the elders, for I obey your precepts. I have kept my feet from every evil path so that I might obey your word. I have not departed from your laws, for you yourself have taught me. How sweet are your words to my taste, sweeter than honey to my mouth! I gain understanding from your precepts, therefore I hate every wrong path. (Psalm 119:97-104)

Jesus answered, "It is written: 'Man does not live on bread alone, but on every word that comes from the mouth of God.'" (Matthew 4:4)

Watch and pray so that you will not fall into temptation. The spirit is willing, but the body is weak. (Matthew 26:41)

Jesus: "[Father] Sanctify them by the truth; your word is truth." (John 17:17)

IX. Obedience is a necessary requirement if God is to hear our prayers.

If I had cherished sin in my heart, the Lord would not have listened... (Psalm 66:18)

If anyone turns a deaf ear to the law, even his prayers are detestable. (Proverbs 28:9)

We know that God does not listen to sinners. He listens to the godly man who does his will. (John 9:31)

X. Righteousness allows us to know God's will.

Therefore, I urge you, brothers, in view of God's mercy, to offer your bodies as living sacrifices, holy and pleasing to God - this is your spiritual act of worship. Do not conform any longer to the patterns of this world, but be transformed by the renewing of your mind. Then you will be able to test and approve what God's will is - his good, pleasing and perfect will. (Romans 12:1, 2)

XI. Our sanctification is for the purpose of glorifying God.

Jesus: "This is to my Father's glory, that you bear much fruit, showing yourselves to be my disciples." (John 15:8)

With this in mind, we constantly pray for you, that our God may count you worthy of his calling, and that by his power he may fulfill every good purpose of yours and every act prompted by your faith. We pray this so that the name of our Lord Jesus may be glorified in you, and you in him, according to the grace of our God and the Lord Jesus Christ. (II Thessalonians 1:11, 12)

But you [God's elect] are a chosen people, a royal priesthood, a holy nation, a people belonging to God, that you may declare the praises of him who called you out of darkness into his wonderful light. Once you were not a people, but now you are the people of God; once you had not received mercy, but now you have received mercy. Dear friends, I urge you, as aliens and strangers in the world, to abstain from sinful desires, which war against your soul. Live such good lives among the pagans that, though they accuse you of doing wrong, they may see your good deeds and glorify God on the day he visits us. (I Peter 2:9-12)

Part of sanctification is overcoming anger and resentment. If we are to overcome our anger and resentment we must make progress toward sanctification. The two processes feed on each other.

Chapter Five
Things That Disrupt Our Fellowship with God

The Bible tells us about the security true believers have in their relationship with God through Christ.

My [Jesus'] sheep listen to my voice; I know them, and they follow me. I give them eternal life, and they shall never perish; no one can snatch them out of my hand. My Father, who has given them to me, is greater than all; no one can snatch them out of my Father's hand. (John 10:27-29)

Who shall separate us from the love of Christ? Shall trouble or hardship or persecution or famine or nakedness or danger or sword? As it is written: "For your sake we face death all day long; we are considered as sheep to be slaughtered." No, in all these things we are more than conquerors through him who loved us. For I am convinced that neither death nor life, neither angels nor demons, neither the present nor the future, nor any powers, neither height nor depth, nor anything else in all creation, will be able to separate us from the love of God that is in Christ Jesus our Lord. (Romans 8:35-39)

Satan can disrupt the fellowship we have with our Savior by tempting us to commit sin that affects the closeness we have in our relationship with God.

Even though nothing can separate true believers from the love of God and the security of their salvation, Satan can disrupt the fellowship we have with our Savior. The way Dr. Ron Stewart, a local pastor here in Knoxville, has said it is that the devil is trying to take away our anointing (Radio Broadcast).

I am writing these things to you about those who are trying to lead you astray. As for you, the anointing you received from him [the Son] remains in you, and you do not need anyone to teach you. But as his anointing teaches you about all things and as that anointing is real, not counterfeit - just as it has taught you, remain in him. (I John 2:26, 27)

Consider the concept of anointing in the Old and New Testaments.

According to R. Laird Harris in *Theological Wordbook of the Old Testament*, the word *mashah* had a fourfold theological significance:

1. The word indicated an authorized separation for God's service. Moses anointed Aaron "to sanctify him". While representing a position of honor, it also represented increased responsibility. Both Saul and David were called to account for their sin with the reminder, "I [the Lord] anointed you king."
2. Though the person who did the anointing might have been a priest or prophet, God was the authorizing agent.
3. Divine enablement was understood to accompany the anointing.
4. The word was associated with the coming promised deliverer, the Messiah. **(1)**

These ideas about the meaning of anointing seem to be reflected in the Greek New Testament word *chrio*. According to *Vine's Expository Dictionary of New Testament Words*, the word *chrio*, translated anoint, is confined to sacred and symbolic anointing. **(2)**

Now it is God who makes both us and you stand firm in Christ. He anointed [*chrio*] us, set his seal of ownership on us, and put his Spirit in our hearts as a deposit, guaranteeing what is to come. (II Corinthians 1:21, 22)

Another Hebrew Old Testament word for anointing is *suk*. **(3)** This word may be used of anointing the body with olive oil, particularly after bathing, especially for its fragrant effect. This idea of a sweet smell is reflected in the following passage in II Corinthians:

But thanks be to God, who always leads us in triumphal procession in Christ and through us spreads everywhere the fragrance of the knowledge of him. For we are to God the aroma of Christ among those who are being saved and those who are perishing. To the one we are the smell of death; to the other, the fragrance of life. And who is equal to such a task? (II Corinthians 2:14-16)

It is part of the normal Christian life to seek to maintain both aspects of our anointing. Believers are instructed to remain [abide] in Christ. According to Bauer, Arndt, and Gingrich's *A Greek-English Lexicon of the New Testament*, the Greek word *menoo* means to remain or stay or to live, dwell, or lodge. It speaks of Christians in their relationship to God and of God in His relationship to Christians. It means to remain in fellowship. **(4)** In John 15, Jesus describes the closeness believers must have with the Son and the Father if the believers are to abide or remain in Christ and bear spiritual fruit.

I [Jesus] am the true vine, and my Father is the gardener. He cuts off every branch in me that bears no fruit, while every branch that does bear fruit he prunes so that it will be even more fruitful. You are already clean because of the word I have spoken to you. Remain in me, and I will remain in you. No branch can bear fruit by itself; it must remain in the vine. Neither can you bear fruit unless you remain in me. I am the vine; you are the branches. If a man remains in me and I in him, he will bear much fruit; apart from me you can do nothing. If anyone does not remain in me, he is like a branch that is thrown away and withers; such branches are picked up, thrown into the fire and burned. If you remain in me and my words remain in you, ask whatever you wish, and it will be given you. This is to my Father's glory, that you bear much fruit, showing yourselves to be my disciples. As the Father has loved me, so have I loved you. Now remain in my love. If you obey my commands, you will remain in my love, just as I have obeyed my Father's commands and remain in his love. I have told you this so that my joy may be in you and that your joy may be complete. My command is this: Love each other as I have loved you. Greater love has no one than this that he lay down his life for his friends. You are my friends if you do what I command. I no longer call you servants, because a servant does not know his master's business. Instead I have called you friends, for everything that I learned from my Father I have made known to you. You did not choose me, but I chose you and appointed you to go and bear fruit - fruit that will last. Then the Father will give you whatever you ask in my name. This is my command: Love each other. (John 15:1-17)

In the above passage, Jesus is the true vine, and the Father is the gardener. The Father is the farmer, a tiller of the ground. He is the vinedresser. It is the Father's job to cultivate the crops. He takes away the branches that do not bear fruit and prunes or cleanses those that do bear fruit. It glorifies the Father when we, as believers, bear much fruit. Bearing fruit is the external evidence that we are His disciples (verse 8). We cannot bear fruit unless we abide in Christ; we must continue or remain in Him. Without Him, we can do nothing. If we keep His commandments, His joy will remain in us, and our joy will be full (verse 11). We have not chosen Jesus, but He has chosen us to go and bear fruit - fruit that will remain (verse 16).

Please note, "Remain in me, and I will remain in you," verse 4 and "If a man remains in me and I in him" verse 5 of John 15. In addition to considering how we can be able to abide in Christ, we must consider what it takes to get Him to abide in us. In John 15:10, Jesus said, "If you obey my commands, you will remain in my love..." In John 15:13, 14, He says, "Greater love has no one than this, that he lay down his life for his friends. You are my friends if you do what I command." In John 15:12, He says, "My command is this: Love each other as I have loved you," and in John 15:17, He says, "This is my command: Love each other." I believe these passages in John 15 sum up what we must do to abide in Christ and get Him to abide in us. We must love (obey) God and love (serve) each other.

What causes the Lord to turn a deaf ear to His people? What can we do that causes the Lord to separate from fellowship with us? What disrupts the communion of our spirits with His Spirit? We aren't abiding in Christ if we willfully commit acts that create a situation where the Lord will not hear us. It breaks fellowship with God if we have unconfessed sin in our lives. If we've made a profession of faith, there are some things we just aren't supposed to do.

If we claim to have fellowship with him yet walk in the darkness we lie and do not live by the truth. (I John 1:6)

The Bible gives examples of situations when sin separated people from their God.

1. Sexual immorality and idolatry.

Consider the story of Balaam and the children of Israel in Numbers 22-25, 31. On their way to the Promised Land, the Israelites traveled

73

to the plains of Moab and camped along the Jordan River across from Jericho. Balak son of Zippor saw all that Israel had done to the Amorites, and the Moabites were terrified because there were so many people. Balak, son of Zippor, the king of Moab, sent messengers to summon Balaam son of Beor. Balak wanted Balaam to curse the Israelites. The elders of Moab and Midian took the fee for divination with them and gave Balaam Balak's message. That night, Balaam met with God and asked Him to curse the Israelites. God told Balaam not to curse the Israelites because they were blessed.

The next morning, Balaam told the Moabite princes he could not go back with them. The princes returned to Balak and told him that Balaam refused to come with them. Balak sent other princes who told Balaam that he would be rewarded handsomely for cursing the Israelites. That night God came to Balaam and told him to go with them but to only do what He told him to do.

Balaam got up the next morning, saddled his donkey and left with the princes of Moab. Balaam must have had some evil intent because God was very angry when he went. The angel of the Lord stood in the donkey's path three times. Three times Balaam beat the donkey to get her going again. Finally, the donkey spoke to Balaam, rebuking him for beating her. The Lord opened Balaam's eyes, and he saw the angel of the Lord, standing in the road with his sword drawn. The admonition to speak only what God told him was repeated. God warned Balaam that he was on a reckless path. Eventually Balaam met with Balak, and Balak asked Balaam to curse the Israelites. God would only allow Balaam to bless the Israelites.

Balaam devised a plan for the Moabite and Midianite women to seduce the Israelite men to commit sexual immorality and idolatry. Then the Lord would have to turn His back on the Israelites.

They [the women] were the ones who followed Balaam's advice and were the means of turning the Israelites away from the Lord in what happened at Peor, so that a plague struck the Lord's people. (Numbers 31:16)

The Lord sent a plague on the Israelites, but it was lifted when Phinehas the priest took his spear and killed Zimri son of Salu, a Simeonite, and his Midianite partner. The plague was lifted, but the number of Israelites who died in the plague was 24,000 (Numbers 25).

In Numbers 31, God told Moses to take vengeance on the Midianites. The Israelites killed Balaam with the sword. Consider these words in Revelation, to the angel of the church in Pergamum:

Nevertheless, I have a few things against you: You have people there who hold to the teaching of Balaam, who taught Balak to entice the Israelites to sin by eating food sacrificed to idols and by committing sexual immorality. (Revelation 2:14)

2. Complaining, faithlessness, rebellion.

Let us note what the Israelites did after the Lord led them to Kadesh Barnea (Numbers 13 & 14). They sent out spies into the promised land to bring a report about what the land was like, whether the people who lived there were strong or weak, few or many, whether the land was good or bad, and whether the towns were unwalled or fortified. On their return, the spies reported, "We went into the land to which you sent us, and it does flow with milk and honey! Here is its fruit. But the people who live there are powerful, and the cities are fortified and very large…We can't attack those people; they are stronger than we are." The Israelites were afraid and rebelled against the command of the Lord their God. They allowed their emotions to control their sense of reason, their trust in God. They treated the Lord with contempt. They refused to believe in Him. They were disobedient and grumbled against the Lord. They were unwilling to go up into the land. When the Lord heard what the Israelites said, He was angry and solemnly swore that not one of them would enter the land except Caleb, son of Jephunneh, and Joshua, son of Nun. The Israelites would suffer for their sins and know what it was like to have the Lord against them. They would meet their end in the desert, and there they would die. Consider Moses' summary of the subsequent events as recorded in the first chapter of Deuteronomy:

Then you replied, "We have sinned against the Lord. We will go up and fight, as the Lord our God commanded us," so every one of you put on his weapons, thinking it easy to go up into the hill country. But the Lord said to me, "Tell them, 'Do not go up and fight, because I will not be with you. You will be defeated by your enemies.'" So I told you, but you would not listen. You rebelled against the Lord's command and in your arrogance you marched up into the hill country. The Amorites who lived in those hills came out against you; they chased you like a swarm of bees and beat you down from Seir all the way to Hormah. You came back and wept before the Lord, but he paid no attention to your weeping and turned a deaf ear to you. And so you stayed in Kadesh many days..." (Deuteronomy 1:41-46a)

Later at Kadesh (Numbers 20), the people were without water. The people gathered in opposition to Moses and Aaron. The Lord said to Moses, "Speak to that rock before their eyes and it will pour out its water." Moses and Aaron gathered the assembly together in front of the rock, and Moses said to them, "Listen, you rebels, must we bring you water out of this rock?" Then Moses raised his arm and struck the rock twice with his staff, rather than speaking to the rock as the Lord had said. Water gushed out, and the community and their livestock drank. But the Lord said to Moses and Aaron, "Because you did not trust in me enough to honor me as holy in the sight of the Israelites, you will not bring this community into the land I give them." Consider Moses' reflection about what happened next as recorded in Deuteronomy 3.

At that time I pleaded with the Lord: "O Sovereign Lord, you have begun to show to your servant your greatness and your strong hand. For what god is there in heaven or on earth who can do the deeds and mighty works you do? Let me go over and see the good land beyond the Jordan - that fine hill country and Lebanon." But because of you the Lord was angry with me and would not listen to me. "That is enough," the Lord said. "Do not speak to me anymore about this matter." (Deuteronomy 3:23-26)

In Deuteronomy 31, the Lord spoke to Moses and predicted Israel's rebellion, which was soon to occur after their entrance into the Promised Land. God also told Moses how He would respond to that apostasy.

And the Lord said to Moses: "You are going to rest with your fathers, and these people will soon prostitute themselves to the foreign gods of the land they are entering. They will forsake me and break the covenant I made with them. On that day I will become angry with them and forsake them; I will hide my face from them, and they will be destroyed. Many disasters and difficulties will come upon them, and on that day they will ask, "Have not these disasters come upon us because our God is not with us?" And I will certainly hide my face on that day because of all their wickedness in turning to other gods. (Deuteronomy 31:16-18)

3. Disobedience.

After Moses died, Joshua became the leader of the Israelites. Consider God's words to Joshua:

I will give you every place where you set your foot, as I promised Moses . . . No one will be able to stand up against you all the days of your life. As I was with Moses, so I will be with you; I will never leave you nor forsake you . . . Be careful to obey all the law my servant Moses gave you; do not turn from it to the right or to the left, that you may be successful wherever you go. Do not let this Book of the Law depart from your mouth; meditate on it day and night; so that you may be careful to do everything written in it. Then you will be prosperous and successful. Have I not commanded you? Be strong and courageous. Do not be terrified; do not be discouraged, for the Lord your God will be with you wherever you go. (Joshua 1:3–9)

Joshua confidently led the Israelites across the Jordan River and into the Promised Land. With the victory at Jericho, the conquest of Canaan had begun. But the Israelites subsequently suffered defeat at Ai. The defeat was God's punishment for Achan's sin. Achan had taken some of the plunder from the conquest at Jericho, something the Lord had expressly forbidden (Joshua 6:17-19).

Consider Joshua's reaction to the situation as initially he was not aware of the reason for the defeat:

Then Joshua tore his clothes and fell facedown to the ground before the ark of the Lord, remaining there till evening. The elders of Israel did the same, and sprinkled dust on their heads. And Joshua said, "Ah, Sovereign Lord, why did you ever bring this people across the Jordan to deliver us into the hands of the Amorites to destroy us? If only we had been content to stay on the other side of the Jordan! O Lord, what can I say, now that Israel has been routed by its enemies? The Canaanites and the other people of the country will hear about this and they will surround us and wipe out our name from the earth. What then will you do for your own great name?" (Joshua 7:6–9)

Note the Lord's response to Joshua:

The Lord said to Joshua, "Stand up! What are you doing down on your face? Israel has sinned; they have violated my covenant which I commanded them to keep. They have taken some of the devoted things; they have stolen, they have lied, they have put them with their own possessions. That is why the Israelites cannot stand against their enemies; they turn their backs and run because they have been made liable to destruction. I will not be with you anymore unless you destroy whatever among you is devoted to destruction. (Joshua 7:10-12)

Achan was identified and punished.

4. Hypocritical worship of God without true repentance, without obedience, and without love for and service to our brothers.

The Lord spoke to the Israelites through the prophets about the importance of obedience if they were to maintain their relationship with Him. For example, public worship of God means nothing if our hearts are not in it or if we do not treat our neighbor well.

The Lord says: "These people come near to me with their mouth and honor me with their lips, but their hearts are far from me. (Isaiah 29:13a)

My [the Lord's] people come to you [Ezekiel], as they usually do, and sit before you to listen to your words, but they do not put them into practice. With their mouths they express devotion, but their hearts are greedy for unjust gain. (Ezekiel 33:31)

We must love God and love others. If we turn a deaf ear to God when He calls, He will not hear us when we call.

"The multitude of your sacrifices - what are they to me?" says the Lord. "I have more than enough of burnt offerings, of rams and the fat of fattened animals; I have no pleasure in the blood of bulls and lambs and goats. When you come to appear before me, who has asked this of you, this trampling of my courts? Stop bringing meaningless offerings! Your incense is detestable to me. New moons, Sabbaths and convocations - I cannot bear your evil assemblies. Your New Moon festivals and your appointed feasts my soul hates. They have become a burden to me; I am weary of bearing them. When you spread out your hands in prayer, I will hide my eyes from you; Even if you offer many prayers, I will not listen. Your hands are full of blood; wash and make yourselves clean. Take your evil deeds out of my sight! Stop doing wrong, learn to do right! Seek justice, encourage the oppressed. Defend the cause of the fatherless, plead the case of the widow. Come now let us reason together," says the Lord. "Though your sins are like scarlet, they shall be as white as snow; Though they are red as crimson, they shall be like wool." (Isaiah 1:11-18)

Shout it aloud, do not hold back. Raise your voice like a trumpet. Declare to my people their rebellion and to the house of Jacob their sins. For day after day they seek me out; they seem eager to know my ways, as if they were a nation that does what is right and has not forsaken the commands of its God. They ask me for just decisions and seem eager for God to come near them. "Why have we fasted," they say, "and you have not seen it? Why have we humbled ourselves, and you have not noticed?" Yet on the day of your fasting, you do as you please and exploit all your workers. Your fasting ends in quarreling and strife, and in striking each other with wicked fists. You cannot fast as you do today and expect your voice to be heard on high. Is this the kind of fast I have chosen, only a day for a man to humble himself? Is it only for bowing one's head like a reed and for lying on sackcloth and ashes? Is that what you call a fast, a day acceptable to the Lord? Is not this the kind of fasting I have chosen: to loosen the chains of injustice and untie the cords of the yoke, to set the oppressed free and break every yoke? Is it not to share your food with the hungry and to provide the poor wanderer with shelter - when you see the naked, to clothe him, and not turn away from your own flesh and blood? Then your light will break forth like the dawn, and your healing will quickly appear; then your righteousness will go before you, and the glory of the Lord will be your rear guard. Then you will call, and the Lord will answer; you will cry for help, and he will say: Here am I. If you do away with the yoke of oppression, with the pointing finger and malicious talk, and if you spend yourselves in behalf of the hungry and satisfy the needs of the oppressed, then your light will rise in the darkness, and your night will become like the noonday. The Lord will guide you always; he will satisfy your needs in a sun-scorched land and will strengthen your frame. You will be like a well-watered garden, like a spring whose waters never fail. (Isaiah 58:1-11)

The *MacArthur Study Bible* makes the following comment about Isaiah 58:3-7: "The people complained when God did not recognize their religious actions, but God responded that their fastings had been only half-hearted. Hypocritical fasting resulted in contention, quarreling, and pretense, excluding the possibility of genuine prayer to God. Fasting consisted of more than just an outward ritual and a mock repentance; it involved penitence over sin and humility, disconnecting from sin and oppression of others, feeding the hungry, and acting humanely toward those in need." **(5)**

Surely the arm of the Lord is not too short to save, nor his ear too dull to hear. But your iniquities have separated you from your God; your sins have hidden his face from you, so that he will not hear. For your hands are stained with blood, your fingers with guilt. Your lips have spoken lies, and your tongue mutters wicked things. No one calls for justice; no one pleads his case with integrity. They rely on empty arguments and speak lies; they conceive trouble and give birth to evil. (Isaiah 59:1-4)

"Will you steal and murder, commit adultery and perjury, burn incense to Baal and follow other gods you have not known, and then come and stand before me in this house, which bears my Name, and say, 'We are safe' - safe to do all these detestable things? Has this house, which bears my Name, become a den of robbers to you? But I have been watching!" Declares the Lord. "Go now to the place in Shiloh where I first made a dwelling for my Name, and see what I did to it because of the wickedness of my people Israel. While you were doing all these things, declares the Lord, I spoke to you again and again, but you did not listen; I called you, but you did not answer. Therefore, what I did to Shiloh I will do to the house that bears my Name, the temple you trust in, the place I gave to you and your fathers. I will thrust you from my presence, just as I did all your brothers, the people of Ephraim [the Northern Kingdom of Israel]. So do not pray for this people nor offer any plea or petition for them; do not plead with me, for I will not listen to you. Do you not see what they are doing in the towns of Judah and in the streets of Jerusalem? The children gather wood, the fathers light the fire, and the women knead the dough and make cakes of bread for the Queen of Heaven. They pour out drink offerings to other gods to provoke me to anger. But am I the one they are provoking?" Declares the Lord. "Are they not rather harming themselves, to their own shame?" (Jeremiah 7:9-19)

Then the Lord said to me, "There is a conspiracy among the people of Judah and those who live in Jerusalem. They have returned to the sins of their forefathers, who refused to listen to my words. They have followed other gods to serve them. Both the house of Israel and the house of Judah have broken the covenant I made with their forefathers. Therefore this is what the Lord says: 'I will bring on them a disaster they cannot escape. Although they cry out to me, I will not listen to them.' The towns of Judah and the people of Jerusalem will go and cry out to the gods to whom they burn incense, but they will not help them at all when disaster strikes. You have as many gods as you have towns, O Judah; and the altars you have set up to burn incense to that shameful god Baal are as many as the streets of

Jerusalem. Do not pray for this people, because I will not listen when they call to me in the time of distress." (Jeremiah 11:9-14)

This is what the Lord says about his people: "They greatly love to wander; they do not restrain their feet. So the Lord does not accept them; he will now remember their wickedness and punish them for their sins." Then the Lord said to me, "Do not pray for the well-being of this people. Although they fast, I will not listen to their cry; though they offer burnt offerings and grain offerings, I will not accept them. Instead I will destroy them with the sword, famine and plague." (Jeremiah 14:10-12)

For this is what the Lord, the God of Israel, says about the houses in this city and the royal palaces of Judah that have been torn down to be used against the siege ramps and the sword in the fight with the Babylonians: "They will be filled with the dead bodies of the men I will slay in my anger and wrath. I will hide my face from this city because of all its wickedness." (Jeremiah 33:4, 5)

Then he [the Lord] brought [in visions] me [Ezekiel] to the entrance to the north gate of the house of the Lord, and I saw a woman sitting there, mourning for Tammuz [Sumerian god of vegetation]. He said to me, "Do you see this, son of man? You will see things that are even more detestable than this." He then brought me into the inner court of the house of the Lord, and there at the entrance to the temple, between the portico and the altar, were about twenty-five men. With their backs toward the temple of the Lord and their faces toward the east, they were bowing down to the sun in the east. He said to me, "Have you seen this, son of man? Is it a trivial matter for the house of Judah to do the detestable things they are doing here? Must they also fill the land with violence and continually provoke me to anger? Look at them putting the branch to their nose! Therefore I will deal with them in anger; I will not look on them with pity or spare them. Although they shout in my ears, I will not listen to them." (Ezekiel 8:14-18)

Therefore say to the house of Israel: "This is what the Sovereign Lord says: Will you defile yourselves the way your fathers did and lust after vile images? When you offer your gifts - the sacrifice of your sons in the fire - you continue to defile yourselves with all your idols to this day. Am I to let you inquire of me, O house of Israel? As surely as I live, declares the Sovereign Lord, I will not let you inquire of me." (Ezekiel 29:30, 31)

And the word of the Lord came again to Zechariah: "This is what the Lord Almighty says: 'Administer true justice; show mercy and compassion to one another. Do not oppress the widow or the fatherless, the alien or the poor. In your hearts do not think evil of each other.' But they refused to pay attention; stubbornly they turned their backs and stopped up their ears. They made their hearts as hard as flint and would not listen to the law or to the words that the Lord Almighty had sent by his Spirit through the earlier prophets. So the Lord Almighty was very angry. "When I called, they did not listen; so when they called, I would not listen," says the Lord Almighty. "I scattered them with a whirlwind among the nations, where they were strangers. The land was left so desolate behind them that no one could come or go. This is how they made the pleasant land desolate." (Zechariah 7:8-14)

According to Harris, *Theological Wordbook of the Old Testament*, both words for *called* in the passage above are from the Hebrew *qara*. The root *qr'* denotes primarily the enunciation of a specific message. That message is customarily addressed to a specific recipient and is intended to elicit a specific response. It may refer to God's calling a person or a people to a specific task. It may also be used of people who cry out urgently to God for help; frequently the context has to do with a critical or chronic need. **(6)**

There are other verses in the poetic books of the Old Testament that carry the same idea regarding certain standards for God's people, what is expected of them if they are to maintain fellowship with God.

Lord, who may dwell in your sanctuary? Who may live on your holy hill? He whose walk is blameless and who does what is righteous, who speaks the truth from his heart and has no slander on his tongue, who does his neighbor no wrong and casts no slur on his fellowman, who despises a vile man but honors those who fear the Lord, who keeps his oath even when it hurts, who lends his money without usury and does not accept a bribe against the innocent. He who does these things will never be shaken. (Psalm 15)

If a man shuts his ears to the cry of the poor, he too will cry out and not be answered. (Proverbs 21:13)

The New Testament epistles also speak of acts of disobedience that affect our relationship with the Lord. The concept is not exclusive to the Old Testament.

For, "Whoever would love life and see good days must keep his tongue from evil and his lips from deceitful speech. He must turn from evil and do good; he must seek peace and pursue it. For the eyes of the Lord are on the righteous and his ears are attentive to their prayer, but the face of the Lord is against those who do evil." (I Peter 3:10-12)

The New Testament makes references about higher standards for certain categories of people. There are higher standards for leaders in the church.

An elder must be blameless, the husband of but one wife, a man whose children believe and are not open to the charge of being wild and disobedient. Since an overseer is entrusted with God's work, he must be blameless - not overbearing, not quick-tempered, not given to drunkenness, not violent, not pursuing dishonest gain. Rather he must be hospitable, one who loves what is good, who is self-controlled, upright, holy and disciplined. He must hold firmly to the trustworthy message as it has been taught, so that he can encourage others by sound doctrine and refute those who oppose it. (Titus 1:6-9)

There are higher standards for those who teach the word to others.

Not many of you should presume to be teachers, my brothers, because you know that we who teach will be judged more strictly. (James 3:1)

In *The MacArthur Study Bible*, John MacArthur writes as follows:

Verse 3:1 teachers. This word is translated "master" in the gospels and refers to a person who functions in an official teaching or preaching capacity…stricter judgment…This is not meant to discourage true teachers, but to warn the prospective teacher of the role's seriousness. **(7)**

There are high standards for people who partake of the Lord's Supper.

Therefore whoever eats the bread or drinks the cup of the Lord [Holy Communion] in an unworthy manner will be guilty of sinning against the body and blood of the Lord. A man ought to examine himself before he eats of the bread and drinks of the cup. For anyone who eats and drinks without recognizing the body of the Lord eats and drinks judgment on himself. That is why many among you are weak and sick, and a number of you have fallen asleep [died]. But if we judged ourselves, we would not come under judgment. When we are judged by the Lord, we are being disciplined so that we will not be condemned with the world. (I Corinthians 11:27-32)

In *The MacArthur Study Bible*, John MacArthur writes:

Verses 11:27, 29 in an unworthy manner. i.e. ritualistically, indifferently, with an unrepentant heart, a spirit of bitterness, or any other ungodly attitude. In **11:27**

83

guilty. To come to the Lord's Table clinging to one's sin does not only dishonor the ceremony, but it also dishonors His body and blood, treating lightly the gracious sacrifice of Christ for us. It is necessary to set all sin before the Lord (v. 28), then partake, so as not to mock the sacrifice for sin by holding on to it. **11:29 judgment**. i.e. chastisement. **not discerning the Lord's body**. When believers do not properly judge the holiness of the celebration of Communion, they treat with indifference the Lord Himself - His life, suffering, and death. **(8)**

There are high standards for those who approach God in prayer. In *Introductory Lectures in Systematic Theology*, Henry Clarence Thiessen writes as follows:

The most important question as to the manner of prayer is the condition of the heart of the one praying. Murray calls Jesus' words, "If ye abide in me" (John 15:7), "the all-inclusive condition" to answered prayer. Andrew Murray, *With Christ in the School of Prayer* (New York: Fleming H. Revell Co., n.d.), p. 160. This is true and it resolves itself into many subdivisions. To abide in Him implies freedom from known sin (Ps. 66:18; Isa. 59:1, 2; Prov. 28:9), unselfishness in our requests (Jas. 4:2, 3), asking according to His will (I John 5:14), forgiveness of those who have wronged us (Matt. 6:12; Mark 11:25), asking in Christ's name (John 14:13; 15:16; 16:23, 24), praying in the Spirit (Eph. 6:18; Jude 20), asking in faith (Jas. 1:6, 7; Matt. 21:22), and earnestness and perseverance in our supplications (Jas. 5:16; Luke 18:1-8; Col. 4:2). **(9)**

It would be beneficial to keep in mind the condition of our hearts as we pray, especially if we are offering intercessory prayer for someone we particularly care about.

We are supposed to consider the consequences of what we do.

When I was a child, my granddad told me a story of something that had happened when he was in his twenties. I thought to myself, "Do you suppose he realized that one day he would get old?" I then realized that someday, I would be old as well, and I needed to do all I could to get my life ready for old age.

A horrible and shocking thing has happened in the land: The prophets prophecy lies, the priests rule by their own authority, and my people love it this way. But what will you do in the end? (Jeremiah 5:30, 31)

Joy is gone from our hearts; our dancing has turned to mourning. The crown has fallen from our head. Woe to us, for we have sinned! (Lamentations 5:15, 16)

But wisdom is proved right by all her children. (Luke 7:35)

About Luke 7:35, *The MacArthur Study Bible* reads as follows: "True wisdom is vindicated by its consequences – what it produces." **(10)**

God cannot be mocked. A man reaps what he sows. The one who sows to please his sinful nature, from that nature will reap destruction; the one who sows to please the Spirit, will from the Spirit reap eternal life. Let us not become weary in doing good, for at the proper time we will reap a harvest if we do not give up. (Galatians 6:7b-9)

Consider the meaning of prudence as recorded in *The American Heritage College Dictionary*.

Prudence: 1. The state, quality, or fact of being prudent. 2. Careful management; economy. Synonyms: prudence, discretion, foresight, forethought, or circumspection. These nouns refer to the exercise of good judgment, common sense, and even caution, especially in practical matters. Discretion suggests wise self-restraint, as in resisting a rash impulse. Foresight implies the ability to foresee and make provision for what may happen: the foresight to plan. Forethought suggests advance consideration of future eventualities.

Circumspection implies discretion, as out of concern for moral or social repercussions. **(11)**

It is unwise to treat God with contempt or profane His name.

The Hebrew word for treat with contempt in Leviticus 22:9 is translated *profane* in the KJV. According to R. Laird Harris in *Theological Wordbook of the Old Testament*, *halal* means to profane, defile, pollute, or desecrate. The word *halal* is associated with uncleanness. To profane is to misuse the name of God, the Sabbath, or the holy place, and so desecrate it. The word may be used of any action that controverts God's planned order. **(12)**

The Lord said to Moses, "How long will these people *treat me with contempt*? How long will they refuse to believe in me, in spite of all the miraculous signs I have performed among them? (Numbers 14:11)

85

The Hebrew word for *treat with contempt* in Numbers 14:11 is also translated *provoke* in the KJV. According to R. Laird Harris in *Theological Wordbook of the Old Testament*, *na'as* means to *despise* or *abhor*. To the despiser, nothing that is God's is considered holy. Thus, he not only deprecates God's power and ability to carry out His threats, but his contemptuous view of God leads him to prefer sin to God and to express his contempt in a conscious way. **(13)**

He who oppresses the poor shows contempt for their Maker, but whoever is kind to the needy honors God. (Proverbs 14:31)

He who mocks the poor shows contempt for their Maker; whoever gloats over disaster will not go unpunished. (Proverbs 17:5)

The Hebrew word for showing contempt in Proverbs 14:31 and 17:5 is translated *reproacheth* in the KJV. According to R. Laird Harris in *Theological Wordbook of the Old Testament*, the Hebrew word *harap* carries the connation of casting blame or scorn on someone. The word may be used in the sense of imputing blame or guilt to someone in order to harm his character. *Harap* is the antithesis of the Hebrew word *kabed* (honor) and may be understood as disgrace or dishonor. In some contexts, the word *taunt* is an acceptable translation. The word may bear the nuance of mocking or defiance. **(14)**

But Ephraim [Israel] has bitterly provoked him [the Lord] to anger; his Lord will leave upon him the guilt of his bloodshed and will repay him for his *contempt*. (Hosea 12:14)

The Hebrew word for contempt in Hosea 12:14 is translated *reproach* in the KJV. According to R. Laird Harris in *Theological Wordbook of the Old Testament*, the Hebrew word *herpa* is a derivative of *harap*, as above, and basically carries the same meaning. **(15)**

If we wish to have a right relationship with the Lord, it would also seem prohibitive to do things the Lord hates.

There are six things the Lord hates, seven that are detestable to him: haughty eyes, a lying tongue, hands that shed innocent blood, a heart that devises wicked

86

schemes, feet that are quick to rush into evil, a false witness who pours out lies and a man who stirs up dissension among brothers. (Proverbs 6:16-19)

In Proverbs 8, wisdom is personified and is giving an oration.

I, wisdom, dwell together with prudence; I possess knowledge and discretion. To fear the Lord is to hate evil; I hate pride and arrogance, evil behavior and perverse speech. (Proverbs 8:12, 13)

Consider some words from the prophets.

For I, the Lord, love justice; I hate robbery and iniquity In my faithfulness I will reward them [my people] and make an everlasting covenant with them. (Isaiah 61:8)

I [the Lord God Almighty] hate, I despise your religious feasts; I cannot stand your assemblies. Even though you bring me burnt offerings and grain offerings, I will not accept them. Though you bring choice fellowship offerings, I will have no regard for them. Away with the noise of your songs! I will not listen to the music of your harps. But let justice roll on like a river, righteousness like a never-ending stream! (Amos 5:21-24)

The Sovereign Lord has sworn by himself - the Lord God Almighty declares: "I abhor the pride of Jacob and detest his fortresses; I will deliver up [hand over] the city and everything in it." (Amos 6:8)

"These are the things you are to do: Speak the truth to each other, and render true and sound judgment in your courts; do not plot evil against your neighbor, and do not love to swear falsely. I hate all this," declares the Lord. (Zechariah 8:16, 17)

It would make better sense to do the things that please God and or, to put it another way, to cooperate with God as He does the things that bring Him pleasure.

I [David] know, my God, that you test the heart and are pleased with integrity. (I Chronicles 29:17a)

May those who delight in my [David's] vindication shout for joy and gladness may they always say, "The Lord be exalted, who delights in the well-being of his servant." (Psalm 35:27)

His pleasure is not in the strength of a horse, nor his delight in the legs of a man; the Lord delights in those who fear him, who put their hope in his unfailing love. (Psalm 147:10, 11)

For the Lord takes delight in his people; he crowns the humble with salvation. (Psalm 149:4)

My son, do not despise the Lord's discipline and do not resent his rebuke, because the Lord disciplines those he loves, as a father the son he delights in. (Proverbs 3:11, 12)

The Lord abhors dishonest scales, but accurate weights are his delight. (Proverbs 11:1)

The Lord detests men of perverse heart but he delights in those whose ways are blameless. (Proverbs 11:20)

The Lord detests lying lips, but he delights in men who are truthful. (Proverbs 12:22)

And he made known to us the mystery of his will according to his good pleasure, which he purposed in Christ, to be put into effect when the times will have reached their fulfillment - to bring all things in heaven and on earth together under one head, even Christ. (Ephesians 1:9, 10)

Finally brothers, we instructed you how to live in order to please God, as in fact you are living. Now we ask you and urge you in the Lord Jesus to do this more and more. (I Thessalonians 4:1)

And without faith it is impossible to please God, because anyone who comes to him must believe that he exists and that he rewards those who earnestly seek him. (Hebrews 11:6)

In order to deal properly with anger and resentment, we need to cooperate with what God is doing in our lives. We need His power in order to succeed. We must avoid things that disturb the closeness of our fellowship with Him. We must seek to please Him in all we do. In the next chapter, let us consider what the New Testament commands us to do.

Chapter Six
The New Testament Commandments

Peeple often talk about the Ten Commandments, those in the Old Testament, given by God to Moses on Mount Sinai. There are many commandments in the New Testament as well.

Let me state initially that keeping the law does not put us in right relationship with God. Salvation is by grace through faith. What counts is a new creation.

For it is by grace you have been saved, through faith – and this is not from yourselves, it is the gift of God – not by works, so that no one can boast. For we are God's workmanship, created in Christ Jesus to do good works, which God prepared in advance for us to do. (Ephesians 2:8-10)

David Jeremiah writes: "**2:10** Christians are saved **for good works**, not by their works." **(1)**

May I [Paul] never boast except in the cross of our Lord Jesus Christ, through which the world has been crucified to me, and I to the world. Neither circumcision [works of the law] nor uncircumcision means anything; what counts is a new creation. (Galatians 6:14, 15)

Wayne Grudem writes: "As the gospel comes to us, God speaks through it to summon us to himself (effective calling) and to give us new spiritual life (regeneration) so that we are enabled to respond in faith. Effective calling is thus God the Father speaking powerfully to us, and regeneration is God the Father and God the Holy Spirit working powerfully in us, to make us alive. **(2)**

After we are saved, however, and as we live our daily lives, obedience is of paramount importance.

Circumcision is nothing and uncircumcision is nothing. Keeping God's commands is what counts. (I Corinthians 7:19)

Let us consider the Greek words for New Testament commandments. These are the words for command and commandment according to Vine. **(3)** It is to be noted here that the various lexicons, concordances, etc. do not always completely line up with each other.

GREEK WORDS FOR COMMAND (Verbs)

I. **Diatasso** – signifies to set in order, appoint, command. **(4)** The word frequently denotes to arrange, appoint, or prescribe, e.g. of what was appointed for tax collectors to collect; of the tabernacle, as appointed by God for Moses to make; of the arrangements appointed by Paul with regard to himself and his travelling companions; of the rule the Apostle "ordained" for all the churches in regard to marital conditions; of what the Lord "ordained" in regard to the support of those who proclaimed the Gospel; of the Law as Divinely "ordained," or administered, through angels, by Moses. In Titus 1:5, A.V., "had appointed thee," the sense is rather that of commanding, R.V., "gave thee charge." **(5)**

Bauer, Arndt, and Gingrich say the word means to order, direct, or command. **(6)** Consider examples:

After Jesus had finished <u>instructing</u> his twelve disciples, he went on from there to teach and preach in the towns of Galilee. (Matthew 11:1)

For information about what that instruction included see Matthew chapter ten.

There [Corinth] he [Paul] met a Jew named Aquila, a native of Pontus, who had recently come from Italy with his wife Priscilla, because Claudius <u>had ordered</u> all the Jews to leave Rome. (Acts 18:2a)

Nevertheless, each one should retain the place in life that the Lord assigned to him and to which God has called him. This is the rule I <u>lay down</u> in all the churches. (I Corinthians 7:17)

In I Corinthians 7:10a, Paul writes, "To the married I give this command (not I, but the Lord)". In I Corinthians 7:12a, he writes,

90

"To the rest I say this (I, not the Lord)." And in I Corinthians 7:17b, he writes, "This is the rule I lay down in all the churches." And finally, in 7:25b, he writes, "I have no command from the Lord, but I give a judgment as one who by the Lord's mercy is trustworthy."

About the origin of these teachings, John MacArthur writes:

7:12 to the rest.…I say. Not a denial of inspiration or an indication that Paul is giving human opinion, but simply a way of saying that Jesus had not spoken on this and God had not previously given revelation on the matter, as Paul was then writing. **(7)**

Personally, I believe Paul is saying that God has not spoken to him on the matter, but what he is recommending makes the most sense to him. MacArthur further writes that the issue in I Corinthians 7:17-24 is one of contentment. People should be content to serve the Lord where they are, until He leads them elsewhere. **(8)**

Diatasso is used sixteen times in the New Testament. **(9)** On one occasion, the word is used to refer to God directing Moses how to build the tabernacle. The word is used three times of Jesus instructing His disciples. It is used once, after the ascension, of the Lord about one of His commandments. The word is used of John the Baptist, giving a command to the tax collectors. The word is used twice of Jesus and then Paul giving non-moral commands (i.e. give the girl something to eat; reserve me a place on a ship). It is used four times of Paul, either directly or indirectly giving advice to churches. Once the word is used of the fact that the Old Testament Law was put into effect through angels by a mediator. Three times *diatasso* is used of a man giving orders to another man or men. However, these are not weighty issues such as "Thou shalt not kill," or "Thou shalt not steal."

II. **Epo** – denotes to speak, to bid, or command. **(10)** According to Liddell and Scott, the word means say, call, or name. It was probably invented as the present tense of *eipon*. **(11)** *Eipon* is used as the aorist tense of *lego,* to speak, to say and sometimes has the meaning of commanding or bidding. **(12)**

Bauer, Arndt, and Gingrich say the word *eipon* means to say or speak. There are various modifications in meaning resulting from the context, for instance with commands and requests. **(13)**

Consider examples:

Then Jesus said to the crowds and to his disciples: "The teachers of the law and the Pharisees sit in Moses' seat. So you must obey them and do everything they <u>tell</u> you. But do not do what they do, for they do not practice what they preach. (Matthew 23:1-3)

When he [Jesus] had taken the seven loaves and given thanks, he broke them and gave them to his disciples to set before the people, and they did so. They had a few small fish as well; he gave thanks for them and also <u>told</u> the disciples to distribute them. (Mark 8:6b, 7)

But Martha was distracted by all the preparations that had to be made. She came to him [Jesus] and asked, "Lord, don't you care that my sister [Mary] has left me to do the work by myself? <u>Tell</u> her to help me!" (Luke 10:40)

In the right context, this word can be appropriate for situations when a command is given, but when that is the case, it is often less significant than a moral command from God.

By my count, the Greek word e*po* is used 947 times in the New Testament. **(14)** The word usually means say or said. In certain contexts, the word can mean command or bid. According to Wigram, there are eight times in the KJV where the word is translated *command* and five times where the word is translated *bid.* **(15)** It appears to me that, in those verses, the word is generally used of something other than giving moral commands. In Matthew 16:12 and 23:3, the word *epo* is used of giving moral direction, but it does not seem to be used for specific commandments.

III. **Entello** – signifies to enjoin upon, to charge with; it is used in the middle voice in the sense of commanding or giving commandment. **(16)** An alternate form is *entellomai*, to order, command, or enjoin. **(17)**

92

"Charge" has multiple meanings which include "to impose a task or responsibility." **(18)** Enjoin means to direct or impose by authoritative order or with urgent admonition, to forbid or prohibit or to put an injunction on. **(19)**

Bauer, Arndt, and Gingrich say the word *entello* means command, order, or give orders. **(20)** Consider examples:

Then the eleven disciples went to Galilee, to the mountain where Jesus had told them to go. When they saw him, they worshipped him, but some doubted. Then Jesus came to them and said, "All authority in heaven and on earth has been given to me. Therefore go and make disciples of all nations, baptizing them in the name of the Father and of the Son and of the Holy Spirit, and teaching them to obey everything I have <u>commanded</u> you. And surely I am with you always, to the very end of the age." (Matthew 28:16-20)

The teachers of the law and the Pharisees brought in a woman caught in adultery. They made her stand before the group and said to Jesus, "Teacher, this woman was caught in the act of adultery. In the law Moses <u>commanded</u> us to stone such women. Now what do you say?" (John 8:3-5)

. . .but the world must learn that I [Jesus] love the Father and that I do exactly what my Father has <u>commanded</u> me. (John 14:31a)

The word *entello* is used 17 times in the New Testament. **(21)** Two times it refers to an Old Testament commandment. Two times, the word refers to a command given by Moses about divorce and once about Moses commanding the people to stone women caught in adultery (John 8:1-11). This New Testament passage is not in the earliest manuscripts. I can't find the command in the first five books of the Old Testament. In Leviticus 20:10, it says that the adulterer and the adulteress must be put to death, but I don't read anything about stoning them. Once the word is used referring to commands of God the Father to Jesus. In two different gospels the word refers to the event when the devil tempted Jesus to throw Himself off the temple and quoted Psalm 91:11, 12: "He [God] will command his angels concerning you, and they will lift you up in their hands, so that you will not strike your foot against a stone." The New Testament describes four times when Jesus used this word in reference to moral commands and twice when His command was not of a moral nature. On one occasion, Acts speaks of the Lord commanding Paul and

Barnabas to take the gospel to the Gentiles. On two occasions the New Testament describes situations when a man gave a command to a man or to men.

The Greek word *entello* is in line with what we think of when we hear about someone giving true commands and includes moral commands from God.

IV. **Epitasso** – signifies to appoint over, put in charge, to put upon one as a duty. **(22)** It means to set or arrange over, to charge, command, is rendered "enjoin" in Philemon 8. **(23)** Enjoin means to direct or impose with authority and emphasis. **(24)**

Bauer, Arndt, and Gingrich say the Greek word *epitasso* means order or command. **(25)** Consider examples:

The people were all so amazed that they asked each other, "What is this? A new teaching – and with authority! He [Jesus] even gives orders to evil spirits and they obey him." (Mark 1:27)

Then Jesus directed them to have all the people sit down in groups on the green grass. (Mark 6:39)

At this the high priest Ananias ordered those standing near Paul to strike him on the mouth. (Acts 23:2)

Epitasso is used ten times in the New Testament. **(26)** Six times the word is used of commands of Jesus: once a non-moral command at the feeding of the five thousand to have all the people to sit on the grass, four times of Jesus' commands to evil spirits, and once of His command to the wind and the raging waters. On one occasion, Paul was sending the slave Onesimus back to Philemon and spoke of commanding him to forgive and reinstate Onesimus. However, rather than command him, he was appealing to Philemon to do the right thing on the basis of love. Three times, the word is used of a man in authority giving a command to another man or men. *Epitasso* seems to be more about following orders in a chain of command or in a hierarchy, rather than a moral command from a Holy God.

V. **Keleuo** – to urge, incite, order. **(27)**

Bauer, Arndt, and Gingrich say the word means command, order, or urge. **(28)** See examples:

When Jesus saw the crowd around him, he gave orders to cross to the other side of the lake. (Matthew 8:18)

Going to Pilate, he [Joseph of Arimathea] asked for Jesus' body, and Pilate ordered that it be given to him. (Matthew 27:58)

Chief priests and Pharisees: "Sir," they said, "we remember that while he [Jesus] was still alive that deceiver said, 'After three days I will rise again.' So [to Pilate] give the order for the tomb to be made secure until the third day." (Matthew 27:63, 64a)

The Greek word *keleuo* is used twenty-seven times in the New Testament. **(29)** Four times it used of Jesus giving a command not related to morals, e.g., cross to the other side of the lake; sit on the grass. Once the word is used when Peter requested that Jesus command him to come to Him, walking on the water. Twenty-two times it is used of a man or men giving a command to another man or men.

The word *keleuo* means to give an order or command, but I don't find it used with any moral commands.

VI. **Parangello** – to announce beside, to pass on an announcement, give the word, order, give a charge, command. **(30)** The word means to hand on an announcement from one to another. It usually denotes to command or to charge.

Bauer, Arndt, and Gingrich say the word *parangello* means to give orders, command, instruct, direct of all kinds of persons in authority, worldly rulers, Jesus, the apostles. **(31)** Consider examples:

These twelve Jesus sent out with the following instructions: "Do not go among the Gentiles or enter any town of the Samaritans. Go rather to the lost sheep of Israel." (Matthew 10:5, 6)

95

When he [the demon-possessed man] saw Jesus, he cried out and fell at his feet, shouting at the top of his voice, "What do you want with me, Jesus, Son of the Most High God? I beg you, don't torture me!" For Jesus had <u>commanded</u> the evil spirit to come out of the man. (Luke 8:28, 29a)

Having brought the apostles, they made them appear before the Sanhedrin to be questioned by the high priest. "We <u>gave you strict orders</u> not to teach in this name," he said. "Yet you have filled Jerusalem with your teaching and are determined to make us guilty of this man's blood." (Acts 5:27, 28)

The Greek word *parangello* is used, in one form or another, a total of thirty times in the New Testament. **(32)** Three times the word is used referring to moral commands of God or His command to the disciples to preach the gospel, referring to God as God (Acts 17:30), Jesus (Acts 10:42), or the Lord (I Corinthians 7:10). Seven times, the word is used in the gospels or Acts, referring to Jesus giving out instructions to the disciples or the people about how to, or not to, carry out the ministry. Once each, it is used in reference to Jesus and Paul casting out evil spirits. Eight times, the word is used in reference to Paul's instructions to the church, either directly, or through Timothy. Once, the word is used by Paul, as he describes to Timothy how he should carry on his life's work. Seven times it refers to the word of men in authority, telling other men what, or what not, to do.

The Greek word *parangello* seems to carry more moral weight than *keleuo*.

VII. **Prostasso** – to arrange or set in order towards; hence to prescribe, give command. **(33)**

Bauer, Arndt, and Gingrich say the word means command, order, prescribe something, give orders concerning someone. **(34)** See examples:

When Joseph woke up, he did what the angel of the Lord had <u>commanded</u> him and took Mary home as his wife. But he had no union with her until she gave birth to a son. And he gave him the name Jesus. (Matthew 1:24, 25)

Jesus sent him away at once with a strong warning: "See that you [the man cleansed

96

from leprosy] don't tell this to anyone. But go, show yourself to the priest and offer the sacrifices that Moses commanded for your cleansing, as a testimony to them." (Mark 1:43, 44)

MacArthur writes that the priest's acceptance of the man's offering would be public affirmation of his cure and cleansing. **(35)**

So I [Cornelius] sent for you [Peter] immediately, and it was good of you to come. Now we are all here in the presence of God to listen to everything the Lord has commanded you to tell us. (Acts 10:33)

The word *prostasso* is used seven times in the New Testament. **(36)** In three different gospels, it is used to describe the same story of Jesus commanding the man healed of leprosy to show himself to the priest and offer the sacrifices that Moses commanded for his cleansing, as a testimony to them. Once the word is used of a command Jesus gave to the disciples that was one of a non-moral nature, for them to bring Him the donkey and colt for the triumphal entry. Once the Greek word *prostasso* is used of the command of the angel of the Lord to Joseph to not be afraid to take Mary as his wife, because what was conceived in her was from the Holy Spirit. The word is used twice in Acts 10 to describe Peter's visit to the house of Cornelius. The first time, Cornelius said that the people were all there to listen to everything God had commanded Peter to tell them. Later, the word is used to describe Peter's reaction when he realized they had received the gift of the Holy Spirit. He ordered that they be baptized in the name of Jesus Christ.

Prostasso appears to be a true command of solemn importance, but I don't believe any of its seven uses in the New Testament apply to present day believers.

GREEK WORDS FOR COMMANDMENT (nouns)

I. **Diatagma** – signifies that which is imposed by decree or law. It stresses the concrete character of the commandment. **(37)** Bauer, Arndt, and Gingrich say the word means edict, command. **(38)** See example:

By faith Joseph, when his end was near, spoke about the exodus of the Israelites from Egypt and gave instructions about his bones. By faith Moses' parents hid him for three months after he was born, because they saw he was no ordinary child, and they were not afraid of the king's edict. (Hebrews 11:22, 23)

Diatagma appears to be a very authoritative word for command, but according to *The Englishman's Greek Concordance of the New Testament*, the word is only used once in the New Testament, in Hebrews 11:23 **(39)**, and then is used of a command from an earthly ruler.

II. **Entolee** – akin to *entello* above, denotes, in general, an injunction, charge, precept, or commandment. It is the most frequent term for commandment in the New Testament and is used of moral and religious precepts. The word is frequently used in the gospels, especially that of John, and in his epistles. **(40)**

Bauer, Arndt, and Gingrich say the word means command(ment), order.

1. Of men
    a. Of official decrees
    b. Of the commands of other persons in high position: father, apostles, Jewish teachings
2. Of divine authorities, of imperial decrees
    a. Of the commandments of the Old Testament law
    b. Of divine commandments
    c. Of God's commands to Christ
    d. Of the precepts of Jesus
    e. Of the commands of the angel of repentance
    f. Of the whole Christian religion as thought of as a new law. **(41)**

See examples:

But the chief priests and Pharisees had given orders that if anyone found out where Jesus was, he should report it so that they might arrest him. (John 11:57)

A new command I [Jesus] give you: Love one another. As I have loved you, so you must love one another. By this all men will know that you are my disciples, if you love one another. (John 13:34, 35)

But sin, seizing the opportunity afforded by the <u>commandment</u> ["Do not covet."], produced in me every kind of covetous desire. For apart from the law, sin is dead. (Romans 7:8)

The Greek word *entolee* is the most frequent term used of moral and religious commands. The word *entolee* is used, in one form or another, a total of sixty-eight times in the New Testament. **(42)** The word refers to an Old Testament command thirty-three times. It refers to a command of God the Father to God the Son four times and from the Father to men thirteen times. Entolee is used of the commands of Jesus ten times. Paul uses the word to give a general command from the Lord twice and a personal command to Timothy once. There are five times when the word is used by a man, or men in authority, to another man or men.

This Greek noun *entollee* is in line with what we think of when we hear about someone giving true moral commands, and the word includes moral commands from God.

III. **Entalma** – marks more especially the thing commanded, a commission. **(43)**

Bauer, Arndt, and Gingrich say the word means commandment. **(44)** See examples:

They worship me [Jesus] in vain; their <u>teachings</u> are but rules taught by men. (Matthew 15:9)

They worship me [Jesus] in vain; their <u>teachings</u> are but rules taught by men. (Mark 7:7)

These [basic principles of this world] are all destined to perish with use, because they are based on human commands and <u>teachings</u>. (Colossians 2:22)

According to *The Englishman's Greek Concordance of the New Testament* the above three passages are the only times *entalma* is used in the New Testament **(45)**, and every time, it refers to the

99

commandments of men.

IV. **Epitagee** – stresses the authoritativeness of the command. **(46)**

According to Bauer Arndt, and Gingrich, the word means command, order, or injunction. **(47)** See examples:

Now to him who is able to establish you by my gospel and the proclamation of Jesus Christ, according to the mystery hidden for long ages past, but now revealed and made known through the prophetic writings by the <u>command</u> of the eternal God, so that all nations might believe and obey him – to the only wise God be glory forever through Jesus Christ! Amen. (Romans 16:25-27)

Paul, an apostle of Christ Jesus by the <u>command</u> of God our Savior and of Christ Jesus our hope… (I Timothy 1:1)

These, then, are the things you should teach. Encourage and rebuke with all <u>authority</u>. Do not let anyone despise you. (Titus 2:15)

The Greek word *epitagee* is used seven times in the New Testament. **(48)** The word is used three times as a command of God. Once the word is used when Paul is telling Titus how to conduct his ministry. Three times, Paul uses the word when he says certain ideas are good ideas, but they are not a command. The word is not often used in the New Testament, but it is a very strong word, and stresses the authority of the person making the command.

The following is a summary of how the different Greek words for command are used in the New Testament.

Not used for moral commands in the New Testament:
 epo
 epitasso
 keleuo
 diatagma
 entalma

Used for moral commands in the New Testament but none apply to present day believers:

prostasso

Sometimes used for moral commands in the New Testament:
diatasso
parangello

Strongest use for moral commands in the New Testament:
entello
entolee
epitage

Classification of the New Testament Commandments

1. The Bible commands us to believe in the name of the God's Son, Jesus Christ.

Dear friends, if our hearts do not condemn us, we have confidence before God and receive from him anything we ask, because we obey his commands [*entolee*] and do what pleases him. And this is his command [*entolee*]: to believe in the name of his Son, Jesus Christ, and to love one another as he commanded [*didomi + entolee*] us. Those who obey his commands [*entolee*] live in him, and he in them. (I John 3:21-24a)

According to Bauer, Arndt, and Gingrich, *didomi* means give, grant, or impose. **(49)**

Consider the poor outcome for those who do not obey the command to believe in the name of Jesus.

If they [false teachers] have escaped the corruption of the world by knowing our Lord and Savior Jesus Christ and are again entangled in it and overcome, they are worse off at the end than they were at the beginning. It would have been better for them not to have known the way of righteousness, than to have known it and then to turn their backs on the sacred command [*entolee*] that was passed on to them. (II Peter 2:20, 21)

Regarding II Peter 2:20, MacArthur writes: "Peter notes that at some point in time these false teachers and their followers wanted to escape

101

the moral contamination of the world system and sought religion, even Jesus Christ…But these false teachers had never genuinely been converted to Christ. They heard the true gospel and moved toward it, but then rejected the Christ of that gospel. That is apostasy." **(50)** They had not truly responded in obedience to the command of I John 3:22, 23 to believe in the name of God's Son, Jesus Christ.

If we deliberately keep on sinning after we have received the knowledge of the truth, no sacrifice for sins is left, but only a fearful expectation of judgment and of raging fire that will consume the enemies of God. Anyone who rejected the law of Moses died without mercy on the testimony of two or three witnesses. How much more severely do you think a man deserves to be punished who has trampled the Son of God under foot, who has treated as an unholy thing the blood of the covenant that sanctified him, and who has insulted the Spirit of grace? (Hebrews 10:26-29)

2. We are commanded to love God and to love others.

Hearing that Jesus had silenced the Sadducees, the Pharisees got together. One of them, an expert in the law, tested him with this question: "Teacher, which is the greatest commandment [*entolee*] in the Law?" Jesus replied: "'Love the Lord your God with all your heart and with all your soul and with all your mind.' This is the first and greatest commandment [*entolee*]. And the second is like it: 'Love your neighbor as yourself.' All the Law and the Prophets hang on these two commandments [*entolee*]." (Matthew 22:34-40)

In the above passage, Jesus is quoting Deuteronomy 6:4, 5 and Leviticus 19:18.

Let no debt remain outstanding, except the continuing debt to love one another, for he who loves his fellowman has fulfilled the law. The commandments [actual word not in the Greek text, Westcott and Hort, p. 371], "Do not commit adultery," "Do not murder," "Do not steal," "Do not covet," and whatever other commandment [*entolee*] there may be, are summed up in this one rule: "Love your neighbor as yourself." Love does no harm to its neighbor. Therefore love is the fulfillment of the law. (Romans 13:8-10)

The entire law is summed up in a single command [the Greek here is *logos*, meaning *word*, Westcott & Hort, p. 426]: "Love your neighbor as yourself." (Galatians 5:14)

Dear friends, I am not writing you a new command [*entolee*] but an old one, which you have had since the beginning. The old command [*entolee*] is the message you have heard. Yet I am writing you a new command [*entolee*]; its truth is seen in him and you, because the darkness is passing and the true light is already shining. Anyone who claims to be in the light but hates his brother is still in darkness. Whoever loves his brother lives in the light, and there is nothing in him to make him stumble. But whoever hates his brother is in the darkness and walks around in the darkness; he does not know where he is going, because the darkness has blinded him. (I John 2:7-11)

MacArthur writes: "**2:7 new.** Not referring to 'new' in the sense of time but something that is fresh in quality, kind or form; something that replaces something else that has been worn out. **new commandment...old commandment.** John makes a significant word play here. Though he doesn't state here what the command is, he does in 2 John 5, 6. It is to love. Both of these phrases refer to the same commandment of love." **(51)**

Our love for God is demonstrated by our obedience to His commandments.

"If you love me [Jesus], you will obey what I command [*entolee*]. And I will ask the Father, and he will give you another Counselor [the Holy Spirit] to be with you forever – the Spirit of truth. The world cannot accept him, because it neither sees him nor knows him. But you know him, for he lives with you and will be in you. I will not leave you as orphans; I will come to you. Before long, the world will not see me anymore, but you will see me. Because I live, you also will live. On that day you will realize that I am in my Father, and you are in me, and I am in you. Whoever has my commands [*entolee*] and obeys them, he is the one who loves me. He who loves me will be loved by my Father, and I too will love him and show myself to him." Then Judas (not Judas Iscariot) said, "But Lord, why do you intend to show yourself to us and not to the world?" Jesus replied, "If anyone loves me, he will obey my teaching. My Father will love him, and we will come to him and make our home with him. He who does not love me will not obey my teaching." (John 14:15-24a)

We know that we have come to know him [God] if we obey his commands [*entolee*]. The man who says, "I know him," but does not do what he commands [*entolee*] is a liar, and the truth is not in him. But if anyone obeys his word, God's love is truly made complete in him. This is how we know we are in him: whoever claims to live in him must walk as Jesus did. (I John 2:3-6)

This is love for God: to obey his commands [*entolee*]. (I John 5:3a)

3. God commands people to repent of sin.

Therefore since we are God's offspring, we should not think that the divine being is like gold or silver or stone – an image made by man's design and skill. In the past God overlooked such ignorance, but now he commands [*parangello*] all people everywhere to repent. (Acts 17:29, 30)

4. We are commanded to obey our parents.

Children obey your parents in the Lord, for this is right. "Honor your father and mother" which is the first commandment [*entolee*] with a promise "that it may go well with you and that you may enjoy long life on the earth." (Ephesians 6:1-3)

5. We are commanded to remember that Jesus is coming again, and we are to live holy and godly lives as we look forward to the day of His coming.

But you, man of God, flee from all this [the love of money and its consequences], and pursue righteousness, godliness, faith, love, endurance and gentleness. Fight the good fight of faith. Take hold of the eternal life to which you were called when you made your good confession in the presence of many witnesses. In the sight of God, who gives life to everything, and of Christ Jesus, who while testifying before Pontius Pilate made the good confession, I charge [*parangello*] you to keep this command [*entolee*] without spot or blame until the appearing of our Lord Jesus Christ… (I Timothy 6:11-14)

Dear friends, this is now my second letter to you. I have written both of them as reminders to stimulate you to wholesome thinking. I want you to recall the words spoken in the past by the holy prophets and the command [*entolee*] given by our Lord and Savior through your apostles. First of all, you must understand that in the last days scoffers will come, scoffing and following their own evil desires. They will say, "Where is this 'coming' he promised? Ever since our fathers died, everything goes on as it has since the beginning of creation." But they deliberately forget that long ago by God's word the heavens existed and the earth was formed out of water and by water. By these waters also the world of that time was deluged and destroyed. By the same word the present heavens and earth are reserved for fire, being kept for the Day of Judgment and destruction of ungodly men. But do not forget this one thing, dear friends: With the Lord a day is like a thousand years, and a thousand years are like a day. The Lord is not slow in keeping his promise, as some understand slowness. He is patient with you, not wanting anyone to perish, but everyone to come to repentance. But the day of the Lord will come like a thief. The heavens will disappear with a roar; the elements will be destroyed by fire, and the earth and everything in it will be laid bare. Since everything will be destroyed in this way, what kind of people ought you to be? You ought to live holy and godly lives as you look forward to the day of God and speed its coming. That day will bring about the destruction of the heavens by fire, and the elements will melt in the heat. But in keeping with this promise we are looking forward to a new heaven and a new earth, the home of righteousness. So then, dear friends, since you are looking forward to this, make every effort to be found spotless, blameless and at peace with him. (II Peter 3:1-14)

6. A wife must not separate from her husband, but if she does, she must remain unmarried or be reconciled to her husband. A husband must not divorce his wife.

To the married I give this command [*parangello*] (not I, but the Lord): A wife must not separate from her husband. But if she does, she must remain unmarried or else be reconciled to her husband. And a husband must not divorce his wife. (I Corinthians 7:10, 11)

Marriage vows are for as long as both parties shall live. My son says that when a person is dating, he/she is usually trying to decide whether or not that person is the right one for marriage. Once they are married, that person is the right one.

7. When believers come together for worship and mutual edification, they should be eager to prophesy, speak forth God's truth, but everything should be done in a fitting and orderly way.

According to Bauer, Arndt, and Gingrich, the Greek word *propheeteuo* (English word *prophesy*) has three meanings:

1. proclaim a divine revelation, 2. reveal what is hidden, and lastly, 3. foretell the future. (52)

What then shall we say, brothers? When you come together, everyone has a hymn, or a word of instruction, a revelation, a tongue or an interpretation. All of these must be done for the strengthening of the church. If anyone speaks in a tongue, two – or at the most three – should speak, one at a time, and someone must interpret. If there is no interpreter, the speaker should keep quiet in the church and speak to himself and God. Two or three prophets should speak, and the others should weigh carefully what is said. And if a revelation comes to someone who is sitting down, the first speaker should stop. For you can all prophesy in turn so that everyone may be instructed and encouraged. The spirits of prophets are subject to the control of prophets. For God is not a God of disorder but of peace. As in all the congregations of the saints, women should remain silent in the churches. They are not allowed to speak, but must be in submission, as the law says. If they want to inquire about something, they should ask their own husbands at home; for it is disgraceful for a woman to speak in church. Did the word of God originate with you? Or are you the only people it has reached? If anybody thinks he is a prophet or spiritually gifted, let him acknowledge that what I am writing to you is the Lord's command [entolee]. If he ignores this, he himself will be ignored. Therefore, my brothers, be eager to prophesy, and do not forbid speaking in tongues. But everything should be done in a fitting and orderly way. (I Corinthians 14:26-40)

8. Believers are commanded to keep away from every brother who is idle [disorderly].

In the name of the Lord Jesus Christ, we command [parangello] you, brothers, to keep away from every brother who is idle and does not live according to the teaching you received from us. For you yourselves know how you ought to follow our example. We were not idle when we were with you, nor did we eat anyone's food without paying for it. On the contrary, we worked night and day, laboring and toiling so that we would not be a burden to any of you. We did this, not because we do not have the right to such help, but in order to make ourselves a model for you to follow. For even when we were with you, we gave you this rule: "If a man will not work, he shall not eat." We hear that some among you are idle. They are not busy; they are busybodies. Such people we command [parangello] and urge in the Lord Jesus Christ to settle down and earn the bread they eat. And as for you, brothers, never tire of doing what is right. (II Thessalonians 3:6-13)

The Greek word for idle in II Thessalonians 3:6 and 3:11 is the adjective *ataktos*. Bauer, Arndt, and Gingrich say the word means not in proper order, undisciplined, disorderly, or insubordinate. **(53)**
In II Thessalonians 3:11, Paul refers to these people as busybodies. The Greek word is *periergazomai*. According to Bauer, Arndt, and Gingrich, the word means to do something unnecessary or useless, have undue anxiety about something, or meddle in other people's matters. **(54)** It sounds to me as if they are codependent, that they have difficulty setting or respecting boundaries and also have issues with conflict avoidance. Codependent people often go around stirring up trouble.

106

It's been my experience that those who will not work often have other negative character traits.

In his *Believer's Bible Commentary*, William MacDonald writes as follows:

It seems clear that some of the saints at Thessalonica had stopped working for a living because they were so intently waiting for the Lord's return. Paul does not encourage this as a spiritual attitude, but proceeds to give definite instructions as to how to deal with such brethren.

His instructions are in the form of a command to **withdraw from every brother who walks disorderly,** this is one who does not keep in step with the others, but refuses to work, and who sponges off others (see vv. 10, 11). Believers should show their disapproval of such **a brother** by refusing to mingle with him socially. **The tradition which** the Thessalonians **received from** Paul was one of tireless industry, hard work, and self-support. **(55)**

One thing I'm grateful for, though I was not so grateful at the time, is that when I was growing up, my dad taught me to work.

9. We are commanded to not put our hope in wealth and to use what wealth we have to help others.

Command [*parangello*] those who are rich in this present world not to be arrogant nor to put their hope in wealth, which is so uncertain, but to put their hope in God, who richly provides us with everything for our enjoyment. Command [*parangello*] them to do good, to be rich in good deeds, and to be generous and willing to share. In this way they will lay up treasure for themselves as a firm foundation for the coming age, so that they may take hold of the life that is truly life. (I Timothy 6:17-19)

This command to the rich applies to most of us who are blessed to have been born in the United States.

10. We are commanded to walk in the truth.

It has given me great joy to find some of your [the chosen lady's] children walking in the truth, just as the Father commanded [*entolee* + *lambano*] us. (II John 4)

According to Vine, *lambano* denotes either to take or receive. **(56)**

The King James Version puts the verse this way:

I rejoiced greatly that I found of my children walking in truth, as we have received a commandment [*entolee*] from the Father. (II John 4)

Of course, the truth is what God says, not what we hear from the world.

11. We are commanded to study the Bible and be able to discern truth from falsehood. We are to sit under pastors who teach accurately the truth of God's word. We are commanded not to teach false doctrine.

As I [Paul] urged you when I went into Macedonia, stay there in Ephesus so that you may command [*parangello*] certain men not to teach false doctrines any longer nor to devote themselves to myths and endless genealogies. These promote controversies rather than God's work – which is by faith. The goal of this command [*parangellia*] is love, which comes from a pure heart and a good conscience and a sincere faith. Some have wandered away from these and turned to meaningless talk. They want to be teachers of the law, but they do not know what they are talking about or what they so confidently affirm. (I Timothy 1:3-7)

The Spirit clearly says that in the latter times some will abandon the faith and follow deceiving spirits and things taught by demons. Such teachings come through hypocritical liars, whose consciences have been seared as with a hot iron. They forbid people to marry and order them to abstain from certain foods, which God created to be received with thanksgiving by those who believe and who know the truth. For everything God created is good, and nothing is to be rejected if it is received with thanksgiving, because it is consecrated by the word of God and prayer. If you point these things out to the brothers, you will be a good minister of Christ Jesus, brought up in the truths of the faith and of the good teaching that you have followed. Have nothing to do with godless myths and old wives tales; rather, train yourself to be godly. For physical training is of some value, but godliness has value for all things, holding promise for both the present life and the life to come. This is a trustworthy saying that deserves full acceptance (and for this we labor and strive), that we have put our hope in the living God, who is the Savior of all men, and especially of those who believe. Command [*parangello*] and teach these things. Don't let anyone look down on you because you are young, but set an example for the believers in speech, in life, in love, in faith and in purity. Until I come devote yourself to the public reading of Scripture, to preaching and to teaching. Do not neglect your gift, which was given you through a prophetic message when the body of elders laid their hands on you. Be diligent in these matters; give yourself wholly to them, so that everyone may see your progress. Watch your life and doctrine closely. Persevere in them, because if you do, you will save both yourself and your hearers. (I Timothy 4:1-16)

12. We are commanded to endure patiently.

Since you [the Church in Philadelphia] have kept my command [*logos* – word] to endure patiently, I will also keep you from the hour of trial that is going to come upon the whole world to test those who live on the earth. (Revelation 3:10)

13. God commands that the gospel of Jesus Christ be proclaimed to all nations, and we, as believers, are commanded to share in that proclamation.

Then [after the resurrection] the eleven disciples went to Galilee, to the mountain where Jesus had told them to go. When they saw him, they worshipped him; but some doubted. Then Jesus came to them and said, "All authority in heaven and on earth has been given to me. Therefore go and make disciples of all nations, baptizing them in the name of the Father and of the Son and of the Holy Spirit, teaching them to obey everything I have commanded [*entello*] you. And surely I am with you always, to the very end of the age." (Matthew 28:16-20)

Then Peter began to speak [to the people at the house of Cornelius, a Gentile]: "I now realize how true it is that God does not show favoritism but accepts men from every nation who fear him and do what is right. You know the message God sent to the people of Israel, telling the good news of peace through Jesus Christ, who is Lord of all. You know what has happened throughout Judea, beginning in Galilee after the baptism that John preached – how God anointed Jesus of Nazareth with the Holy Spirit and power, and how he went around doing good and healing all who were under the power of the devil, because God was with him. We are witnesses of everything he did in the country of the Jews and in Jerusalem. They killed him by hanging him on a tree, but God raised him from the dead on the third day and caused him to be seen. He was not seen by all the people, but by witnesses whom God had already chosen – by us who ate and drank with him after he rose from the dead. He commanded [*parangello*] us to preach to the people and to testify that he is the one whom God appointed as judge of the living and the dead. All the prophets testify about him that everyone who believes in him receives forgiveness of sins through his name." (Acts 10:34-43)

On the next Sabbath, almost the whole city gathered to hear the word of the Lord. When the Jews saw the crowds, they were filled with jealously and talked abusively against what Paul was saying. Then Paul and Barnabas answered them boldly: "We had to speak the word of God to you first. Since you reject it and do not consider yourselves worthy of eternal life, we now turn to the Gentiles. For this is what the

Lord has commanded [*entello*] us." "'I have made you [singular] a light for the Gentiles, that you may bring salvation to the ends of the earth.'"

When the Gentiles heard this, they were glad and honored the word of the Lord; and all who were appointed for eternal life believed." (Acts 13:44-48)

The Old Testament quote in Acts 13:47b is from Isaiah 49:6. In his *Believer's Bible Commentary – Old Testament*, William MacDonald writes as follows: "In chapters 49 through 53 [of Isaiah], God is dealing with His people because of their rejection of the Messiah. This is the book of the Suffering Servant of Jehovah. **49:1-6** The **servant** of Jehovah in chapter 49 may seem to be the nation of Israel in verses 1-3, but only the Lord Jesus fully answers to the text…God called Him not only to bring about the spiritual rebirth of Israel, but also to bring salvation **to the Gentiles**." **(57)**

In his *The MacArthur Study Bible*, John MacArthur writes regarding Isaiah 49:6: "Paul applied this verse to his ministry to the Gentiles on his first missionary journey" (Acts 13:47). **(58)** I see that Paul, in Acts 13:47a, does write: "the Lord has commanded us." I believe Paul is saying that, since he is a follower of Jesus, he is commanded to emulate the example of Jesus and follow in His steps, to be a light to the world.

Paul, a servant of God and an apostle of Jesus Christ for the faith of God's elect and the knowledge of the truth that leads to godliness – a faith and knowledge resting on the hope of eternal life, which God, who does not lie, promised before the beginning of time, and at his appointed season he brought his word to light through the preaching entrusted to me by the command [*epitage*] of God our Savior… (Titus 1:1-3)

Our individual ministries are determined by the command of God. Notice the authority of the Greek word used for command. Our responsibility should not be taken lightly.

For more information about how Paul received the message of the gospel and what the message contained, please see Galatians 1:11, 12, 15-17; Ephesians 1:3-14; and I Corinthians 15:1-8.

110

Summary of the New Testament Commandments

1. The Bible commands us to believe in the name of God's Son, Jesus Christ.
2. We are commanded to love God and to love others.
3. God commands people to repent of sin.
4. We are commanded to obey our parents.
5. We are commanded to remember that Jesus is coming again, and we are to live holy and godly lives as we look forward to the day of His coming.
6. A wife must not separate from her husband, but if she does, she must remain unmarried or be reconciled to her husband. A husband must not divorce his wife.
7. When believers come together for worship and mutual edification, they should be eager to prophesy, speak forth God's truth, but everything should be done in a fitting and orderly way.
8. Believers are commanded to keep away from every brother who is idle [disorderly].
9. We are commanded to not put our hope in wealth and to use what wealth we have to help others.
10. We are commanded to walk in the truth.
11. We are commanded to study the Bible and be able to discern truth from falsehood. We are to sit under pastors who teach accurately the truth of God's word. We are commanded not to teach false doctrine.
12. We are commanded to endure patiently.
13. God commands that the gospel of Jesus Christ be proclaimed to all nations, and we, as believers, are commanded to share in that proclamation.

Now in the next chapter, let us look at some of the many reasons why we obey God.

Chapter Seven
Reasons to Obey God

Salvation is by grace alone, through faith (Ephesians 2:8, 9). However, although it is not a work of the law, exercising our faith is an act of obedience.

And this is his [God's] command: to believe in the name of his Son, Jesus Christ, and to love one another as he commanded us. (I John 3:23)

Even though salvation is by grace through faith, after we are saved, works do matter. I don't believe God judges us on our performance, but He does expect our obedience. In order to have the power to properly deal with anger and resentment we must do what God says. We must do so if we want to maintain fellowship with Him and want His power to operate in our lives. There are many reasons for us to be obedient. There are many different reasons for us to serve the Lord.

1. We are obedient because of guilt and fear of discipline and judgment.

Our fathers disciplined us for a little while as they thought best; but God disciplines us for our good, that we may share in his holiness. No discipline seems pleasant at the time, but painful. Later on, however, it produces a harvest of righteousness and peace for those who have been trained by it. (Hebrews 12: 10, 11)

Since you call on a Father who judges each man's work impartially, live your lives as strangers here in reverent fear. (I Peter 1:17)

If anyone sees his brother commit a sin that does not lead to death, he should pray and God will give him life. I refer to those whose sin does not lead to death. There is a sin that leads to death. I am not saying that he should pray about that. All wrongdoing is sin, and there is sin that does not lead to death. (I John 5:16, 17)

There is a sin that leads to death.

2. We are obedient because we are thankful for our salvation and want to please God.

One man considers one day more sacred than another; another man considers every day alike. Each one should be fully convinced in his own mind. He who regards one day as special, does so to the Lord. He who eats meat, eats to the Lord, for he gives thanks to God; and he who abstains, does so to the Lord and gives thanks to God. For none of us lives to himself alone and none of us dies to himself alone. If we live, we live to the Lord; and if we die, we die to the Lord. So, whether we live or die, we belong to the Lord. (Romans 14:5-8)

I speak to sensible people; judge for yourselves what I say. Is not the cup of thanksgiving for which we give thanks a participation in the blood of Christ? And is not the bread that we break a participation in the body of Christ? (I Corinthians 10:15, 16)

For Christ's love compels us, because we are convinced that one died for all, and therefore all died. And he died for all, that those who live should no longer live for themselves but for him who died for them and was raised again. (II Corinthians 5:14, 15)

Be very careful, then, how you live - not as unwise but as wise, making the most of every opportunity, because the days are evil. Therefore do not be foolish, but understand what the Lord's will is. Do not get drunk on wine, which leads to debauchery. Instead, be filled with the Spirit. Speak to one another with psalms, hymns, and spiritual songs. Sing and make music in your heart to the Lord, always giving thanks to God the Father for everything, in the name of our Lord Jesus Christ. (Ephesians 5:15-20)

Therefore, since we are receiving a kingdom that cannot be shaken, let us be thankful, and so worship God acceptably with reverence and awe, for our "God is a consuming fire." (Hebrews 12:28)

So then, those who suffer according to God's will should commit themselves to their faithful Creator and continue to do good. (I Peter 4:19)

This is love: not that we loved God, but that he loved us and sent his Son as an atoning sacrifice for our sins. Dear friends, since God so loved us, we also ought to love one another. (I John 4:10, 11)

We love because he [God] first loved us. (I John 4:19)

This is love: that we walk in obedience to his [the Father's] commands. As you have heard from the beginning, his command is that you walk in love. (II John 6)

113

3. We are obedient because we have a responsibility to live the Christian life as it should be lived, to reflect God's nature in our lives. After making a profession of faith, we are not to profane His holy name by living ungodly lives.

God is concerned about what kind of appearance He makes to the world. He cares about how the speech and actions of His people reflect on His name. Christians are not to profane God's name. One Hebrew word for profane is *halal*. According to Brown, Driver, and Briggs, the word means to pollute, defile, desecrate, violate, dishonor, or treat as common the holiness of God. **(1)** We are not to willfully take any action which controverts God's planned order. **(2)** God wants us to glorify Him. It profanes God's name when we want to be like the world. We are to be holy, separate, apart from the world. Holy things are not to be defiled. We are not to do anything that reflects negatively on our Savior.

Do not swear falsely by my name and so profane the name of your God. I am the Lord. (Leviticus 19:12)

They [Old Testament priests] must be holy to their God and must not profane the name of their God. Because they present the offerings made to the Lord by fire, the food of their God, they are to be holy. (Leviticus 21:6)

Keep my commands and follow them. I am the Lord. Do not profane my holy name. I must be acknowledged as holy by the Israelites. I am the Lord, who makes you holy and who brought you out of Egypt to be your God. I am the Lord. (Leviticus 22:31-33)

But the children rebelled against me. They did not follow my decrees, they were not careful to keep my laws - although the man who obeys them will live by them - and they desecrated my Sabbaths. So I said I would pour out my wrath on them and spend my anger against them in the desert. But I withheld my hand, and for the sake of my name I did what would keep it from being profaned in the eyes of the nations in whose sight I had brought them out. (Ezekiel 20:21, 22)

Her [Judah's] priests do violence to my law and profane my holy things; they do not distinguish between the holy and the common; they teach that there is no difference between the unclean and the clean; they shut their eyes to the keeping of my Sabbaths, so that I am profaned among them. (Ezekiel 22:26)

And wherever they [the Israelites] went among the nations they profaned my holy name, for it was said of them, "These are the Lord's people, and yet they had to leave his land." I had concern for my holy name, which the house of Israel profaned among the nations where they had gone. Therefore say to the house of Israel, "This is what the Sovereign Lord says: It is not for your sake, O house of Israel, that I am going to do these things, but for the sake of my holy name, which you have profaned among the nations where you have gone. I will show the holiness of my great name, which has been profaned among the nations, the name you have profaned among them. Then the nations will know that I am the Lord, declares the Sovereign Lord, when I show myself holy through you before their eyes. For I will take you out of the nations; I will gather you from all the countries and bring you back into your own land." (Ezekiel 36:20-24)

They [the Israelites] trample on the heads of the poor as upon the dust of the ground and deny justice to the oppressed. Father and son use the same girl and so profane my [The Lord's] holy name. (Amos 2:7)

"Everything is permissible for me" - but not everything is beneficial. "Everything is permissible for me" - but I will not be mastered by anything. "Food for the stomach and the stomach for food" - but God will destroy them both. The body is not meant for sexual immorality, but for the Lord, and the Lord for the body. By his power God raised the Lord from the dead, and he will raise us also. Do you not know that your bodies are members of Christ himself? Shall I then take the members of Christ and unite them with a prostitute? Never! Do you not know that he who unites himself with a prostitute is one with her in body? For it is said, "The two will become one flesh." But he who unites himself with the Lord is one with him in spirit. Flee from sexual immorality. All other sins a man commits are outside his body, but he who sins sexually sins against his own body. Do you not know that your body is a temple of the Holy Spirit, who is in you, whom you have received from God? You are not your own; you were bought at a price. Therefore honor God with your body. (I Corinthians 6:12-20)

Be imitators of God, therefore as dearly loved children and live a life of love, just as Christ loved us and gave himself up for us as a fragrant offering and sacrifice to God. But among you there must not be even a hint of sexual immorality, or of any kind of impurity, or of greed, because these are improper for God's holy people. Nor should there be obscenity, foolish talk or coarse joking, which are out of place, but rather thanksgiving. (Ephesians 5:1-4)

I also want women to dress modestly, with decency and propriety, not with braided hair or gold or pearls or expensive clothes, but with good deeds, appropriate for women who profess to worship God. (I Timothy 2:9, 10)

115

4. We are obedient because God has made each of us a new creation. The Lord guides us, and He gives us the will and power to obey.

A man's steps are directed by the Lord. How then can anyone understand his own way? (Proverbs 20:24)

Lord, you establish peace for us; all that we have accomplished you have done for us. (Isaiah 26:12)

Although the Lord gives you the bread of adversity and the water of affliction, your teachers will be hidden no more; with your own eyes you will see them. Whether you turn to the right or to the left, your ears will hear a voice behind you, saying, "This is the way; walk in it." (Isaiah 30:20, 21)

Through him and for his name's sake we received grace and apostleship to call people from among all the Gentiles to the obedience that comes from faith. (Romans 1:5)

For if you live according to the sinful nature, you will die; but if by the Spirit you put to death the misdeeds of the body, you will live, because those who are led by the Spirit of God are sons of God. (Romans 8:13, 14)

Therefore, if anyone is in Christ, he is a new creation; the old has gone, the new has come! (II Corinthians 5:17)

We proclaim him, admonishing and teaching everyone with all wisdom, so that we may present everyone perfect in Christ. To this end I labor, struggling with all his energy, which so powerfully works in me. (Colossians 1:28, 29)

To God's elect...who have been chosen according to the foreknowledge of God the Father, through the sanctifying work of the Spirit, for obedience to Jesus Christ. (I Peter 1b, 2a)

No one who is born of God will continue to sin, because God's seed remains in him; he cannot go on sinning, because he has been born of God. (I John 3:9)

We know that anyone born of God does not continue to sin; the one who was born of God keeps him safe, and the evil one cannot harm him. (I John 5:18)

5. We are obedient because we desire the joy of the experience.

Having the assurance of my salvation brings joy to my soul. It brings joy to my soul when I'm alone with the Lord in the morning, and God

116

Almighty speaks to me. It thrills my soul when I discover a new truth in Scripture or when I find a thread running through the Bible that no one has told me about before. It brings joy to my soul when God uses me to bless others. It thrills my soul that the God, who flung the universe into existence, allows me to participate in what He is doing.

Then King David said to the whole assembly: "My son Solomon, the one whom God has chosen, is young and inexperienced. The task is great, because this palatial structure is not for man but for the Lord God. With all my resources I have provided for the temple of my God - gold for the gold work, silver for the silver, bronze for the bronze, iron for the iron and wood for the wood, as well as onyx for the settings, turquoise, stones of various colors, and all kinds of fine stone and marble - all of these in large quantities. Besides, in my devotion to the temple of my God I now give my personal treasures of gold and silver for the temple of my God, over and above everything I have provided for this holy temple: three thousand talents [about 110 tons] of gold (gold of Ophir) and seven thousand talents [about 260 tons] of refined silver, for the overlaying of the walls of the buildings, for the gold work and the silver work, and for all the work to be done by the craftsman. Now, who is willing to consecrate himself today to the Lord?" Then the leaders of the families, the officers of the tribes of Israel, the commanders of thousands and the commanders of hundreds, and the officials in charge of the king's work gave willingly. They gave toward the work on the temple of God five thousand talents [about 190 tons] and ten thousand darics [about 185 lb.] of gold, ten thousand talents [about 375 tons] of silver, eighteen thousand talents [about 675 tons] of bronze and a hundred thousand talents [about 3,750 tons] of iron. Any who had precious stones gave them to the treasury of the temple of the Lord in the custody of Jehiel the Gershonite. The people rejoiced at the willing response of their leaders, for they had given freely and wholeheartedly to the Lord. David the king also rejoiced greatly. (I Chronicles 29:1-9)

They assembled at Jerusalem in the third month of the fifteenth year of Asa's reign. At that time they sacrificed to the Lord seven thousand head of cattle and seven thousand sheep and goats from the plunder they had brought back. They entered into a covenant to seek the Lord, the God of their fathers, with all their heart and soul. All who would not seek the Lord, the God of Israel, were to be put to death, whether small or great, man or woman. They took an oath to the Lord with loud acclamation, with shouting and with trumpets and horns. All Judah rejoiced about the oath because they had sworn it wholeheartedly. They sought God eagerly, and he was found by them. So the Lord gave them rest on every side. (II Chronicles 15:10-15)

The whole assembly then agreed to celebrate the festival seven more days; so for

117

another seven days they celebrated joyfully. Hezekiah king of Judah provided a thousand bulls and seven thousand sheep and goats for the assembly, and the officials provided them with a thousand bulls and ten thousand sheep and goats. A great number of priests consecrated themselves. The entire assembly of Judah rejoiced, along with the priests and Levites and all who had assembled from Israel, including the aliens who had come from Israel and those who lived in Judah. There was great joy in Jerusalem, for since the days of Solomon son of David king of Israel there had been nothing like this in Jerusalem. The priests and the Levites stood to bless the people and God heard them, for their prayer reached heaven, his holy dwelling place. (II Chronicles 30:23-27)

How lovely is your dwelling place, O Lord Almighty! My soul yearns, even faints, for the courts of the Lord; my heart and my flesh cry out for the living God. (Psalm 84:1, 2)

I rejoice in following your [the Lord's] statutes as one rejoices in great riches. I meditate on your precepts and consider your ways. I delight in your decrees; I will not neglect your word. (Psalm 119:14-16)

I rejoiced with those who said to me, "Let us go to the house of the Lord." (Psalm 122:1)

How precious to me are your thoughts, O God! How vast is the sum of them! Were I to count them, they would outnumber the grains of sand. (Psalm 139:17, 18a)

Yes, Lord, walking in the way of your laws, we wait for you; your name and renown are the desire of our hearts. My soul yearns for you in the night; in the morning my spirit longs for you. (Isaiah 26:8, 9a)

Therefore, since we have been justified through faith, we have peace with God through our Lord Jesus Christ, through whom we have gained access by faith into this grace in which we now stand. And we rejoice in the hope of the glory of God. (Romans 5:1, 2)

Now I [Paul] want you to know, brothers, that what has happened to me has really served to advance the gospel. As a result, it has become clear throughout the whole palace guard and to everyone else that I am in chains for Christ. Because of my chains, most of the brothers in the Lord have been encouraged to speak the word of God more courageously and fearlessly. It is true that some preach Christ out of envy and rivalry, but others out of goodwill. The latter do so in love, knowing that I am put here for the defense of the gospel. The former preach Christ out of selfish ambition, not sincerely, supposing they can stir up trouble for me while I am in chains. But what does it matter? The important thing is that in every way, whether from false motives or true, Christ is preached. And because of this I rejoice. (Philippians 1:12-18a)

6. We are obedient because we care about the next generation.

When some couples first marry, especially if they are living in a different city from their parents, they may have a tendency to skip church. Later, when children come along, they once again begin to worship in church because they want their children to become godly people.

Only be careful, and watch yourselves closely so that you do not forget the things your eyes have seen or let them slip from your heart as long as you live. Teach them to your children and to their children after them. Remember the day you stood before the Lord your God at Horeb, when he said to me [Moses], "Assemble the people before me to hear my words so that they may learn to revere me as long as they live in the land and may teach them to their children." (Deuteronomy 4:9, 10)

In the future, when your son asks you, "What is the meaning of the stipulations, decrees and laws the Lord our God has commanded you?" tell him: "We were slaves of Pharaoh in Egypt, but the Lord brought us out of Egypt with a mighty hand. Before our eyes the Lord sent miraculous signs and wonders - great and terrible - upon Egypt and Pharaoh and his whole household. But he brought us out of there to bring us in and give us the land he promised on oath to our forefathers. The Lord commanded us to obey all these decrees and to fear the Lord our God, so that we might always prosper and be kept alive, as is the case today. And if we are careful to obey all this law before the Lord our God, as he has commanded us, that will be our righteousness." (Deuteronomy 6:20-25)

Fix these words of mine in your hearts and minds; tie them as symbols on your hands and bind them on your foreheads. Teach them to your children, talking about them when you sit at home and when you walk along the road, when you lie down and when you get up. Write them on the doorframes of your houses and on your gates, so that your days and the days of your children may be many in the land that the Lord swore to give your forefathers, as many as the days that the heavens are above the earth. (Deuteronomy 11:18-21)

Train a child in the way he should go, and when he is old he will not turn from it. (Proverbs 22:6)

I will give them [the people of Israel and Judah] singleness of heart and action, so that they will always fear me for their own good and the good of their children after them. (Jeremiah 32:39)

Fathers do not exasperate your children; instead bring them up in the training and instruction the Lord. (Ephesians 6:4)

7. We are obedient because we want to be used to bless others.

There have been situations when I was upset about something, but I controlled my tongue because I didn't want to mess up my testimony.

During the night Paul had a vision of a man of Macedonia standing and begging him, "Come over to Macedonia and help us." After Paul had seen the vision, we got ready at once to leave for Macedonia, concluding that God had called us to preach the gospel to them. (Acts 16:9, 10)

From Miletus, Paul sent to Ephesus for the elders of the church. When they arrived, he said to them: "You know how I lived the whole time I was with you, from the first day I came into the province of Asia. I served the Lord with great humility and with tears, although I was severely tested by the plots of the Jews. You know that I have not hesitated to preach anything that would be helpful to you but have taught you publicly and from house to house. (Acts 20:17-20)

And now, compelled by the Spirit, I [Paul] am going to Jerusalem, not knowing what will happen to me there. I only know that in every city the Holy Spirit warns me that prison and hardships are facing me. However, I consider my life worth nothing to me, if only I may finish the race and complete the task the Lord Jesus has given me - the task of testifying to the gospel of God's grace. (Acts 20:22-24)

What, after all, is Apollos? And what is Paul? Only servants, through whom you came to believe - as the Lord assigned to each his task. I planted the seed, Apollos watered it, but God made it grow. So neither he who plants nor he who waters is anything, but only God, who makes things grow. The man who plants and the man who waters have one purpose, and each will be rewarded according to his own labor. For we are God's fellow workers; you are God's field, God's building. (I Corinthians 3:5-9)

"Everything is permissible" - but not everything is beneficial. "Everything is permissible" - but not everything is constructive. Nobody should seek his own good, but the good of others. (I Corinthians 10:23, 24)

Do not cause anyone to stumble, whether Jews, Greeks or the church of God - even as I try to please everybody in every way. For I am not seeking my own good but the good of many, so that they may be saved. (I Corinthians 10:32, 33)

Follow the way of love and eagerly desire spiritual gifts, especially the gift of prophecy...everyone who prophesies speaks to men for their strengthening, encouragement and comfort...he who prophesies edifies the church. (I Corinthians 14:1-4)

120

According to *Vine's Expository Dictionary of New Testament Words*, prophecy is the speaking forth of the mind and counsel of God. **(3)** It is the declaration of that which cannot be known by natural means. It is not, primarily, foretelling the future.

And pray for us, too, that God may open a door for our message, so that we may proclaim the mystery of Christ, for which I am in chains. Pray that I may proclaim it clearly, as I should. Be wise in the way you act toward outsiders; make the most of every opportunity. Let your conversation be always full of grace, seasoned with salt, so that you may know how to answer everyone. (Colossians 4:3-6)

In the New Testament, the word mystery, as above, is a term related to prophecy. The Greek word *musteerion* refers to the secret thoughts, plans, and dispensations of God, hidden from human reason and from all other comprehension below the divine level. Mysteries must be revealed to those for whom they are intended **(4)**. They are too profound for human ingenuity.

We sent Timothy, who is our brother and God's fellow worker in spreading the gospel of Christ, to strengthen and encourage you in your faith, so that no one would be unsettled by these trials. You know quite well that we were destined for them. (I Thessalonians 3:2, 3)

Therefore encourage one another and build each other up, just as in fact you are doing. (I Thessalonians 5:11)

8. We are obedient in expectation of blessings in this life; they may be in the physical realm, or mental, or spiritual. I have learned that it is hard for me to approach the throne of grace with confidence, so that I may receive mercy and find grace to help me in my time of need, if I have a guilty conscience. We are obedient so we can experience all that God has for us in this life. We are obedient because obedience gets us ready to do battle with the forces of evil.

In expectation of blessings in this life includes serving God and knowing God as ends in themselves. According to Paul, compared to knowing God, everything else is rubbish (Philippians 3:7-11).

Knowing God requires keen spiritual eyesight. Willful sin leads to spiritual blindness (Romans 1:18-25; Ephesians 4:17-19). If we want to know God, we must be obedient to His word.

If the Lord delights in a man's way, he makes his steps firm; though he stumble, he will not fall, for the Lord upholds him with his hand. (Psalm 37:23, 24)

The righteous will flourish like a palm tree, they will grow like a cedar of Lebanon; planted in the house of the Lord, they will flourish in the courts of our God. They will still bear fruit in old age, they will stay fresh and green, proclaiming, "The Lord is upright; he is my Rock, and there is no wickedness in him." (Psalm 92:12-15)

Blessings crown the head of the righteous, but violence overwhelms the mouth of the wicked. (Proverbs 10:6)

To the man who pleases him, God gives wisdom, knowledge and happiness. (Ecclesiastes 2:26a)

But blessed is the man who trusts in the Lord, whose confidence is in him. He will be like a tree planted by the water that sends out its roots by the stream. It does not fear when heat comes; its leaves are always green. It has no worries in a year of drought and never fails to bear fruit. (Jeremiah 17:7, 8)

"Bring the whole tithe into the storehouse, that there may be food in my house. Test me in this," says the Lord Almighty, "and see if I will not throw open the floodgates of heaven and pour out so much blessing that you will not have room enough for it." (Malachi 3:10)

So when you give to the needy, do not announce it with trumpets, as the hypocrites do in the synagogues and on the streets, to be honored by men. I tell you the truth, they have received their reward in full. But when you give to the needy, do not let your left hand know what your right hand is doing, so that your giving may be in secret. Then your Father, who sees what is done in secret, will reward you. (Matthew 6:2-4)

So do not worry saying, "What shall we eat?" or "What shall we drink?" or "What shall we wear?" For the pagans run after all these things, and your heavenly Father knows that you need them. But seek first his kingdom and his righteousness, and all these things will be given to you as well. (Matthew 6:31-33)

So the Pharisees and teachers of the law asked Jesus, "Why don't your disciples live according to the tradition of the elders instead of eating their food with 'unclean' hands?" He replied, "Isaiah was right when he prophesied about you hypocrites; as it is written: "'These people honor me with their lips, but their hearts are far from me. They worship me in vain; their teachings are but rules taught by men.' You have let go of the commands of God and are holding on to the traditions of men." (Mark 7:5-8)

We don't want our worship to be in vain. It is not a good thing to harbor resentment while we are trying to worship God.

Give, and it will be given to you. A good measure, pressed down, shaken together and running over, will be poured into your lap. For with the measure you use, it will be measured to you. (Luke 6:38)

Why do you call me, "Lord, Lord,' and do not do what I say? I will show you what he is like who comes to me and hears my words and puts them into practice. He is like a man building a house, who dug down deep and laid the foundation on rock. When a flood came, the torrent struck that house but could not shake it, because it was well built. But the one who hears my words and does not put them into practice is like a man who built a house on the ground without a foundation. The moment the torrent struck that house, it collapsed and its destruction was complete. (Luke 6:46-49)

As Jesus was saying these things, a woman in the crowd called out, "Blessed is the mother who gave you birth and nursed you." He replied, "Blessed rather are those who hear the word of God and obey it," (Luke 11:27, 28)

When we hear His words, we are supposed to put them into practice.

Not only so, but we also rejoice in our sufferings, because we know that suffering produces perseverance; perseverance, character; and character, hope. And hope does not disappoint us, because God has poured out his love into our hearts by the Holy Spirit, whom he has given us. (Romans 5:3-5)

Am I not free? Am I not an apostle? Have I not seen Jesus our Lord? Are you not the result of my work in the Lord? Even though I may not be an apostle to others, surely I am to you! For you are the seal of my apostleship in the Lord. (I Corinthians 9:1, 2)

Slaves, obey your earthly masters with respect and fear, and with sincerity of heart, just as you would obey Christ. Obey them not only to win their favor when their eye is on you, but like slaves of Christ, doing the will of God from your heart. Serve wholeheartedly, as if you were serving the Lord, not men, because you know that the Lord will reward everyone for whatever good he does, whether he is slave or free. (Ephesians 6:5-8)

Do not merely listen to the word, and so deceive yourselves. Do what it says. Anyone who listens to the word but does not do what it says is like a man who looks at his face in a mirror and, after looking at himself, goes away and immediately forgets what he looks like. But the man who looks intently into the perfect law that gives freedom, and continues to do this, not forgetting what he has heard, but doing it - he will be blessed in what he does. (James 1:22-25)

Finally, all of you, live in harmony with one another; be sympathetic, love as brothers, be compassionate and humble. Do not repay evil with evil or insult with insult, but with blessing, because to this you were called so that you may inherit a blessing. (I Peter 3:8, 9)

9. We are obedient in expectation of rewards in the life hereafter.

Do not store up for yourselves treasures on earth, where moth and rust destroy, and where thieves break in and steal. But store up for yourselves treasures in heaven, where moth and rust do not destroy, and where thieves do not break in and steal. For where your treasure is, there your heart will be also. (Matthew 6:19-21)

Then Jesus said to his disciples, "If anyone would come after me, he must deny himself and take up his cross and follow me. For whoever wants to save his life will lose it, but whoever loses his life for me will find it. What good will it be for a man if he gains the whole world, yet forfeits his soul? Or what can a man give in exchange for his soul? For the Son of Man is going to come in his Father's glory with his angels, and then he will reward each person according to what he has done." (Matthew 16:24-27)

I [Jesus] tell you, use worldly wealth to gain friends for yourselves, so that when it is gone, you will be welcomed into eternal dwellings. (Luke 16:9)

Do not work for food that spoils, but for food that endures to eternal life, which the Son of Man will give you. (John 6:27)

God "will give to each person according to what he has done." To those who by persistence in doing good seek glory, honor and immortality, he will give eternal life. (Romans 2:6, 7)

By the grace God has given me, I laid a foundation as an expert builder, and someone else is building on it. But each one should be careful how he builds. For no one can lay any foundation other than the one already laid, which is Jesus Christ. If any man builds on this foundation using gold, silver, costly stones, wood, hay or straw, his work will be shown for what it is, because the Day will bring it to light. It will be revealed with fire, and the fire will test the quality of each man's work. If what he has built survives, he will receive his reward. If it is burned up, he will suffer loss; he himself will be saved, but only as one escaping through the flames. (I Corinthians 3:10-15)

Do you not know that in a race all the runners run, but only one gets the prize? Run in such a way as to get the prize. Everyone who competes in the games goes into strict training. They do it to get a crown that will not last; but we do it to get a crown that will last forever. Therefore I do not run like a man running aimlessly; I do not fight like a man beating the air. No, I beat my body and make it my slave so that after I have preached to others, I myself will not be disqualified for the prize. (I Corinthians 9:24-27)

Once you were alienated from God and were enemies in your minds because of your evil behavior. But now he has reconciled you by Christ's physical body through death to present you holy in his sight, without blemish and free from accusation - if you continue in your faith, established and firm, not moved from the hope held out in the gospel. (Colossians 1:21-23a)

For what is our hope, our joy, or the crown in which we will glory in the presence of our Lord Jesus when he comes? Is it not you? Indeed, you are our glory and joy. (I Thessalonians 2:19, 20)

People we have nurtured in the faith will be to our glory when Christ returns.

For I [Paul] am already being poured out like a drink offering, and the time has come for my departure. I have fought the good fight, I have finished the race, I have kept the faith. Now there is in store for me the crown of righteousness, which the Lord, the righteous Judge, will award to me on that day - and not only to me, but also to all who have longed for his appearing. (II Timothy 4:6-8)

Women received back their dead, raised to life again. Others were tortured and refused to be released, so that they might gain a better resurrection. (Hebrews 11:35)

To the elders among you, I appeal as a fellow elder, a witness of Christ's sufferings and one who will share in the glory to be revealed: Be shepherds of God's flock that is under your care, serving as overseers - not because you must, but because you are willing, as God wants you to be; not greedy for money, but eager to serve; not lording it over those entrusted to you, but being examples to the flock. And when the Chief Shepherd appears, you will receive the crown of glory that will never fade away. (I Peter 5:1-4)

God is love. Whoever lives in love lives in God, and God in him. In this way, love is made complete among us so that we will have confidence on the Day of Judgment, because in this world we are like him. (I John 4:16b, 17)

Do not be afraid of what you are about to suffer. I tell you, the devil will put some of you in prison to test you, and you will suffer persecution for ten days. Be faithful, even to the point of death, and I will give you the crown of life. (Revelation 2:10)

Then I heard a voice from heaven say, "Write: Blessed are the dead who die in the Lord from now on." "Yes," says the Spirit, "they will rest from their labor, for their deeds will follow them." (Revelation 14:13)

Summary of Reasons to Obey God

1. We are obedient because of guilt and fear of discipline and judgment.
2. We are obedient because we are thankful for our salvation and want to please God.
3. We are obedient because we have a responsibility to live the Christian life as it should be lived, to reflect God's nature in our lives. After making a profession of faith, we are not to profane His holy name by living ungodly lives.
4. We are obedient because God has made each of us a new creation. The Lord guides us, and He gives us the will and power to obey.
5. We are obedient because we desire the joy of the experience.
6. We are obedient because we care about the next generation.
7. We are obedient because we want to be used to bless others.
8. We are obedient in expectation of blessings in this life; they may be in the physical realm, or mental, or spiritual. I have learned that it is hard for me to approach the throne of grace with confidence, so that I may receive mercy and find grace to help me in my time of need, if I have a guilty conscience. We are obedient so we can experience all that God has for us in this life. We are obedient because obedience gets us ready to do battle with the forces of evil.
9. We are obedient in expectation of rewards in the life hereafter.

In the next chapter, we'll consider God's sovereignty and how He orders the events in our lives for our benefit and for His glory.

Chapter Eight
God's Sovereignty

God is in charge of everything we encounter in this life, both the things that seem to be good and the things that seem to be bad. When people mistreat us or life is hard, what we endure ultimately falls under the control of God's sovereignty. We need to understand how God is using our experiences to guide us to our ultimate destination. We need to understand how God is using our afflictions to mold each of our characters to make them closer to the likeness of Jesus. We need to understand how sufferings teach us things that make us better able to minister to others with similar affliction. Along the road of life, bad things happen. When we understand that God is truly sovereign, it should help us control the anger we may feel about our difficult circumstances.

God may allow us to take our lives in all sorts of strange directions, and let all sorts of things happen to us, to help us reach His ultimate purpose for us. Consider Paul's words to the men of Athens:

The God who made the world and everything in it is the Lord of heaven and earth and does not live in temples built by hands. And he is not served by human hands, as if he needed anything, because he himself gives all men life and breath and everything else. From one man he made every nation of men that they should inhabit the whole earth; and he determined the times set for them and the exact places where they should live. God did this so that men would seek him and perhaps reach out for him and find him, though he is not far from each one of us. "For in him we live and move and have our being." As some of your own poets have said, "We are his offspring." (Acts 17:24-28)

Consider the case of Joseph in the book of Genesis (chapters 37, 39-50). Joseph was the favored child of Jacob. His stepbrothers resented the fact. One time, when his stepbrothers were out grazing the flocks, Jacob sent Joseph to check on them. The brothers stripped him of his richly ornamented robe and threw him into a cistern. Then they sold him as a slave to the Ishmaelites, who took him to Egypt. Potiphar, one of Pharaoh's officials, the captain of the guard, purchased Joseph. When Potiphar saw that the Lord was with Joseph, he put Joseph in charge of his household. Potiphar's wife made false accusations about Joseph, and he was thrown in prison. Joseph found favor in the eyes of the prison warden. He was put in charge of all those held in the prison.

Sometime later, Pharaoh's chief cupbearer and chief baker were imprisoned. The captain of the guard assigned them to Joseph. One night both of the men had dreams. Joseph correctly interpreted the dreams. Things turned out just as Joseph had predicted. The chief cupbearer was restored to his position, but the chief baker was hanged. The chief cupbearer forgot his promise to help Joseph. Joseph remained in prison two more years. Later, when Pharaoh had a dream that his magicians could not interpret, the chief cupbearer remembered Joseph. Joseph was summoned, and he correctly interpreted the dream about the coming famine. Joseph was placed in charge of the whole land of Egypt, second in authority only to Pharaoh.

Because of the famine, Joseph's brothers came to Egypt to buy grain. Joseph recognized them, and eventually Joseph moved his father's family to Egypt and took care of them. After Jacob died, Joseph's brothers feared retribution. Consider these words in Genesis, chapter 50.

When Joseph's brothers saw that their father was dead, they said, "What if Joseph holds a grudge against us and pays us back for all the wrongs we did to him?" So they sent word to Joseph saying, "Your father left these instructions before he died: 'This is what you are to say to Joseph. I ask you to forgive your brothers the sins and the wrongs they committed in treating you so badly.' Now please forgive the sins of the servants of the God of your father." When the message came to him, Joseph wept. His brothers then came and threw themselves down before him. "We are your slaves," they said. But Joseph said to them, "Don't be afraid. Am I in the place of God? You intended to harm me, but God intended it for good to accomplish what is now being done, the saving of many lives. So then, don't be afraid. I will provide for you and your children." And he reassured them and spoke kindly to them. (Genesis 50:15-21)

Consider also these words in other passages of Scripture:

In his heart a man plans his course, but the Lord determines his steps. (Proverbs 16:9)

For you, O God, tested us; you refined us like silver. You brought us into prison and laid burdens on our backs. You let men ride over our heads; we went through fire and water, but you brought us to a place of abundance. (Psalm 66:10-12)

Before I was afflicted, I went astray, but now I obey your word. You are good, and what you do is good; teach me your decrees. Though the arrogant have smeared me with lies, I keep your precepts with all my heart. Their hearts are callous and unfeeling, but I delight in your law. It was good for me to be afflicted so I might learn your decrees. The law from your mouth is more precious to me than thousands of pieces of silver and gold. Your hands made me and formed me; give me understanding to learn your commands. May those who fear you rejoice when they see me, for I have put my hope in your word. I know, O Lord, that your laws are righteous, and in faithfulness you have afflicted me. May your unfailing love be my comfort, according to your promise to your servant. (Psalm 119:67-76)

Consider it pure joy, my brothers, whenever you face trials of many kinds, because you know that the testing of your faith develops perseverance. Perseverance must finish its work so that you may be mature and complete, not lacking anything. If any of you lacks wisdom, he should ask God, who gives generously to all without finding fault, and it will be given to him. (James 1:2-5)

We need to understand how sufferings teach us things that make us better able to minister to others with similar affliction.

Praise be to the God and Father of our Lord Jesus Christ, the Father of compassion and the God of all comfort, who comforts us in all our troubles, so that we can comfort those in any trouble with the comfort we ourselves have received from God. For just as the sufferings of Christ flow over into our lives, so also through Christ our comfort overflows. If we are distressed, it is for your comfort and salvation; if we are comforted, it is for your comfort, which produces in you patient endurance of the same sufferings we suffer. (II Corinthians 1:3-6)

Let me share with you some of the details about my journey. When I was seven years old, I accepted Jesus Christ as my Savior. At the age of twelve, I learned about having the assurance of my salvation (I

129

John 5:13). The next year, I dedicated my life to the Lord Jesus Christ.

When I was in the seventh grade, I learned I was pretty smart. I took an IQ test and was told that my reading comprehension was that of a freshman in college. I felt a tremendous responsibility to make the right vocational choice so that I could be of service to the Lord in the best possible way. Later, when I was a freshman in high school, one of my friends said, "While I'm here at Central [high school], I'm going to take all the math and science I can." I thought to myself, that's a pretty good idea, and so I did the same thing.

In the fall of 1960, I began college at the University of Tennessee in Knoxville (UTK). I was very indecisive about what to study, the right choice for a major. By actual count, I changed my major at least seventeen times. I was in pre-med three different times. I remember sitting in Greek class one day and saying to myself, "What am I doing here?" My third year in college, I went to Bryan College in Dayton, Tennessee, to take courses related to the Bible. I was searching for meaning and direction in life. The first week I was at Bryan, we had a series of evening meetings. I learned I didn't need to worry about the rest of my life. If I would just abide in Christ, He would get me where I needed to be. I was later to learn about II Chronicles 20:12b: "We do not know what to do, but our eyes are upon you [our God]." At Bryan, I took two semesters of Old Testament Survey and one semester each of Bible Geography and a Christian Education course about teaching Sunday school. The book of the Bible we taught from in the Christian Education course was the book of Nehemiah. I finished up three years of Greek and took a year of Hebrew.

The summer quarter of 1963, I was back at UTK. I had decided to major in Physics. In summer school I began with the initial Physics course the physics majors took, not the somewhat easier course usually taken by the pre-med students. Because of the Physics major, I also started a second year of calculus. It had been two years since I had finished my first year of calculus. During fall quarter, I had a conversation with a friend who had been one of my lab partners in Zoology. He had been trying to get me to go back into pre-med. When I told him about how much fun I was having taking the courses as a Physics major, he said, "What are you going to do, have fun or help people?" The words pierced my heart, and I applied for medical school. I was accepted for the class starting in the fall of 1964. I was able to finish up the necessary pre-med courses at UTK during winter and spring quarters of 1964. As it seemed the natural thing to do, I finished out my year of Physics in the same series of courses (for those who are Physics majors). I seemed to have a knack for math, so I finished the second year of calculus. The math class was a five-hour course, and I always made A's in math. I took calculus to keep my grade point average up.

During winter quarter of 1964, I set my eye on a young lady in my Math and Physics classes. I had seen her around, and she attracted my attention. Her name was Barbara Jean Overton. I noticed that her hands and arms did not work right. I had been sitting in Physics class with another girl I had dated. I really didn't have much long-term interest in her, but winter quarter was almost over, and I was not going to create any issues with the other girl so late in the term by telling her I didn't want to sit with her anymore. One day a friend said, referring to the latter girl, "You're wasting your time with that girl. She'll date you for two years and not like you any better than she did when she first started dating you. What you need is a girl who's kind of shy. Then when she starts liking you, you'll really have something, like that Miss Overton over there."

I had another friend in Math class. He was a good friend of Barbara's next-door neighbor. He and Barbara knew each other. One day, as we were getting ready for our final examination in math class, the friend and I were in the hallway chatting. Barbara was on her way into the classroom and spoke to him. After she passed by, thinking about the problems with her hands and arms, I asked him, "What's wrong with her?" He replied, "Her daddy won't let her do anything." I said, "What?" He said, "Her daddy won't let her do anything. He keeps a gun over the mantel to drive away all the boys." I concluded Barbara was a girl who had been protected, and I decided I wanted a date with her. A few days later, I saw her sitting in her car in a parking lot studying. I spoke to her and invited myself into her car. We began dating. I was soon to learn that Barbara had had polio in the third grade, and at that time, she had missed a year of school.

That next fall, I traveled to Memphis to begin medical school. Our long-distance relationship did not fare so well, and after about eighteen months, my feelings for Barbara were almost non-existent. I had no negative feelings about her; I just hardly had any feelings at all. I told her the truth about how I felt. That spring of 1966, she came to Memphis for a few days to try to get something going again in our relationship. She arrived unannounced. She called one of my classmates who had let Barbara use her apartment in Memphis over the previous Thanksgiving weekend, and my classmate told me Barbara was in town. I called Barbara at the hotel, and we agreed to see each other. We also spent some time with a married couple with whom I had become friends. I had a part-time job with a physiology professor doing research. My fellow worker was in law school at Memphis State and had a part-time job feeding the mice. Barbara returned home on a Sunday morning. That afternoon, I was in the Physiology building, studying in the office of the professor. The couple came in. Joyce said, "Barbara really cares about you. She has lost fifteen pounds worrying about you." Her words touched my heart, and I made contact with Barbara again.

Over the next several months our relationship continued but was fairly cool. Barbara graduated from UTK summer quarter 1966. She was certified to teach Mathematics and Science in high school. She told me she wanted to get a job in Memphis. I told her if she wanted to come to Memphis that was okay, but I couldn't promise her anything. When she looked into the possibility of a position in Memphis, she found there were no openings. She made arrangements to teach in a small town to the north, in Missouri. She and her mother were getting ready to go to that town to finalize the deal and look for a place for her to live. Just before they walked out the door, the telephone rang. The call was from the Memphis school system. They had a need for someone to teach math. Barbara began teaching at Treadwell High School in Memphis in the fall of 1966. We always figured the events were the Lord's timing.

During that fall, I spent a lot of time with Barbara, but there was no discussion about any long-term commitment. There was also no kissing. She had a car, and I rode home to Knoxville with her for Christmas vacation. I had a job as an extern at the Tennessee Psychiatric Hospital, and because of the need for someone to cover during Christmas holidays, I took a bus back to Memphis the day after Christmas. I must have really bonded with her the previous few months. After I returned to Memphis, I was very lonely. Actually, I was miserable. When Barbara returned to Memphis, I told her I loved her and wanted to get married. She let me know she had been dating someone else, and then she added, "And besides I'm not going to marry you because you're too fat!" I found out the main reason she wanted the job in Memphis was not to be with me but to get out of Knoxville. She wanted to be on her own and not be told by her family how to live her life. We continued to see each other, and I started losing weight. After about three weeks, she agreed to marry me. We were married in June 1967. From January to June, 1967, I did lose sixty-five pounds.

After finishing medical school, I did an internship and spent two years in the army. My year in Vietnam had a profound effect on my perspective in dealing with pain and suffering. Following discharge from the army, I did two years training in Internal Medicine and a two-year Nephrology fellowship at UT in Memphis. I finished my Nephrology fellowship in December 1974. By that time, Barbara and I had two children. The medical subspecialties were not so well developed then, and so I went into private practice in Roanoke, Virginia, with a general internist who had been one of my mentors during my internship there at Roanoke Memorial Hospitals. After several months, Barbara became very unhappy about the long hours

I was working and also about the lack of money. We had overbought on a house. She made up her mind we were going to leave Roanoke, and I got tired of hearing it. After a year and a half, we left Roanoke, bound for Florence, Alabama.

I joined an internal medicine group in Florence. I noticed that many of the children of my elderly patients had left Florence in search of better jobs. As their folks got older, I could tell it was hard for those men and women to help look after them from long-distance. I also noticed that many of them returned to Florence after retirement. My mother visited us twice while we were in Florence. She had no ulterior motive; she just wanted to spend time with us. I became reacquainted with her. Always before, during our visits to our hometown of Knoxville, I had been pulled in so many different directions, there was never any time to spend just talking to my mother. While she was there for the second visit, one of my medical school classmates called on the telephone to tell me that two nephrologists in Knoxville were looking for a third nephrologist to help them open a dialysis unit. I had a desire to return home, but I wasn't sure what to do.

One morning, as I was reading my Bible, I came across these words in Revelation 3:8: "I have placed before you an open door that no one can shut." I took these words as a sign that we should return to Knoxville. When I telephoned one of the nephrologists about the position, I was told that their minds were not completely made up, but they had pretty much already decided on someone else. I figured they wouldn't want too many nephrologists in the area, and if I went ahead and moved to Knoxville, they would take me. In November 1977, we returned to Knoxville. I began doing emergency room work, waiting for a decision to be made. After I was told another nephrologist had been chosen for that position, I was crushed. I was overwhelmed with a sense of betrayal. I thought God had led me to Knoxville and then abandoned me. It took me two days to work through my feelings. I decided that if God shut one door, He would open another. I started my own practice. I have lived in the area since that time. I practiced nephrology, out of the same office for 32 years. The Lord had opened a door for me; I had not realized which one it was. The office was three miles from my childhood home. I was able to visit my mother, usually twice a week, for twenty-five years until she died.

I want to offer a few observations about these events.

1. If I hadn't been so indecisive about a major during my education, I would not have been taking that particular first year Physics course and second year Calculus my fourth year in college and would never have met Barbara. The math and that particular physics I was taking were not courses I needed in preparation for medical school anyway.
2. If Barbara had not had polio in the third grade and missed a year of school, I would never have met her; we would have had no classes together.
3. If Barbara had not had polio during her childhood and developed the deformity in her arms and hands, I likely would not have paid as much attention to her.
4. If it were not for the comments made by my two friends, I probably would never have dated her.
5. If Barbara had not been sitting in that car studying, there's a good chance I would never have asked her out. Spring quarter had started, and I had no more classes with her.
6. If my medical school classmate had not told me Barbara was in Memphis, we likely would not have gotten back together.
7. If I had not had the research job, I wouldn't have known the couple from the physiology department, and the lady would not have told me how much Barbara cared for me. I doubt my heart would have gone out to Barbara.
8. If Barbara had not been able to get the job in Memphis, we would likely have never married.
9. If we had stayed in Florence, my two sons would have a totally different experience growing up.
10. If it had not been for what I learned during my two previous

practice experiences, I likely would not have done so well with starting my own practice.

I believe that before the foundation of the world, it was ordained that I would marry Barbara and be married to her for thirty-five years, that I would be her spousal caregiver for five years until she died of breast cancer, and that I would write a book about our experiences and about tribulation in general called *Finding Strength in Weakness - A Study of Tribulation and our Appropriate Response.* **(1)** God has used that book to change many lives.

God uses our relationships and our experiences to mold each one of us into a unique individual. Admittedly, there are times when the only way we can trace His hand is in retrospect and then sometimes not at all. We may have to go down what seem like false trails in order for God to get us where we need to be and to be prepared for the job He wants us to do.

During my first two years in college, my sense of insecurity had caused me to wander down many of those false trails of study. Later, when I took the Medical College Admission Test, used to assess the general knowledge of the applicant, it was as if the person making out the test looked at my transcript, with all those strange courses I took while I was floundering around and used that as a guide to making out the test. I remember specifically there was a question on the test about ancient Greek plays. I had taken a course about Greek plays. There was also a question about the Torah.

We are expected to learn from life's trials. One of the things we are supposed to learn from life's trials is humility. We learn we are not in charge of our own destinies. God also gets us ready to use what each of us has learned to minister to the people in our individual and unique spheres of influence. There are some things we cannot learn except by experiencing them. For example, people in the waiting room of a Pediatric Intensive Care Unit understand each other's concerns. Families in the waiting room of a dialysis unit understand each other. Combat veterans are able to share battlefield experiences, and they understand each other. Chuck Colson's experience while he was incarcerated led to a world-wide prison ministry. Joni Eareckson Tada's ministry to the disabled came after her diving accident and the resultant quadriplegia.

Jesus was willing to experience life and death on earth so He could better understand our struggles and so He could overcome them and be our Savior. Consider these passages from the book of Hebrews:

But we see Jesus, who was made a little lower than the angels, now crowned with glory and honor because he suffered death, so that by the grace of God he might taste death for everyone. In bringing many sons to glory, it was fitting that God, for whom and through whom everything exists, should make the author of their salvation perfect through suffering. Both the one who makes men holy and those who are made holy are of the same family. So Jesus is not ashamed to call them brothers...Since the children have flesh and blood, he [Jesus] too shared in their humanity so that by his death he might destroy him who holds the power of death - that is, the devil - and free those who all their lives were held in slavery by their fear of death. For surely it is not angels he helps, but Abraham's descendants. For this reason he had to be made like his brothers in every way, in order that he might become a merciful and faithful high priest in service to God, and that he might make atonement for the sins of the people. Because he himself suffered when he was tempted, he is able to help those who are being tempted. (Hebrews 2:9-18)

Therefore, since we have a great high priest who has gone through the heavens, Jesus the Son of God, let us hold firmly to the faith we profess. For we do not have a high priest who is unable to sympathize with our weaknesses, but we have one who has been tempted in every way, just as we are - yet was without sin. (Hebrews 4:14, 15)

During the days of Jesus' life on earth, he offered up prayers and petitions with loud cries and tears to the one who could save him from death, and he was heard because of his reverent submission. Although he was a son, he learned obedience from what he suffered and, once made perfect he became the source of eternal salvation for all who obey him. (Hebrews 5:7-9)

For the law appoints as high priests men who are weak; but the oath, which came after the law, appointed the Son, who has been made perfect forever. (Hebrews 7:28) (For the oath see Psalm 110, especially verse four)

Notice in three different places in Hebrews that Jesus' experiences on earth made Him perfect (complete): Hebrews 2:10, Hebrews 5:8, 9, and Hebrews 7:28. Hebrews 2:10 tells us that it was God the Father who made Jesus perfect through suffering. Hebrews 5:8, 9 tell us that Jesus learned obedience from what He suffered and the experience made Him complete. Hebrews 7:28 tells us that Jesus was made perfect forever. Regarding the use of the Greek word *teleioo* in Hebrews 2:10; 5:9; and 7:28, Bauer, Arndt, and Gingrich tell us, "This is usually understood to mean the *completion* and *perfection* of Jesus by overcoming earthly limitations." **(2)**

esus was willing to experience life and death on earth so He could better ur struggles, and so He could overcome His own struggles and become o

Consider some of the abuse Jesus tolerated:

1. While Jesus was in agony in the Garden of Gethsemane, His closest friends slept. (Matthew 26:40-45)
2. Jesus was betrayed by Judas, a man who was in His inner circle. (Mark 14:43-46)
3. During the arrest in Gethsemane, Jesus' disciples deserted Him and fled. (Mark 14:50)
4. After making the statement that he would never fall away from Jesus, Peter denied Him three times. (Mark 14:29-31) During the third denial: "Just as he [Peter] was speaking, the rooster crowed. The Lord turned and looked straight at Peter. Then Peter remembered the word the Lord had spoken to him: 'Before the rooster crows today, you will disown me three times.' And he went outside and wept bitterly." (Luke 22:60b-62)
5. While on trial before the Sanhedrin, one of the officials struck Jesus in the face. (John 18:22)
6. The men who were guarding Jesus began mocking and beating Him. The governor's soldiers spit in His face and struck Him with

their fists. They made fun of Him. They blindfolded Him and demanded, "Prophesy! Who hit you?" and they said many other insulting things to Him. (Matthew 26:67, 68; Mark 14:65; Luke 22:63-65)

7. The whole assembly led Jesus off to Pilate. When Pilate learned Jesus was a Galilean, he sent Him to Herod Antipas. Herod and his soldiers ridiculed and mocked Jesus. Dressing Him in an elegant robe, they sent Him back to Pilate. (Luke 23:11)

8. The crowd demanded that Jesus be crucified. (Luke 23:20-24)

9. Pilate took Jesus and had Him flogged. The soldiers twisted together a crown of thorns and put it on his head. They clothed him in a purple robe and put a staff in His right hand. They ridiculed him. They spit on Him and took the staff and struck Him on the head again and again. (Matthew 27:27-30; John 19:1-3)

10. The Roman soldiers crucified Jesus. (Matthew 27:35; Luke 23:33)

11. The crowd hurled insults at Jesus. (Matthew 27:39, 40; Mark 15:29, 30)

12. The Roman soldiers mocked Jesus. (Luke 23:36)

There were times during His ministry when Jesus became angry such as when He cleansed the temple (Matthew 21:12, 13; Mark 11:15-17; Luke 19:45, 46; John 2:13-17), but He did not become angry about the abuse He received during His arrest, trial, or crucifixion.

Beginning with His arrest, it is apparent from the text that Jesus was looking at the situation from an eternal perspective. He was no longer pleading with the Father to be spared the agony of the cross (Luke 22:42). Consider the words He spoke and when He was silent.

At the Time of the Arrest:

"Rise, let us go! Here comes my betrayer!" (Matthew 26:46)

To Judas: "Friend, do what you came for…" (Matthew 26:50)

To Judas: "Judas, are you betraying the Son of Man with a kiss?" (Luke 22:48b)

To the detachment of soldiers and some officials from the chief priests and Pharisees: "Jesus, knowing all that was going to happen to him, went out and asked them, "Who is it you want?" "Jesus of Nazareth," they replied." "I am he," Jesus said. (And Judas the traitor was standing there with them.) When Jesus said, "I am he," they drew back and fell to the ground. Again he asked them, "Who is it you want?" And they said, "Jesus of Nazareth." "I told you that I am he," Jesus answered. "If you are looking for me, then let these men go." This happened so that the words he had spoken would be fulfilled: "I have not lost one of those you gave me." (John 18:4-9)

To Peter after he cut off the ear of the high priest's servant: "Put your sword back in its place," Jesus said to him, "for all who draw the sword will die by the sword. Do you think I cannot call on my Father, and he will at once put at my disposal more than twelve legions of angels? But how then would the Scriptures be fulfilled that say it must happen in this way?" (Matthew 26:52-54)

Jesus commanded Peter, "Put your sword away! Shall I not drink the cup the Father has given me?" (John 18:11)

To the arresting party: "Am I leading a rebellion," said Jesus, "that you have come out with swords and clubs to capture me? Every day I was with you, teaching in the temple courts, and you did not arrest me. But the Scriptures must be fulfilled." (Mark 14:48, 49)

At the Trial before the Sanhedrin:

Meanwhile, the high priest questioned Jesus about his disciples and his teaching. "I have spoken openly to the world," Jesus replied. "I always taught in synagogues or at the temple, where all the Jews came together. I said nothing in secret. Why question me? Ask those who heard me. Surely they know what I said." When Jesus said this, one of the officials nearby struck him in the face. "Is this the way you answer the high priest?" he demanded. "If I said something wrong," Jesus replied, "testify as to what is wrong. But if I spoke the truth, why did you strike me?" (John 18:19-23)

At daybreak the council of the elders of the people, both the chief priests and the teachers of the law, met together, and Jesus was led before them. "If you are the Christ," they said, "tell us." Jesus answered, "If I tell you, you will not believe me, and if I asked you, you would not answer. But from now on, the Son of Man will be seated at the right hand of the mighty God." They all asked, "Are you then the Son of God?" He replied, "You are right in saying I am." (Luke 22:66-70)

At the Trial before Pilate:

Meanwhile Jesus stood before the governor [Pilate], and the governor asked him, Are you the king of the Jews?" "Yes, it is as you say," Jesus replied. (Matthew 27:11)

The chief priests accused him of many things. So again Pilate asked him, "Aren't you going to answer? See how many things they are accusing you of." But Jesus still made no reply, and Pilate was amazed. (Mark 15:3-5)

Pilate then went back inside the palace, summoned Jesus and asked him, "Are you the king of the Jews?" "Is this your own idea," Jesus asked, "or did others talk to you about me?" "Am I a Jew?" Pilate replied. "It was your people and your chief priests who handed you over to me. What is it you have done?" Jesus said, "My kingdom is not of this world. If it were my servants would fight to prevent my arrest by the Jews. But now my kingdom is from another place." "You are a king, then!" said Pilate. Jesus answered, "You are right in saying I am a king. In fact, for this reason I was born, and for this I came into the world, to testify to the truth. Everyone on the side of truth listens to me." "What is truth?" Pilate asked. (John 18:33-38a)

The Jews insisted, "We have a law, and according to that law he must die, because he claimed to be the Son of God." When Pilate heard this, he was even more afraid, and he went back inside the palace. "Where do you come from?" he asked Jesus, but Jesus gave him no answer. "Do you refuse to speak to me?" Pilate said. "Don't you realize I have power either to free you or to crucify you?" Jesus answered, "You would have no power over me if it were not given to you from above. Therefore the one who handed me over to you is guilty of a greater sin." (John 19:7-11)

On the Way to Golgotha:

As they led him away, they seized Simon from Cyrene, who was on his way in from the country, and put the cross on him and made him carry it behind Jesus. A large number of women followed him, including women who mourned and wailed for him. Jesus turned and said to them, "Daughters of Jerusalem, do not weep for me; weep for yourselves and for your children. For the time will come when you will say, 'Blessed are the barren women, the wombs that never bore and the breasts that never nursed!'" Then they will say to the mountains, "Fall on us!" and to the hills, "Cover us!" For if men do these things when the tree is green, what will happen when it is dry? (Luke 23:26-31)

During the Crucifixion:

Jesus said, "Father forgive them, for they do not know what they are doing." (Luke 23:34a)

When we look at life from an eternal perspective, it helps us get our priorities straight. When I am talking with someone about the difficulties of life, and that person flippantly quotes platitudes such as, "Just turn it over to the Lord and then get out of the way," I know that person has never experienced brokenness. He doesn't know what it is like to have lost all hope. He does not understand what it is like to experience a tragedy that brings him to the end of his own resources and causes him to have to trust God, trust Him because there is nothing else left in whom or in which to trust. That person does not understand what it is like to be in a situation so overwhelming that it brings him to his knees. He does not understand such things as the death of a loved one who is more precious than life itself.

We should remember God's sovereignty the next time we have a tendency to ruminate about the resentment we feel because of what a person or persons has done to us or how any type of tribulation has wounded us. The Lord has a reason for what He allows to happen to us, and we must trust Him.

Just before He ascended into heaven, Jesus said to His disciples, "But you will receive power when the Holy Spirit comes on you; and you will be my witnesses in Jerusalem, and in all Judea and Samaria, and to the ends of the earth" (Acts 1:8). The Greek word translated "witness" is *martys*. It is the word from which we get the English word "martyr." The English word "martyr" refers to someone who is a witness by his death. **(3)** Greek words similar to *martys* include *martyreo*, meaning to bear witness, *martyria*, meaning testimony, and *martyrion*, that which serves as testimony or proof. **(4)**

Each Christian, in his own way, will become a witness for Christ. Believers who have made a decision to follow Christ, become subject

142

to attacks by Satan. The question is not *if* it will happen, but *when* it will happen. We will be on the receiving end of the flaming arrows of the evil one (Ephesians 6:16), the enemy of our souls. How we react to his attacks will be a witness of what the Spirit of God has done in our lives. We may either have a testimony of a mature relationship with the Father or a testimony that we are still spiritual infants. Most of us will fall somewhere in between. We will be witnesses to others of what God has done in our lives during our tribulation, both by our words and our deeds, whether we make positive statements or negative ones.

Having a ministry is a normal part of the Christian life. God formed our individual set of circumstances to help make each one of us become the unique person he/she is. He arranged our individual spheres of influence. How does the maltreatment you've experienced and your anger about it fit in with the ministry God has for your life? Will it negatively impact your ministry, or will you work through your anger and will the way you were able to work through that anger be a part of your ministry? Take what you've learned through your experiences and allow God to use you as a conduit of His grace rather than letting the experiences derail you. One saying I've often heard is that life is not fair. God is fair, though we don't always understand His ways. Would you exchange eternal blessings for convenience in this life? I hope not! Do not allow yourself to be on the road toward becoming a bitter old man or woman.

When people offend us, the natural reaction is anger. In the next chapter we'll consider what anger most often is. Anger is usually the flesh. It is most often self. It is most often sin.

Chapter Nine

Recognizing Anger as a Sin of the Flesh

My favorite definition of anger is one I heard from my sister years ago: "Anger is that feeling that wells up inside us when our sense of justice is violated." Of course our sense of justice is flawed by the world, the flesh, and the devil. I heard another definition at a malpractice seminar: "Anger is that passion or emotion that is aroused when we don't get what we expect." This latter definition fits in with the thought that to overcome anger, one of the things we need to practice is acceptance; we need to expect less. We'll take up the subject of acceptance in chapter eleven. The *American Heritage College Dictionary* defines anger as "a strong feeling of displeasure or hostility." **(1)** Anger is said to be the strongest of all emotions.

In his letter to the Ephesians, Paul writes, "Be ye angry, and sin not:" (Ephesians 4:26a – KJV). I've heard many a person quote this verse and say that it's okay to be angry; we just have to be careful and not sin in our response to the particular situation. Personally, I don't believe anger is okay. There are too many other verses of scripture that say anger is bad.

My NIV Bible says that Ephesians 4:26a is a quotation from Psalm 4:4a. The KJV and ASV render Psalm 4:4a as follows: "Stand in awe, and sin not:" The NIV renders the phrase, "In your anger do not sin." The word in the Hebrew text for stand in awe or be ye angry is *ragaz*. According to Strong **(2)**, the word means to quiver with any violent emotion, especially anger or fear. Harris says that the word is used to express agitation growing out of some deeply rooted emotion. The term refers to the agitation itself, and the underlying emotion is to be recognized only from context. This term expresses the trembling of the world's inhabitants before God's appearance in judgment. **(3)**

In his commentary on Psalms, Spurgeon writes, "This psalm is apparently intended to accompany the third [psalm] and make a pair with it. If the last [third psalm] may be entitled The Morning Psalm, this [psalm] from its matter is equally deserving of the title of The Evening Hymn." **(4)** The psalm is about communion with God. We have been given some biblical references to people who met the Lord, for example Job (Job 42:1-6) and Isaiah (Isaiah 6:5). I would think the natural reaction to being in the presence of God would be to be overwhelmed with a sense of His majesty and to quake or shake or tremble.

The wording, in Greek, in both the Septuagint **(5)** and the New Testament text **(6)** is the same, "*Orgizesthe kai mee amartanete.*" The Septuagint is a translation of the Word of God. But the New Testament text is the Word of God. I'm not sure that the translation from Hebrew to Greek in the Septuagint is accurate, but the original Greek text of the New Testament does say, "*Orgizesthe kai mee amartanete.*"

The Greek word for, "Be ye angry," in Ephesians 4:26a is *orgizoo*. The word means to be angry at someone due to something, or be angry at or with someone. **(7)** Regarding *orgizoo*, Vine writes, "to provoke, to arouse to anger, is used in the Middle Voice in the eight places where it is found, it signifies to be angry or wroth. It is said of individuals, in Matthew 5:22; 18:34; 22:7; Luke 14:21; 15:28, and Ephesians 4:2 (where a possible meaning is 'be angry with yourselves'); of nations, Revelation 11:18; of Satan as the Dragon, 12:17. " **(8)**

In their book, *A Manual Grammar of the Greek New Testament*, Dana and Mantey write concerning the middle voice: "Here we approach one of the most distinctive and peculiar phenomena of the Greek language. It is impossible to describe, adequately or accurately, in terms of English idiom, for English knows no approximate parallel." **(9)**

145

"The middle voice is that use of the verb which describes the subject as participating in the results of the action." **(10)** "It is scarcely possible to formulate a single definition of its basal function which could be applied to all its actual occurrences. No single principle can be found to cover all the cases...It is an appropriate warning that Robertson gives in saying that we must not fall into the error of explaining the force of the middle by the English translation **(11)**...Any analysis of the uses of the middle is more or less arbitrary." **(12)**

If we are not completely sure how to translate the middle voice, it seems to me unwise to base a firm theological conclusion that it's okay to be angry based on Ephesians 4:26a, especially if it contradicts other passages in scripture about the subject. I'm sure that the text doesn't say to try to become angry. Consider a couple of alternate translations for Hebrews 4:26a from Curtis Vaughn's *The Word*:

"If angry, beware of sinning" - *The New Testament in Modern Speech,* Richard Francis Weymouth, "If you do get angry, you must stop sinning in your anger" - *The New Testament: A Translation in the Language of the People*, Charles B. Williams **(13)**

In his book, *Theological Wordbook of the Old Testament*, R. Laird Harris has a paragraph about Ephesians 4:26 in the information about the Hebrew word *ragaz*.

The NT (Ephesians 4:26) which is taken from the LXX [Septuagint] is variously interpreted also. Perhaps best is Meyer's suggestion that the negative force applies to the second imperative, "In being angry do not sin." i.e., do not sin by anger. Or NIV: In your anger do not sin." **(14)**

Personally, I'm going to make the following application in my life: The way I see it, no matter how hard I try to control my temper, and no matter how hard I strive for sanctification, there will be times when I will become angry. In those situations, by

the grace of God and the power of the Holy Spirit, I will do my best to control it and not multiply my sin in thought, word, or deed. I'm going to do everything I can to understand anger in general, understand my own heart and my own anger, understand how the Lord would have me act when anger begins, when my emotions start to get out of control, accept the things I can't or have no authority to change, and find ways to deal with anger in a constructive way, especially if it's my responsibility as a leader to help resolve some of the issues.

What about righteous indignation?

Righteous indignation is said to be an emotional reaction to something that is wrongful, unjust, or evil. It seems to me that it is very difficult to differentiate between righteous indignation and anger related to selfishness or pride. Some people have false motives and are in denial about them. Our mental mechanisms, such as denial and rationalization may operate at the preconscious level. Regarding denial, people may "deny what they perceive, think or feel in a traumatic situation, either saying something to the effect that it cannot be so, or else trying to invalidate something intolerable by deliberately ignoring its existence." **(15)**

Rationalization "consists of the justification of otherwise unacceptable, ego-alien thought, feeling or action, through the misuse and distortion of facts and through employing a pseudologic. Rationalization is a common device in everyday life where people explain away their own defects, failures and misdeeds, as well as those of persons they love and admire – for example, by saying that everyone else does the same thing, or by giving a rationale which they think up after the thing has already been done." **(16)**

In medical school I learned that rationalization is a subconscious mental mechanism when someone does something for one reason but convinces himself he is doing it for another, more socially acceptable reason.

When people discuss the matter of righteous indignation, they often bring up Jesus cleansing the temple of the moneychangers. He did so at least twice.

When it was almost time for the Jewish Passover, Jesus went up to Jerusalem. In the temple courts he found men selling cattle, sheep and doves, and others sitting at tables exchanging money. So he made a whip out of cords, and drove all from the temple area, both sheep and cattle; he scattered the coins of the money changers and overturned their tables. To those who sold doves he said, "Get these out of here! How dare you turn my Father's house into a market!" His disciples remembered that it is written: "Zeal for your house will consume me" (John 2:13-17).

John 2:17b is a quote of Psalm 69:9a.

According to *The Narrated Bible in Chronological Order* the above event occurred during the first Passover of Jesus' ministry A.D. 27. **(17)**

Jesus also cleansed the temple on Monday of Holy Week (the day after Palm Sunday).

On reaching Jerusalem, Jesus entered the temple area and began driving out those who were buying and selling there. He overturned the tables of the money changers and the benches of those selling doves, and would not allow anyone to carry merchandise through the temple courts. And as he taught them, he said, "Is it not written: 'My house will be called a house of prayer for all nations?' But you have made it 'a den of robbers.'" (Mark 11:15-17)

According to *The Reese Chronological Bible* this "second cleansing of the temple" occurred in A. D. 29. **(18)**

In my mind, whatever Jesus did was good. He was/is God and it is God's prerogative to become angry. It doesn't convince me I should do anything of a similar nature. I am not omniscient, and I do not always understand other people's motives. He does. In my mind, if we want to understand righteous indignation, we must at least consider some biblical examples of righteous indignation said to occur in men.

Phineas the priest, son of Eleazer, grandson of Aaron was zealous for God. He was incensed over the Moabites and their tempting of the Israelite men to indulge in sexual immorality and idolatry. He drove a spear through Zimri and his partner.

While Israel was staying in Shittim, the men began to indulge in sexual immorality with Moabite women, who invited them to the sacrifices of their gods. The people ate and bowed down before these gods. So Israel joined in worshipping the Baal of Peor. And the Lord's anger burned against them. The Lord said to Moses, "Take all the leaders of these people, kill them and expose them in broad daylight before the Lord, so that the Lord's fierce anger may turn away from Israel." So Moses said to Israel's judges, "Each of you must put to death those of your men who have joined in worshipping the Baal of Peor." Then an Israelite man brought to his family a Midianite woman right before the eyes of Moses and the whole assembly of Israel while they were weeping at the entrance to the Tent of Meeting. When Phinehas son of Eleazer, the son of Aaron, the priest, saw this, he left the assembly, took a spear in his hand and followed the Israelite into the tent. He drove the spear through both of them – through the Israelite and into the woman's body. Then the plague against the Israelites stopped; but those who died in the plague numbered 24,000. The Lord said to Moses, "Phinehas son of Eleazer, the son of Aaron, the priest, has turned my anger away from the Israelites; for he was as zealous as I am for my honor among them, so that in my zeal I did not put an end to them. Therefore tell him I am making my covenant of peace with him. He and his descendants will have a covenant of a lasting priesthood, because he was zealous for the honor of his God and made atonement for the Israelites." (Numbers 25:1-13)

King Saul became angry when Nahash the Ammonite wanted to gouge out the right eye of the Israelite men from Jabesh Gilead.

Nahash the Ammonite went up and besieged Jabesh Gilead. And all the men of Jabesh said to him, "Make a treaty with us, and we will be subject to you." But Nahash the Ammonite replied, "I will make a treaty with you only on the condition that I gouge out the right eye of every one of you and so bring disgrace on all Israel." The elders of Jabesh said to him, "Give us seven days so we can send messengers throughout Israel; if no one comes to rescue us, we will surrender to you." When the messengers came to Gibeah of Saul and reported these terms to the people, they all wept aloud. Just then Saul was returning from the fields, behind his oxen, and he asked, "What is wrong with the people? Why are they weeping?" Then they repeated to him what the men of Jabesh had said. When Saul heard their words, the Spirit of God came upon him in power, and he burned with anger...The next day Saul separated his men into three divisions; during the last watch of the night they broke into the camp of the Ammonites and slaughtered them until the heat of the day. Those who survived were scattered, so that no two of them were left together. (I Samuel 11:1-6, 11)

Jonathan, son of King Saul, became angry when he realized his father Saul wanted to kill David.

So David hid in the field, and when the new moon festival came, the king [Saul] sat down to eat. He sat in his customary place by the wall, opposite Jonathan, and Abner sat next to Saul, but David's place was empty. Saul said nothing that day, for he thought, "Something must have happened to David to make him ceremonially unclean – surely he is unclean." But the next day, the second day of the month, David's place was empty again. Then Saul said to his son Jonathan, "Why hasn't the son of Jesse come to the meal, either yesterday or today?" Jonathan answered, "David earnestly asked me for permission to go to Bethlehem. He said, 'Let me go, because our family is observing a sacrifice in the town and my brother has ordered me to be there. If I have found favor in your eyes, let me get away to see my brothers.' That is why he has not come to the king's table." Saul's anger flared up at Jonathan and he said to him, "You son of a perverse and rebellious woman! Don't I know that you have sided with the son of Jesse to your own shame and to the shame of the mother who bore you? As long as the son of Jesse lives on this earth, neither you nor your kingdom will be established. Now send and bring him to me, for he must die!" "Why should he be put to death? What has he done?" Jonathan asked his father. But Saul hurled his spear at him to kill him. Then Jonathan knew that his father intended to kill David. Jonathan got up from the table in fierce anger; on that second day of the month he did not eat, because he was grieved at his father's shameful treatment of David. (I Samuel 20:24-34)

King David was angry because of the story about the rich man butchering the poor man's only sheep.

The Lord sent Nathan to David. When he came to him, he said, "There were two men in a certain town, one rich and the other poor. The rich man had a very large number of sheep and cattle, but the poor man had nothing except one little ewe lamb he had bought. He raised it, and it grew up with him and his children. It shared his food, drank from his cup and even slept in his arms. It was like a daughter to him. Now a traveler came to the rich man, but the rich man refrained from taking one of his own sheep or cattle to prepare a meal for the traveler who came to him. Instead he took the ewe lamb that belonged to the poor man and prepared it for the one who had come to him." David burned with anger against the man and said to Nathan, "As surely as the Lord lives, the man who did this deserves to die! He must pay for that lamb four times over, because he did such a thing and had no pity." Then Nathan said to David, "You are the man! Why did you despise the word of the Lord by doing what is evil in his eyes? You struck down Uriah the Hittite with the sword and took his wife to be your own." (II Samuel 12:1-7a, 9a)

Let's review the text and consider what authority each of these men had to respond to his own individual situation the way he did. Before Phineas killed Zimri, God's order had already gone out to kill those who were participating in the revelry. (Numbers 25:4, 5) Saul had the authority to take action in his situation, because he had been chosen king (I Samuel 10:20-26). Jonathan's anger did not result in any action directly against his father, but he did warn David of his father's intent to kill him. The thing that David's anger required was repentance.

Consider definitions for two Hebrew words translated indignation in the Old Testament.

Indignation [horror – KJV] grips me because of the wicked, who have forsaken your [the Lord's] law. (Psalm 119:53)

The Hebrew word for indignation or horror in Psalm 119:53 is *zal'apa.* According to Brown, Driver, and Briggs, the word means raging heat. **(19)**

I [Jeremiah] never sat in the company of revelers, never made merry with them; I sat alone because your hand was on me and you had filled me with indignation. (Jeremiah 15:17)

The Hebrew word for indignation in Jeremiah 15:17 is *za'am.* Harris says the basic idea of this word is expressing intense anger. **(20)**

Consider two stories from The New Testament. I'm sure Paul must have been very angry.

Later Paul said to Barnabas, "Let us go back and visit the brothers in all the towns where we preached the word of the Lord and see how they are doing." Barnabas wanted to take John, also called Mark, with them, but Paul did not think it wise to take him, because he had deserted them in Pamphylia and had not continued with them in the work. They had such a sharp disagreement that they parted company.

Barnabas took Mark and sailed for Cypress, but Paul chose Silas and left, commended by the brothers to the grace of the Lord. (Acts 15:36-40)

When we were going to the place of prayer, we were met by a slave girl who had a spirit by which she predicted the future. She earned a great deal of money for her owners by fortune-telling. This girl followed Paul and the rest of us, shouting, "These men are servants of the Most High God, who are telling you the way to be saved." She kept this up for many days. Finally Paul became so troubled that he turned around and said to the spirit, "In the name of Jesus Christ I command you to come out of her!" At that moment the spirit left her. (Acts 16:16-18)

Paul wrote Galatians to counter Judaizing false teachers who were undermining the central New Testament doctrine of justification by faith. They were ignoring the express decree of the Jerusalem Council (Acts 15:23-29) and taught that Gentiles must keep the Mosaic Law **(21)**, including the requirement of circumcision. Paul wrote about them as follows:

As for those agitators, I wish they would go the whole way and emasculate [castrate] themselves! (Galatians 5:12)

When our passions are aroused, we may not be able to interpret our own feelings correctly. We're all born with a conscience, a sense of right and wrong. As we go through life, we learn which actions are right and which are wrong. We may not have good teachers.

We need to consider the fact that when someone has a sense that something is not right, it doesn't necessarily mean the person is correct in his thinking. Our own individual sense of justice is under the influence of evil.

Consider three examples of indignation in the gospels.

The blind and the lame came to him [Jesus] at the temple, and he healed them. But when the chief priests and the teachers of the law saw the wonderful things he did and the children shouting in the temple area, "Hosanna to the Son of David," they were *indignant*. (Matthew 21:14, 15)

While Jesus was at Bethany in the home of a man known as Simon the Leper, a woman came to him with an alabaster jar of very expensive perfume, which she

152

poured on his head as he was reclining at the table. When the disciples saw this, they were *indignant.* "Why this waste?" they asked. This perfume could have been sold at a high price and the money given to the poor." Aware of this, Jesus said to them, "Why are you bothering this woman? She has done a beautiful thing to me. The poor you will always have with you, but you will not always have me. When she poured this perfume on my body, she did it to prepare me for burial. I tell you the truth, wherever this gospel is preached throughout the world, what she has done will also be told, in memory of her." (Matthew 26:6-13)

Indignant because Jesus had healed on the Sabbath, the synagogue ruler said to the people, "There are six days for work. So come and be healed on those days, not on the Sabbath." (Luke 13:14)

In each of the three above passages from the New Testament, the Greek word *aganakteo* is the word translated *indignant.* The word means be aroused, *indignant,* or be angry at someone or at something. **(22)** In each of these passages, the *indignant* persons were in the wrong. It seems to me that the Bible does not make a clear distinction between *indignation* and anger. I'm not sure we can either. We don't even understand our own hearts.

There is a place for righteous indignation, but I am not sure we can always recognize when it happens. In any given situation, we may or may not have the authority to do anything about whatever is making us angry. The United States is supposed to be a country based on the rule of law. We don't need to give in to the urge to let our emotions and actions go unchecked. We need to deal with our emotions and go through the proper channels to resolve our issues.

The heart is deceitful above all things and beyond cure. Who can understand it? (Jeremiah 17:9)

You were taught, with regard to your former way of life, to put off your old self, which is being corrupted by its deceitful desires; (Ephesians 4:22)

See to it, brothers, that none of you has a sinful unbelieving heart that turns away from the living God. But encourage one another daily, as long as it is called today, so that none of you may be hardened by sin's deceitfulness. (Hebrews 3:12, 13)

The Behaviorists have a concept referred to as Fundamental

Attribution Error. As individuals, we don't know so much about other people's circumstances, and therefore, we have a tendency to explain their behavior based on our perception of their personalities. Conversely, we know about our own circumstances, and we tend to overemphasize situational factors as determining any aberrant behavior and underemphasize the role of our own personalities (*Wikipedia*).

I have four questions for people to consider in each situation:

1. How do I know it is righteous *indignation*?
2. Why do I care?
3. How do I know I'm accurate in my assessment of the situation?
4. How does that affect what I do?

For personal affronts, the New Testament emphasizes forgiveness. We are to take the initiative in promoting reconciliation (Matthew 18:15-17; Matthew 5:23, 24). For moral failure, we are to go to the person, and it that doesn't work, ostracize him (I Corinthians 5:1, 2, 5, 9-13; Galatians 6:1; II Timothy 4:2; Titus 3:9, 10). For cataclysmic occurrences, such as war, tragic accidents, or natural disasters, we must take our comfort in the sovereignty of God (Isaiah 30:15a; Habakkuk 3:16-19a; Philippians 4:6, 7). In my mind, the important thing about anger is not how we categorize it but what we do about it.

Perhaps Christians exhibit too much so-called *righteous indignation.* That may be why unbelievers often view Christ-followers as angry, hostile, and hateful people, people to be avoided. It reminds me of the old Joan Baez song *One Tin Soldier.* The refrain goes like this:

Go ahead and hate your neighbor
Go ahead and cheat a friend.
Do it in the name of heaven
You can justify it in the end.
But there won't be any trumpets blowing

Come the judgment day.
On the bloody morning after
One tin soldier rides away. (taken off the internet)

My first book, *Finding Strength in Weakness*, came out in 2001. Several weeks later my wife and I had a booth at the national meeting of the American Association of Christian Counselors at the Opryland Hotel in Nashville, TN. One night we were catching a bus to a special event. I heard one of the employees say, "I'll be glad when we get rid of these Christians!"

In the New Testament, I see a completely different picture.

Make it your ambition to lead a quiet life, to mind your own business and to work with your hands just as we told you, so that your daily life will win the respect of outsiders and so that you will not be dependent on anybody. (1 Thessalonians 4:11, 12)

Live such good lives among the pagans that, though they accuse you of doing wrong, they may see your good deeds and glorify God on the day he visits us. (1 Peter 2:12)

Anger is a sin of the flesh.

I remember when I first realized that understanding my anger was not very complicated. It was just the flesh; it was just my sinful nature expressing itself.

The Greek word translated flesh (sinful nature in the NIV) is *sarx*. According to Bauer, Arndt, and Gingrich, the word can have several meanings:

1. The material that covers the bones of a human or animal body.
2. The body itself.
3. A man of flesh and blood.
4. Human or mortal nature, earthly descent.
5. Corporeality, physical limitation(s), life here on earth.
6. The external or outward side of life, as it appears to the eye of an unregenerate person, that which is natural or earthly...wise people

according to human standards...boast of one's outward circumstances, i.e. descent, manner of life, etc.

7. In Paul's thought especially, the flesh is the willing instrument of sin, and is subject to sin to such a degree that wherever flesh is, all forms of sin are likewise present, and no good thing can live in the *sarx*. **(23)**

There are many ways the flesh asserts itself and gets out of control. There are many ways the flesh can become a willing instrument of unrighteousness.

I do not understand what I do. For what I want to do I do not do, but what I hate to do. And if I do what I do not want to do, I agree that the law is good. As it is, it is no longer I myself who do it, but it is sin living in me. I know that nothing good lives in me, that is, in my sinful nature [my flesh]. For I have the desire to do what is good, but I cannot carry it out. For what I do is not the good I want to do; no, the evil I do not want to do – this I keep on doing. Now if I do what I do not want to do, it is no longer I who do it, but it is sin living in me that does it. So I find this law at work: When I want to do good, evil is right there with me. For in my inner being I delight in God's law; but I see another law at work in the members of my body, waging war against the law of my mind and making me a prisoner of the law of sin at work within my members. What a wretched man I am! Who will rescue me from this body of death? Thanks be to God – through Jesus Christ our Lord! (Romans 7:15-25a)

Many of us are slaves to our bodies. We eat and drink when our bodies tell us to do so. We urinate and defecate on command. We go to sleep and awaken as instructed. Many of us are also under the control of our passions, i.e. love, joy, hatred, or anger, and are dominated by them. We need to find a way to control our own bodies, including our passions.

No, I beat my body and make it my slave so that after I have preached to others, I myself will not be disqualified for the prize. (I Corinthians 9:27)

It is God's will that you should be sanctified: that you should avoid sexual immorality; that each of you should learn to control his own body in a way that is holy and honorable, not in passionate lust like the heathen, who do not know God; (I Thessalonians 4:3-5)

We have to be especially careful about our thought life. Wayne Grudem writes: "We may define sin as follows: Sin is any failure to conform to the moral law of God in act, attitude, or nature…Sin includes not only individual acts such as stealing or lying or committing murder, but also attitudes that are contrary to the attitudes God requires of us. We see this already in the Ten Commandments, which not only prohibit sinful actions but also wrong attitudes…You shall not covet your neighbor's wife [Exodus 20:17]…The Sermon on the Mount also prohibits sinful attitudes such as anger (Matthew 5:22) or lust (Matthew 5:28). Paul lists attitudes such as jealousy, anger, and selfishness (Galatians 5:20) as things that are works of the flesh…a life that is pleasing to God is one that has moral purity not only in its actions, but also in its desires of the heart." **(24)**

We take captive every thought to make it obedient to Christ. (II Corinthians 10:5b)

Some people say that it's okay to become angry; a person just has to be careful that he does not sin in response to the anger. That's like saying fornication and adultery are bad, but lust is okay. Consider these words of Jesus in the Sermon on the Mount: "You have heard that it was said, 'Do not commit adultery.' But I tell you that anyone who looks at a woman lustfully has already committed adultery with her in his heart." (Matthew 5:27, 28)

Saying that anger itself is not a sin is like saying stealing is sinful, but coveting is not a sin. The Ten Commandments make the issue clear, "You shall not covet your neighbor's house. You shall not covet your neighbor's wife, or his manservant or maidservant, his ox or donkey, or anything that belongs to your neighbor" (Exodus 20:17).

Jesus Himself said that anyone who is angry with his brother will be subject to judgment.

"You have heard that it was said to the people long ago, 'Do not murder, and anyone who murders will be subject to judgment.' But I tell you that anyone who

157

is angry with his brother will be subject to judgment. Again, anyone who says to his brother, 'Raca,' is answerable to the Sanhedrin. But anyone who says, 'You fool!' will be in danger of the fire of hell." (Matthew 5:21, 22)

There are several verses in the epistles dealing with malice and slander and how damaging they are. In regard to malice, the Greek word *kakia*, in the moral sense, refers to depravity or wickedness; it can also mean malice, ill will, malignity, trouble, or misfortune. **(25)** The American Heritage College dictionary says malice is a desire to harm others or see others suffer. **(26)** I take it that it includes the desire for something bad to happen to someone else.

Remind the people to be subject to rulers and authorities, to be obedient, to be ready to do whatever is good, to slander no one, to be peaceable and considerate, and to show true humility toward all men. At one time we too were foolish, disobedient, deceived and enslaved by all kinds of passions and pleasures. We lived in malice and envy, being hated and hating one another. (Titus 3:1-3)

Therefore, rid yourselves of all malice and all deceit, hypocrisy, envy, and slander of every kind. (I Peter 2:1)

Regarding slander, in Ephesians 4:31, Colossians 3:8, and Titus 3:2 the Greek words *blaspheemeo* and *blaspheemia* refer to, in our relationships to men, injuring the reputation of, reviling, defaming, using abusive speech, or slandering. **(27)** In I Peter 2:1, the Greek word *katalalia* denotes evil speech, slander, or defamation. **(28)** We dare not share publicly the negative feelings we have toward others. If a confrontation is necessary, we are to go to that person alone (Matthew 18:15-17). According to Bauer, Arndt, and Gingrich, *A Greek-English Lexicon of the New Testament*, *katalalia* is "injurious to faith." **(29)** It is apparent from Scripture that sin leads to spiritual blindness (see chapter three).

If someone considers himself religious and yet does not keep a tight rein on his tongue, he deceives himself and his religion is worthless. (James 1:26)

We must find a way to tame the tongue through the power of the Holy Spirit.

Some thoughts recently became more real to me one morning as I was reading through Psalms. Psalm 39 is a psalm of David. In the first two and a half verses, David was trying to control the anger he felt toward his enemies. But when he kept silent, the anger increased.

I said, "I will watch my ways and keep my tongue from sin; I will put a muzzle on my mouth as long as the wicked are in my presence." But when I was silent and still, not even saying anything good, my anguish increased. My heart grew hot within me, and as I meditated, the fire burned... (Psalm 39:1-3a)

In verses 4-6, David reflects on his relationship with the Lord and the brevity of life. It appears to me that by verse 7, David begins to develop a little humility. In verse 8, he comes to realize that his own sin is part of the problem. In verse 9, he exhibits some contrition, and he realizes that ultimately God is responsible for his circumstances. In verses 10-12a, David appeals to the Lord for relief.

"But now, Lord, what do I look for? My hope is in you. Save me from all my transgressions; do not make me the scorn of fools. I was silent; I would not open my mouth, for you are the one who has done this. Remove your scourge from me; I am overcome by the blow of your hand. You rebuke and discipline men for their sin; you consume their wealth like a moth - each man is but a breath. Hear my prayer, O Lord, listen to my cry for help; be not deaf to my weeping. (Psalm 39:7-12a)

Patience and Forbearance

I believe having patience and forbearance is part of our obedience to the second great commandment, the commandment to love others. The word patient in I Corinthians 13:4 is rendered *suffereth long* in the KJV and is translated from the Greek verb *makrothumeo*. According to Bauer, Arndt, and Gingrich it means have patience or wait. It means forbearing especially toward someone. **(30)** *Webster's New Collegiate Dictionary 150th Anniversary Edition* defines forbearance as "a refraining from the enforcement of something (as a debt, right, or obligation) that is due." **(31)** Forbearance means leniency. To forbear is to hold oneself back especially with an effort of self-restraint. Regarding forbearance, *The American Heritage*

159

College Dictionary includes the meanings of "tolerance and restraint in the face of provocation" and "the act of a creditor who refrains from enforcing a debt when it falls due." **(32)**

I therefore, the prisoner of the Lord, beseech you that ye walk worthy of the vocation wherewith ye are called, with all lowliness and meekness, with longsuffering, forbearing one another in love; endeavoring to keep the unity of the Spirit in the bond of peace. (Ephesians 4:1-3 - KJV)

According to Ephesians 4:1-3, forbearing helps us in keeping the unity of the Spirit in the bond of peace. In my own experience, letting myself calm down after becoming angry helps me deal with a situation assertively rather than aggressively. I have trouble reconciling Ephesians 4:1-3 with Ephesians 4:26b, "Do not let the sun go down while you are still angry." I guess Ephesians 4:26b must be talking about calming down our angry emotions rather than resolving all the issues. It must be one of those commandments that is an ideal, that we keep working toward but may not be fully realized this side of heaven. Conventional wisdom would tell us that *stuffing* our anger leads to all sorts of somatic complaints as well as being a factor leading to an eventual emotional blowup. Of course, conventional wisdom leaves out the power of the Holy Spirit as He calms us down and helps us to forgive and accept.

Most of the time I was in medical school, I had no car. I had a friend who was in law school at Memphis State. We would do things together. When he picked me up, he was always late. I decided he wasn't going to change. I reasoned that I could accept the situation as it was or end the relationship. For the sake of the relationship, I accepted him the way he was.

I am now a senior citizen. Most of the people I know are fairly set in their ways. There are many things I now accept, especially because I've initiated many confrontations, over the years, that have done more harm than good. I remember a nasty letter I wrote to a man, several years ago, because I didn't like something he wrote in an article. He has since passed away. Regarding the letter, my wife said,

"Did that letter do you any good?" I had to admit that my answer was in the negative. There are so many things we may become angry about that don't make that much difference anyway.

The Bible teaches us that God loves us. He is patient and forbearing with us. "We love because he first loved us." (I John 4:19)

The Lord is not slow in keeping his promise, as some understand slowness. He is patient [*macrothumeo*] with you, not wanting anyone to perish, but everyone to come to repentance. (II Peter 3:9)

Consider these words of Paul to Timothy, his son in the faith.

I thank Christ Jesus our Lord, who had given me strength, that he considered me faithful, appointing me to his service. Even though I was once a blasphemer and a persecutor and a violent man, I was shown mercy because I acted in ignorance and unbelief. The grace of our Lord was poured out on me abundantly, along with the faith and love that are in Christ Jesus. Here is a trustworthy saying that deserves full acceptance: Christ Jesus came into the world to save sinners - of whom I am the worst. But for that very reason I was shown mercy so that in me, the worst of sinners, Christ Jesus might display his unlimited patience [*makrothumia*] as an example for those who would believe on him and receive eternal life. (I Timothy 1:12-16)

According to Bauer, Arndt, and Gingrich, *makrothumia* is a noun meaning patience, steadfastness, or endurance. It also means forbearance or patience toward others. **(33)** *Vine's Expository Dictionary of New Testament Words* lists other Greek words for the English concept of forbearance.

ANOCHE...a holding back...denotes forbearance, a delay of punishment, Romans 2:4; 3:25, in both places of God's forbearance with men; in the latter passage His forbearance is the ground, not of His forgiveness, but of His *praetermission* [see below] of sins, His withholding punishment. In 2:4, it represents a suspense of wrath which must eventually be exercised unless the sinner accepts God's conditions; in 3:25 it is connected with the passing over of sins in times past, previous to the atoning work of Christ.

Note: Cp. The noun *epieikeia*, Acts 24:4, "clemency" [disposition to be merciful and especially to moderate the severity of punishment due]; II Corinthians 10:1, "gentleness." Synonymous with this are *makrothumia*, longsuffering, and *hupomone*, patience (see Colossians 1:11). *Anoche* and *makrothumia* are used

161

together in Romans 2:4. See also Ephesians 4:2 (where [the verb form *anecho*], is used in this combination). Trench (Syn.) and Abbott-Smith (Lex.) state that *hupomone* expresses patience with regard to adverse things, *makrothumia* patience with regard to antagonistic persons...

Longsuffering is that quality of self-restraint in the face of provocation which does not hastily retaliate or promptly punish; it is the opposite of anger and is associated with mercy, and is used of God, Exodus 34:6 [Septuagint]; Romans 2:4; I Peter 3:20. Patience is the quality that does not surrender to circumstances or succumb under trial; it is the opposite of despondency and is associated with hope. **(34)**

Of course there are times when God is not patient. There is a sin unto death (I John 5:16, 17). The Bible gives examples of people struck down because of their sin. For example, Nadab and Abihu (Leviticus 10), Korah and his followers (Numbers 16), Ananias and Sapphira (Acts 5) and King Herod Agrippa I (Acts 12). Sometimes God exhibits forbearance and sometimes He doesn't. It's His choice, and His only standard is His own character. We don't know how long God will continue in His forbearance with us, so we best not get too cozy with our sin.

The Free Dictionary by Farlex defines *praetermission* [or pretermission] as follows: "To disregard intentionally or allow to pass unnoticed or unmentioned." Through the years God has had plenty of justification to take my life. In His forbearance, He chose to overlook my sin. Also, His Spirit was with me, preventing me from doing other bad things that would have really ruined my life. He spared me in anticipation of what He was later going to do in my heart.

But now a righteousness from God, apart from the law, has been made known, to which the Law and the Prophets testify. This righteousness from God comes through faith in Jesus Christ to all who believe. There is no difference, for all have sinned and fall short of the glory of God, and are justified freely by his grace through the redemption that came by Christ Jesus. God presented him as a sacrifice of atonement, through faith in his blood. He did this to demonstrate his justice, because in his forbearance he had left the sins committed beforehand unpunished – he did this to demonstrate his justice at the present time, so as to be just and the one who justifies those who have faith in Jesus. (Romans 3:21-26)

162

From what I can see, God's forbearance with the Old Testament saints extends to present day Christians as well. God has been so patient with me and has shown so much forbearance with me, when something happens that I don't like, and I start to get a little resentful, I need to remember God's forbearance with me. I believe I've lived long enough to have some judgment about which situations require confrontation and which don't. I don't need to be angry to confront someone when necessary.

I also need to realize God understands the situation better than I do, that He is all-powerful, and that He loves me. I need to practice more forbearance with other people and with myself. I've reached some conclusions about patience and forbearance from other passages in the New Testament. While the list of how we are supposed to act in I Corinthians 13:4-7 is fairly comprehensive, it is not exhaustive. Within the additional passages below are other lists that tell us how we are supposed to act. The thing that ties all these concepts together is love. It's about loving God and loving our neighbors as ourselves.

A man's wisdom gives him patience; it is to his glory to overlook an offense. (Proverbs 19:11)

1. Our patience and forbearance are powered by the Spirit of God.

For this reason, since the day we heard about you, we have not stopped praying for you and asking God to fill you with the knowledge of his will through all spiritual wisdom and understanding. And we pray this in order that you may live a life worthy of the Lord and may please him in every way: bearing fruit in every good work, growing in the knowledge of God, being strengthened with all power according to his glorious might so that you may have great endurance and patience, and joyfully giving thanks to the Father, who has qualified you to share in the inheritance of the saints in the kingdom of light. (Colossians 1:9-12)

2. Our patience and forbearance are evidence that we have a relationship with God.

The acts of the sinful nature are obvious: sexual immorality, impurity and debauchery; idolatry and witchcraft; hatred, discord, jealousy, fits of rage, selfish

163

ambition, dissensions, factions and envy; drunkenness, orgies, and the like. I warn you, as I did before, that those who live like this will not inherit the kingdom of God. But the fruit of the Spirit is love, joy, peace, patience, kindness, goodness, faithfulness, gentleness and self-control. Against such things there is no law. Those who belong to Christ Jesus have crucified the sinful nature with its passions and desires. Since we live by the Spirit, let us keep in step with the Spirit. Let us not become conceited, provoking and envying each other. (Galatians 5:19-26)

Discord, fits of rage, dissensions, factions, and provoking each other are acts of the sinful nature and are in conflict with the Spirit. They are the opposite of loving our neighbor.

3. Believers' patience and forbearance with each other promote unity in the Spirit.

Be completely humble and gentle; be patient, bearing with one another in love. Make every effort to keep the unity of the Spirit through the bond of peace. (Ephesians 4:2, 3)

Therefore, as God's chosen people, holy and dearly loved, clothe yourselves with compassion, kindness, humility, gentleness and patience. Bear with each other and forgive whatever grievances you may have against one another. Forgive as the Lord forgave you. And over all these virtues put on love, which binds them all together in perfect unity. (Colossians 3:12-14).

4. Our patience and forbearance during times of affliction are part of our ministry.

We put no stumbling block in anyone's path, so that our ministry will not be discredited. Rather as servants of God we commend ourselves in every way: in great endurance; in troubles, hardships and distresses; in beatings, imprisonments and riots; in hard work, sleepless nights and hunger; in purity, understanding, patience and kindness; in the Holy Spirit and in sincere love… (II Corinthians 6:3-6)

5. Our patience and forbearance lead to blessings from God.

Brothers, as an example of patience in the face of suffering, take the prophets who spoke in the name of the Lord. As you know, we consider blessed those who have persevered. You have heard of Job's perseverance and have seen what the Lord finally brought about. The Lord is full of compassion and mercy. (James 5:10, 11)

6. Patience and forbearance are required for us to receive our eternal reward.

God is not unjust; he will not forget your work and love you have shown him as you have helped his people and continue to help them. We want each of you to show this same diligence to the very end, in order to make your hope sure. We do not want you to become lazy, but to imitate those who through faith and patience inherit what has been promised. (Hebrews 6:10-12)

Forgiveness

In order to help readers understand what it means to forgive, I offer the meanings of the three Hebrew and three Greek words for forgive, as used in the original text. According to R. Laird Harris in *Theological Wordbook of the Old Testament*, the Hebrew verb *kapar* means make an atonement, make reconciliation, or purge. **(35)** The parent noun *kippur* is used in the expression, "Yom Kippur" meaning Day of Atonement. Yom Kippur was celebrated on the tenth day of the seventh month of the Jewish calendar [September-October]. On that day the high priest entered the inner sanctuary of the temple to make reconciling sacrifices for the sins of the entire nation in accordance with the rites described in Leviticus 16. "On that day only would the high priest enter within the inner veil bearing the [goat] blood of the sin offering (cf. Hebrews 9:7). A second goat was released as an escape goat [scapegoat] to symbolize the total removal of sin." **(36)**

According to Harris, the Hebrew verb *nasa* has three separate meanings, to lift up, to bear or carry or support, and to take or take away. "The meaning 'to lift up' is used both literally and figuratively in many phrases, i.e. 'To lift up the hand' in taking an oath...in doing violence...as a signal...and in punishment...'To lift up one's head' in restoration to honor." **(37)** This latter definition reminds me of a phrase I sometimes hear when one of the players at the ball park has just made some kind of mistake and seems dejected; the phrase is, "Get your head up!" The use of the verb to mean "to take, or take away" stresses the taking away, forgiveness, or pardon of sin, iniquity, and transgression. "So characteristic is this action of taking away sin, that it is listed as one of God's attributes...Sin can be forgiven and forgotten because it is taken up and carried away." **(38)**

According to Harris, the Hebrew verb *salah* is used in Scripture solely of God. The word "is used of God's offer of pardon and forgiveness to the sinner. Never does this word in any of its forms refer to people forgiving each other." In the Old Testament, real atonement and forgiveness were available for all sins except those of the defiant and unrepentant sinner...who "despised the word of the Lord." "The experience of forgiveness in the Old Testament was personally efficacious, although objectively the basis and grounds of forgiveness awaited the death [and resurrection] of Christ." **(39)**

In the New Testament the main word for *forgive* is the Greek verb *aphieemi*. According to Bauer, Arndt, and Gingrich, it means *leave, let go,* or *send away*. It is the word used for canceling a debt. **(40)** It is the word used for *leave* in Matthew 4:20 when Peter and Andrew left their nets to follow Jesus. **(41)** *Aphiemi* is the word used by Jesus in Matthew 6:14. **(42)**

For if you forgive men when they sin against you. Your heavenly Father will also forgive you. (Matthew 6:14)

There are a couple of other Greek words in the New Testament that may be translated forgive. *Charizomai* means to give freely or graciously as a favor. It can mean give - remit, forgive, [or] pardon. **(43)** It is the word used in Acts 27:24, quoting an angel of God, who is speaking to Paul, during a storm on the Mediterranean Sea. "...Do not be afraid, Paul. You must stand trial before Caesar; and God has graciously given you the lives of all who sail with you."

According to Bauer, Arndt, and Gingrich, the word *apoluo* means to set free, release, [or] pardon. It can also mean let go, send away, [or] dismiss **(44)**. It is the word used for "forgive" in Luke 6:37. "Do not judge, and you will not be judged. Do not condemn, and you will not be condemned. Forgive, and you will be forgiven."

Vine's Expository Dictionary of New Testament Words, says the word means to loose from or release. In Luke 6:37, it refers to setting a person free as a quasi-judicial act. **(45)** According to Goodrick's *The NIV Exhaustive Concordance, apoluo* is most often translated release, send away, or divorce. It is translated *forgive* in the New Testament only that one time. **(46)**

Forgiving Others

To be healthy spiritually, we need to be able to forgive others. If we have an oppressive feeling of resentment for someone, we need to forgive and let it go. It removes a tremendous burden from our shoulders. Let me share an example of a time when my wife and I needed to forgive and let go of oppressive feelings. We started building a house in 1981. Those were the days of sixteen to eighteen percent interest rates. After the ordeal of building the house, all the arrangements and all the decisions, we had a sixty thousand dollar overrun, money that was spent over and beyond the money from other sources. After we moved into the house, there were several things that needed more attention. It was a struggle to get the contractor to come back and fix them. When we did get him back, we would give him a list of eight or ten things that needed correction. He would fix one of them, and then we would not hear from him again until we called him. We were becoming upset over and over and over again. Finally, I decided that the only way we could have any peace of mind was to accept the house as it was, forgive the contractor for things he should have done but didn't, and if there was other work needed for the house, to hire another contractor to come in and take care of it. Once we decided to do that, a tremendous weight lifted off our shoulders.

The New Testament appeals to us to forgive others on several different levels. We are encouraged to forgive on the basis of love. Ideally when we forgive, it should be spontaneous, not forced.

Therefore, although in Christ I could be bold and order you to do what you ought to do, yet I appeal to you on the basis of love. I then, as Paul—an old man and now also a prisoner of Christ Jesus—I appeal to you for my son Onesimus, who became my son while I was in chains. Formerly he was useless to you, but now he has become useful both to you and to me. I am sending him - who is my very heart - back to you . . . So if you consider me a partner, welcome him as you would welcome me. If he has done you any wrong or owes you anything, charge it to me. (Philemon 8-12, 17, 18)

The debt that that other person owes us is insignificant compared with the debt we owe God.

Therefore the kingdom of heaven is like a king who wanted to settle accounts with his servants. As he began the settlement, a man who owed him ten thousand talents was brought to him. Since he was not able to pay, the master ordered that he and his wife and his children and all that he had be sold to repay the debt. The servant fell on his knees before him, "Be patient with me," he begged, "and I will pay back everything." The servant's master took pity on him, canceled the debt and let him go. But when that servant went out, he found one of his fellow servants who owed him a hundred denarii. He grabbed him and began to choke him. "Pay back what you owe me!" he demanded. His fellow servant fell to his knees and begged him, "Be patient with me, and I will pay you back." But he refused. Instead, he went off and had the man thrown into prison until he could pay the debt. When the other servants saw what had happened, they were greatly distressed and went and told their master everything that had happened. Then the master called the servant in. "You wicked servant," he said, "I cancelled all that debt of yours because you begged me to. Shouldn't you have had mercy on your fellow servant just as I had on you?" In anger his master turned him over to the jailers to be tortured, until he could pay back all he owed. This is how my heavenly Father will treat each of you unless you forgive your brother from your heart. (Matthew 18:23–35)

Jesus said that if we do not forgive others, the Father will not forgive us:

For if you forgive men when they sin against you, your heavenly Father will also forgive you. But if you do not forgive men their sins, your Father will not forgive your sins. (Matthew 6:14, 15)

If we do not forgive, it gives Satan a foothold in our lives. Consider Paul's words:

"In your anger do not sin." Do not let the sun go down while you are still angry, and do not give the devil a foothold . . . Do not let any unwholesome talk come out of your mouths, but only what is helpful for building others up according to their needs, that it may benefit those who listen . . . Get rid of all bitterness, rage and anger, brawling and slander, along with every form of malice. Be kind and compassionate to one another, forgiving each other, just as in Christ God forgave you. (Ephesians 4:26–32)

Note that verse thirty-one tells us to get rid of all anger.

My dear brothers, take note of this: Everyone should be quick to listen, slow to speak and slow to become angry, for man's anger does not bring about the righteous life that God desires. (James 1:19, 20)

The soul and spirit of a Christian should not be like a household that is divided against itself. We are reminded in Colossians 1:13 that the Father has rescued us from the dominion of darkness. If we are angry and resentful, it is difficult to have fellowship with God. It is futile to be bitter toward our fellow man.

Chapter Ten
Overcoming the Sins
of the Flesh

How do we overcome the sins of the flesh?

We overcome by the grace of God, flowing from all three persons of the Trinity.

For those God foreknew he also predestined to be conformed to the likeness of his Son, that he might be the firstborn among many brothers. And those he predestined, he also called; those he called, he also justified; those he justified, he also glorified. (Romans 8:29, 30)

For the grace of God that brings salvation has appeared to all men. It teaches us to say "No" to ungodliness and worldly passions, and to live self-controlled, upright and godly lives in this present age... (Titus 2:11, 12)

Who will bring any charge against those whom God has chosen? It is God who justifies. Who is he that condemns? Christ Jesus, who died – more than that, who was raised to life – is at the right hand of God and is also interceding for us. (Romans 8:33, 34)

Therefore He [Jesus] is able to save completely those who come to God through him, because he always lives to intercede for them. (Hebrews 7:25)

In the same way, the Spirit helps us in our weakness. We do not know what we ought to pray for, but the Spirit himself intercedes for us with groans that words cannot express. And he who searches our hearts knows the mind of the Spirit, because the Spirit intercedes for the saints in accordance with God's will. (Romans 8:26, 27)

We overcome through hearing and heeding the great and precious promises of Jesus. We gain spiritual maturity through God's power and our own obedience.

His [Jesus Christ's] divine power has given us everything we need for life and godliness through our knowledge of him who called us by his own glory and goodness. Through these he has given us his very great and precious promises, so that through them you may participate in the divine nature and escape the corruption in the world caused by evil desires. For this very reason, make every effort to add to your faith goodness; and to goodness, knowledge; and to knowledge, self-control; and to self-control, perseverance; and to perseverance, godliness; and to godliness, brotherly kindness; and to brotherly kindness, love. For if you possess these qualities in increasing measure, they will keep you from being ineffective and unproductive in your knowledge of our Lord Jesus Christ. But if anyone does not have them, he is nearsighted and blind, and has forgotten that he has been cleansed from his past sins. Therefore, my brothers, be all the more eager to make your calling and election sure. For if you do these things, you will never fall, and you will receive a rich welcome into the eternal kingdom of our Lord and Savior Jesus Christ. (II Peter 1:3-11)

In this passage we see an opportunity for spiritual progress based on a combination of what God does and what we do. Believers have been foreordained for life and godliness through Jesus Christ, but we have to cooperate with Him to bring our holiness to fruition. We must make every effort to add to our faith goodness, knowledge, self-control, perseverance, godliness, brotherly kindness, and love. As an example of our need to cooperate with what God is doing in our lives, consider that we can't have knowledge of spiritual things if we never open our Bibles or fellowship with other believers. We can't hear and heed the promises of Jesus if we never find out what they are. We can't learn how to live godly lives if we never practice doing so. We will not learn to persevere if we never give it a try. It helps us make our calling and election sure when we see a long-term pattern of growth in our Christian lives. The phrase, "possess these qualities in increasing measure," in II Peter 1:8 confirms the idea that obtaining godliness [sanctification, holiness] in this life is a process.

Jesus made many promises. Let us review a few of them. Jesus' promises are often conditional.

Just as Moses lifted up the snake in the desert, so the Son of Man must be lifted up, that everyone who believes in him may have eternal life. For God so loved the world that he gave his one and only Son, that whoever believes in him shall not perish but have eternal life. For God did not send his Son into the world to condemn the world, but to save the world through him. Whoever believes in him is not condemned, but whoever does not believe stands condemned already because he has not believed in the name of God's one and only Son. (John 3:14-18)

Jesus answered [the woman of Samaria], "Everyone who drinks this water [from the well] will be thirsty again, but whoever drinks the water I give him [spiritual life] will never thirst. Indeed, the water I give him will become in him a spring of water welling up to eternal life." (John 4:13)

I [Jesus] tell you the truth, whoever hears my word and believes him who sent me has eternal life and will not be condemned; he has crossed from death to life. I tell you the truth, a time is coming and has now come when the dead will hear the voice of the Son of God and those who hear will live. For as the Father has life in himself, so he has granted the Son to have life in himself. And he has given him the authority to judge because he is the Son of Man. Do not be amazed at this, for a time is coming when all who are in their graves will hear his voice and come out – those who have done good will rise to live, and those who have done evil will rise to be condemned. (John 5:24-29)

Then Jesus declared, "I am the bread of life. He who comes to me will never go hungry, and he who believes in me will never be thirsty. But as I told you [the crowd], you have seen me and still do not believe. All that the Father gives me will come to me, and whoever comes to me I will never drive away. For I have come down from heaven not to do my will but to do the will of Him who sent me. And this is the will of Him who sent me that I shall lose none of all that He has given me, but raise them up at the last day. For my Father's will is that everyone who looks to the Son and believes in him shall have eternal life, and I will raise him up at the last day." (John 6:35-40)

I [Jesus] am the resurrection and the life. He who believes in me will live, even though he dies; and whoever lives and believes in me will never die. (John 11:25b, 26a)

We overcome through living in the Spirit

Paul had much to say about turning our back on the world and putting to death our earthly nature. Our salvation is by faith alone, but it doesn't mean works are unimportant. We are called to a holy life. Holiness in our deeds helps us keep in step with the Spirit.

In his book, *Mere Christianity*, C. S. Lewis writes he had previously assumed that if a human mind once accepts a thing as true, the person would automatically go on regarding it as true until some real reason for reconsideration emerges. Lewis had assumed that the human mind is ruled by reason, but he eventually concluded his assumption was incorrect. He realized there is a battle between faith and reason on one side and emotion [passion] and imagination on the other. **(1)**

Supposing a man's reason had once decided that the weight of evidence argues for the truth of Christianity. Lewis concluded that in the following few weeks, the man's emotions would rise up and make an attempt to destroy his beliefs. Lewis wasn't referring to any real new grounds for losing his convictions. He was talking about moments when the man's mood rises up against his logic. **(2)**

Let me give an example of the conflict that can occur when a person's mood rises up against his/her logic. In chapter eight, I mentioned my first book, *Finding Strength in Weakness*. I wrote that book during my wife's long illness with breast cancer. The book was written in order for me to work through my own pain and to be an encouragement to others. The conflict between reason and emotion is illustrated in a card I received from a lady who was reading the book. She was in the emotional aftermath of a personal disaster that affected her and her whole family. The letter reads in part as follows: "I read up to the early section which describes how people can feel God has abandoned them. I had to lay the book down and cry for many minutes before I could resume reading. I don't know how I can be so torn - to know so clearly with my head that God is here and at work for Good and to feel so deeply betrayed in my heart...this card is to let you know you have ministered to my spirit in a time of anguish and trouble."

Lewis said faith is the art of holding on to things a person's reason has once accepted as true in spite of his/her changing moods. This rebellion of a man's moods against his real self will come sooner or later anyway; that rebellion is why faith is such a necessary virtue. **(3)**

The first step is to recognize the fact that moods will change. The next step is to be sure that some of the main doctrines of Christianity are held before a person's mind for some time every day through prayer, religious readings, and church attendance. Lewis says that we need to be continually reminded of what we believe. Neither our Christian beliefs nor any other will automatically remain alive in our minds. They must be fed. **(4)**

We cannot discover our inability to keep God's law except by trying our very hardest and then failing. This effort leads up to the vital moment when we turn to God and say, "You must do this; I can't." The sense in which a Christian leaves it to God is that he puts all his trust in Christ: trusts that Christ will somehow share with him the perfect human obedience which He carried out from His birth to His crucifixion: that Christ will make the man more like Himself and, in a sense, make good his deficiencies. **(5)**

And, in yet another sense, handing everything over to Christ does not, of course, mean that a man stops trying. To trust Jesus means, of course, trying to do all that He says. There would be no sense in saying a man trusted a person if he would not take the person's advice. Thus, if he really handed himself over to Jesus, it must follow that he is trying to obey Him. But he is trying in a new way, a less worried way. Not doing these things in order to be saved, but because Jesus has begun to save the man already. Not hoping to get to heaven as a reward for his actions, but inevitably wanting to act in a certain way because a first faint gleam of heaven is already inside him. **(6)**

Christians have often disputed as to whether what leads the Christian home [to heaven] is good actions or faith in Christ. It does seem to Lewis like asking which blade in a pair of scissors is most necessary. One set of Christians is accused of saying, "Good actions are all that matters." The other set is accused of saying, "Faith is all that matters." The Bible really seems to clinch the matter when it puts the two things together in one amazing sentence. In the first part it looks as if everything depends on us and our good actions. In the second part it looks as if God does everything, and we do nothing. **(7)**

…continue to work out your salvation with fear and trembling, for it is God who works in you to will and to act according to his good purpose. (Philippians 2:12b, 13)

According to Lewis, some people try to understand and separate into compartments, exactly what God does and what man does when God and man are working together. God is not like that. He is inside us as well as outside. **(8)**

In order to have control over our passions, we must draw upon God's power. One mechanism is through reasoning.

In seems to me that to be effectual, our reasoning has to be based on our study of the word of God and guided by the Holy Spirit. The process of sanctification requires God's power, but we must be intentional in our cooperation with Him. I've heard Ravi Zacharias say that we can train our appetites. We can also train our habits.

When we become angry, we experience the battle between reason and emotion. In order to overcome anger, we must allow our faith to overcome the fire kindled by our passions. The power for victory in this setting is the Holy Spirit. To have the Holy Spirit at work in our lives requires obedience to the commands of God. When we come to Jesus for help with our anger, He doesn't want to just deal with our anger; He wants to deal with all of our sin. Let us consider some other sources to gain additional insight about the tension that exists between passion, on the one hand, and reason on the other.

The definition of passion as found in Webster's New Collegiate Dictionary includes the following meanings:

1. Emotion
2. The emotions as distinguished from reason
3. An intense, driving, or overmastering feeling
4. An outbreak of anger
5. Ardent affection or love
6. A strong liking for or devotion to some activity, object, or concept **(9)**

Passion, fervor, ardor, enthusiasm, and zeal each have a shared meaning element: intense emotion compelling action. **(10)**

For when we were controlled by the sinful nature, the sinful passions aroused by the law were at work in our bodies, so that we bore fruit for death. (Romans 7:5)

One Greek word for passion is pathos. According to Bauer, Arndt, and Gingrich, the word also may refer to that which is endured or experienced, i.e. suffering. The word is used in reference to the physical sufferings of Christ. Pathos may also refer to other kinds of passion, especially of a sexual nature, such as lustful passion, or disgraceful passions. **(11)**

In *Hatch and Redpath's Corcordance to the Septuagint*, the Greek word *pathos* is shown to occur only twice in the Old Testament, in Job 30:31 and Proverbs 25:20. However, in IV Maccabees, a book in the Apocrypha, the word *pathos*, in one form or another, is used 63 times. **(12)** First, let me offer some disclaimers about IV Maccabees:

1. The book was written during the 400 years between the Old and New Testaments. Protestants do not count the Apocrypha as part of the canon of scripture.

2. During this time period, there were no prophets from God.

3. Prior to the day of Pentecost, there was no indwelling of the Holy Spirit.

There appears to be some wisdom in the book, and it seems prudent to consider what it says. This translation of the Septuagint into English was carried out by Sir Lancelot C.L. Brenton in 1851. **(13)** IV Maccabees tells us that we should be able to control our passions through reason.

If, then, reasoning appears to hold the mastery over the passions which stand in the way of temperance, such as gluttony and lust, it surely also and manifestly has the rule over affections which are contrary to justice, such as malice; and of those which are hindrances to manliness, as wrath, and pain and fear. (IV Maccabees 1:3, 4)

Wrath is an affection, common to pleasure and to pain, if anyone will pay attention when it comes upon him. And there exists in pleasure a malicious disposition, which is the most multiform of all the affections. In the soul it is arrogance, and love of money, and vaingloriousness [doing things to be noticed or appreciated], and contention, and faithlessness, and the evil eye [an eye or glance held capable of inflicting harm]. In the body it is greediness and gormandizing [devouring food gluttonously], and solitary gluttony. As pleasure and pain are, therefore, two growths of the body and the soul, so there are many offshoots of these passions. And reasoning, the universal husbandman, purging, and pruning these severally, and binding round, and watering, and transplanting, in every way improves the materials of the morals and affections. For reasoning is the leader of the virtues, but it is the sole ruler of the passions. (IV Maccabees 1:24-30a)

Now temperance consists of a command over the lusts. But of the lusts, some belong to the soul, others to the body: and over each of these classes the reasoning appears to bear sway. For whence is it, otherwise, that when urged on to forbidden meats, we reject the gratification which would ensue from them? Is it not because reasoning is able to command the appetites? I believe so. (IV Maccabees 1:31-35)

To *punch someone's buttons* has both anger provoking and sexual connotations. The thing common to both is passion.

177

Consider some New Testament passages about passion.

Now to the unmarried and the widows I say: It is good for them to stay unmarried, as I am. But if they cannot control themselves, they should marry, for it is better to marry than to burn with passion. (I Corinthians 7:8, 9)

The Greek word for burn with passion in I Corinthians 7:9 is the verb *puroo* meaning to set on fire or burn up. It can literally mean to burn. But figuratively it can also mean to burn or be inflamed with sympathy, readiness to aid, or indignation. It can mean to burn with sexual desire. The word may also mean to make red hot, cause to glow, or heat thoroughly...by such heating precious metals are tested and refined...[it] makes a comparison between the refining influence of fire on metals with the effect that fiery trials have in removing impurities from Christians. **(14)**

As noted in the previous paragraph, passion can have a good connotation (sympathy, readiness to aid). When talking with seminary students about their life goals, Howard Hendrix used to ask them, "What is your passion? What do you like to do? What keeps you awake at night?"

Those who belong to Christ Jesus have crucified the sinful nature with its passions and desires. (Galatians 5:24)

For the grace of God that brings salvation has appeared to all men. It teaches us to say "No" to ungodliness and worldly passions, and to live self-controlled, upright and godly lives in this present age, (Titus 2:11, 12)

At one time we too were foolish, disobedient, deceived and enslaved by all kinds of passions and pleasures. We lived in malice and envy, being hated and hating one another. (Titus 3:3)

The Greek word for passionate or passions in I Thessalonians 4:3 and Titus 2:12 and 3:3 is *epithymia*. According to Bauer, Arndt, and Gingrich, the word can be used in several ways. As a neutral term, the word can mean desire for much business. In a good sense, it means eagerly desire or great longing. Used in a bad sense as a desire for something forbidden. **(15)**

As obedient children, do not conform to the evil desires you had when you lived in ignorance. But just as he who called you is holy, so be holy in all you do: for it is written: "Be holy, because I am holy." (I Peter 1:14-16)

The Mind

Neuroscientists have discovered that the human brain operates very much like a personal computer. Whatever we record or program into our human computer's memory remains there indefinitely until it is removed or replaced. Everything we perceive through our five senses is programmed into our subconscious minds, as are our thoughts. It is the brain's responsibility to take care of us, and it does so by how it responds to what it perceives and what it remembers. **(16)** Unfortunately, in the natural man, much of what the brain does is flawed.

Please allow me to explain three Hebrew words from the Old Testament and three Greek words used in the New Testament that may refer to the mind.

The Hebrew word Leb is translated heart, mind, or midst. *Leb* may refer to the organ of the body called the heart, but *Leb* may also refer to the inner part or middle of a thing **(17)**, e.g. "deep in the heart of Texas." The understanding of the meaning of the word in the individual verses where it is used depends on the context. A related word, *Lebab*, can be used of the inner man, as contrasted to the outer man. **(18)**

"Lebab is often compounded with *'soul'* for emphasis, as in II Chronicles 15:12; 'and they entered into a covenant to seek the Lord God of their fathers with all their heart and with all their soul'" (cf. II Chronicles 15:15). **(19)**

In his *Theological Wordbook of the Old Testament*, R. Laird Harris puts *leb* and *lebab* together under the same heading and writes,

Concrete meanings of leb referred to the internal organ and to analogous physical

179

locations. However, in its abstract meanings, "heart" became the richest biblical term for the totality of man's inner or immaterial nature. In biblical literature it is the most frequently used term for man's immaterial personality functions as well as the most inclusive term for them since, in the Bible, virtually every immaterial function of man is attributed to the "heart." **(20)**

According to the *Hebrew to English Index – Lexicon of the Old Testament* in the *NIV Exhaustive Concordance*, the Hebrew word *leb* is used 600 times in the Old Testament. The word is translated *heart* 310 times, *hearts* 74 times, *mind* 21 times, and *judgment* 11 times. All the other English words used to translate *leb* occur ten times or less. **(21)**

Nepesh, life, soul, creature, person, appetite, mind **(22)** is translated 'heart' fifteen times in the KJV. Each time it connotes the 'inner man': 'For as he thinketh in his heart [*nepesh*], so is he' (Proverbs 23:7). **(23)** Harris writes that the original, concrete meaning of the word was probably "to breathe." The word can refer to one's spiritual/volitional appetite, that is, "desire" or "will." It is frequently used in connection with the emotional states of joy and bliss. Since personal existence by its very nature involves drives, appetites, desires, and will, *napesh* denotes the "life" of an individual. It is also equivalent to "self." The word *nepesh* is used 755 times in the Old Testament. In the *Septuagint*, it is translated 600 times by the Greek word *psyche* (English word *soul*). In its most synthetic use *nepesh* stands for the entire person. **(24)** Regarding the Greek word *psyche*, Bauer Arndt, and Gingrich write, "It is often impossible to draw hard and fast lines between the meanings of this many-sided word." **(25)**

Nous is a Greek word for mind. Speaking generally, the word denotes the seat of reflective consciousness, comprising the faculties of perception and understanding, and those of feeling, judging, and determining. The word *nous* denotes the faculty of knowing, the seat of understanding. **(26)**

Dianoia, another Greek word for mind means literally, a thinking through, or over, a meditation, reflecting. It signifies, like *nous*, the faculty of knowing, understanding, or moral reflection. **(27)**

Kardia, the Greek word for heart, is the name for the chief organ of physical life. By an easy transition the word came to stand for man's entire mental and moral activity [including the mind], both the rational and emotional elements. **(28)**

Let us consider the condition of the heart of natural man and how it is able to transition to the heart of a mature believer.

The mind of unregenerate man is unenlightened. He cannot comprehend the truth.

Unregenerate man is unenlightened; a man's spiritual blindness may even be purposeful. His darkened heart has learned ways of living and dealing with life that are ungodly and counterproductive.

But to this day the Lord has not given you a mind that understands or eyes that see or ears that hear. (Deuteronomy 29:4)

But my [the Lord's] people would not listen to me; Israel would not submit to me. So I gave them over to their stubborn hearts to follow their own devices. (Psalm 81:11, 12)

The heart is deceitful above all things and beyond cure. Who can understand it? (Jeremiah 17:9)

Woe to them [the people of Ephraim, i. e. the Northern kingdom of Israel] because they have strayed from me [the Lord]! Destruction to them, because they have rebelled against me! I long to redeem them but they speak lies against me. They do not cry out to me with their hearts but wail upon their beds. (Hosea 7:13, 14a)

The disciples came to him [Jesus] and asked, "Why do you speak to the people in parables?" He replied, "The knowledge of the secrets of the kingdom of heaven has been given to you, but not to them. Whoever has will be given more, and he will have an abundance. Whoever does not have, even what he has will be taken from him. This is why I speak to them in parables: "Though seeing, they do not see; though hearing, they do not understand." In them is fulfilled the prophecy of Isaiah: "'You will be ever hearing but never understanding; you will be ever seeing but never perceiving. For this people's heart has become calloused; they hardly hear with their ears, and they have closed their eyes. Otherwise they might see with their eyes, and hear with their ears, understand with their hearts and turn, and I would heal them."" (Matthew 13:10-15)

Furthermore, since they [godless and wicked men] did not think it worthwhile to retain the knowledge of God, he gave them over to a depraved mind, to do what ought not to be done. (Romans 1:28)

As for you, you were dead in your transgressions and sins, in which you used to live when you followed the ways of this world and the ruler of the kingdom of the air, the spirit who is now at work in those who are disobedient. All of us also lived among them at one time, gratifying the cravings of our sinful nature and following its desires and thoughts. Like the rest, we were by nature objects of wrath. (Ephesians 2:1-3)

They [the Gentiles] are darkened in their understanding and separated from the life of God because of the ignorance that is in them due to the hardening of their hearts. Having lost all sensitivity, they have given themselves over to sensuality so as to indulge in every kind of impurity, with a continual lust for more. (Ephesians 4:18, 19)

Do not let anyone who delights in false humility and worship of angels disqualify you for the prize. Such a person goes into great detail about what he has seen, and his unspiritual mind puffs him up with idle notions. (Colossians 2:18)

If anyone teaches false doctrines and does not agree to the sound instruction of our Lord Jesus Christ and to godly teaching, he is conceited and understands nothing. He has an unhealthy interest in controversies and quarrels about words that result in envy, strife, malicious talk, evil suspicions and constant friction between men of corrupt mind, who have been robbed of the truth and who think that godliness is a means to financial gain. (I Timothy 6:5)

But mark this: There will be terrible times in the last days. People will be lovers of themselves, lovers of money, boastful, proud, abusive, disobedient to their parents, ungrateful, unholy, without love, unforgiving, slanderous, without self-control, brutal, not lovers of the good, treacherous, rash, conceited, lovers of pleasure rather than lovers of God – having a form of godliness but denying its power. Have nothing to do with them. They are the kind who worm their way into homes and gain control over weak-willed women, who are loaded down with sins and are swayed by all kinds of evil desires, always learning but never able to come to knowledge of the truth. Just as Jannes and Jambres opposed Moses, so also these men oppose the truth – men of depraved minds, who, as far as their faith in concerned, are rejected. (II Timothy 3:1-8)

To the pure, all things are pure, but to these who are corrupted and do not believe, nothing is pure. In fact, both their minds and consciences are corrupted. They claim to know God, but by their actions they deny him. They are detestable, disobedient and unfit for doing anything good. (Titus 1:15, 16)

The Holy Spirit helps the elect understand the truth and then gives them the power to act on it.

Before we can be saved, the Holy Spirit must prepare our hearts. When we are saved, the Holy Spirit comes into our bodies, hearts, and spirits and begins to make changes.

I [the Lord] will give them [the Israelites] an undivided heart and put a new spirit in them; I will remove from them their heart of stone and give them a heart of flesh. Then they will follow my decrees and be careful to keep my laws. They will be my people, and I will be their God. (Ezekiel 11:19, 20)

Listen then to what the parable of the sower means: When anyone hears the message about the kingdom and does not understand it, the evil one comes and snatches away what was sown in his heart. This is the seed sown along the path. The one who received the seed that fell on rocky places is the man who hears the word and at once receives it with joy. But since he has no root, he lasts only a short time. When trouble or persecution comes because of the word, he quickly falls away. The one who received the seed that fell among the thorns is the man who hears the word, but the worries of this life and the deceitfulness of wealth choke it, making it unfruitful. But the one who received the seed that fell on good soil is the man who hears the word and understands it. He produces a crop, yielding a hundred, sixty or thirty times what was sown. (Matthew 13:18-23)

I believe the reason the last man produced a crop is because he understood the message. The Holy Spirit had prepared his heart.

After the resurrection, Jesus had to open the minds of the disciples so they could understand the Scriptures.

Then he [Jesus] opened their [the disciples'] minds so they could understand the Scriptures. He told them, "This is what is written: The Christ will suffer and rise from the dead on the third day, and repentance and forgiveness of sins will be preached in his name to all nations, beginning at Jerusalem. You are witnesses of these things." (Luke 24:45-48)

There are other references to spiritual enlightenment and empowerment in the epistles.

I [Paul] keep asking that the God of our Lord Jesus Christ, the glorious Father, may give you the Spirit of wisdom and revelation, so that you may know him better. I pray also that the eyes of your heart may be enlightened in order that you may know the hope to which he has called you, the riches of his glorious inheritance in the saints... (Ephesians 1:17, 18)

For this reason, since the day we heard about you, we have not stopped praying for you and asking God to fill you with the knowledge of his will through all spiritual wisdom and understanding. And we pray this in order that you may live a life worthy of the Lord and may please him in every way: bearing fruit in every good work, growing in the knowledge of God... (Colossians 1:9, 10)

With this in mind, we constantly pray for you, that our God may count you worthy of his calling, and that by his power he may fulfill every good purpose of yours and every act prompted by your faith. (II Thessalonians 1:11)

We know also that the Son of God has come and has given us understanding, so that we may know him who is true. (I John 5:20a)

We must cooperate with the Holy Spirit as He works to make us holy. For those changes that God wants to make in our lives to be effective, we must do our part in the struggle. Romans chapter 6 speaks of our struggle for holiness. In *Believer's Bible Commentary, New Testament,* William MacDonald calls Romans 6 "The Gospel's Way to Holy Living." He writes as follows:

"It will help us to follow Paul's argument in this chapter if we understand the difference between the believer's position and his practice. His position is his standing in Christ. His practice is what he is or should be in everyday life.

Grace puts us into the position, then teaches us to walk worthy of it. Our position is absolutely perfect because we are in Christ. Our practice should increasingly correspond to our position. It never will correspond perfectly until we see the Savior in heaven, but we should be becoming more and more conformed to His image in the meantime...

It has been helpfully suggested that there are four answers in the chapter to the initial question, Shall we continue in sin?

1. You cannot, because you are united to Christ. Reasoning (vv. 1-11).
2. You need not, because sin's dominion has been broken by grace. Appealing (vv. 12-14).
3. You must not, because it would bring sin in again as your master. Commanding (vv. 15-19).
4. You had better not, for it would end in disaster. Warning (vv. 20-23)." **(29)**

Consider some selected quotations from Romans. Please note the only thing we, as Christians, have any control of in these passages is our obedience. Salvation is by faith alone, but after we are saved, we are required to be obedient to God's Word. In order to be able to obey, we must do so in the power of the Spirit.

True faith produces obedience.

Through him and for his name's sake, we received grace and apostleship to call people from among all the Gentiles to the obedience that comes from faith. (Romans 1:5)

Obedience leads to righteousness.

Don't you know that when you offer yourselves to someone to obey him as slaves, you are slaves to the one whom you obey – whether you are slaves to sin, which leads to death, or to obedience, which leads to righteousness? (Romans 6:16)

According to Bauer, Arndt, and Gingrich, the Greek word *dikaiosunee*, translated *righteousness* in Romans 6:16, means uprightness or justice. The word means righteousness in the sense of fulfilling the divine statutes. Righteousness means character or quality of being right or just, whatever conforms to the revealed will of God. The word can refer to the practice of piety. It means to do what is right. It has to do with righteousness or uprightness as the compelling motive for the conduct of one's whole life. **(30)**

Righteousness leads to holiness.

I put this in human terms because you are weak in your natural selves. Just as you used to offer the parts of your body in slavery to impurity and to ever-increasing wickedness, so now offer them in slavery to righteousness leading to holiness. (Romans 6:19)

The Greek word for holiness in Romans 6:19 is *hagiasmos*, meaning holiness, consecration, or sanctification, the state of being made holy. **(31)** Holiness has to do with the state of being separated or set apart to God. The word *holiness* describes a changed nature, a sanctified heart.

Holiness leads to eternal life.

But now that you have been set free from sin and have become slaves to God, the benefit you reap leads to holiness, and the result is eternal life. (Romans 6:22)

Offering parts of our body in slavery to righteousness and becoming slaves to God mean the same thing. Doing what is right helps along the path to holiness (see John 15:1-17).

Consider these words in James about faith and actions working together.

What good is it, my brothers, if a man claims to have faith but has no deeds? Can such faith save him? Suppose a brother or sister is without clothes and daily food. If one of you says to him, "Go, I wish you well; keep warm and well fed," but does nothing about his physical needs, what good is it? In the same way, faith by itself, if it is not accompanied by action, is dead. But someone will say, "You have faith; I have deeds. Show me your faith without deeds, and I will show you my faith by what I do. You believe there is one God. Good! Even the demons believe that – and shudder. You foolish man, do you want evidence that faith without deeds is useless? Was not our ancestor Abraham considered righteous for what he did when he offered his son Isaac on the altar? You see that his faith and his actions were working together, and *his faith was made complete by what he did.* And the scripture was fulfilled that says, 'Abraham believed God, and it was credited to him as righteousness,' and he was called God's friend. You see that a person is justified by what he does and not by faith alone." (James 2:14-24)

186

The italics in James 2:22 were added for emphasis.

I've heard John Patrick say that freedom means something different to those in the world and to us as believers. People in the world believe that being free means that an individual can do what he wants, as he pleases. In the Christian tradition, freedom means a person becomes free from the tyranny of sin and is free to do what he knows he should do.

We are to live by the Spirit.

So, my brothers, you also died to the law through the body of Christ, so you might belong to another, to him who was raised from the dead, in order that we might bear fruit to God. For when we were controlled by the sinful nature, the sinful passions aroused by the law were at work in our bodies, so that we bore fruit for death. But now, by dying to what once bound us, we have been released from the law so that we serve in a new way of the Spirit, and not in the old way of the written code. (Romans 7:4-6)

So I say, live by the Spirit, and you will not gratify the desires of the sinful nature. For the sinful nature desires what is contrary to the Spirit, and the Spirit what is contrary to the sinful nature. They are in conflict with each other, so that you do not do what you want. But if you are led by the Spirit, you are not under the law. (Galatians 5:16-18)

Since we live by the Spirit, let us keep in step with the Spirit. (Galatians 5:25)

When I was in college, I was taught to report to the Lord for duty every morning. I was taught to turn the day over to Him and expect

Him to take it and use it for His glory. Praying such a prayer does more for me than giving myself a pep talk.

There are many ways we can cooperate with the Spirit.

First, we must be sure we are in the family of God, and after salvation, remain in fellowship with Him. Examine yourselves to see whether you are in the faith; test yourselves. Do you not realize that Christ Jesus is in you – unless, of course, you fail the test? (II Corinthians 13:5)

187

Each one should test his own actions. (Galatians 6:4a)

For the Christian, if an individual is sure he/she is truly saved, and then becomes aware of a sin problem in his/her life, it's time to recognize that sin problem and repent. This is not about losing and regaining salvation; it's about falling away from and then returning into a vibrant relationship with God.

According to Bauer, Arndt, and Gingrich, the Greek word for repent is *metanoeoo*. It means change one's mind. It means feel remorse, repent, or be converted. It may mean turn away from something. **(32)** Vine says the word literally means to perceive afterwards "(meta, after, implying change, *noeo*, to perceive; nous, the mind, the seat of moral reflection), in contrast to *pronoeo* to perceive beforehand, hence signifies to change one's mind or purpose, always in the New Testament, involving a change for the better, an amendment, and always, except in Luke 17:3, 4, of repentance from sin." **(33)** The noun *metanoia* is used of repentance from sin or evil, except in Hebrews 12:17, where the word "repentance" seems to mean, not simply a change in Isaac's mind, but such a change as would reverse the effects of his own previous state of mind. Esau's birthright-bargain could not be recalled; it involved an irretrievable loss. **(34)**

Repentance from sin is necessary both for an unbeliever to come to Christ and for a believer, who is made aware of a sin problem, to make things right with God.

The requirement for repentance, on man's part, is set forth in several verses.

John the Baptist: "Produce fruit in keeping with repentance." (Matthew 3:8; Luke 3:8)

Paul: "I have declared to both Jews and Greeks that they must turn to God in repentance and have faith in our Lord Jesus." (Acts 20:21)

When the Holy Spirit convicts individuals of sin, that is God's gift to us. When we respond in repentance, that response is also God's gift to us.

The God of our fathers raised Jesus from the dead – whom you [members of the Sanhedrin] had killed by hanging him on a tree. God exalted him to his own right hand as Prince and Savior that he might give repentance and forgiveness of sins to Israel. We are witnesses of these things, and so is the Holy Spirit, whom God has given to those who obey him. (Acts 5:30-32)

When they [the circumcised believers in Jerusalem] heard this [that the Gentiles at Cornelius' house had received the Holy Spirit], they had no further objections and praised God saying, "So then God has granted even the Gentiles repentance unto life." (Acts 11:18)

Or do you [the saints in Rome] show contempt for the riches of his kindness, tolerance and patience, not realizing that God's kindness leads you toward repentance? (Romans 2:4)

Those who oppose him [the Lord's servant] he must gently instruct, in the hope that God will grant them repentance leading to a knowledge of the truth, and that they will come to their senses and escape the trap of the devil, who has taken them captive to do his will. (II Timothy 2:25, 26)

Vine writes,

In the New Testament the subject chiefly has reference to repentance from sin, and this change of mind involves both a turning from sin and a turning to God. The parable of the prodigal son is an outstanding example of this. Christ began His ministry with a call to repentance, Matthew 4:17, but the call is addressed, not as in the Old Testament to the nation, but to the individual. **(35)**

Consider some other verses about repentance.

Then Jesus began to denounce the cities in which most of his miracles had been performed, because they did not repent. (Matthew 11:20)

Jesus: "For John came to you [the chief priests and elders] to show you the way of righteousness, and you did not believe him, but the tax collectors and prostitutes did, and even after you saw this, you did not repent and believe him. (Matthew 21:32)

After John was put in prison, Jesus went into Galilee, proclaiming the good news of God. "The time has come," he said. "The kingdom of God is near. Repent and believe the good news!" (Mark: 1:14, 15)

They [the Twelve] went out and preached that people should repent. (Mark 6:12)

189

I [Jesus] have not come to call the righteous, but sinners to repentance. (Luke 5:32)

Now there were some present at that time who told Jesus about the Galileans whose blood Pilate had mixed with their sacrifices [killed]. Jesus answered, "do you think that these Galileans were worse sinners than all the other Galileans because they suffered this way? I tell you, no! But unless you repent, you too will all perish. Or those eighteen who died when the tower in Siloam fell on them – do you think they were more guilty than all the others living in Jerusalem? I tell you, no! But unless you repent, you too will all perish." (Luke 13:1-5)

Jesus, at the end of the parable of the lost sheep: "I tell you that in the same way there will be more rejoicing in heaven over one sinner who repents than over ninety-nine righteous persons who do not need to repent." (Luke 15:7)

He [Jesus] told them, "This is what is written: The Christ will suffer and rise from the dead on the third day, and repentance and forgiveness of sins will be preached in his name to all nations, beginning at Jerusalem." (Luke 24:45-47)

Peter replied, "Repent and be baptized, every one of you, in the name of Jesus Christ for the forgiveness of your sins. And you will receive the gift of the Holy Spirit. The promise is for you and your children and for all who are far off – for all whom the Lord our God will call." (Acts 2:38, 39)

Therefore since we are God's offspring, we should not think that the divine being is like gold or silver or stone – an image made by man's design and skill. In the past God overlooked such ignorance, but now he commands all people everywhere to repent. For he has set a day when he will judge the world with justice by the man he has appointed. He has given proof of this to all men by raising him from the dead. (Acts 17:29-31)

Paul: "So then King Agrippa, I was not disobedient to the vision from heaven. First to those in Damascus, then to those in Jerusalem and in all Judea, and to the Gentiles also, I preached that they should repent and turn to God and prove their repentance by their deeds." (Acts 26:19, 20)

Even if I [Paul] caused you sorrow by my letter [I Corinthians], I do not regret it. Though I did regret it - I see that my letter hurt you, but only for a little while – yet now I am happy, not because you were made sorry, but because your sorrow led you to repentance. For you became sorrowful as God intended and so were not harmed in any way by us. Godly sorrow brings repentance that leads to salvation and leaves no regret, but worldly sorrow brings death. (II Corinthians 7:8-10)

The Lord is not slow in keeping his promise, as some understand slowness. He is patient with you, not wanting to perish, but everyone to come to repentance. (II Peter 3:9)

Jesus to the church in Laodicea: "Those whom I love I rebuke and discipline, so be earnest and repent." (Revelation 3:19)

The rest of mankind that were not killed by these plagues [after the sixth angel who sounded his trumpet] still did not repent of the work of their hands; they did not stop worshipping demons, and idols of gold, silver, bronze, stone and wood – idols that cannot see or hear or walk. Nor did they repent of their murders, their magic arts, their sexual immorality or their thefts. (Revelation 9:20, 21)

The fourth angel poured out his bowl on the sun, and the sun was given power to scorch people with fire. They were seared by the intense heat and they cursed the name of God, who had control over these plagues, but they refused to repent and glorify him. The fifth angel poured out his bowl on the throne of the beast, and his kingdom was plunged into darkness. Men gnawed their tongues in agony and cursed the God of heaven because of their pains and their sores, but they refused to repent of what they had done. (Revelation 16:8-11)

Observations from these last sixteen passages:

Jesus performed many miracles, but often people did not repent. Except for a few of them, the religious leaders of Jesus' day did not repent. Jesus preached that the kingdom of God was near; people were to repent and believe the good news. It is not the righteous but sinners who are called to repentance. Affliction comes to both the righteous and sinners; it is a warning to people that judgment is coming. If people don't repent of their sin, they will perish. Heaven rejoices when a sinner repents. It was prophesied that Christ would suffer and rise from the dead on the third day; repentance and forgiveness of sin would be preached to all nations. Repentance and baptism, in the name of Jesus Christ, were preached for the forgiveness of sins; the people would receive the gift of the Holy Spirit. The promise was for them, their children, and many who were in distant lands, for all whom the Lord would call. God commands all people, everywhere to repent. The day is coming when Jesus will judge the world; His resurrection proves the truth of His message. Paul was not disobedient to the vision from heaven; he preached

191

repentance, turning to God, and *people proving their repentance by their deeds*. Godly sorrow [for sins] brings repentance that leads to salvation and leaves no regret. The spiritual benefits make the sorrow worthwhile. Worldly sorrow brings death. The Lord is patient, wanting everyone to come to repentance. The Lord rebukes and disciplines those He loves, so people should be earnest and repent. Despite severe affliction, some people refuse to repent. In my view, they don't want to bow the knee.

To live in the Spirit, we must program new information into our brains.

Much of the new information we send into our brains replaces the old, faulty information. We must develop a new set of habits. I believe it is safe to assume that anything we do in obedience to Jesus Christ reprograms our brains in a positive way; sin has the opposite effect. Consider the references to the bad information that may be written on or contained within our hearts.

Judah's sin is engraved with an iron tool, inscribed with a flint point, on the tablets of their hearts and on the horns of their altars. (Jeremiah 17:1)

Make a tree good and its fruit will be good, or make a tree bad and its fruit will be bad, for a tree is recognized by its fruit. You brood of vipers, how can you who are evil say anything good? For out of the overflow of the heart the mouth speaks. The good man brings good things out of the good stored up in him, and the evil man brings evil things out of the evil stored up in him. (Matthew 12:33-35)

There are several references on the programming of right information into our hearts.

These commandments that I [the Lord] give you [the Israelites] today are to be upon your hearts. Impress them on your children. Talk about them when you sit at home and when you walk along the road, when you lie down and when you get up. (Deuteronomy 6:6, 7)

Circumcise your hearts, therefore, and do not be stiff-necked any longer. (Deuteronomy 10:16)

According to R. Laird Harris, circumcision symbolized God's covenant with Abraham and his descendants. It was the mark of submission to the sovereign will of God. **(36)**

Consider these words of wisdom, as she is personified in the book of Proverbs, as she speaks to the simple ones, the mockers, and the fools.

My son, if you accept my words and store up my commands within you, turning your ear to wisdom and applying your heart to understanding, and if you call out for insight and cry aloud for understanding, and if you look for it as silver and search for it as hidden treasure, then you will understand the fear of the Lord and find the knowledge of God... Then you will understand what is right and just and fair – every good path. For wisdom will enter your heart, and knowledge will be pleasant to your soul. (Proverbs 2:1-5, 9, 10)

Let love and faithfulness never leave you; bind them around your neck; write them on the tablet of your heart. (Proverbs 3:3)
My son, keep my words and store up my commands within you. Keep my commands and you will live; guard my teachings as the apple of your eye. Bind them on your fingers; write them on the tablet of your heart. (Proverbs 7:1-3)

There are many other references to providing our hearts with new information.

Apply your heart to instruction and your ears to words of knowledge. (Proverbs 23:12)

"This is the covenant I will make with the house of Israel after that time," declares the Lord. "I will put my law in their minds and write it on their hearts." (Jeremiah 31:33)

Therefore, I urge you, brothers, in view of God's mercy, to offer your bodies as living sacrifices, holy and pleasing to God – this is your spiritual act of worship. Do not conform any longer to the pattern of this world, but be transformed by the renewing of your mind. Then you will be able to test and approve what God's will is – his good, pleasing and perfect will. (Romans 12:1, 2)

As believers, we are to offer our bodies as living sacrifices, holy and pleasing to God – this is our spiritual act of worship. We are not to conform any longer to the pattern of the world. We are to be holy.

We are to be transformed by the renewing of our minds. In our own strength, we don't have the ability to renew our minds. That requires the power of the Holy Spirit. For the Holy Spirit to act in our lives, we must stay connected to the source of our spiritual power. Staying connected requires obedience, loving God, and loving others. (John 15)

The Holy Spirit is required for us to reprogram our brains and change our hearts. The Holy Spirit provides increased perception and understanding. He removes the old faulty information and gradually replaces it with the new - with spiritual maturity. We cooperate with the program by, among other things, keeping our minds on the things of the Spirit, studying the Scriptures, and experiencing mutual edification in community with friends of like-minded persuasion. We need to be circumspect. We are to be attentive, to be aware of what works for good in our lives and what doesn't. We must pay attention to the consequences of what we do. Jesus said, "Wisdom is proved right by all her children" (Luke 7:35). If we are prudent, we will be able to test and approve what God's will is – His good, pleasing, and perfect will. We will be able to experience His purpose for our lives.

It seems to me that in some ways, living the Christian life is like starting one's own business, going to college, or training as an athlete. There is an ongoing evaluation and reevaluation of what the person is doing. A person "tests the waters" again and again to find out what works and what doesn't work.

You show that you are a letter from Christ, the result of our ministry, written not with ink but with the Spirit of the living God, not on tablets of stone but on tablets of human hearts. (II Corinthians 3:3)

So I tell you this, and insist on it in the Lord, that you must no longer live as the Gentiles do, in the futility of their thinking. (Ephesians 4:17)

The Holy Spirit also testifies to us about this. First he says: "This is the covenant I will make with them after that time, says the Lord. I will put my laws in their hearts, and I will write them on their minds." (Hebrews 10:15, 16)

Come near to God and he will come near to you. Wash your hands, you sinners, and purify your hearts, you double-minded. (James 4:8)

In our everyday encounters, we can reinforce the good information written on our hearts or the bad. We can stay true to God's word and support the good information, or we can give in to temptation and augment the effect of the bad. For a person with anger issues, it reinforces bad behavior when we give in to our anger and react aggressively. There is something about the adrenaline rush and the feeling of power that reinforces the bad behavior.

For believers, the Bible gives several ways to replace the bad information programmed into our brains (onto our hearts). It's all part of learning to live in the Spirit.

1. Bible study and meditation.

The Bible tells us to abide in Jesus' word. (John 5:38; John 8:31; John 15:7; I John 2:14) Then we will know the truth, and the truth will set us free. (John 8:32) The Greek word for *abide* is *menoo*. The word is found it each of these four verses. It means to remain, stay, live, dwell, or lodge. **(37)** I take it to mean that we must study our Bibles and meditate on God's word; we must let it permeate our inner parts.

When he [the future king of Israel] takes the throne of his kingdom, he is to write for himself on a scroll a copy of this law, taken from that of the priests, who are Levites. It is to be with him, and he is to read it all the days of his life so that he may learn to revere the Lord his God and follow carefully all the words of this law and these decrees. (Deuteronomy 17:18, 19)

Words of the Lord to Joshua: "Be strong and very courageous. Be careful to obey all the law my servant Moses gave you; do not turn from it to the right or to the left, that you may be successful wherever you go. Do not let this Book of the Law depart from your mouth; meditate on it day and night, so that you may be careful to do everything written in it." (Joshua 1:7,8a)

How can a young man keep his way pure? By living according to your [the Lord's]

195

word. I seek you with all my heart; do not let me stray from your commands. I have hidden your word in my heart that I might not sin against you. (Psalm 119:9-11)

O how I love your law! I meditate on it all day long. Your commands make me wiser than my enemies, for they are ever with me. I have more insight than all my teachers, for I meditate on your statutes. I have more understanding than the elders, for I obey your precepts. (Psalm 119:97-100)

Do your best to present yourself to God as one approved, a workman who does not need to be ashamed and who correctly handles the word of truth. (II Timothy 2:15)

For the word of God is living and active. Sharper than any double-edged sword, it penetrates even to dividing soul and spirit, joints and marrow; it judges the thoughts and attitudes of the heart. (Hebrews 4:12)

2. Obedience.

Obedience to the precepts of Scripture is required if what we learn there is to help us.

Do not merely listen to the word, and so deceive yourselves. Do what it says. Anyone who listens to the word but does not do what it says is like a man who looks at his face in a mirror and, after looking at himself, goes away and immediately forgets what he looks like. But the man who looks intently into the perfect law that gives freedom, and continues to do this, not forgetting what he has heard, but doing it – he will be blessed in what he does. (James 1:22-25)

To live the Christian life as it should be lived, we must remain connected to the source of our spiritual power.

I [Jesus] am the vine; you are the branches. If a man remains in me and I in him, he will bear much fruit; apart from me you can do nothing... If you obey my commands, you will remain in my love, just as I have obeyed my Father's commands and remain in his love. (John 15: 5, 10)

Those who live according to the sinful nature have their minds set on what that nature desires; but those who live in accordance with the Spirit have their minds set on what the Spirit desires. The mind of sinful man is death, but the mind controlled by the Spirit is life and peace; the sinful mind is hostile to God. It does not submit to God's law, nor can it do so. Those controlled by the sinful nature cannot please God. You, however, are controlled not by the sinful nature but by the Spirit, if the Spirit of God lives in you. And if anyone does not have the Spirit of

Christ, he does not belong to Christ. But if Christ is in you, your body is dead because of sin, yet your spirit is alive because of righteousness. And if the Spirit of him who raised Jesus from the dead is living in you, he who raised Christ from the dead will also give life to your mortal bodies through his Spirit, who lives in you. Therefore, brothers, we have an obligation – but it is not to the sinful nature, to live according to it. For if you live according to the sinful nature, you will die; but if by the Spirit you put to death the misdeeds of the body, you will live, because those who are led by the Spirit of God are sons of God. (Romans 8:5-14)

So I tell you this, and insist on it in the Lord, that you must no longer live as the Gentiles do, in the futility of their thinking. They are darkened in their understanding and separated from the life of God because of the ignorance that is in them due to the hardening of their hearts. Having lost all sensitivity, they have given themselves over to sensuality so as to indulge in every kind of impurity, with a continual lust for more. You, however, did not come to know Christ that way. Surely you heard of him and were taught in him in accordance with the truth that is in Jesus. You were taught, with regard to your former way of life, to put off your old self, which is being corrupted by its deceitful desires; to be made new in the attitude of your minds; and to put on the new self, created to be like God in true righteousness and holiness. Therefore each of you must put off falsehood and speak truthfully to his neighbor, for we are members of one body. "In your anger do not sin": Do not let the sun go down while you are still angry, and do not give the devil a foothold. He who has been stealing must steal no longer, but must work, doing something useful with his own hands, that he may have something to share with those in need. Do not let any unwholesome talk come out of your mouths, but only what is helpful for building others up according to their needs, that it may benefit those who listen. And do not grieve the Holy Spirit of God, with whom you were sealed for the day of redemption. Get rid of all bitterness, rage and anger, brawling and slander, along with every form of malice. Be kind and compassionate to one another, forgiving each other, just as in Christ God forgave you. Be imitators of God, therefore, as dearly loved children and live a life of love, just as Christ loved us and gave himself up for us as a fragrant offering and sacrifice to God. But among you there must not even be a hint of sexual immorality, or any other kind of impurity, or of greed, because these are improper for God's holy people. Nor should there be obscenity, foolish talk or course joking, which are out of place, but rather thanksgiving. For of this you can be sure: no immoral, impure or greedy person - such a man is an idolater - has any inheritance in the kingdom of Christ and of God. Let no one deceive you with empty words, for because of such things God's wrath comes on those who are disobedient. Therefore do not be partners with them. For you were once darkness, but now you are light in the Lord. Live as children of light (for the fruit of the light consists in all goodness, righteousness and truth) and find out what pleases the Lord. Have nothing to do with the fruitless deeds of darkness, but rather expose them. For it is shameful even to mention what the disobedient do in secret. But everything exposed by the light becomes visible, for it is the light that makes everything visible. This is why it is said: "Wake up, O sleeper, rise from the dead, and Christ will shine on you." Be very careful, then, how you live - not as unwise but as wise, making the most of every opportunity, because the days are evil. Therefore do not be foolish, but understand what the Lord's will is. Do not get drunk on wine, which leads to debauchery. Instead, be filled with the Spirit. Speak to one another with psalms, hymns and spiritual songs. Sing and make music in your heart to the Lord, always giving thanks to God the Father for everything, in the name of our Lord Jesus Christ. Submit to one another out of reverence for Christ. (Ephesians 4:17-5:21)

Therefore prepare your minds for action; be self-controlled; set your hope fully on the grace to be given you when Jesus Christ is revealed. As obedient children, do not conform to the evil desires you had when you lived in ignorance. But just

as he who called you is holy, so be holy in all you do; for it is written: "Be holy, because I am holy." (I Peter 1:13-16)

Obedience includes controlling the tongue.

Therefore each of you must put off falsehood and speak truthfully to his neighbor, for we are all members of one body. (Ephesians 4:25)

Do not let any unwholesome talk come out of your mouths, but only what is helpful for building others up according to their needs, that it may benefit those who listen. (Ephesians 4:29)

Get rid of all bitterness, rage and anger, brawling and slander, along with every form of malice. (Ephesians 4:31)

Nor should there be obscenity, foolish talk or coarse joking, which are out of place, but rather thanksgiving. (Ephesians 5:4)

But now you must rid yourselves of all such things as these: anger, rage, malice, slander, and filthy language from your lips. Do not lie to each other, since you have taken off your old self with its practices and have put on the new self, which is being renewed in knowledge in the image of its creator. (Colossians 3:8-10)

If anyone considers himself religious and yet does not keep a tight rein on his tongue, he deceives himself and his religion is worthless. (James 1:26)

We all stumble in many ways. If anyone is never at fault in what he says, he is a perfect man, able to keep his whole body in check. (James 3:2)

Likewise the tongue is a small part of the body, but it makes great boasts. Consider what a great forest is set on fire by a small spark. The tongue also is a fire, a world of evil among the parts of the body. It corrupts the whole person, sets the whole course of his life on fire, and is itself set on fire by hell. (James 3:5, 6)

But no man can tame the tongue. It is a restless evil, full of deadly poison. (James 3:8)

3. Prayer.

As for me [Samuel], far be it me that I should sin against the Lord by failing to pray for you [Israelites]. (I Samuel 12:23a)

Look to the Lord and his strength; seek his face always. (I Chronicles 16:11)

Consider this verse from Psalm 86, a prayer of David.

Teach me your way, O Lord, and I will walk in your truth; give me an undivided heart, that I may fear your name. (Psalm 86:11)

Psalm 90 is a prayer of Moses.

Teach us to number our days aright, that we may gain a heart of wisdom. (Psalm 90:12)

Consider other passages from the Bible about prayer.

He who dwells in the shadow of the Most High will rest in the shadow of the Almighty. (Psalm 91:1)

But when you pray, go into your room, close the door and pray to your Father, who is unseen. Then your Father, who sees what is done in secret, will reward you. (Matthew 6:6)

Watch and pray so that you will not fall into temptation. The spirit is willing, but the body is weak. (Matthew 26:41)

Then Jesus told his disciples a parable to show them that they should always pray and not give up. (Luke 18:1)

Finally, "Be strong in the Lord and in his mighty power. Put on the full armor of God so that you can take your stand against the devil's schemes. For our struggle is not against flesh and blood, but against the rulers, against the authorities, against the powers of this dark world and against the spiritual forces of evil in the heavenly realms. Therefore put on the full armor of God, so that when the day of evil comes, you may be able to stand your ground, and after you have done everything, to stand. Stand firm then, with the belt of truth buckled around your waist, with the breastplate of righteousness in place, and with your feet fitted with the readiness that comes from the gospel of peace. In addition to all this, take up the shield of faith, with which you can extinguish all the flaming arrows of the evil one. Take the helmet of salvation and the sword of the Spirit, which is the word of God. And pray in the Spirit on all occasions with all kinds of prayers and requests. With this in mind, be alert and always keep on praying for all the saints." (Ephesians 6:10-18)

Devote yourselves to prayer, being watchful and thankful. (Colossians 4:2)
...pray continually... (I Thessalonians 5:17)

4. Crucifying the sinful nature.

Vine says that the Greek noun *stauros* meaning *cross* is metaphorically used of the renunciation of the world that characterizes the true Christian life. He also says that the verb *stauroo* signifies the act of crucifixion and is used metaphorically of the putting off of the flesh with its passions and lusts. A similar verb *sustauroo* is used metaphorically of spiritual identification with Christ in His death. **(38)**

For we know that our old self was crucified with him so that the body of sin might be done away with, that we should no longer be slaves to sin – because anyone who has died has been freed from sin. (Romans 6:6, 7)

Those who belong to Christ Jesus have crucified the sinful nature with its passions and desires. (Galatians 5:24)

You were taught, with regard to your former way of life, to put off your old self, which is being corrupted by its deceitful desires; to be made new in the attitude of your minds; and to put on the new self, created to be like God in true righteousness and holiness. (Ephesians 4:22-24)

Be imitators of God, therefore, as dearly loved children... (Ephesians 5:1)

Put to death, therefore, whatever belongs to your earthly nature: sexual immorality, impurity, lust, evil desires and greed, which is idolatry. (Colossians 3:5)

Do not lie to each other, since you have taken off your old self with its practices and put on the new self, which is being renewed in knowledge in the image of its Creator. (Colossians 3:9, 10)

Therefore, since we are surrounded by such a great cloud of witnesses, let us throw off everything that hinders and the sin that so easily entangles, and let us run with perseverance the race marked out for us. Let us fix our eyes on Jesus, the author and perfecter of our faith, who for the joy set before him endured the cross, scorning its shame, and sat down at the right hand of the throne of God.
Consider him who endured such opposition from sinful men, so that you will not grow weary and lose heart. (Hebrews 12:1-3)

We should be able to anticipate some of the problems that may come up related to our sinful natures. The five foolish virgins were expected to make provision for the oil needed for their lamps. (Matthew 25:1-13) Similarly, we should anticipate and make provision for our issues with anger. We ought to be able to reason through predictable situations ahead of time. It would also seem prudent to deal with underlying problems that may predispose to anger, such as unresolved grief, failure to set boundaries, or irresponsibility with money. (See chapter eleven)

5. Keeping our minds and hearts on the things of the Spirit, rather than the things of the sinful nature.

Those who live according to the sinful nature have their minds set on what that nature desires; but those who live according to the Spirit have their minds set on what the Spirit desires. (Romans 8:5)

The hour has come for you to wake up from your slumber, because our salvation is nearer now than when we first believed. The night is nearly over; the day is almost here. So let us put aside the deeds of darkness and put on the armor of light. Let us behave decently, as in the daytime, not in orgies and drunkenness, not in sexual immorality and debauchery, not in dissension and jealously. Rather clothe yourselves with the Lord Jesus Christ, and do not think about how to gratify the desires of the sinful nature. (Romans 13:11b-14)

In the KJV, Romans 13:14b says, "Make no provision for the flesh, to fulfill the lusts thereof." According to *Webster's Dictionary*, provision means "the quality or state of being prepared beforehand," or "a stock of needed materials or supplies." **(39)** Provision is translated from the Greek noun *pronoia*. According to Bauer, Arndt, and Gingrich the word means foresight or care. **(40)** Liddell and Scott include the meaning of crimes committed with design. **(41)** The related verb *pronoeo* includes the meaning of think of or plan beforehand. **(42)** One example would be that a young man who has a problem with pornography might have a subscription to a pornographic magazine or may have purchased the adult channels available through his cable television provider. That's planning ahead for sin.

So we fix our eyes not on what is seen, but on what is unseen. For what is seen is temporary, but what is unseen is eternal. (II Corinthians 4:18)

Finally, brothers, whatever is true, whatever is noble, whatever is right, whatever is pure, whatever is lovely, whatever is admirable – if anything is excellent or praiseworthy – think about such things. Whatever you have learned or received or heard from me, or seen in me – put it into practice. And the God of peace will be with you. (Philippians 4:8, 9)

Since then, you have been raised with Christ, set your hearts on things above, where Christ is seated at the right hand of God. Set your minds on things above, not on earthly things. (Colossians 3:1, 2)

Therefore, holy brothers, who share in the heavenly calling, fix your thoughts on Jesus, the apostle and high priest whom we confess. (Hebrews 3:1)

Dear friends, this is now my second letter to you. I have written both of them as reminders to stimulate you to wholesome thinking. (II Peter 3:1)

6. Mutual edification in community.

It's been said that progressive sanctification occurs best in community.

I Thessalonians 4:13-18 speaks of the Coming of the Lord. Verse 18 says, "Therefore encourage each other with these words." The KJV says, "Comfort one another with these words." The Greek word used here is *parakaleo*. According to Bauer, Arndt, and Gingrich, the word means comfort, encourage, or cheer up. It can also mean call to one's side, summon to one's aid, or call upon for help. **(43)** We can't comfort another person during his/her affliction unless we take the time to listen to his story. We need to let the other person talk about what he wants to talk about. Talking about a tragic loss helps a person accept the reality of that loss and work through the pain of grief. **(44)** To comfort someone properly, it may be necessary for us to listen long enough to experience his/her pain. Taking the time to listen is good training for the listener.

For people to function together well in a group, it requires a certain amount of give and take. It requires working together. In this situation there are also times when submission is required. The attribute of submission helps us as we seek to be made holy.

Marriage and parenthood teach us humility and submission if we will allow it. There are times when insisting on our own way is counterproductive. Insisting on our own way may not work out very well if we have a strong-willed child. We need to be circumspect. Compromises may be necessary. We may have to pick our battles. Sometimes we have to ask ourselves, "What's the objective?" Is it to have our own way or to raise children who become true believers and good citizens? As our children grow up, we may reach a point when it is time to stop trying to control them and start relating to them.

A person has to learn humility and submission to get along with others; he has to learn humility and submission to get along with God.

During my thirty-five years practicing medicine, my patients taught me how to act. So did my colleagues and employees. I've learned over the years to not try to control other people.

It is important for us not to do anything that may have a detrimental effect on a young believer's spirit or on believers who have convictions different from our own. For example, most religions of the ancient Near East had laws regarding sacrifices to their gods. Part of the ritual was for the supplicants to eat some of the sacrifice, believing that the gods and the people became closer by partaking of the same animal. **(45)** Because of such a practice, some believers in the early church had a fear of eating any meat; they thought it was wrong to eat meat that might have been sacrificed to idols. Paul had a few words to say about the situation.

Therefore let us stop passing judgment on one another. Instead make up your mind not to put any stumbling block or obstacle in your brother's way. As one who is in the Lord Jesus, I am fully convinced that no food is unclean in itself. But if anyone regards something as unclean, then for him it is unclean. If your brother is distressed because of what you eat, you are no longer acting in love. Do not by your eating destroy your brother for whom Christ died. Do not allow what you consider good to be spoken of as evil. For the kingdom of God is not a matter of eating and drinking, but of righteousness, peace and joy in the Holy Spirit, because anyone who serves Christ in this way is pleasing to God and approved by men. Let us therefore make every effort to do what leads to peace and to mutual edification. Do not destroy the work of God for the sake of food. All food is clean, but it is wrong for a man to eat anything that causes someone else to stumble. It is better not to eat meat or drink wine or to do anything else that will cause your brother to fall. (Romans 14:13-21)

I appeal to you, brothers, in the name of our Lord Jesus Christ, that all of you agree with one another so that there may be no divisions among you and that you may be perfectly united in mind and thought. (I Corinthians 1:10)

It was he [Christ] who gave some to be apostles, some to be prophets, some to be evangelists, and some to be pastors and teachers, to prepare God's people for works of service, so that the body of Christ [the church] may be built up until we all reach unity in the faith and in the knowledge of the Son of God and become mature, attaining to the whole measure of the fullness of Christ. (Ephesians 4:11-13)

Let the peace of Christ rule in your hearts, since as members of one body you were called to peace. And be thankful. Let the word of Christ dwell in you richly as you teach and admonish one another with all wisdom, and as you sing psalms, hymns and spiritual songs with gratitude in your hearts to God. And whatever you do, whether in word or deed, do it all in the name of the Lord Jesus, giving thanks to God the Father through him. (Colossians 3:15-17)

We must choose our friends wisely. In order to have mutual edification with friends in community, we may need to get new friends.

Blessed is the man who does not walk in the counsel of the wicked or stand in the way of sinners or sit in the seat of mockers. But his delight is in the law of the LORD, and on his law he meditates day and night. He is like a tree planted by streams of water, which yields its fruit in season and whose leaf does not wither. Whatever he does prospers. Not so the wicked! They are like chaff that the wind blows away. Therefore the wicked will not stand in the judgment, nor sinners in the assembly of the righteous. For the Lord watches over the way of the righteous, but the way of the wicked will perish. (Psalm 1)

Do not set foot on the path of the wicked or walk in the way of evil men. (Proverbs 4:14)

Do not make friends with a hot-tempered man, do not associate with one easily angered, or you may learn his ways and get yourself ensnared. (Proverbs 22:24, 25)

But now I am writing you that you must not associate with anyone who calls himself a brother but is sexually immoral or greedy, an idolater or a slanderer, a drunkard or a swindler. With such a man do not even eat. (I Corinthians 5:11)

Do not be misled. "Bad company corrupts good character." (I Corinthians 15:33)

7. Avoidance of alcohol and substance abuse and perhaps other addictive forms of behavior.

Alcohol and substance abuse often cause people to be preoccupied with feeding their addiction. Such behavior may affect their work ethic. Regular use of alcohol may interfere with their ability to do their job and provide for their families. It may predispose to other social problems.

Do not join those who drink too much wine or gorge themselves on meat, for drunkards and gluttons become poor, and drowsiness clothes them in rags. (Proverbs 23:20, 21)

Who has woe? Who has sorrow? Who has strife? Who has complaints? Who has needless bruises? Who has bloodshot eyes? Those who linger over wine, who go to sample bowls of mixed wine. Do not gaze at wine when it is red, when it sparkles in the cup, when it goes down smoothly! In the end it bites like a snake and poisons like a viper. Your eyes will see strange sights and your mind imagine confusing things. You will be like one sleeping on the high seas, lying on top of the rigging. (Proverbs 23:29–34)

It is not for kings, O Lemuel – not for kings to drink wine, nor for rulers to crave beer, lest they drink and forget what the law decrees, and deprive all the oppressed of their rights. (Proverbs 31:4, 5)

Woe to those who rise early in the morning to run after their drinks, who stay up late at night till they are inflamed with wine. They have harps and lyres at their banquets, tambourines and flutes and wine, but they have no regard for the deeds of the LORD, no respect for the work of his hands. (Isaiah 5:11, 12)

And these also stagger from wine and reel from beer: [Ephraim's] Priests and prophets stagger from beer and are befuddled with wine; they reel from beer, they stagger when seeing visions, they stumble when rendering decisions. All the tables are covered with vomit and there is not a spot without filth. (Isaiah 28:7, 8)

John MacArthur writes regarding Isaiah 28:7: "Drunkenness had infected even the religious leadership of the nation resulting in false spiritual guidance of the people. **(46)**

Do you not know that the wicked will not inherit the kingdom of God? Do not be deceived: Neither the sexually immoral nor idolaters nor adulterers nor male prostitutes nor homosexual offenders nor thieves nor the greedy nor drunkards nor slanderers nor swindlers will inherit the kingdom of God. (I Corinthians 6:9, 10)

Do not get drunk on wine, which leads to debauchery. Instead be filled with the Spirit. (Ephesians 5:18)

The Greek word for *debauchery* is *ascheemoon* and means *shameful*, *unpresentable*, or *indecent*. **(47)**

Alcohol and substance abuse affect a person's judgment and reduce his inhibitions. Such habits may predispose him to anger and other sins.

Wine is a mocker and beer a brawler; whoever is led astray by them is not wise. (Proverbs 20:1)

David Jeremiah writes: "Wine and strong drink are personified as troublemakers... Such beverages cloud one's thinking and judgment, hampering the ability to make wise decisions. **(48)**

According to *Alcohol Alert*, published by the National Institute on Alcohol Abuse and Alcoholism, (No. 38, October 1997), there is a two-way association between alcohol consumption and violent or aggressive behavior. Intoxication alone does not cause violence. However, alcohol may encourage aggression or violence by disrupting normal brain function. Alcohol weakens brain mechanisms that normally restrain impulsive behaviors, including inappropriate aggression. In many studies, subjects exhibited increased aggressiveness in proportion to increasing alcohol consumption. **(49)**

On the other hand, alcohol consumption may promote aggression because people expect it to do so. Research using real or mock alcoholic beverages demonstrated that people who believe they have consumed alcohol may act more aggressively. **(50)** When I was in the Army in Viet Nam, I noticed that too much alcohol was often associated with aggressive behavior. Some of the aggressiveness was probably fostered by the idea that if confronted later about their behavior, the men could blame it on the alcohol.

People who use alcohol and drugs use them as a means to lift their spirits. But the reality of the situation is that regular use of such agents eventually destroys emotional stability. As such behavior becomes more compulsive, the self-concept suffers. **(51)** People involved in substance abuse subconsciously create defense mechanisms in an effort to maintain emotional stability. They often repress their true feelings about themselves and project their self-hatred onto others. **(52)** Their memory is affected, and they become unaware of the fact that they are on a downward spiral to emotional death. **(53)**

There are other forms of addictive behavior besides substance abuse. People may habitually eat too much. They may have a sexual addiction. They may have a problem with impulse buying or habitually spending too much money. Gambling may be an addiction. These addictive behaviors may provide some relief and a temporary escape from the stresses of life. There is often a biological basis for many of these forms of behavior, but it is still wise to find a way to control them.

8. Living lives of humility and service to others.

Humility and service to others help us produce fruit in keeping with our new nature and help us live in the Spirit. It helps reorient our brains. Jesus said, "It is more blessed to give than to receive" (Acts 20:35b). Giving should make us thankful for what we have and teach us humility.

The brother in humble circumstances ought to take pride in his high position. But the one who is rich should take pride in his low position, because he will pass away like a wild flower. For the sun rises with scorching heat and withers the plant; its blossom falls and its beauty is destroyed. In the same way, the rich man will fade away even while he goes about his business. (James 1:9-11)

In their book *The Meaning of Marriage*, Keller and Keller write, "The introductory statement for Paul's famous paragraph on marriage in Ephesians is verse 5:21: 'Submit to one another out of reverence for Christ.'" In English this is usually rendered as a separate sentence, but that hides from readers an important point that Paul is making. In the Greek text, verse 21 is the last clause in the long previous sentence in which Paul describes several marks of a person who is "filled with the Spirit." The last mark of Spirit fullness is in this last clause: It is a loss of pride and self-will that leads a person to humbly serve others." **(54)**

We are to produce fruit in keeping with our new nature. Service to others helps us grow in grace.

But the fruit of the Spirit is love, joy, peace, patience, kindness, goodness, faithfulness, gentleness and self-control. (Galatians 5:22, 23a)

Be imitators of God, therefore, as dearly loved children and live a life of love, just as Christ loved us and gave himself up for us as a fragrant offering and sacrifice to God. (Ephesians 5:1, 2)

For you were once darkness, but now you are light in the Lord. Live as children of light (for the fruit of the light consists in all goodness, righteousness, and truth)… (Ephesians 5:9)

Be very careful, then, how you live – not as unwise but as wise, making the most of every opportunity, because the days are evil. (Ephesians 5:15, 16)

Performing acts of service provides evidence that a person has new life in Christ. For someone who claims to be a believer, serving others, as he should, demonstrates repentance from sin and a true conversion. It is visible proof that each of us is a new creation. *They'll know us by the love we have for the brothers.*

If a man shuts his ears to the cry of the poor, he too will cry out and not be answered. (Proverbs 21:13)

But when you give to the needy, do not let your left hand know what your right hand is doing, so that your giving may be in secret. Then your Father, who sees what is done in secret, will reward you. (Matthew 6:3, 4)

Do not store up for yourselves treasures on earth, where moth and rust destroy, and where thieves break in and steal. But store up for yourselves treasures in heaven, where moth and rust do not destroy, and where thieves do not break in and steal. For where your treasure is, there your heart will be also. (Matthew 6:19-21)

Religion that God our Father accepts as pure and faultless is this: to look after orphans and widows in their distress and to keep oneself from being polluted by the world. (James 1:27)

What good is it, my brothers, if a man claims to have faith but has no deeds? Can such faith save him? Suppose a brother or sister is without clothes and daily food. If one of you says to him, "Go, I wish you well; keep warm and well fed," but does nothing about his physical needs, what good is it? In the same way, faith by itself, if not accompanied by action, is dead. (James 2:14-17)

We know that we have passed from death to life, because we love our brothers. Anyone who does not love remains in death. (I John 3:14)

Serving others is an act of obedience. Obedience is a requirement if we are to stay connected to the source of life. Serving others allows us to keep in step with the Spirit. It allows the Holy Spirit's power to flow through our lives. Actions that demonstrate evidence of a changed heart result in God's blessings. Focusing on the needs of others helps empty us of self. It teaches us patience. Focusing on meeting the needs of others is the opposite of false pride, which is at the root of the sins of the flesh. Meeting someone else's needs is a way to give the other person encouragement.

Give generously to him [your poor brother] and do so without a grudging heart; then because of this the Lord your God will bless you in all your work and in everything you put your hand to. (Deuteronomy 15:10)

Sell your possessions and give to the poor. Provide purses for yourselves that will not wear out, a treasure in heaven that will not be exhausted, where no thief comes near and no moth destroys. For where your treasure is, there your heart will be also. (Luke 12:33, 34)

By serving others, we learn submission. When we make known our intention to serve someone else, it may lead us into doing more than we actually wanted to do. It may take more time than we had allotted. Such a situation may require submission to the other person's needs. Of course, in some situations, it may be necessary to set boundaries. Some people may want to take more from us than we are able to give. We may need to use some judgment.

There may be other negative aspects of serving others. When a person's primary goal is to be of service to someone else, he may be expected to do things he doesn't want to do. He may not be appreciated as much as he thinks he should be. He may have to deal with indifference or even hostility. On occasion, he may have to suppress a negative response.

Altruism goes against the Darwinian theory of survival of the fittest. It's an act of submission to serve someone we don't like. It can be an act of submission to put another's welfare before our own, to regard another as better than ourselves. Also consider that the other person may not have the resources to return the favor. Giving to those who cannot repay is one of the highest forms of service.

Then Jesus said to his host, "When you give a luncheon or dinner, do not invite your friends, your brothers or relatives, or your rich neighbors; if you do they will invite you back and so you will be repaid. But when you give a banquet, invite the poor, the crippled, the lame, the blind, and you will be blessed. Although they cannot repay you, you will be repaid at the resurrection of the righteous." (Luke 14:12-14)

Consider Jesus' example. He learned to submit.

During the days of Jesus' life on earth, he offered up prayers and petitions with loud cries and tears to the one who could save him from death, and he was heard because of his reverent submission. Although he was a son, he learned obedience from what he suffered… (Hebrews 5:7, 8)

Consider Jesus' example of servanthood.

Your attitude should be the same as that of Christ Jesus: Who being in very nature God, did not consider equality with God something to be grasped, but made himself nothing, taking the very nature of a servant, being made in human likeness. And being found in appearance as a man, he humbled himself and became obedient to death – even death on a cross! (Philippians 2:5-8)

All of the material in this section may sound very legalistic to some people. Let me offer two analogies that may shed a little more light on my perspective regarding these issues. On the subject of how long I remain alive on this earth, I'm trusting the Lord for my destiny. The Bible tells us that "The Lord brings death and makes alive; he brings down to the grave and raises up" (I Samuel 2:6).

The day of our death was appointed before we were born.

Man's days are determined; you [God] have decreed the number of his months and set limits he cannot exceed. (Job 14:5)

All the days ordained for me were written in your [the Lord's] book before one of them came to be. (Psalm 139:16b)

Consider Jesus' words in the Beatitudes.

Who of you by worrying can add a single hour to his life? (Matthew 6:27)

Even though the day of my death was appointed before I was born, the fact doesn't excuse me from being a good steward of this old body. I am still held responsible to keep my doctor's appointments, take my medicine, watch my diet, and get adequate sleep and exercise. I'm also trusting the Lord for my livelihood.

The Lord sends poverty and wealth… (I Samuel 2:7a)

Jesus had some words about provision for our food and clothing.

So do not worry, saying, "What shall we eat?" or "What shall we drink?" or "What shall we wear?" For the pagans run after all these things, and your heavenly Father knows that you need them. But seek first his kingdom and his righteousness, and all these things will be given to you as well. (Matthew 6:31-33)

Even though I'm trusting the Lord for my sustenance, that fact doesn't excuse me from working for a living, from generating my own income. I'm still expected to make wise decisions about how I spend God's money, including giving to the Lord's work and to the poor and putting money back for a rainy day. I'm still expected to spend less than I make.

Consider three other passages about work, written by Paul.

He who has been stealing must steal no longer, but must work, doing something useful with his own hands, that he may have something to share with those in need. (Ephesians 4:28)

Make it your ambition to lead a quiet life, to mind your own business and to work with your hands, just as we told you, so that your daily life will win the respect of outsiders and so that you will not be dependent on anybody. (I Thessalonians 4:11, 12)

For even when we were with you, we gave you this rule: "If a man will not work, he shall not eat." (II Thessalonians 3:10)

Progressive sanctification in this life is a process and requires work.

Therefore, my dear friends, as you have always obeyed – not only in my presence, but now much more in my absence – continue to work out your salvation with fear and trembling, for it is God who works in you to will and to act according to his good purpose. (Philippians 2:12)

The normal Christian life is characterized by work. Our own individual ministry is a work of the Lord in us and frequently serves both the Lord and our fellowman.

Therefore, my dear brothers, stand firm. Let nothing move you. Always give yourselves fully to the work of the Lord, because you know that your labor in the Lord is not in vain. (I Corinthians 15:58)

And God is able to make all grace abound to you, so that in all things, at all times, having all that you need, you will abound in every good work. (II Corinthians 9:8)

From him [Christ] the whole body, joined and held together by every supporting ligament, grows and builds itself up in love, as each part does its work. (Ephesians 4:16)

Consider these words to the church in Ephesus:

I [Jesus] know your deeds, your hard work and your perseverance. (Revelation 2:2a)

Our works will be judged.

By the grace God has given me [Paul], I laid a foundation as an expert builder, and someone else is building on it. But each one should be careful how he builds. For no one can lay any foundation other than the one already laid, which is Jesus Christ. If any man builds on this foundation using gold, silver, costly stones, wood, hay or straw, his work will be shown for what it is, because the Day will bring it to light. It will be revealed with fire, and the fire will test the quality of each man's work. If what he has built survives, he will receive his reward. If it is burned up, he will suffer loss; he himself will be saved, but only as one escaping through the flames. (I Corinthians 3:10-15)

I Corinthians 3:11-13, in part, reads, "no one can lay any foundation other than the one already laid, which is Jesus Christ. If any man builds on this foundation...his work will be shown for what it is." This passage is another example of the truth that our good works don't mean a thing unless we've already become children of God by faith in Jesus Christ. I Corinthians 3:15, "If it is burned up, he will suffer loss; he himself will be saved, but only as one escaping through the flames," is also further evidence that salvation is not by works.

Therefore we are always confident and know that as long as we are at home in the body we are away from the Lord. We live by faith, not by sight. We are confident, I say, and would prefer to be away from the body and at home with the Lord. So we make it our goal to please him, whether we are at home in the body or away from it. For we must all appear before the judgment seat of Christ, that each one may receive what is due him for the things done while in the body, whether good or bad. (II Corinthians 5:6-10)

Whatever you do, work at it with all your heart, as working for the Lord, not for men, since you know that you will receive an inheritance from the Lord as a reward. It is the Lord Christ you are serving. (Colossians 3:23)

To grow spiritually we must be attentive to the voice of God.

We don't overcome the flesh by following a formula; we do so by practicing a lifestyle. The process is a struggle for righteousness that will never end, at least not this side of heaven. If we try to accomplish anything spiritually by using a formula, the things listed in our formula are just things we think we are supposed to do to achieve holiness. They leave out God's intervention as He speaks to us day-by-day and step-by-step.

Although the Lord gives you the bread of adversity and the water of affliction, your teachers will be hidden no more; with your own eyes you will see them.

Whether you turn to the right or to the left, your ears will hear a voice behind you saying, "This is the way; walk in it." (Isaiah 30:20, 21)

God speaks to us, but for us as individuals to get the message, we have to listen. As we process each day's events, we need to be expectant about what God will tell us, showing us what to do to help make us more holy. One main way He speaks to us is to bring to our minds Bible verses we have learned over the years. He can't do that for us if we don't know our Bibles.

Let me offer an example of anticipating what the Lord was about to reveal. When I first went into medical practice, I wanted to provide my patients with spiritual comfort as well as physical comfort, I wanted them to experience healing in their souls and spirits as well as in their bodies. I collected a list of Bible verses that the Lord used

214

to give encouragement to many people. The Lord provided the verses from many sources including my own private reading of the Bible, Scripture passages from readings in church, and from Christian tapes and radio. In order to collect these verses, especially from Christian radio, I had to keep my wits about me. I had to anticipate. I had to notice the citations and then act quickly and write them down before I forgot the references. The list of passages are as follows: Job 5:7; Matthew 5:1-12; Matthew 6:25-34; Romans 5:3-5; Romans 8:18-39; I Corinthians 10:13; II Corinthians 1:3-5; II Corinthians 4:7-10; II Corinthians 12:1-10; I Thessalonians 5:18; II Timothy 1:7; James 1:2-5; I Peter 1:6, 7; and Revelation 21:1-4.

God may speak to us in several ways.

1. Through His Word.

I have hidden your [the Lord's] word in my heart that I might not sin against you. (Psalm 119:11)

Do your best to present yourself to God as one approved, a workman who does not need to be ashamed and who correctly handles the word of truth. (II Timothy 2:15)

All Scripture is God-breathed and is useful for teaching, rebuking, correcting and training in righteousness, so that the man of God may be thoroughly equipped for every good work. (II Timothy 3:16, 17)

2. By the Holy Spirit.

But the Counselor, the Holy Spirit, whom the Father will send in my name, will teach you all things and will remind you of everything I [Jesus] have said to you. (John 14:26)

But I [Jesus] tell you the truth: It is for your good that I am going away. Unless I go away, the Counselor will not come to you; but if I go, I will send him to you. When he comes, he will convict the world of guilt in regard to sin and righteousness and judgment: (John 16:7, 8)

But when he, the Spirit of truth, comes, he will guide you into all truth. (John 16:13a)

However as it is written: "No eye has seen, no ear has heard, no mind has conceived what God has prepared for those who love him" – but God has revealed it to us by his Spirit. The Spirit searches all things, even the deep things of God. For who among men knows the thoughts of a man except the man's spirit within him? In the same way no one knows the thoughts of God except the Spirit of God. We have not received the Spirit of the world but the Spirit who is from God, that we may understand what God has freely given us. This is what we speak, not in words taught by human wisdom but in words taught by the Spirit, expressing spiritual truths in spiritual words. The man without the Spirit does not accept the things that come from the Spirit of God, for they are foolishness to him, because they are spiritually discerned. (I Corinthians 2:9-14)

3. By what we hear from others.

What we hear from others includes what we read in books, what we hear in church, and what we hear over such things as Christian recordings or radio. It also may include normal conversation.

Vine says that prophecy "signifies the speaking forth of the mind and counsel of God…With the completion of the canon of Scripture prophecy apparently passed away, (I Cor. 13:8, 9). In his measure the teacher has taken the place of the prophet…The difference is that, whereas the message of the prophet was a direct revelation of the mind of God for the occasion, the message of the teacher is gathered from the completed revelation contained in the Bible." **(55)**

If we listen to what we hear and combine it with a sensitivity derived from the Holy Spirit, God can use other believers and even unbelievers to speak forth His truth to us, to teach us about wisdom and help us make wise decisions.

Therefore encourage one another and build each other up, just as in fact you are doing. (I Thessalonians 5:11)

4. Through our experiences.

Before I was afflicted I went astray, but now I obey your word. (Psalm 119:67)

Our fathers disciplined us for a little while as they thought best; but God disciplines us for our good, that we may share in his holiness. (Hebrews 12:10)

216

How we react to the difficulties of life can be a signal to us, as individuals, of what we really are like on the inside. Ways we can know our own hearts includes observing how we react to a rebuke, such as noticing what things make us angry. Making decisions and observing consequences, good or bad, helps us develop wisdom.

We are not to grieve or quench the Holy Spirit.

Do not grieve (Ephesians 4:30) or quench (I Thessalonians 5:19 - KJV) the Holy Spirit of God. In his book, *The Holy Spirit*, Billy Graham talks about grieving or quenching the Holy Spirit. He says that almost any wrong action Christians may take can be included under one of these two headings. **(56)** Mr. Graham further writes that we can grieve only a person who loves us. Whatever is unlike Christ in conduct, speech, or disposition grieves the Spirit of grace. **(57)** The Holy Spirit imparts to us joy, peace, and gladness of heart, but when we grieve Him, this ministry is suspended. **(58)** Mr. Graham also writes, "The word quench means 'to put out, to put a damper on.' **(59)** When we quench the Spirit, we put the fire out…A fire goes out when the fuel supply is withdrawn. When we do not stir up souls, when we do not use the means of grace, when we fail to pray, witness, or read the Word of God, the fire of the Holy Spirit is banked. These things are channels through which God gives us the fuel that keeps the fire burning…When we criticize, act unkindly, belittle the work of others by careless or unappreciative words, we smother the fire and put it out." **(60)**

We are to commit our way unto the Lord and trust Him to sanctify us.

The information in this chapter makes me realize that I don't even understand my own mind and feel even less in control of it, especially my subconscious mind. The thought makes me feel even more uncertain about how I proceed. It increases my dependency on the Spirit. When I was a junior in college, I learned to abide in Christ and trust Him to get me where I needed to be vocationally. Just as I abided in Christ and trusted Him to get me where I needed to be vocationally, I need to trust Him to get me where I need to be spiritually.

Commit your works to the Lord, and your thoughts will be established. (Proverbs 16:3 - NKJ)

About Proverbs 16:3, John MacArthur writes:

16:3 Commit. Literally "roll upon" in the sense of both total trust and submission to the will of God; He will fulfill your righteous plans. **(61)**

Trust in the Lord with all your heart, and lean not on your own understanding, but in all your ways acknowledge Him, And He shall direct your paths. (Proverbs 3:5, 6)

Commit your way to the Lord, Trust also in Him, And He shall bring it to pass. He shall bring forth your righteousness as the light, and your justice as the noonday. Rest in the Lord, and wait patiently for Him; do not fret because of him who prospers in his way, Because of the man who brings wicked schemes to pass. Cease from anger, and forsake wrath; do not fret – it only causes harm. (Psalm 37:5-8 – NKJ)

Therefore, I urge you, brothers, in view of God's mercy, to offer your bodies as living sacrifices. Holy and pleasing to god. This is your spiritual act of worship. Do not conform any longer to the pattern of this world, but we transformed by the renewing of your mind. Then you will be able to test and approve what God's will is - his – good, pleasing and perfect will. (Romans 12:1, 2)

Regarding Romans 12:1, 2 John MacArthur writes, in part, as follows:**present your bodies as a living sacrifice.** Under the Old Covenant, God accepted the sacrifices of dead animals. But because of Christ's ultimate sacrifice, the OT sacrifices are of no longer any effect (*Heb. 9:11, 12*). For those in Christ, the only acceptable worship is to offer themselves completely to the Lord. Under God's control, the believer's yet unredeemed body must be yielded to Him as an instrument of righteousness. **do not be conformed.** "Conformed" refers to assuming an outward expression that does not reflect what is really inside, a kind of masquerade or act. The word's form implies that Paul's readers were already allowing this to happen and must stop… **renewing of your mind.** This kind of transformation can only occur as the Holy Spirit changes our thinking through consistent study and meditation of Scripture…The renewed mind is one saturated with and controlled by the Word of God. **(62)**

Vine writes, "of believers, Romans 12:2, "be ye transformed," the obligation being to undergo a complete change which, under the power of God, will find expression in character and conduct…The present continuous tenses indicate a process. **(63)**

Now the Lord is the Spirit, and where the Spirit of the Lord is, there is freedom. And we, who with unveiled faces all reflect the Lord's glory, are being transformed into likeness with ever-increasing glory, which comes from the Lord, who is the Spirit. (11 Corinthians 3:17, 18)

Regarding 11 Corinthians 3:17, John MacArthur writes as follows:
there is liberty [freedom]. Freedom from sin and the futile attempt to keep the demands of the law as a means of earning righteousness (cf. John 8:32-36; Romans 3:19, 20). The believer is no longer in bondage to the law's condemnation and Satan's dominion. **(64)**

About II Corinthians 3:18, John MacArthur writes,

Being transformed: A continual, progressive transformation…
Into the same image. As they gaze at the glory of the Lord, believers are continually being transformed into Christlikeness. The ultimate goal of the believer is to be like Christ (cf. Romans 8:29; Philippians 3:12-14; 1 John 3:2), and by continually focusing on Him the Spirit transforms the believer more and more into His image. **(65)**

The Greek word used in Romans 12:2 and II Corinthians 3: 18 is *metamorphoo*. According to Bauer, Arndt, and Gingrich the word means *transform*, or *change in form*. It can speak of a transformation that is outwardly visible or one that is invisible to the physical eye. **(66)** Metamorphosis is the term used to describe the changing of a caterpillar into a butterfly.

Therefore we do not lose heart. Though outwardly we are wasting away, yet inwardly we are being renewed day by day. For our light and momentary troubles are achieving for us an eternal glory that far outweighs them all. (II Corinthians 4:16, 17)

John MacArthur writes:

The growth and maturing process of the believer is constantly occurring. While the physical body is decaying, the inner self of the believer continues to grow and mature into Christlikeness. **(66)**

But by faith we eagerly await through the Spirit the righteousness for which we hope. (Galatians 5:5)

…being confident of this, that he [God] who began a good work ion you will carry it on to completion until the day of Christ Jesus. (Philippians 1:6)

Therefore, rid yourselves of all malice and all deceit, hypocrisy, envy, and slander of every kind. Like newborn babies, crave pure spiritual milk [pure milk of the word – NKJ], so that by it you may grow up in your salvation, now that you have tasted that the Lord is good. (I Peter 2:1-3)

But grow in the grace and knowledge of our Lord and Savior Jesus Christ. (II Peter 3:18a)

The Christian life is a process. To learn certain things, sometimes a Christian has to learn other things first.

In college, there are many different types of courses that we can take. There are some courses, especially upper-division courses a student may not sign up for unless he has had the necessary prerequisite courses. For example, he cannot sign up for Organic Chemistry until he has taken General Chemistry. He cannot sign up for Differential Equations until he has successfully completed Calculus.

When medical schools are considering whether or not to admit certain applicants, they like to accept people who have had a broad Liberal Arts education. But there are still certain prerequisites. I was accepted for medical school in November 1963 for the class entering the fall of 1964. But the acceptance was contingent on me completing all the required premedical courses. In winter and spring quarters, I completed two quarters of Physical Chemistry, One quarter of Embryology, and the third quarter each of Physics and Organic Chemistry.

Similarly, in God's schoolroom, we have to learn and understand some things before He can teach us other things. However, for the process of sanctification to continue, we must walk in obedience.

His [our God and Savior Jesus Christ] divine power has given us everything we need for life and godliness through our knowledge of him who called us by his own glory and goodness. Through these he has given us his very great and precious promises, so that through them you may participate in the divine nature and escape the corruption in the world caused by evil desires. (II Peter 1:3, 4)

What the Bible teaches me is that the main thing I need to overcome the flesh [my sinful nature] is the fullness of the Godhead living within me. When I accepted Christ as my Savior, the fullness of the Godhead came into my heart. It is my responsibility, by His power, to keep in step with Him and triumph over the flesh and over the powers and authorities, utilizing the power that is already there.

Chapter Eleven
Anger Management

In my mind, the important thing about anger is not how we categorize it but what we do about it. There are things we can do to prevent anger, and, once it develops, there are things we can do to control it.

The New Testament offers guidelines on our appropriate response to personal affront.

You have heard that it was said, "Eye for eye and tooth for tooth." But I [Jesus] tell you, do not resist an evil person. If someone strikes you on the right cheek, turn to him the other also. And if someone wants to sue you and take your tunic, let him have your cloak as well. If someone forces you to go one mile, go with him two miles. Give to the one who asks you, and do not turn away from the one who wants to borrow from you. (Matthew 5:38-42)

You have heard that it was said, "Love your neighbor and hate your enemy." But I [Jesus] tell you: Love your enemies and pray for those who persecute you, that you may be sons of your Father in heaven. He causes his sun to rise on the evil and the good, and sends rain on the righteous and the unrighteous. If you love those who love you, what reward will you get? Are not even the tax collectors doing that? And if you greet only your brothers, what are you doing more than others? Do not even pagans do that? Be perfect, therefore, as your heavenly Father is perfect. (Matthew 5:43-48)

Give to everyone who asks you, and if anyone takes what belongs to you, do not demand it back. (Luke 6:30)

We are not to take revenge.

Do not repay evil for evil. Be careful to do what is right in the eyes of everybody. If it is possible, as far as it depends on you, live at peace with everyone. Do not take revenge, my friends, but leave room for God's wrath, for it is written: "it is mine to avenge; I will repay," says the Lord. On the contrary: "If your enemy is hungry, feed him; if he is thirsty, give him something to drink. In doing this you will heap burning coals on his head." Do not be overcome by evil, but overcome evil with good. (Romans 12:17-21)

Do not let any unwholesome talk come out of your mouths, but only what is helpful for building others up according to their needs, that it may benefit those who listen. (Ephesians 4:29)

Let your gentleness be evident to all. (Philippians 4:5a)

Consider Jesus' example. When he was on the cross, what was done to Him was morally wrong. However, Jesus forgave those who crucified him:

When they came to the place called the Skull, there they crucified him, along with the criminals - one on his right, the other on his left. Jesus said, 'Father forgive them for they do not know what they are doing." (Luke 23:33, 34a)

We are to take the initiative in promoting reconciliation.

There are many Scripture passages that speak to the way we are to handle interpersonal conflict. For example, Jesus had some fairly specific words to say regarding attempts to resolve such issues. If someone sins against us, we are supposed to go to the person about the fault.

Jesus: "If your brother sins against you, go and show him his fault, just between the two of you. If he listens to you, you have won your brother over. But if he will not listen, take one or two others along, so that "every matter may be established by the testimony of two or three witnesses." If he refuses to listen to them, tell it to the church; and if he refuses to listen even to the church, treat him as you would a pagan or a tax collector." (Matthew 18:15-17)

Also, if someone has something against us, we are supposed to go to him/her about it.

Therefore, if you are offering your gift at the altar and there remember that your brother has something against you, leave your gift there in front of the altar. First go and be reconciled to your brother; then come and offer your gift. (Matthew 5:23, 24)

Mutual edification may require confrontation. For us to build each other up in the faith, it may require us to meet with our brothers and challenge them about certain types of behavior that may need to change.

223

The New Testament gives us guidelines concerning how to confront wrongdoing:

It is actually reported that there is sexual immorality among you, and of a kind that does not occur even among pagans: A man has his father's wife. And you are proud! Shouldn't you rather have been filled with grief and have put out of your fellowship the man who did this? Hand this man over to Satan, so that the sinful nature may be destroyed and his spirit saved on the day of the Lord. I [Paul] have written you in my letter not to associate with sexually immoral people – not at all meaning the people of this world who are immoral, or the greedy and swindlers, or idolaters. In that case you would have to leave this world. But now I am writing you that you must not associate with anyone who calls himself a brother but is sexually immoral or greedy, an idolater or a swindler. With such a man do not even eat. What business is it of mine to judge those outside the church? Are you not to judge those inside? God will judge those outside. "Expel the wicked man from among you." (I Corinthians 5:1, 2, 5, 9-13)

Brothers, if someone is caught in a sin, you who are spiritual should restore him gently. But watch yourself, or you also may be tempted. (Galatians 6:1)

Let the peace of Christ rule in your hearts, since as members of one body you were called to peace. And be thankful. Let the word of Christ dwell in you richly as you teach and admonish [warn or instruct] one another with all wisdom, and as you sing psalms, hymns and spiritual songs with gratitude in your hearts to God. And whatever you do, whether in word or deed, do it all in the name of the Lord Jesus, giving thanks to God the Father through him. (Colossians 3:15-17)

Preach the Word; be prepared in season and out of season; correct, rebuke and encourage – with great patience and careful instruction. (II Timothy 4:2)

But avoid foolish controversies and genealogies and arguments and quarrels about the law, because these are unprofitable and useless. Warn a divisive person once, and then warn him a second time. After that have nothing to do with him. (Titus 3:9, 10)

For situations such as personal tragedy or cataclysmic events that affect individuals or multitudes of people, such as war, tragic accidents, or natural disasters, we must take our comfort in the sovereignty of God.

This is what the Sovereign Lord, the Holy One of Israel, says: "In repentance and rest is your salvation, in quietness and trust is your strength... (Isaiah 30:15a)

Consider Habakkuk's response when he was told that God was sending the Chaldeans to judge Judah:

I heard and my heart pounded, my lips quivered at the sound; decay crept into my bones, and my legs trembled. Yet I will wait patiently for the day of calamity to come on the nation invading us. Though the fig tree does not bud and there are no grapes on the vines, though the olive crop fails and the fields produce no food, though there are no sheep in the pen and no cattle in the stalls, yet I will rejoice in the Lord, I will be joyful in God my Savior. The Sovereign Lord is my strength; he makes my feet like the feet of a deer, he enables me to go on the heights. (Habakkuk 3:16-19a)

Do not be anxious about anything, but in everything, by prayer and petition, with thanksgiving, present your requests to God. And the peace of God, which transcends all understanding, will guard your hearts and your minds in Christ Jesus. (Philippians 4:6, 7)

There are many reasons to control anger.

1. We control anger because anger is sin, a manifestation of our sinful nature.

Consider some passages about the nature of anger. There are many more examples in the text of this chapter; I ask you to read on.

Refrain from anger and turn from wrath; do not fret – it leads only to evil. (Psalm 37:8)

The acts of the sinful nature are obvious: sexual immorality, impurity and debauchery; idolatry and witchcraft; hatred, discord, jealousy, fits of rage, selfish ambition, dissensions, factions and envy; drunkenness, orgies, and the like. I warn you, as I did before, that those who live like this will not inherit the kingdom of God. (Galatians 5:19-21)

"In your anger do not sin": Do not let the sun go down while you are still angry, and do not give the devil a foothold. (Ephesians 4:26, 27)

Put to death, therefore, whatever belongs to your earthly nature: sexual immorality, impurity, lust, evil desires and greed, which is idolatry. Because of these, the wrath of God is coming. You used to walk in these ways, in the life you once lived. But now you must rid yourselves of all such things as these: anger, rage, malice, slander, and filthy language from your lips. (Colossians 3:5-8)

2. We control anger because it leads to multiple physical complaints.

Physical manifestations of anger include difficulty sleeping, rapid heartbeat, chest tightness, increased blood pressure, headache, back pain, and gastric and duodenal ulcers. Anger is associated with an increased risk for heart attack and stroke. **(1)**

3. We control our anger over adverse circumstances because it shows a lack of trust in the character and justice of God.

When people encounter affliction, they often respond in anger. They may become angry with God. They see the man down the street, who appears to be making no effort to please God, living an apparently trouble-free life. They think whatever is happening to them should be happening to someone else. Job had such feelings.

Does it please you [God] to oppress me [Job], to spurn the work of your hands, while you smile on the schemes of the wicked? (Job 10:3)

People, who are suffering, may get the idea that serving God is not worth the bother.

You have said, "It is futile to serve God. What did we gain by carrying out his requirements and going about like mourners before the Lord Almighty? But now we call the arrogant blessed. Certainly the evildoers prosper, and even those who challenge God escape." Then those who feared the Lord talked with each other, and the Lord listened and heard. A scroll of remembrance was written in his presence concerning those who feared the Lord and honored his name. "They will be mine," says the Lord Almighty, "in the day when I make up my treasured possession. I will spare them, just as in compassion a man spares his son who serves him. And you will again see the distinction between the righteous and the wicked, between those who serve God and those who do not." (Malachi 3:14-18)

God expects us to trust Him, trust that He is working for our ultimate good.

For men are not cast off by the Lord forever. Though he brings grief, he will show compassion, so great is his unfailing love. For he does not willingly bring affliction or grief to the children of men. (Lamentations 3:31-33)

226

And we know that in all things God works for the good of those who love him, who have been called according to his purpose. For those God foreknew he also predestined to be conformed to the likeness of his Son, that he might be the firstborn among many brothers. And those he predestined he also called; those he called, he also justified; those he justified, he also glorified. What, then, shall we say in response to this? If God is for us, who can be against us? He who did not spare his own Son, but gave him up for us all – how will he not also, along with him, graciously give us all things? Who will bring any charge against those whom God has chosen? It is God who justifies. Who is he that condemns? Christ Jesus, who died – more than that, who was raised to life – is at the right hand of God and is also interceding for us. Who shall separate us from the love of Christ? Shall trouble or hardship or persecution or famine or nakedness or danger or sword? As it is written: "For your sake we face death all day long; we are considered as sheep to be slaughtered." No, in all these things we are more than conquerors through him who loved us. For I am convinced that neither death nor life, neither angels nor demons, neither the present nor the future, nor any powers, neither height nor depth, nor anything else in all creation, will be able to separate us from the love of God that is in Christ Jesus our Lord. (Romans 8:28-39)

Consider it pure joy, my brothers, whenever you face trials of many kinds, because you know that the testing of your faith develops perseverance. Perseverance must finish its work so that you may be mature and complete, not lacking anything. If any of you lacks wisdom, he should ask God, who gives generously to all without finding fault, and it will be given to him. But when he asks, he must believe and not doubt, because he who doubts is like a wave of the sea, blown and tossed by the wind. That man should not think he will receive anything from the Lord; he is a double-minded man, unstable in all he does. (James 1:2–8)

But if you suffer for doing good and you endure it, this is commendable before God. To this you were called, because Christ suffered for you, leaving you an example, that you should follow in his steps. "He committed no sin, and no deceit was found in his mouth." When they hurled their insults at him, he did not retaliate; when he suffered, he made no threats. Instead, he entrusted himself to him who judges justly. (1 Peter 2:20b–23)

We may not understand what God is doing until we get to heaven.

All these people [Old Testament saints] were still living by faith when they died. They did not receive the things promised; they only saw them and welcomed them from a distance. And they admitted that they were aliens and strangers on earth. People who say such things show they are looking for a country of their own. If they had been thinking of the country they had left, they would have had opportunity to return. Instead they were longing for a better country – a heavenly one. Therefore God is not ashamed to be called their God, for he has prepared a city for them…Others were tortured and refused to be released, so that they might gain a better resurrection. Some faced jeers and flogging, while still others were chained and put in prison. They were stoned; they were sawed in two; they were put to death by the sword. They went about in sheepskins and goatskins, destitute, persecuted and mistreated – the world was not worthy of them. They wandered in deserts and mountains, and in caves and holes in the ground. These were all commended for their faith, yet none of them received what had been promised. God had planned something better for us so that only together with us would they be made perfect. (Hebrews 11:13-16, 35b-40)

Then I saw a new heaven and a new earth, for the first heaven and the first earth had passed away, and there was no longer any sea. I saw the Holy City, the new Jerusalem, coming down out of heaven from God, prepared as a bride, beautifully dressed for her husband. And I heard a loud voice from the throne saying, "Now the dwelling of God is with men, and he will live with them. They will be his people, and God himself will be with them and be their God. He will wipe every tear from their eyes. There will be no more death or mourning or crying or pain, for the old order of things has passed away." (Revelation 21:1-4)

My wife's mother had a lymphoma. She was sick for many years before she finally passed away at a relatively young age. Her favorite song was *Farther Along*. The first stanza and chorus went like this.

Tempted and tried we're oft made to wonder Why it should be thus all the day long, While there are others living about us, Never molested tho in the wrong. Farther along we'll know all about it, Farther along we'll understand why; Cheer up, my brother, live in the sun-shine, we'll understand it all by and by. **(2)**

We must place our confidence in the Lord our God.

4. We control anger because it separates us from God's power in our lives.

So I tell you this, and insist on it in the Lord, that you must no longer live as the Gentiles do, in the futility of their thinking. They are darkened in their understanding and separated from the life of God because of the ignorance that is in them due to the hardening of their hearts…You were taught, with regard to your former way of life, to put off your old self, which is being corrupted by its deceitful desires; to be made new in the attitude of your minds; and to put on the new self, created to be like God in true righteousness and holiness…In your anger do not sin: Do not let the sun go down while you are still angry, and do not give the devil a foothold…Get rid of all bitterness, rage and anger, brawling and slander, along with every form of malice. Be kind and compassionate to one another, forgiving each other, just as in Christ God forgave you. (Ephesians 4:17, 18, 22-24, 26, 27, 31, 32)

5. We control anger because it stunts our spiritual growth.

My dear brothers, take note of this: Everyone should be quick to listen, slow to speak and slow to become angry, for man's anger does not bring about the righteous life that God desires. Therefore, get rid of all moral filth and the evil [overflow of wickedness - NKJV] that is so prevalent and humbly accept the word planted in you, which can save you. (James 1:19-21)

William MacDonald writes as follows regarding James 1:21:

Another way to manifest ourselves as first fruits of His creatures is to **lay aside all filthiness and overflow of wickedness**. These vices are likened to soiled garments which are to be set aside once for all. **Filthiness** includes every form of impurity, whether spiritual, mental, or physical. The expression **"overflow of wickedness"** may refer to those forms of evil which are a holdover from our unconverted days. It may refer to sins that **overflow** from our lives and touch the lives of others. Or it may refer to abounding evil, in which case James is not so much describing an excess of evil, but the intensely wicked character which evil has. The over-all meaning is clear. In order to receive the truth of the word of God, we must be morally clean. **(3)**

Hebrews 12:1 carries a similar idea in reference to the laying aside of evil.

Therefore, since we are surrounded by such a great cloud of witnesses, let us throw off everything that hinders and the sin that so easily entangles, and let us run with perseverance the race marked out for us. (Hebrews 12:1)

6. We control anger because it ensnares us and can get us off course; it can dominate our lives.

The Book of Esther is a story of the Jews in captivity in Susa, the winter capital of the Persian Empire, during the reign of Ahasuerus, in the 5th Century B. C. Esther was an orphan, raised by her older cousin, Mordecai. Esther and Mordecai were Jews. In chapter two of the Book of Esther, Esther was chosen to be queen. She had never revealed to the king that she was a Jewess. There was hostility between Mordecai and a man named Haman. When Haman was given a seat of honor higher than that of all the other nobles, the royal officials at the king's gate knelt down and paid honor to Haman, but Mordecai would not do so. Mordecai's refusal to bow down to Haman enraged him, and Haman looked for a way to kill all the Jews throughout the whole kingdom. John MacArthur writes in his *The MacArthur Study Bible*:

The historical genesis for the drama played out between Mordecai (a Benjamite descendant of Saul) and Haman (an Agagite) goes back almost 1,000 years when the Jews exited from Egypt and were attacked by the Amalekites, whose lineage began with Amalek, grandson of Esau. God pronounced His curse on the Amalekites, which resulted in their total elimination as a people. Although Saul received orders to kill all the Amalekites, including their king Agag, he disobeyed and incurred God's displeasure. Samuel finally hacked Agag into pieces (I Samuel 15:32, 33 [NKJV]). Because of his lineage from Agag, Haman carried deep hostility toward the Jews **(4)**.

Haman advised King Ahasuerus that the Jews did not obey the king's orders, and it was not in his best interest to tolerate them. An order went out to kill all the Jews, young and old, women and children, on the thirteenth day of the twelfth month of the Jewish calendar year. Mordecai sent a message to Esther to urge her to go into the king's presence to beg for mercy and plead with him for her people. She agreed to do so, but since she had not been summoned, it was at the risk of her own life. When Esther approached the king, he held out his golden scepter to show that he was pleased with her.

Esther invited the king and Haman to a special banquet. Consider these words about Haman after the banquet:

Haman went out that day happy and in high spirits. But when he saw Mordecai at the king's gate and observed he neither rose nor showed fear in his presence, he was filled with rage against Mordecai. Nevertheless, Haman restrained himself and went home. Calling together his friends and Zeresh, his wife, Haman boasted to them about his vast wealth, his many sons, and all the ways the king had honored him and how he had elevated him above the other nobles and officials. "And that's not all," Haman added. "I'm the only person Queen Esther invited to accompany the king to the banquet she gave. And she has invited me along with the king tomorrow. But all this gives me no satisfaction as long as I see that Jew Mordecai sitting at the king's gate." His wife Zeresh and all his friends said to him, "Have a gallows built, seventy-five feet high, and ask the king in the morning to have Mordecai hanged on it. Then go with the king to the dinner and be happy." This suggestion delighted Haman, and he had the gallows built. (Esther 5:9-14)

At the banquet the following evening with the king and Haman, Esther asked the king to spare her life and the lives of her people. She revealed to the king that she was a Jew and their adversary was Haman. Haman was hanged on the gallows prepared for Mordecai. The law could not be changed. The king published an edict granting the Jews in every city the right to assemble and protect themselves. In the citadel of Susa alone, the Jews killed five hundred men and the ten sons of Haman. The Jews established the celebration of Purim as a time of feasting and joy, commemorating the time when the Jews obtained relief from their enemies, their sorrow was turned into joy, and their mourning into a day of celebration.

If Haman had not been so uncontrollably angry, perhaps there would have been no Book of Esther. Haman destroyed himself and his family for no good reason.

7. We control our anger because it affects the way we represent God to others. It may cause us to model bad habits for our families. In a professing Christian, an aggressive anger style profanes God's name.

Moses had a problem with anger. As a young man, he killed an Egyptian who had been beating a Hebrew (Exodus 2:11–15). Subsequently, Moses fled to Midian. After God spoke to Moses from the burning bush, he returned to Egypt to give Pharaoh God's message. When Pharaoh would not accept the message, Moses became angry with Pharaoh (Exodus 11:4–10).

After the Israelites left Egypt, when they were in the wilderness, God sent manna from heaven. Moses told the people to eat all they gathered. No one was to keep any of it until morning. Some of them paid no attention to Moses. They kept part of it until morning, but by then was full of maggots and had begun to smell. So Moses was angry with them. (Exodus 16:20)

While Moses was on Mount Sinai communicating with God, the Israelites made a golden calf and worshipped it (Exodus 32). When Moses came down from the mountain and saw the calf and the dancing, his anger burned. He broke the tablets of the Ten Commandments. He ground the calf to powder, scattered it on the water, and forced the Israelites to drink it. He had 3000 of the Israelites killed.

The people quarreled with Moses at Rephidim because they were thirsty (Exodus 17:1–7). Moses replied, "Why do you quarrel with me? Why do you put the Lord to the test?" When he struck the rock, water came out. Moses called the place *massah* which means "testing" and *meribah* meaning "quarreling."

Moses became angry when his authority was questioned by Korah, Dathan, and Abiram (Numbers 16:15).

At Kadesh, the Israelites again had no water and quarreled with Moses (Numbers 20:1–13). The Lord told Moses to take the staff and speak to the rock. Moses and Aaron gathered the assembly together in front of the rock. Moses said, "Listen, you rebels, must we bring you water out of this rock?" Moses struck the rock twice rather than speaking to it as God had instructed. Water gushed out. The Lord said to Moses, "Because you did not trust in me enough to honor me as holy in the sight of the Israelites, you will not bring this community into the land I give them" (Numbers 20:12).

Moses' fate ought to be a lesson to us to not lose patience with those God has called us to serve. In his *Believer's Bible Commentary – Old*

Testament, William MacDonald quotes G. Campbell Morgan:

By this manifestation of anger, which as we have said was so very natural, the servant of God misrepresented God to the people. His failure was due to the fact that for the moment his faith failed to reach the highest level of activity. He still believed in God, and in His power: but he did not believe in Him to sanctify Him in the eyes of his people. The lesson is indeed a very searching one. Right things may be done in so wrong a way as to produce evil results. There is a hymn in which we may miss the deep meaning, if we are not thoughtful. "Lord, speak to me that I may speak in living echoes of thy tone." That is far more than a prayer that we may be able to deliver the Lord's message. It is rather that we may do so in His tone, with His temper. That is where Moses failed, and for this failure he was excluded from the Land. **(5)**

Consider also the part the Israelites played in Moses' anger as described in the following passage from Psalms:

By the waters of Meribah, they [the Israelites] angered the Lord, and trouble came to Moses because of them; for they rebelled against the Spirit of God, and rash words came from Moses' lips. (Psalm 106:32, 33)

This story should also be a lesson to us to not be too hard on those who are in authority over us.

Obey your leaders and submit to their authority. They keep watch over you as men who must give an account. Obey them so that their work will be a joy, not a burden, for that would be of no advantage to you. (Hebrews 13:17)

The other side of the coin is worth mentioning. John Calvin said that rulers are responsible to the people they govern for how they act. I don't believe in the divine right of kings. There are proper ways to confront wrongdoing in the people who are in authority over us.

8. We control anger because it affects our ability to think logically; it affects our judgment.

I've experienced times when my anger has spiraled out of control. My mouth got going, and I couldn't stop it. The word rage applies to anger that is uncontrolled. I was thinking about my anger one day, and these words came to mind:

When I'm angry, I'm less aware; I'm too preoccupied to be in communion with God. When I'm angry, I'm not humble; my sinful nature is in control. When I'm angry, I'm not teachable; my sinful nature is in control. When I'm angry, I'm not submissive to God; my sinful nature is in control. When I'm angry, I'm not obedient to God; my sinful nature is in control. When I'm angry, I'm not trusting God; my sinful nature is in control. When I'm angry, I'm not at peace; my sinful nature is in control. When I exhibit rage, I'm not in control; my sinful nature is in control. When I'm angry, I'm guilty of presuming too much in my own behalf and of rebelling against God.

9. We control anger because it divides us from others.

The Bible tells us to love our neighbor. Jesus said it was the second of the two great commandments.

Hearing that Jesus had silenced the Sadducees, the Pharisees got together. One of them, an expert in the law, tested him with this question: "Teacher, which is the greatest commandment in the law?" Jesus replied, "'Love the Lord your God with all your heart and with all your soul and with all your mind.' This is the first and greatest commandment. And the second is like it: 'Love your neighbor as yourself.' All the Law and the Prophets hang on these two commandments." (Matthew 22:34-40)

In I Corinthians 13, we are told what love does.

Love is patient, love is kind. It does not envy, it does not boast, it is not proud. It is not rude, it is not self-seeking, it is not easily angered, it keeps no record of wrongs. Love does not delight in evil but rejoices with the truth. It always protects, always trusts, always hopes, always perseveres. (I Corinthians 13:4-7)

In 1974, when I was a senior Nephrology fellow, I attended the national meeting of the American Society of Nephrology. At the meeting, I met another Nephrology fellow who was working with one of the most honored Nephrologists in the country, at one of the most esteemed medical centers in the country. Someone asked him what it was like to work with that man. His response was as follows: "He has feet of clay." His mentor was just a man, like anyone else.

234

Apparently, there were times when he became angry and was not very nice. I suspect his legacy was tarnished.

Years later, I was on a mission trip to a third world country. I was traveling by car with a man who was a prominent Christian leader. There was a young man riding on a bicycle in front of us. The man on the bicycle gave an arm signal and attempted to turn left into a village. Just as he did so, the driver of our car started to pass him on the left. There was a collision. I don't believe the bicycle rider was hurt very badly. But the Christian leader became very angry with the bicycle rider and said some unkind things. From my perspective, it was our driver who was at fault. After that incident, I didn't have quite as much respect for the man as I had had before. Our anger often gets in the way of our human relationships.

A gentle answer turns away wrath, but a harsh word stirs up anger. (Proverbs 15:1)

A hot-tempered man stirs up dissension, but a patient man calms a quarrel. (Proverbs 15:18)

Better to live in a desert than with a quarrelsome and ill-tempered wife. (Proverbs 21:19)

An angry man stirs up dissension, and a hot-tempered one commits many sins. (Proverbs 29:22)

For as churning the milk produces butter, and as twisting the nose produces blood, so stirring up anger produces strife. (Proverbs 30:33)

Let us not become conceited, provoking and envying each other. (Galatians 5:26)

The Greek word for provoke in Galatians 5:26 is *prokaleo* and is one of the verbs in the New Testament with that meaning. Vine says the word means "to call forth, as to a contest, hence to stir up what is evil in another." **(6)**

I [Paul] want men everywhere to lift up holy hands in prayer, without anger or disputing. (I Timothy 2:8)

10. We control anger because it may cause us to do things that have harmful effects, i.e. hurtful words, physical abuse, and/or murder. There can be untoward results for the perpetrator as well. The consequences may be long-standing.

Consider the story of Simeon and Levi and their anger (Genesis 34). Jacob bought some land in the city of Shechem in Canaan and settled there. One day, Jacob's daughter Dinah went out to visit the women of the land. Shechem (a man), son of Hamor the Hivite, ruler of the area, took her and violated her. Shechem's heart was drawn to Dinah. Shechem loved Dinah. He asked his father to obtain her to be his wife. Hamor and Shechem went to talk with Jacob. Jacob's sons had just come in from the fields. They were filled with grief and fury because of what Shechem had done to their sister. They replied deceitfully to Shechem and Hamor. The consent for marriage would only be given if the Shechemites circumcised all their males. Only then would Jacob's family intermarry with the Shechemites. Hamor and Shechem presented the proposal to their fellow townsman, and they agreed to be circumcised. Much of the reason they agreed is because Jacob was a man of wealth (Genesis 34:23). Three days after the circumcisions had been completed, while all the men were still in pain, two of Jacob's sons, Simeon and Levi, took their swords and attacked the unsuspecting city, killing every male. The sons of Jacob carried off all the plunder. Then Jacob said to Simeon and Levi, "You have brought trouble on me by making me a stench to the Canaanites and Perizzites, the people living in this land. We are few in number, and if they join forces against me and attack me, I and my household will be destroyed." But they replied, "Should he have treated our sister like a prostitute?"

When Jacob was about to die, he had some last words for his sons. Consider his words concerning Simeon and Levi.

Simeon and Levi are brothers – their swords are weapons of violence. Let me not enter their council, let me not join their assembly, for they have killed men in their anger and hamstrung oxen as they pleased. Cursed be their anger, so fierce, and their fury so cruel! I will scatter them in Jacob and disperse them in Israel. (Genesis 49:5-7)

236

After the Israelites entered the Promised Land, the Levites became the priests and were dispersed throughout Israel (Joshua 14:4b; 18:7a; 21:1-42). The Simeonites received their territory dispersed within the allotment for Judah (Joshua 19:1, 9).

Judah was the fourth son of Jacob. Consider Jacob's words about Judah's kingship. The words spoke not only about Jacob's descendants being rulers of the country of Israel, but the prophecy was also messianic in nature.

Judah, your brothers will praise you; your hand will be on the neck of your enemies; your father's sons will bow down to you. You are a lion's cub, O Judah; you return from the prey, my son. Like a lion he crouches and lies down, like a lioness – who dares to rouse him? The scepter will not depart from Judah, nor the ruler's staff from between his feet, until he comes to whom it belongs and the obedience of the nations is his. He will tether his donkey to a vine, his colt to the choicest branch; he will wash his garments in wine, his robes in the blood of grapes. His eyes will be darker than wine, his teeth whiter than milk. (Genesis 49:8-12)

The descendants of Judah, Jacob's fourth son, were chosen for royalty, both for earthly kingship and to bring forth the Messiah. Reuben was disqualified because he slept with his father's concubine (Genesis 35:22) and defiled his father's bed (Genesis 49:4). Simeon and Levi were disqualified because of the slaughter at Shechem.

Many of the same anger issues are present in the story of Jacob and Esau (Genesis 27). Over the centuries there were ongoing problems between the Israelites (descendants of Jacob) and the Edomites (descendants of Esau).

Consider the story of David, Nabal, and Abigail, Nabal's wife (I Samuel 25). David was on the run from Saul and had moved down into the desert of Maon. David sent men to Nabal, telling him they wished him well, and reminded Nabal that they had not mistreated his men. They asked him for leftovers.

Please give your servants and your son David whatever you can find for them. (I Samuel 25:8b)

Nabal hurled insults at them and brushed them off. David became very angry and prepared to attack Nabal and his men. He planned to kill all the males. When Abigail found out what was going on, she sent a large provision of food to David. Consider her words to him:

Please forgive your servant's offense, for the Lord will certainly make a lasting dynasty for my master, because he fights the Lord's battles. Let no wrongdoing be found in you as long as you live. Even though someone is pursuing you to take your life, the life of my master will be bound securely in the bundle of the living by the Lord your God. But the lives of your enemies he will hurl away as from the pocket of a sling. When the Lord has done for my master every good thing he promised concerning him and has appointed him leader over Israel, my master will not have on his conscience the staggering burden of needless bloodshed or having avenged himself. (I Samuel 25:28-31a)

David said to Abigail, "Praise be to the Lord, the God of Israel, who has sent you today to meet me. May you be blessed for your good judgment and for keeping me from bloodshed this day and from avenging myself with my own hands. (I Samuel 25:32, 33)

Ten days later, the Lord struck Nabal, and he died. David was thankful God had kept him from doing wrong.

I have some words for people with a continuing, poorly controlled, anger problem: Get help now before you really hurt someone or something happens to you that can't be fixed. You may need to meet with a pastor, Licensed Clinical Social Worker, Behaviorist, Psychologist, Psychiatrist, or the like. Don't lose your family or your career. Don't end up doing jail time.

11. We control anger because we are commanded to do so.

The end of a matter is better than its beginning, and patience is better than pride. Do not be quickly provoked in your spirit, for anger resides in the lap of fools. (Ecclesiastes 7:8, 9)

Let us behave decently, as in the daytime, not in orgies and drunkenness, not in sexual immorality and debauchery, not in dissension and jealousy. (Romans 13:13)

Be completely humble and gentle; be patient, bearing with one another in love. Make every effort to keep the unity of the Spirit through the bond of peace. (Ephesians 4:2, 3)

And the Lord's servant must not quarrel; instead he must be kind to everyone, able to teach, not resentful. Those who oppose him he must gently instruct, in the hope that God will grant them repentance leading them to a knowledge of the truth... (II Timothy 2:24, 25)

If anyone considers himself religious and yet does not keep a tight rein on his tongue, he deceives himself and his religion is worthless. (James 1:26)

We all stumble in many ways. If anyone is never at fault in what he says, he is a perfect man, able to keep his whole body in check. When we put bits into the mouths of horses to make them obey us, we can turn the whole animal. Or take ships as an example. Although they are so large and are driven by strong winds, they are steered by a very small rudder wherever the pilot wants to go. Likewise the tongue is a small part of the body, but it makes great boasts. Consider what a great forest is set on fire by a small spark. The tongue is also a fire, a world of evil among the parts of the body. It corrupts the whole person, sets the whole course of his life on fire, and is itself set on fire by hell. All kinds of animals, birds, reptiles and creatures of the sea are being tamed and have been tamed by man. But no man can tame the tongue. It is a restless evil, full of deadly poison. With the tongue we praise our Lord and Father, and with it we curse men, who have been made in God's likeness. Out of the same mouth come praise and cursing. My brothers, this should not be. Can both fresh water and salt [bitter] water flow from the same spring? My brothers, can a fig tree bear olives, or a grapevine bear figs? Neither can a salt spring produce fresh water. (James 3:2-12)

Do not repay evil with evil or insult with insult, but with blessing, because to this you were called so that you may inherit a blessing. For, "Whoever would love life and see good days must keep his tongue from evil and his lips from deceitful speech." (I Peter 3:9, 10)

Not controlling our anger is an act of disobedience. Obedience is a prerequisite if we are to abide in Christ and experience His power in our lives.

12. We control anger because it makes good sense to do so.

When words are many, sin is not absent, but he who holds his tongue is wise. (Proverbs 10:19)

A man who lacks judgment derides his neighbor, but a man of understanding holds his tongue. (Proverbs 11:12)

A fool shows his annoyance at once, but a prudent man overlooks an insult. (Proverbs 12:16)

239

Reckless words pierce like a sword, but the tongue of the wise brings healing. (Proverbs 12:18)

A fool's talk brings a rod to his back, but the lips of the wise protect them. (Proverbs 14:3)

A wise man fears the Lord and shuns evil, but a fool is hotheaded and reckless. A quick-tempered man does foolish things, and a crafty man is hated. (Proverbs 14:16, 17)

A patient man has great understanding, but a quick-tempered man displays folly. (Proverbs 14:29)

Better a patient man then a warrior, a man who controls his temper than one who takes a city. (Proverbs 16:32)

Better a dry crust with peace and quiet than a house full of feasting, with strife. (Proverbs 17:1)

A fool's lips bring him strife, and his mouth invites a beating. A fool's mouth is his undoing, and his lips are a snare to his soul. (Proverbs 18:6, 7)

A hot-tempered man must pay the penalty; if you rescue him, you will have to do it again. (Proverbs 19:19)

It is to a man's honor to avoid strife, but every fool is quick to quarrel. (Proverbs 20:3)

He who guards his mouth and his tongue keeps himself from calamity. (Proverbs 21:23)

Like one who seizes a dog by the ears is a passer-by who meddles in a quarrel not his own. (Proverbs 26:17)

Mockers stir up a city, but wise men turn away anger. (Proverbs 29:8)

A fool gives full vent to his anger, but a wise man keeps himself under control. (Proverbs 29:11)

If a ruler's anger rises against you, do not leave your post; calmness can lay great errors to rest. (Ecclesiastes 10:4)

13. We control anger because anger invites God's judgment.

You have heard that it was said to the people long ago, "Do not murder, and anyone who murders will be subject to judgment." But I tell you that anyone who is angry with his brother will be subject to judgment. Again, anyone who says to his brother "Raca [empty-headed]," is answerable to the Sanhedrin. But anyone who says, "You fool!" will be in danger of the fire of hell. (Matthew 5:21-22)

Make a tree good and its fruit will be good, or make a tree bad and its fruit will be bad, for a tree is recognized by its fruit. You brood of vipers, how can you who are evil say anything good? For out of the overflow of the heart the mouth speaks. The good man brings good things out of the good stored up in him, and the evil man brings evil things out of the evil stored up in him. But I [Jesus] tell you that men will have to give account on the Day of Judgment for every careless word they have spoken. For by your words you will be acquitted, and by your words you will be condemned. (Matthew 12:36, 37)

As I study the verses in the concordance about anger and its synonyms, I see that the Bible has many references to God's anger about the various sins of mankind. He is God and it's His prerogative to be angry about sin. We are not God, and the way I see it, we need to cool down.

Causative Factors Related to Anger

1. Our Own Folly.

Of the multiple causative factors related to anger, I believe that one of the main factors to consider is our own folly. Often we become angry about things that are not worth the trouble. Recently I was taking my stepdaughter's father-in-law home from the doctor. I was making a left turn into the subdivision. I had to pause because a car was coming from the other direction. The man in the car behind me blew his horn. I could see in the rear view mirror that he was making an obscene gesture. I said to Jim, "What was that about?" Jim thought perhaps I had not turned on my blinker soon enough to suit the man. I pondered the fact that if I hadn't turned on my blinker at all, and the man had run into the back of my car, the accident would have been his fault. The man's anger seemed so useless and futile, a lot of internal agitation for nothing.

A man's own folly ruins his life, yet his heart rages against the Lord. (Proverbs 19:3)

Words from a wise man's mouth are gracious, but a fool is consumed by his own lips. At the beginning his words are folly; at the end they are wicked madness – and the fool multiplies words. (Ecclesiastes 10:12-14a)

When men tell you to consult mediums and spiritists, who whisper and mutter, should not a people inquire of their God? Why consult the dead on behalf of the living? To the law and to the testimony! If they do not speak according to this word, they have no light of dawn. Distressed and hungry, they will roam through the land; when they are famished, they will become enraged and, looking upward, will curse their king and their God. Then they will look toward the earth and see only distress and darkness and fearful gloom, and they will be thrust into utter darkness. (Isaiah 8:19-22)

Then I heard a loud voice from the temple saying to the seven angels, "Go, pour out the seven bowls of God's wrath on the earth."...The fourth angel poured out his bowl on the sun, and the sun was given power to scorch people with fire. They were seared by the intense heat and they cursed the name of God, who had control over these plagues, but they refused to repent and glorify him. The fifth angel poured out his bowl on the throne of the beast, and his kingdom was plunged into darkness. Men gnawed their tongues in agony and cursed the God of heaven because of their pains and their sores, but they refused to repent of what they had done. (Revelation 16:1, 8-11)

For some people, it was their own bad decisions that brought about their difficult circumstances. Perhaps for them, anger control should begin with humility, submission, and repentance. They might do well to draw nigh to God, hoping they haven't drifted too far away, and praying He will draw nigh to them.

I'm convinced that many people have to reconcile the issues between themselves and God and their own issues with themselves, before they can straighten out their anger issues with others.

2. Unmet emotional needs.

False ideas or unidentified issues in our subconscious thinking may affect our emotions in the wrong way and lead to aberrant behavior. At a conference, I heard it said by Dr. Paul Meier that 80% of our thinking occurs in the subconscious.

Unmet emotional needs in infancy and childhood, such as lack of adequate physical touch, can have longstanding effects. It's been shown that when children's emotional needs are not met, their personalities do not develop properly. Often bad experiences are repressed, and they don't even remember the nature of the incidents that affected them.

When deep resentment fails to resolve, there may be issues going on within our souls and spirits, things we haven't identified yet that prevent resolution of the pathologic thoughts and feelings that proceed from our sinful natures. An example would be having parents with an aggressive anger style or being on the receiving end of repeated maltreatment or exploitation. There are certain negative experiences in later life that can also predispose to the development of anger.

With careful self-examination, it may be possible for someone with an aggressive anger style to discover something within his own makeup that predisposes him to anger. Whether or not he is able to determine, by himself, the nature of the issue, he needs to seek ways to promote resolution. It may be necessary to invite counsel from others.

3. Lack of a father at home to provide needed male attention for the daughters and to control the aggressive tendencies of the sons.

Isaiah 58:6, 7 gives a list of actions God regards as appropriate behavior. Isaiah 58:7b reads as follows: "and not to turn away from your own flesh and blood?" As I ponder Isaiah 58:7b, several thoughts come to mind. One thought is about the Israelites sacrificing their infants to the pagan male deity Molech.

The Lord said to Moses, "Say to the Israelites: 'Any Israelite or any alien living in Israel who gives any of his children to Molech must be put to death. The people of the community are to stone him. I will set my face against that man and I will cut him off from his people; for by giving his children to Molech, he has defiled my sanctuary and profaned my holy name. If the people of the community close their

243

eyes when that man gives one of his children to Molech and they fail to put him to death, I will set my face against that man and his family and will cut off from their people both him and all who follow him in prostituting themselves to Molech. (Leviticus 20:1-5)

In *Theological Wordbook of the Old Testament,* R. Laird Harris writes as follows:

Molech [or Moloch]…[is] the name…for the pagan male deity…to whom apostate Israelites sacrificed infants in the valley of Hinnon immediately south of Jerusalem…Pious horror of the practice, with lurid – perhaps accurate description – is to be found in Jewish sources. David Kimchi says the image of Moloch was of brass and was hollow. A fire was kindled within the idol. When the extended hands became hot, Moloch's priest taking the babe from its father's hand, placed it in Moloch's hands to the accompaniment of drums to prevent the father from hearing the screams of his dying offspring. **(7)**

I suspect part of the reason for sacrificing an infant to Molech was to avoid trying to meet the needs of a crying baby. The modern-day approach to the inconvenience of parenthood is abortion or abandonment. There are too many women forced to survive as heads of single parent families.

Another thing you do: You flood the Lord's altar with tears. You weep and wail because he no longer pays attention to your offerings or accepts them with pleasure from your hands. You ask, "Why?" It is because the Lord is acting as the witness between you and the wife of your youth, because you have broken faith with her, though she is your partner, the wife of your marriage covenant. Has not the Lord made them one? In flesh and spirit they are his. And why one? Because he was seeking godly offspring. So guard yourself in your spirit, and do not break faith with the wife of your youth. "I hate divorce," says the Lord God of Israel, "and I hate a man's covering himself with violence as well as with his garment," says the Lord Almighty. So guard yourself in your spirit, and do not break faith. (Malachi 2:13-16)

Notice that one reason God wants stable marriages is because He desires godly offspring.

There are other words in the New Testament about how men are supposed to treat their wives. Husbands are commanded to have sacrificial love for their wives.

244

Husbands, love your wives, just as Christ loved the church and gave himself up for her… (Ephesians 5:25)

Husbands, in the same way be considerate as you live with your wives, and treat them with respect as the weaker partner and as heirs with you of the gracious gift of life, so that nothing will hinder your prayers. (I Peter 3:7)

I've often heard it said that the best thing a father can do for his children is to love their mother. Agape love is something a person decides to do. It requires intentionality.

Fathers can anger their children both by sins of omission and sins of commission. They can anger children both by physical and emotional abuse as well as neglect and indifference.

Fathers, do not exasperate your children; instead bring them up in the training and instruction of the Lord. (Ephesians 6:4)

In the *MacArthur Study Bible*, John MacArthur writes the following in reference to Ephesians 6:4.

6:4 fathers. The word [fathers] technically refers to male parents, but was also used of parents in general. Since Paul had been speaking of both parents (vv. 1-3) he probably had both in mind here. The same word is used in Heb. 11:23 for Moses' parents. **do not provoke.** In the pagan world of Paul's day, and even in many Jewish households, most fathers ruled their families with rigid and domineering authority. The desires and welfare of wives and children were seldom considered. The apostle makes clear that a Christian father's authority over his children does not allow for unreasonable demands and strictures that might drive his children to anger, despair, and resentment, **training and admonition of the Lord**. This calls for systematic discipline and instruction, which brings children to respect the commands of the Lord as the foundation of all life, godliness, and blessing. Cf. Proverbs 13:24; Hebrews 12:5-11. **(8)**

In his book, *Uncommon*, Tony Dungy writes regarding the need for a father's nurturing in both girls and boys:

Studies have shown that the father's relationship with his daughter will be the primary predictor in the success of her marriage, relationships with men, and her sexual behavior prior to marriage…if she isn't treated well by her father, or has no father in the home to nurture her, love her, and make her feel secure, she will attempt to fill that void through relationships with other men. As for our sons, if there is no father to model proper behavior for them, they will never learn what it means to be a man or a father. **(9)**

In his book, *Bringing up Boys*, Dr. James Dobson has this to say about the importance of fathers in molding a young man's character.

According to the National Center for Children in Poverty, boys without fathers are twice as likely to drop out of school, twice as likely to go to jail, and nearly four times as likely to need treatment for emotional and behavioral problems as boys with fathers.

Repeatedly during my review of the latest research for this book, I came face-to-face with the same disturbing issue. Boys are in trouble today primarily because their parents, and especially their dads, are distracted, overworked, harassed, exhausted, disinterested, chemically dependent, divorced, or simply unable to cope…all other problems plaguing young males flow from (or are related to) these facts of life in the twenty-first century. Chief among our concerns is the absence of masculine role modeling and mentoring that dads should be providing. Mothers, who also tend to be living on the ragged edge, are left to do a job for which they have had little training or experience. Having never been boys, women often have only a vague notion of how to go about rearing one. Boys are the big losers when families splinter…

Thirty years ago it was believed that poverty and discrimination were primarily responsible for juvenile crime and other behavioral problems. Now we know that family disruption is the real culprit. Despite all the red flags that warn us of the dangers, cavalier attitudes abound with regard to premarital pregnancy, divorce, infidelity, and cohabitation. Some years ago, a greeting-card company started a special Mother's Day program for federal prison inmates. Prisoners received a free card, postage paid, to send to their mothers for Mother's Day. The response was overwhelming! The lines were so long, representatives had to return to the factory to get more cards. The program was so successful, the company decided to come back on Father's Day. What happened on Father's Day? Nothing. There were no lines at all. Not a single inmate wanted to send a card to his father. Truly, a loving relationship with a father has a profound effect on one's life. And the lack of an engaged, active father is a strong determining factor in behavior gone awry. **(10)**

Breaking faith with the wife of our youth, hinders our prayers. It also creates social problems. I believe the two greatest social problems in America today are sexual promiscuity and single parent families. As they are growing up, boys and girls need both parents to teach them what they need to know to mature properly. Many young men and women, who are now growing up are angry and hostile. As a nation, we have abandoned the fixed moral authority of Scripture.

If a child grows up in a home where a parent is missing or does not relate to him well, he needs to seek the Lord to fill that void. Psalm 68:5 tells us that God is a Father to the fatherless. Psalm 27:10 says, "Though my father and mother forsake me, the Lord will receive me." Ultimately, children need to look to the Lord for their emotional support. Without the proper influences, however, it is often easier said than done.

4. Poor modeling of anger response by family members, especially parents.

Fathers, do not irritate *and* provoke your children to anger – do not exasperate them to resentment – but rear them [tenderly] in the training *and* discipline and the counsel *and* admonition of the Lord. (Ephesians 6:4-Amplified)

The Greek word for irritate and provoke is *parorgizo*. Bauer, Arndt, and Gingrich say the word means to make angry **(11)**. Liddell and Scott say the word means to provoke to anger **(12)**. What better way for a parent to anger their children than to be angry and physically or emotionally abusive themselves!

Fathers, do not embitter your children, or they will become discouraged. (Colossians 3:21)

Bauer, Arndt, and Gingrich say the Greek word *erethizo* means to arouse, provoke, mostly in a bad sense, irritate, embitter. **(13)** Liddell and Scott include the meanings of rouse to anger or rouse to fight. The word can mean challenge to a boxing match or incite to rivalry. The word can mean chafe [to irritate by rubbing or to annoy]. **(14)**

God said that He had chosen Abraham to become a great and powerful nation and that all nations on earth would be blessed through him. But the promise required his cooperation. In order for God's purpose to be accomplished, it was necessary for Abraham to teach his children and household after him to do what was right and just (Genesis 18:18, 19). Abraham was an example for good to the children of Israel. We are to be examples for good to those around us, especially our children.

...set an example for the believers in speech, in life, in love, in faith and in purity. (I Timothy 4:12b)

Similarly, encourage the young men to be self-controlled. In everything set them an example by doing what is good. In your teaching show integrity, seriousness and soundness of speech that cannot be condemned, (Titus 2:6-8a)

Train a child in the way he should go, and when he is old he will not turn from it. (Proverbs 22:6)

5. Unresolved grief.

Unresolved grief may cause someone to easily become angered. In the motion picture, *The Sound of Music*, unresolved grief was the problem in the Von Trapp household prior to the arrival of Maria. The Captain could not tolerate anything that reminded him of his deceased wife. He shut up the room where they had given parties. He became angry and scolded Maria for entering the ballroom when she first arrived at his home. The Captain stifled all singing and laughter. The Von Trapp children did not play; they marched. Because of his grief, the Captain was repeatedly angry with his children. Once Maria helped him see the detrimental effect he was having on his children, he had a change of heart. He was finally able to work through his pain and give his children the love they so desperately needed.

People may experience unresolved grief below the level of the conscious mind, hidden down in their subconscious. They may still be experiencing the mental trauma of having had an abusive parent. They may be suffering grief due to a decision that led to untoward results, such as having an abortion. Perhaps no one warned the woman, or the man for that matter, about the high emotional toll that may result from taking the life of her own unborn child.

For a biblical example of unresolved grief, consider Jacob. After he was tricked into believing Joseph was dead, he had unresolved grief for twenty-two years. (Genesis 37:31–35; 42:36, 38; 44:29-31; 45:27b)

Unresolved grief may result in undesirable consequences both for the person involved and for the whole family. For people whose continued grief is affecting their families, realizing what they are doing to their families should help them assume a more proactive role in seeking resolution. In his book, *Grief Counseling and Grief Therapy*, J. William Worden refers to normal or uncomplicated grief and abnormal or complicated bereavement. The former includes those feelings and behaviors that are common after a loss. **(15)** The latter is described as, "The intensification of grief to a level where the person is overwhelmed, resorts to maladaptive behavior, or remains interminably in the state of grief without progression of the mourning process towards completion." **(16)** Psychiatric illness [including anger] may be an expression of such pathological mourning. **(17)**

Worden analyzed the process of mourning based on the concept of tasks. **(18)** In his mind the mourner needs to take action and do something. Worden's tasks of mourning are listed as follows:

1. To accept the reality of the loss—Talking about a loss often helps a person accept the reality of that loss. It may also be helpful for the mourner to visit places that remind him of his painful experiences.
2. To work through the pain of grief—Identifying and expressing feelings is therapeutic.
3. To adjust to an environment in which the deceased is missing, to create a new normal.
4. To emotionally relocate the deceased and move on with life. To take the emotional energy tied up in what was lost and invest it in existing or new relationships.

Rather than looking for ways to avoid the pain of grief, the mourner needs to experience the pain in order to bring the grief to resolution.

It is often helpful for the bereaved to seek emotional support from others. The Bible tells us that we are to encourage one another. Sharing experiences with others, and finding out how they handled similar situations may guide the mourner toward a more effective course of action.

6. Emotional fatigue including stress produced by failure to set appropriate boundaries with others.

I once heard a story about three physicians. One was working at about 80% of capacity, another at about 100% of capacity, and the third at around 120% of what should have been his capacity. People came to each of them with the same three requests. I believe one of the requests was to help out teaching in Sunday school, and another involved each man's wife approaching him about having neighbors over for dinner, so they could get to know them better and perhaps share their faith. The first man was able to figure out a way to be helpful in each case. The second man put them off until a later time. The third became very angry because someone was making more demands on his time.

At a conference at the Focus on the Family headquarters in Colorado Springs, Paul Meier said that if a man doesn't have about an hour a day to call his own, time that he can relax and think and put his feet up, he's probably doing more than the Lord wants him to do.

Moses needed some help in his position as a judge for the Israelites. Because of his father-in-law Jethro, he eventually learned to delegate authority.

The next day Moses took his seat to serve as judge for the people, and they stood around him from morning till evening. When his father-in-law [Jethro] saw all that Moses was doing for the people, he said, "What is this you are doing for the people? Why do you alone sit as judge, while all these people stand around you from morning till evening?" Moses answered him, "Because the people come to me to seek God's will. Whenever they have a dispute, it is brought to me, and I decide between the parties and inform them of God's decrees and laws." Moses' father-in-law replied, "What you are doing is not good. You and these people who come to you will only wear yourselves out. The work is too heavy for you; you cannot handle it alone. Listen now to me and I will give you some advice, and may God be with you. You must be the people's representative before God and bring their disputes to him. Teach them the decrees and laws, and show them the way to live and the duties they are to perform. But select capable men from all the people – men who fear God, trustworthy men who hate dishonest gain – and appoint them as officials over thousands, hundreds, fifties and tens. Have them serve as judges for the people at all times, but have them bring every difficult case to you; the simple cases they can decide for themselves. This will make your load lighter, because they will share it with you. If you do this and God so commands, you will be able to stand the strain, and all these people will go home satisfied." (Exodus 18:13-23)

Even Jesus was able to set boundaries.

As Jesus was getting into the boat, the man who had been demon-possessed begged to go with him. Jesus did not let him, but said, "Go home to your family and tell them how much the Lord has done for you, and how he has had mercy on you." (Mark 5:18, 19)

Someone in the crowd said to him [Jesus], "Teacher, tell my brother to divide the inheritance with me." Jesus replied, "Man, who appointed me a judge or an arbiter between you?" (Luke 12:13, 14)

During the time I was practicing medicine, I often had requests from patients to do things that would have compromised my integrity, such as inappropriately prescribing narcotics. I learned the best way to get them to go away was to not give them what they wanted. The behaviorists have a term for that. It's called extinction, eliminating behavior by withholding reinforcement.

7. Physical illness or injury.

There are physical illnesses that can directly predispose to anger. Many illnesses may do so by affecting brain function and include dementia, strokes, brain tumors, and brain injury, due to such causes as vehicular or industrial accidents. Certain illnesses can non-specifically stimulate metabolism and lead to anger; examples include thyrotoxicosis and pheochromocytoma. Other possible

251

causes of personality change (and anger) include substance abuse and infection.

Regarding the general effects of illness, it is common for someone who is sick or injured to be unhappy about it. In addition to the illness itself, there is an emotional reaction to the illness. And then there are changes in how other people treat them. One lady, who had prided herself on being an excellent Bible teacher, was in the early stages of dementia. When the other women stopped asking her to teach, it hurt her feelings, and she became tearful. When people are hurt, they may experience self-pity; they may dwell on their own sorrows or misfortunes. They may become angry and exhibit anger toward God or anger toward others.

Consider people with cancer. In addition to the cancer itself there are problems associated with the treatment, whether the treatment is surgery, radiation, or chemotherapy. Radical surgery can be crippling. Radiation treatments can severely damage many body systems such as the nervous system, the bone marrow, the gastrointestinal tract, and the endocrine glands. Chemotherapy can suppress the immune system and lead to all sorts of strange infections. The medicine these patients are given may affect both the body and the mind. People being treated for cancer often feel bad. They lose their appetites. Many who are chronically ill are simply unable to eat. Malnutrition may contribute to deterioration in the quality of their lives. People who don't feel well often become difficult to live with. The situation calls for restraint on the part of the patient and patience on the part of the caregiver.

Sometimes, when a person is in the terminal stages of a disease, a state of urgency develops in the patient or in family members. There are certain things a person may think he needs to do, things he feels the need to accomplish prior to death. I've seen it in my own family with my sons, things they felt compelled to do before their mother died. One patient had an extensive "to do" list of things that he thought needed attention, such things as business affairs, estate planning, and home repairs. He was so preoccupied with getting his affairs in order, that when requests came for such things as attending grandchildren's activities, he became angry, thinking family members were imposing on his time. It might have been better for the family members if he had spent more time with them and less time making arrangements.

Over the last fifty years we have made great strides in medicine. People are feeling better and living longer. There is a down side however. We've invented ways for people to suffer that previous generations never dreamed of.

8. Pride.

Pride often creates a sense of entitlement, which leads to increased expectations from others and anger if those expectations are not met.

Pride may prevent someone from submitting to authority. He may think he can do the job better than the one in charge, and he may go around creating disharmony.

When someone is proud, he has tendency to want his own way. Individuals with Narcissistic Personality Disorder often expect to be catered to and are puzzled or even furious when it does not happen. For example, they may assume that they do not have to wait in line and that their priorities are so important others should defer to them. They often get irritated when others fail to cooperate with them. **(19)**

Pride only breeds quarrels, but wisdom is found in those who take advice. (Proverbs 13:10)

The end of a matter is better than its beginning, and patience is better than pride. Do not be quickly provoked in your spirit, for anger resides in the lap of fools (Ecclesiastes 7:8, 9).

Knowledge puffs up, but love builds up. The man who thinks he knows something does not yet know as he ought to know. (I Corinthians 8:1b, 2)

9. Economic pressure.

There's an old saying that goes something like this, "The best way to have plenty of money is to spend less than you make." There are many people who can quote these words but can't apply them to their lives. Some people spend money freely without giving thought to the consequences. Then they're out of money until the next paycheck. There's too much month left at the end of the money. When unexpected expenses come along during the time when they have little money, such as the car breaking down or having an unexpected visit to the emergency room with one of the children, their emotions can be especially volatile.

10. Psychiatric illness.

When someone has significant psychiatric illness, he may need to see a psychiatrist or other mental health care provider. He may or may not need medication to control his emotions.

A. Personality Disorder.

According to the *Diagnostic and Statistical Manuel of Mental Disorders*, anger may be related to a personality disorder.

A personality disorder is an enduring pattern of inner experience and behavior that deviates markedly from the expectations of the individual's culture, is pervasive and inflexible, has an onset in adolescence or early adulthood, is stable over time, and leads to distress or impairment. **(20)**

The personality disorders are grouped into three clusters based on descriptive similarities. Cluster A includes paranoid, schizoid, and schizotypal personality disorders. Individuals with these disorders often appear odd or eccentric. Cluster B includes antisocial, borderline, histrionic, and narcissistic personality disorders. Individuals with these disorders often appear dramatic, emotional, or erratic. Cluster C includes avoidant, dependent, and obsessive-compulsive personality disorders. Individuals with these disorders often appear anxious or fearful. **(21)**

The essential feature of paranoid personality disorder is a pattern of pervasive distrust and suspiciousness of others such that their motives are interpreted as malevolent. **(22)**

Not all problematic behaviors are purely intentional. Some are the result of skill deficits. Replacement behaviors or coping skills may not have been introduced or reinforced yet.

B. Posttraumatic Stress Disorder.

Uncontrolled anger may accompany Posttraumatic Stress Disorder. *Wikipedia* relates the following information about the disorder.

Posttraumatic stress disorder may develop after a person is exposed to one or more traumatic events, such as major stress, sexual assault, terrorism, or other threats on a person's life. The diagnosis may be given when a group of symptoms, such as disturbing recurring flashbacks, avoidance or numbing of memories of the event, and hyperarousal, continue for more than a month after the occurrence of a traumatic event.

Remember, there is also a condition known as *Posttraumatic Growth*. In a speech given to Vietnam veterans, at the Truman Library, on September 12, 2009, by Major General Robert Scales, he made the following statement:

Another reason why Vietnam remains in our consciousness is that the experience has made us better. Don't get me wrong. I'm not arguing for war as a self-improvement course. And I realize that war's trauma has damaged many of our fellow veterans physically, psychologically and morally. But recent research on Post Traumatic Stress Disorder by behavioral scientists has unearthed a phenomenon familiar to most veterans: that the trauma of war strengthens rather than weakens us (They call it Post Traumatic Growth). We know that a near death experience makes us better leaders by increasing our self-reliance, resilience, self-image, confidence and ability to deal with adversity. Combat veterans tend to approach the future wiser, more spiritual and content with an amplified appreciation for life. We know this is true. It's nice to see that the human scientists now agree.

The entire speech is available over the internet and was placed there by The Patriot Files.

C. Paranoid Schizophrenia.

Patients with paranoid schizophrenia have a tendency to become angry, especially if they remain untreated. Consider this information available from *Medical News Today* over the internet:

Paranoid Schizophrenia is a subtype of schizophrenia in which the patient has delusions (false beliefs) that a person or some individuals are plotting against them or members of their family...The majority of people with paranoid schizophrenia...may also have auditory hallucinations – they hear things that are not real. They may also have delusions of personal grandeur...An individual with paranoid schizophrenia may spend a disproportionate amount of time thinking up ways of protecting themselves from their persecutors. Typically, a person with paranoid schizophrenia has fewer problems with memory, dulled emotions and concentration compared to those with other subtypes; which allows them to think and function more successfully. Even so, paranoid schizophrenia is a chronic condition which may eventually lead to complications, including suicidal thoughts and behavior. With proper treatment and support, patients have a very good chance of leading happy and productive lives.

Understanding and controlling the anger response.

Stage One – A triggering event.

Anger usually begins with a triggering or inciting event, something that either happens to a person externally or occurs via an internal thought process. Behaviorists refer to triggering events as antecedents.

Stage Two - A period of increasing intensity of emotion.

Following the triggering event comes a period of fretting or escalation during which the anger builds, but may still be manageable. The length of this period of time is often quite variable.

Refrain from anger and turn from wrath; do not fret—it leads only to evil. (Psalm 37:8)

The Hebrew word for fret in Psalm 37:8 is *harah*. According to R. Laird Harris in *Theological Wordbook of the Old Testament*, the word means "to cause fire to burn". "The Hebrew verb is always used in reference to anger...it emphasizes the 'kindling' of anger like the kindling of a fire...The Hithpael stem occurs four times, always meaning, 'Fret not yourself' (Psalm 37:1, 7-8; Proverbs 24:19). The reflexive thought is: 'Do not kindle yourself' in respect to the wicked, etc. Again a personal subject is implied." **(23)** This is the time when our sense of reason needs to come forth and take over. When we feel anger welling up inside of us, we need to recognize the anger and do what we can to extinguish the fire, while it is more easily managed. There are certain types of phrases that may recur in my mind, letting me know I'm becoming angry. Examples include, "He ran into me on purpose," "He's always late," and "He always talks to me like that." When we realize we are angry and that the anger is increasing, we need to calm ourselves down. Behaviorists would refer to "putting the fire out" as de-escalation. The late Ron Dunn has said that sometimes we need to stop listening to ourselves and start talking to ourselves.

In Psalm 37:8, in the Septuagint, the Hebrew word for fret is translated using the Greek word *parazeeloo*. **(24)** Psalm 37 is Psalm 36 in the Septuagint. The four times *parazeeloo* is used in the New Testament, the word is translated provoke (Romans 10:19; Romans 11:11; Romans 11:14; and I Corinthians 10:22-KJV). **(25)** The word's use in the reflexive thought (Psalm 37:8) tells me that when we fret during a period of escalation in our anger, we are provoking ourselves rather than calming ourselves down.

Starting a quarrel is like breaching a dam; so drop the matter before a dispute breaks out. (Proverbs 17:14)

Without wood a fire goes out; without gossip a quarrel dies down. As charcoal to embers and as wood to fire, so is a quarrelsome man for kindling strife. (Proverbs 26:20, 21)

R. Laird Harris says the Hebrew noun *rib* [strife] is a derivative of the Hebrew verb *rib* meaning strive or contend. He writes that the appearances of *rib*, used as a noun, are in such form that some causative notion (as opposed to mere receptivity) may be expected to be present when this word appears. The word may be used in several ways: To strive in the sense of physical combat or to fight, to quarrel or to chide one another in verbal combat, or to dispute with one another in court. There is also a theological meaning, with God performing either a friendly civil function or prosecuting His own cause. **(26)**

Stage Three - Responding to the angry feelings.

Following the time of fretting comes a response to the situation. The style of the response could be aggressive, suppressive, passive-aggressive, or assertive.

The aggressive anger style: people with this anger style give a vigorous or emotional expression to their angry feelings.

The suppressive anger style: people with this anger style suppress or repress their anger and keep it bottled up inside. It is said that this anger style is the one that most often produces somatic complaints. The symptoms are produced by the effect of anger on the part of the nervous system that is not under voluntary control. At some time in the future, the anger may erupt in an explosive angry outburst. I suspect that, at times, the untoward effects of the suppressive anger style may be overrated.

The passive-aggressive anger style: people with this anger style do not freely express their anger, but it comes out in indirect ways such as lack of cooperation or pouting. They just don't do what they're supposed to do. They may expect the offender to be able to read their minds and figure out what it was that caused the offense.

The assertive anger style: people who utilize this anger style talk through their feelings, negotiate a change in the relationship, and take constructive action to solve a problem. They form a rational argument and express their feelings directly with the person who is the focus of their anger, maintaining respect for the other party. **(27)**

If a response to our angry feelings is indicated, this anger style is the preferred method.

For an example of the assertive anger style, consider the story of Jacob and Laban in the Book of Genesis.

After Jacob deceived Isaac and stole Esau's blessing, Esau nursed a grudge against Jacob. Esau planned to kill Jacob after their father died. When Rebekah heard of Esau's plans, she made arrangements to send Jacob to live with her brother Laban in Paddan Aram.

Then Rebekah said to Isaac, "I'm disgusted with living because of these Hittite women. If Jacob takes a wife from among the women of this land, from Hittite women like these, my life will not be worth living." So Isaac called for Jacob and blessed him and commanded him: "Do not marry a Canaanite woman. Go at once to Paddan Aram, to the house of your mother's father Bethuel. Take a wife for yourself there, from among the daughters of Laban, your mother's brother. (Genesis 27:46-28:1, 2)

Jacob did so, but things did not always go well between Jacob and Laban. Jacob loved Laban's daughter, Rachel. Laban tricked Jacob into marrying Rachel's older sister, Leah, first, and then he was allowed to marry Rachel. Jacob worked for Laban seven years as payment for each of his two daughters. After Joseph was born, Jacob was ready to return to his homeland.

But Laban said to him, "If I have found favor in your eyes, please stay. I have learned by divination that the Lord has blessed me because of you." He added, "Name your wages and I will pay them." Jacob said to him, "You know how I have worked for you and how your livestock has fared under my care. The little you had before I came has increased greatly, and the Lord has blessed you wherever I have been. But now, when may I do something for my own household?" (Genesis 30:27-30)

Jacob and Laban came up with an agreement as to how to divide the sheep. When it became evident that God was blessing Jacob, and he was prospering more that Laban, Laban's sons became upset and Laban's attitude toward Jacob changed. After a total of twenty years in Paddan Aram, the Lord told Jacob to go back to the land of his fathers. Jacob collected his family and his possessions and headed for home. Jacob was unaware that Rachel had stolen her father's household gods. Jacob had not told Laban he was leaving. Three days later, Laban found out Joseph had fled. Taking his relatives with him, he pursued Jacob for seven days and caught up with him in the hill country of Gilead.

Consider the conversation between Jacob and Laban (Genesis 31:26-53a):

Laban: "What have you done? You've deceived me, and you've carried off my daughters like captives in war. Why did you run off secretly and deceive me? You didn't even let me kiss my grandchildren and my daughters goodbye. You have done a foolish thing. I have the power to harm you; but last night the God of your fathers said to me [in a dream], 'Be careful not to say anything to Jacob, either good or bad.' Now you have gone off because you longed to return to your father's house. But why did you steal my gods?"

Jacob: "I was afraid, because I thought you would take your daughters away from me by force. But if you find anyone who has your gods, he shall not live. In the presence of our relatives, see for yourself whether there is anything of yours here with me; and if so, take it."

Laban searched the tents of Jacob, Leah, and the two maidservants but found nothing. Then he came to Rachel's tent. She had put the household gods inside her camel's saddle and was sitting on them.

She told her father she could not stand up because she was having her period. Laban found nothing in Rachel's tent. Joseph was angry.

Jacob: "What is my crime? What sin have I committed that you hunt me down? Now that you have searched through all my goods, what have you found that belongs to your household? Put it here in front of your relatives and mine, and let them judge between the two of us. I have been with you for twenty years now. Your sheep and goats have not miscarried, nor have I eaten rams from your flocks. I did not bring you animals torn by wild beasts; I bore the loss myself. And you demanded payment from me for whatever was stolen by day or night. This was my situation: The heat consumed me in the daytime and the cold at night, and sleep fled from my eyes. It was like this for the twenty years I was in your household. I worked for you fourteen years for your two daughters and six years for your flocks, and you changed my wages ten times. If the God of my father, the God of Abraham and the Fear of Isaac, had not been with me, you would surely have sent me away empty-handed. But God has seen my hardship and the toil of my hands, and last night he rebuked you."

Laban: "The women are my daughters, the children are my children, and the flocks are my flocks. All you see is mine. Yet what can I do today about these daughters of mine, or about the children they have borne? Come now, let's make a covenant, you and I, and let it serve as a witness between us."

260

Jacob took a stone and set it up as a pillar. His relatives took stones and piled them in a heap, and they ate there by the heap. Laban called it Jegar Sahudutha [in Aramaic - witness heap], and Jacob called it Galeed [in Hebrew – witness heap]. It was also called Mizpah [watchtower], because he said, "May the Lord keep watch between you and me when we are away from each other."

Laban: "If you mistreat my daughters or if you take any wives besides my daughters, even though no one is with us, remember that God is a witness between you and me. This heap is a witness and this pillar is a witness, that I will not go past this heap to your side to harm you and that you will not go past this heap and pillar to my side to harm me. May the God of Abraham and the God of Nahor, the God of their father judge between us."

Jacob took an oath in the name of the Fear of his father, Isaac. He offered a sacrifice there and fed his relatives. After the meal, they spent the night. The next morning, Laban kissed his grandchildren and his daughters and blessed them. Then he returned home.

In my opinion, this confrontation between Jacob and Laban in Genesis 31 is a good example of the assertive anger style. There was no cursing, no name-calling, and no angry, irrational threats. Things might have been different had the Lord not intervened.

For another scriptural example of using an assertive anger style, consider I Corinthians 6:1-8. This might be the next step after meeting one on one. The passage carries an element of submission to the spiritual leaders.

If any of you has a dispute with another, dare he take it before the ungodly for judgment instead of before the saints? Do you not know that the saints will judge the world? And if you are to judge the world, are you not competent to judge trivial cases? Do you not know that we will judge angels? How much more the things of this life! Therefore, if you have disputes about such matters, appoint as judges even men of little account in the church! I say this to shame you. Is it possible that there is nobody among you wise enough to judge a dispute between believers? But instead, one brother goes to law against another – and this in front of unbelievers! The very fact that you have lawsuits among you means you have been completely defeated already. Why not rather be wronged? Why not rather be cheated? Instead, you yourselves cheat and do wrong, and you do this to your brothers.

Stage Four - A cooling-down period.

After the response to the situation, there usually follows a cooling down period.

Stage Five – The aftermath.

Finally comes the aftermath. If the anger was expressed in an aggressive style, there may be remorse.

Guidelines for relationships with others and for life's uncertainties.

1. Practice Volitional Love.

Agape (a noun) and *agapao* (a verb) are the characteristic words of Christianity. The Spirit of revelation used them to express ideas previously unknown. A study of extra-biblical literature throws but little light upon their distinctive meaning in the New Testament. Love can be known only from the actions it prompts. God's love is seen in the gift of His Son. It was an exercise of the Divine will in deliberate choice, made without assignable cause save that which lies in the nature of God Himself. Christian love has God for its primary object and expresses itself in implicit obedience to His commandments. *Agapao* love, whether exercised toward the brethren, or toward men generally, is not an impulse from the feelings, it does not always run with the natural inclinations, nor does it spend itself only upon those for some affinity is discovered. Love seeks the welfare of all. **(28)**

You have heard that it was said, "Love your neighbor and hate your enemy." But I [Jesus] tell you: Love your enemies and pray for those who persecute you, that you may be sons of your Father in heaven. He causes his sun to rise on the evil and the good, and sends rain on the righteous and the unrighteous. If you love those who love you, what reward will you get? Are not even the tax collectors doing that? And if you greet only your brothers, what are you doing more than others? Do not even pagans do that? Be perfect, therefore, as your heavenly Father is perfect. (Matthew 5:43-48)

But I [Jesus] tell you who hear me: Love your enemies, do good to those who hate you, bless those who curse you, pray for those who mistreat you. If someone strikes you on one cheek, turn to him the other also. If someone takes your cloak, do not stop him from taking your tunic. Give to everyone who asks you, and if anyone takes what belongs to you, do not demand it back. Do to others as you would have them do to you. If you love those who love you, what credit is that to you? Even "sinners" love those who love them. And if you do good to those who are good to you, what credit is that to you? Even "sinners" do that. And if you lend to those from whom you expect repayment, what credit is that to you? Even "sinners" lend to "sinners," expecting to be repaid in full. But love your enemies, do good to them, and lend to them without expecting to get anything back. Then your reward will be great, and you will be sons of the Most High, because he is kind to the ungrateful and wicked. Be merciful, just as your Father is merciful. (Luke 6:27-36)

Let no debt remain outstanding, except the continuing debt to love one another, for he who loves his fellowman has fulfilled the law. (Romans 13:8)

In 1975, I read *The Kink & I* by James Mallory. **(29)** It was then I learned some things about my relationship with my wife. I learned that how I treated my wife should not depend on how she treated me. I learned that I was responsible to God for how I treated her. If she became angry with me, I did not have to return anger for anger. If we had a conflict, it was up to me to come up with a solution that was good for both of us. I learned not to "keep score." I accepted my wife as she was, God's perfect gift to me. Gradually, I learned to do the same for my children and most of the other people around me.

The main exception to this, the people I had the most difficulty with, were those who were in authority over me. I expected those in authority over me to be perfect, to be *worthy* of my allegiance. My expectations were unreasonable. I could become very resentful if decisions were not made the way I thought they should be made. And once resentments developed, I nurtured them. I stored them away, ready to bring them out at the slightest provocation. God enlightened me about this sin when we were on a mission trip in Guatemala. We were having devotions one morning. The speaker read from 1 Corinthians 13. The phrase, "It [love] keeps no record of wrongs" got my attention. I realized that I was storing up my resentments. I learned to expect less and to be more forgiving. I learned to accept those in authority over me, whether or not they always did exactly as

I thought they should. Their responsibility for what they did was to God, not to me. I was responsible to God to do a good job regardless of the actions of those around me. The concept was tremendously liberating.

My first wife was diagnosed with breast cancer in 1997. About five weeks after the initial diagnosis, her condition deteriorated. She developed severe pain in her left hip and was unable to stand. X-rays demonstrated a pathologic fracture of the pelvis. Because I had read that it might lead to codependency, I didn't want either one of my sons to feel responsible for the care of his mother. I made it plain to them that she was my responsibility, not theirs. I took off work and became her caregiver. I was with her all the time.

When people are together all of the time, it is hard to be nice all of the time. Occasionally angry words are exchanged. One Sunday morning we were watching church on television. The pastor said that he was going to read from Philippians four; I thought to myself, "I don't need to hear about Philippians four. I've heard that fifty times." But as the passage was being read, a little phrase caught my attention: "Let your gentleness be evident to all" (verse 5). I count that revelation as one of God's many acts of grace during our times of difficulty. I realized I needed to let my gentleness be evident to all, especially to my wife.

2. Learn to Forgive.

There are some things I do when I am having trouble forgiving someone. If my resentment is persistent, I remind myself that continued lack of forgiveness, on my part, is rebellion against God, and the thought puts a little fear in my heart. I usually begin to submit, and frequently I feel my attitude begin to change. Sometimes it helps to confess to God my feelings of resentment as sin and then seek deliverance. I put the person on my prayer list and pray regularly for him/her. I try to find something to identify with about that person, something about which, in my heart, to wish him/her success. I try to recognize common interests I have with that person and then make conversation with that person about things that are not related to the issue of my resentment. Two things I definitely try to stay away from are malice (desire to see another suffer) and slander (speak evil of); those things are sin and add fuel to my emotional fire. If the person is an unbeliever, I try to figure out some way to introduce him/her to the Lord Jesus. There are times when forgiveness is difficult, and I have to keep working at it. It may be helpful to turn the situation over to the Lord.

I have found that in some situations, it is easier to go ahead and forgive someone than it is to have to go and meet with him/her about an affront. I know I can't say anything to anybody else about the issue until I have gone to that person first.

3. Practice acceptance.

Acceptance is a state of understanding a difficult situation without becoming agitated or anxious or fretful about it. Acceptance does not mean approval or that a person condones what he is accepting. It means that he sees something and knows it for what it is, without feeling the need to take immediate action against it. Acceptance means understanding something we don't like and being at peace about it. It's about being at peace with things that can't be changed.

When Paul was in jail in Philippi, he accepted his situation and was singing hymns (Acts 16:25). Consider what he later wrote in his letter to the Philippians:

I have learned to be content whatever the circumstances. I know what it is to be in need, and I know what it is to have plenty. I have learned the secret of being content in any and every situation, whether well fed or hungry, whether living in plenty or in want. I can do everything through him who gives me strength. (Philippians 4:11b-13)

Consider Hebrews 10:32-34:

Remember those earlier days after you had received the light, when you stood your ground in a great contest in the face of suffering. Sometimes you were publically exposed to insult and persecution; at other times you stood side by side with those who were so treated. You sympathized with those in prison and joyfully accepted the confiscation of your property, because you knew that you yourselves had better and lasting possessions. (Hebrews 10:32-34)

The Serenity Prayer:

"God, grant me the serenity to accept the things I cannot change, the courage to change the things I can, And the wisdom to know the difference."

According to *Wikipedia*, the *Serenity Prayer* was authored by Reinhold Niebuhr.

When it comes to how people treat us, or the irritating circumstances that recur time after time, we shouldn't expect so much. It makes it easier to accept things as they are. As I've heard it said over and over again, "It is what it is." There are some things that bother us that are not going to change. We might as well get used to them.

A. Accept others.

A man's wisdom gives him patience; it is to his glory to overlook an offense. (Proverbs 19:11)

We who are strong ought to bear with the failings of the weak and not to please ourselves. Each of us should please his neighbor for his good, to build him up. (Romans 15:1, 2)

One day, I saw a woman in the office. She was not in her usual good mood. She was fussing about her daughter-in-law, whom she did not like. Then she began fussing about the time change. We had just gone from Eastern Daylight to Eastern Standard Time. Rather quickly she said that she would just have to accept the time change. It was evident she could do nothing about it. I suggested to her that she needed to accept her daughter-in-law just as she had accepted the time change.

B. Accept challenging circumstances.

Acceptance may come about because of a change in perspective. I entered military service in 1969, right out of my internship. The Army gave me five weeks of orientation at the Medical Field Service School in San Antonio, put some Captain's bars on my collar, and sent me to Vietnam. I was assigned to the 1/69 Armor (tanks) Battalion as its Battalion Surgeon. I was responsible for such things as conducting a medical clinic each morning, providing immunizations, and inspecting latrines.

The Scout Platoon had a mascot, a little black dog who was very friendly. The dog became ill, and over a matter of a few days, died. There was something strange about how the dog acted during those final few days. Its head was sent off to Saigon. As a result of tests performed on the dog's head, the diagnosis of rabies was confirmed. It was the responsibility of the tankers to do the mechanical work on their own tanks. Most of them had minor lacerations on their hands, and the dog had been licking the hands of those tankers. After we found out the dog had died of rabies, members of the Scout Platoon began showing up at my door, expressing concerns about how the dog had licked their hands, including the places where there were breaks in the skin.

All told, it appeared that fourteen members of the Scout Platoon needed prophylactic injections of rabies antitoxin. There were too many men involved to hold them all in base camp for the injections. The battalion commander decided I should fly out to the field every day, in a helicopter, to give them their injections. I was not happy about the idea, but I followed orders. Each day we flew out from Camp Radcliff in An Khe. Once we were in the air, the pilot would radio the Scout Platoon. The men would use their armored vehicles to trample down the grass over a large circular area. The vehicles would then circle the perimeter facing outward. The helicopter would land in the middle of the circle. I would jump out of the helicopter and give the men their injections. Then I would re-board the helicopter, and we would return to base camp. The whole trip took perhaps an hour or more.

One day it rained heavily. We could not get a helicopter. I had to go out in an armored personnel carrier. There was high monkey grass on both sides of the road. The road was not much wider than the vehicle on which we were riding. The trip took all day. I was scared to death the entire time. The next day, when I went out in the helicopter, it hardly bothered me at all! The agitation was gone. I was relieved to be able to use the helicopter again. I had moved from simply following orders (submission) to acceptance (being at peace) because of a change in my perspective. The situation itself had not really changed.

In 1994, the physicians in Tennessee were most upset about a new form of Medicaid, state funded medical care for the poor. It was called Tenncare. It did not bother me so much that we would be expected to give care for very little money. I was used to that. What bothered me was that it seemed we would have no control over the numbers of new patients we would have to take. It seemed as if the insurance companies would have the power to make us take patients. I was afraid that the Tenncare patients would crowd out the rest of my practice. Reluctantly, because of my social conscience and the initiative taken by some primary care physicians at our hospital, I did sign up for Tenncare.

In October 1994, my wife and I went with a People to People delegation to the former U.S.S.R. It was a trip for nephrologists. We met with the physicians there and others who cared for patients with kidney disease in Saint Petersburg and Moscow in Russia, as well as in Minsk, Belarus and Vilnius and Kaunas in Lithuania. While we were there we saw relatively new buildings that were deteriorating because of lack of funds for upkeep. We met physicians who were working full time for a salary of fifty dollars a month. After having dinner with us one evening at a hotel in Saint Petersburg, a plastic surgeon, the Chief of Staff at his hospital, had to leave early. He could not afford a car and had to walk home in the cold. We spoke with nurses in Vilnius who had contracted hepatitis B because they were dialyzing patients without the benefit of gloves. The hospital could not afford to buy them. In Kaunas, we heard about patients who were receiving inadequate dialysis because the health care facilities could not afford to do the lab work necessary to measure dialysis adequacy. The despair exhibited by the medical staff at one pediatric hospital in Minsk was overwhelming.

After I returned home from Eastern Europe, some of the things I had previously been fretting about did not seem so important. Tenncare did not bother me at all. My situation had not changed, but my perspective had changed.

But if you suffer for doing good and you endure it, this is commendable before God. To this you were called, because Christ suffered for you, leaving you an example, that you should follow in his steps. "He committed no sin, and no deceit was found in his mouth. "When they hurled their insults at him, he did not retaliate; when he suffered, he made no threats. Instead he entrusted himself to him who judges justly. He himself bore our sins in his body on the tree, so that we might die to sins and live for righteousness..." (I Peter 2:20b-24a)

C. Accept the difficulties of life.

I came away from Vietnam with painful feelings that would not go away. Of all the difficult situations I encountered in Vietnam, there were two in particular that seemed to affect me the most. While I was a Battalion Surgeon, there was an endocrinologist who held teaching rounds for an hour on Fridays at the 67th Evacuation Hospital in Qui Nhon. I made it down there every Friday I could. I became acquainted with the Battalion Surgeon from one of the infantry units in our area. One week, I invited him to go with me. He called me on the telephone early the morning we were to leave and told me he had better not try to go. His commanding officer was giving him a hard time, and there were some things he needed to stay and do. At the meeting with our commanding officer that evening, I learned he was dead. He had been out checking on some wounded men and had been killed by a land mine. I remember the feeling I had as my spirit dropped with a thud.

Most of the time I was with the 1/69 Armor, our responsibility was to protect Highway 19 between the An Khe Pass and the Mang Yang Pass. For about two months, we ran operations out in the open terrain. I spent several weeks at LZ Hard Times. One day there was an explosion in the Mortar Platoon's trash dump. A man had a second-degree burn that covered 85% of his body. He was afraid he was going to die. I tried to reassure the man and told him I thought he was going to be okay. A few days later, I went to the 67th Evacuation Hospital in Qui Nhon to check on him. I was told he had already been moved out to Japan. It was not long until we received word he was dead. My heart was broken.

I began the practice of medicine in 1975. During the 1980's and 1990's, I didn't think much about Vietnam. The few times I did think about that time in life, I realized I had painful feelings that had not resolved, but I was unable to conceptualize anything to do about them. One of the things that especially troubled me was the sound of whirling helicopter blades. It reminded me of death.

My wife and I attended the 69th Armor Association reunion in Arlington, Virginia, in July 2000. During the wreath-laying ceremony at the Korean War Memorial in Washington, I was touched by the prayer offered by the chaplain. He mentioned in his prayer that Jesus was the only way to God, so I figured he was pretty straight. I spoke with him briefly as we made our way to the Vietnam War Memorial. After the wreath laying ceremony at the Vietnam War Memorial, one man began reading the names of those men from our battalion who had been killed in Vietnam. As he read the names, another man went to the wall and placed a carnation below each name, standing it up against the wall. Their expressions of bereavement and respect tore my heart out. The chaplain could see I was having a hard time. He quietly suggested that I pray the following prayer: "Jesus, I can't handle this, but you can, and I choose to let you do so." After I prayed that prayer, a weight lifted from my shoulders. I was free from the burden I had been carrying around for over thirty years.

Some people would refer to my experience as *turning it over to the Lord.* There is biblical justification for doing such a thing, and often the result is as effective as what I experienced.

Cast your cares on the Lord and he will sustain you… (Psalm 55:22a)

Keep your lives free from the love of money and be content with what you have, because God has said, "Never will I leave you; never will I forsake you." So we say with confidence, "The Lord is my helper; I will not be afraid. What can man do to me?" (Hebrews 13: 5, 6)

Humble yourselves before the Lord, and he will lift you up. (James 4:10)

Cast all your anxiety on him because he cares for you. (I Peter 5:7)

John MacArthur writes regarding I Peter 5:7:

5:7 casting all your care upon Him. This verse partly quotes and partly interprets Ps. 55:22. "Casting" means "to throw something on something," as to throw a blanket on a donkey (Luke 19:35). Christians are to cast all their discontent, discouragement, despair, and suffering on the Lord, and trust Him for knowing what He's doing with their lives…Along with submission (v. 5) and humility (vv. 5,6), trust in God: the third attitude necessary for victorious Christian living. **(30)**

Jesus accepted what could not be changed.

When Jesus was in Gethsemane, the night before the crucifixion, He prayed, "My Father, if it is possible, may this cup be taken from me. Yet not as I will but as you will." That was submission but, in my mind, it was not acceptance. He was still not at peace about the situation. He was still sweating drops of blood. I believe that Jesus accepted his coming crucifixion sometime between then and when He saw the people in the arresting party approaching. Consider His words after He saw them:

"Rise, let us go! Here comes my betrayer!" (Matthew 26:46)

To Judas: "Friend, do what you came for." (Matthew 26:50a)

271

To Peter after he cut off the ear of the high priest's servant: "Put your sword back in its place, for all who draw the sword will die by the sword. Do you think I cannot call on my Father, and he will at once put at my disposal more than twelve legions of angels? But how then would the Scriptures be fulfilled that say it must happen in this way?" (Matthew 26:52–54)

It was Jesus who made sure Peter would have a sword. (Luke 22:35-38)

Also to Peter: "Shall I not drink the cup [accept the destiny] the Father has given me?" (John 18:11b)

I believe the change in the tone of Jesus' words was the result of a change in His perspective. When He prayed, "May this cup be taken from me," He was focusing on the moment. When He asked the rhetorical question, "How then would the Scriptures be fulfilled that say it must happen in this way?" He was focusing on the events with an eternal perspective. How do we develop acceptance? Sometimes it's harder than others. How are we able to see things from a different perspective? How do we have peace? How do we reach a state of contentment? As I see it, we are able to do so by the Spirit and the grace of God. Consider Jesus' words:

Come to me, all you who are weary and burdened, and I will give you rest. Take my yoke upon you and learn from me, for I am gentle and humble in heart, and you will find rest for your souls. For my yoke is easy and my burden is light. (Matthew 11:28–30)

There are other passages that tell us about God's rest, having peace, and experiencing contentment.

My soul finds rest in God alone; my salvation comes from him. He alone is my rock and my salvation; he is my fortress, I will never be shaken. (Psalm 62:1, 2)

He who dwells in the shelter of the Most High will rest in the shadow of the Almighty. I will say of the Lord, "He is my refuge and my fortress, my God in whom I trust." (Psalm 91:1, 2)

Be at rest once more, O my soul, for the Lord has been good to you. (Psalm 116:7)

The fear of the Lord leads to life: Then one rests content, untouched by trouble. (Proverbs 19:23)

You will keep in perfect peace him whose mind is steadfast, because he trusts in you. (Isaiah 26:3)

The fruit of righteousness will be peace; the effect of righteousness will be quietness and confidence forever. (Isaiah 32:17)

The Lord says - your Redeemer, the Holy One of Israel: "I am the Lord your God, who teaches you what is best for you, who directs you in the way you should go. If only you had paid attention to my commands, your peace would have been like a river, your righteousness like the waves of the sea." (Isaiah 48:17, 18)

This is what the Lord says: "Stand at the crossroads and look; ask for the ancient paths, ask where the good way is, and walk in it, and you will find rest for your souls. (Jeremiah 6:16a)

But godliness with contentment is great gain. For we brought nothing into the world, and we can take nothing out of it. But if we have food and clothing, we will be content with that. (I Timothy 6:6-8)

Sometimes, the secret of being content is making up our minds to be content. We need to learn to deal with both good times and bad. Jesus is there to help us get through the daily struggle, to help us have peace and contentment.

When times are good, be happy; but when times are bad, consider: God has made the one as well as the other. (Ecclesiastes 7:14a)

I form the light and create darkness, I bring prosperity and create disaster; I, the Lord, do all these things. (Isaiah 45:7)

It seems to me that most Christians are willing to accept the blessings that come to them because of God's purposes, the things that they want, like, and enjoy, the things that give them pleasure. If we accept the blessings from God that we enjoy, then we should be able to accept everything that happens to us that fits in with God's plan. His plan is to make us more like Jesus Christ.

We need to remember that other people, unless they are under our authority, are not responsible to us for how they act; they are responsible to God.

Who are you to judge someone else's servant? To his own master he stands or falls. (Romans 14:4a)

God doesn't need any vigilante action from us to keep the world in order.

Recently my wife and I spent a week on Sanibel Island, off the western coast of Florida. While we were there, Kay wanted to send Valentine cards to the grandchildren. We could have mailed them from the place we were staying, but the inn had no stamps. The next morning, I went down to the post office with the envelopes. I arrived about 8:40 AM. There was a long line. The door was not to open until 9 AM. The employees were a few minutes late getting the door open. The woman behind me in line was upset. She said, "At home, they have the doors open by 8 AM." She thought the postal workers where she lived were much more efficient.

I said, "I've been on a lot of mission trips, and one of the things they emphasize is to be flexible."

She said, "You're right."

When we trust Christ for our salvation, we do it because we want forgiveness for ourselves, not justice. If we don't want justice for ourselves, why would we expect justice for others? If someone verbally or physically abuses us, chances are that person's relationship with Jesus is not what it should be. We ought to pray for that person that his/her relationship with Jesus will be established or be restored.

Our relationship with God is our most precious possession. It's not worth it to hold on to our anger and let our relationship with Him deteriorate, especially if we have no authority from God to adjudicate the circumstances. Compared to our relationship with the Lord, that thing we're upset about probably doesn't amount to a hill of beans.

4. Live One Day at a Time.

We are not to become mired down by either the failures or the accomplishments of the past. Our emotional stability can be affected by remembering things we've done in the past that failed, and those negative impressions can affect how we interact with others. I've heard it said, "Forget your mistakes, but remember what they taught you."

David wrote that as far as the east is from the west, so far has the Lord removed our transgressions from us (Psalm 103:12). The Lord told the people of Israel, "Forget the former things; do not dwell on the past" (Isaiah 43:18). He also told the people of Israel that they would forget the shame of their youth (Isaiah 54:4).

Years ago, I knew a couple who usually got along very well. When they did have an argument, the mutual agreement was to stick to the issue at hand. If one of them brought up something from the past, the response was, "Don't get historical!"

When we are blessed by the Lord and He causes us to achieve some things for His Kingdom, the things we achieve can lead to pride, and pride can affect how we interact with other people. We may get the idea we are better than they are, and false pride can lead to unreasonable expectations and anger. Many times I've expressed the idea to fellow travelers, while on mission trips to Central America, that we are not better than the people in the villages. The only difference between us and them is that we've received greater blessings from God.

When it came to his accomplishments, Paul's credentials were outstanding. He was of the tribe of Benjamin, circumcised the eighth day, a Hebrew of Hebrews, and a Pharisee. His zeal was demonstrated by the way he persecuted the church, and as for legalistic righteousness, he was faultless. However, he counted all of them but dung (KJV) (Philippians 3:5-8). Paul had no confidence in the flesh (Philippians 3:3).

I [Paul] want to know Christ and the power of his resurrection and the fellowship of sharing in his sufferings, becoming like him in his death, and so, somehow, to attain the resurrection from the dead. Not that I have already obtained all this, or have already been made perfect, but I press on to take hold of that for which Christ Jesus took hold of me. Brothers, I do not consider myself yet to have taken hold of it. But one thing I do: Forgetting what is behind and straining toward what is ahead, I press on toward the goal to win the prize for which God has called me heavenward in Christ Jesus. (Philippians 3:10-14)

When we're angry, it's hard to die to self.

We are not to be overcome by our imaginations about the future. Jesus had some words in reference to worrying about tomorrow.

So do not worry, saying, "What shall we eat?" or "What shall we drink?" or "What shall we wear?" For the pagans run after all these things, and your heavenly Father knows that you need them. But seek first his kingdom and his righteousness, and all these things will be given you as well. Therefore do not worry about tomorrow, for tomorrow will worry about itself. Each day has enough trouble of its own. (Matthew 6:31-34)

Consider this quote from James about the fact that we are not promised tomorrow.

Now listen, you who say, "Today or tomorrow we will go to this or that city, spend a year there, carry on business and make money." Why, you do not even know what will happen tomorrow. What is your life? You are a mist that appears for a little while and then vanishes. Instead, you ought to say, "If it is the Lord's will, we will live and do this or that." (James 4:13-15)

4. Set boundaries.

There are times when it is necessary to set boundaries, to place limits on how we let others treat us. An example of a personal boundary being invaded would be the feeling someone gets when another person gets too close to him or her in the elevator.

Being able to define, set, and maintain proper boundaries helps us in our interpersonal relationships.

We may have to tell someone, "Don't call me after 9 PM." We may have to tell an adult child that it's time for him/her to support himself/herself. With some people, we may have to end a relationship.

An angry man stirs up dissension, and a hot-tempered one commits many sins. (Proverbs 29:22)

R. Laird Harris writes that fools scorn and mock at sin and judgment. The scorner may be described as proud and haughty, incorrigible [not reformable, not manageable], resistant to all reproof, and hating any rebuke. Wisdom and knowledge easily elude him. He must be avoided by all who would live godly lives. One good way to remove contention from a group is to eject the scorner. The wickedness of the scorner is pride. **(31)**

Do not envy wicked men, do not desire their company; for their hearts plot violence, and their lips talk about making trouble. (Proverbs 24:1, 2)

Drive out the mocker [scorner], and out goes strife; quarrels and insults are ended. (Proverbs 22:10)

A few random thoughts about controlling anger through reasoning.

If you think about it, you can probably come up with some better examples.

1. Lessons from the Medical Practice

Some people have a problem with reward dependence. They desperately need positive feedback from others, or the approval of others. They have trouble saying, "No." There are times when we need to say, "No."

We need to set limits on how we let people treat us, and other people need to be able to set limits on how we treat them. When I first entered medical practice in Roanoke, Virginia, one of my female patients wanted me to meet her one evening out, away from the office. I said, "No." Her request overstepped the appropriate boundaries of the doctor-patient relationship. If I had agreed to go, I would have overstepped appropriate boundaries myself.

I remember one especially manipulative patient in Roanoke. I was having difficulty dealing with the things this patient wanted me to do. One colleague's suggestion was this: "If someone tries to get you to do something you do not want to do, just say, 'I can't do that.'"

When I opened the office in Knoxville, my wife set some boundaries. One had to do with telephones. She insisted that in our home, we put in two telephone lines. There was one for regular calls with an unlisted number. The second number was known only to the exchange and the other doctors with whom I was sharing call; it was also unlisted. The first number was turned off at night. The other number was left on in case of emergencies. One night when I was off call, there was an emergency with one of my patients. The doctor covering for me had a question about the patient. He asked the dialysis nurse to ring the number of the more private line. She remembered the number. She called me at that number, a couple of days later, to ask me about another patient. I told her that if she wanted to call me at that number again, that was fine but that I would have the number changed. If she needed to speak with me, she was to dial her number into my pager or call the exchange. I was not abusive about what I said. If people are in the habit of setting limits, they can do so in a nice way.

After I started the practice in Knoxville, I had to make a living. Initially I accepted primary care patients. But later on, as my nephrology practice built up, I was forced to stop taking primary care patients. One of the hardest things I had to do was to explain to friends of mine why I could not be their doctor. Occasionally, I would give in and accept one of them as a patient, but those who were the most insistent that I be their doctor were also the most demanding if I did accept them. For example, they were often less likely to be satisfied with what was offered them at the appointment desk or could be verbally abusive with the employees. "Now look, I am a personal friend of Doctor Black's." Setting boundaries became easier.

Early on in my practice, there was a more senior nephrologist, in a competing group across town, who used to say things and do things to cast doubt on my fund of knowledge and my abilities. I was able to work through my angry emotions by telling myself that he had nothing personal against me; he was just trying to take care of himself. Because I founded our medical practice, it was often my responsibility to deal with the situation when a confrontation with an associate or an employee was necessary. I tried to practice what I was later to learn as the assertive anger style. I tried to maintain respect for the other party. I tried to enter the discussion as a friend and leave as a friend. I tried to call no names, and if possible, make no threats. I tried to make it appear as if I were giving advice for the person's own good, which in reality, was the truth.

Of course, there were times when we needed to separate from an associate if our life goals were incompatible. In that situation, it was even better if we could recognize a problem early on and not associate in the first place. For example, there was one man we were interviewing about joining us. He seemed to know just a little too much about the fee schedule for the different procedures. I mentioned to him that some doctors want the money and are willing to see the patients to get it. Others of us take care of the patients and live on whatever we make; it was always more than we needed anyway. I told him we were like the latter group. After I said that, he started telling me about other offers he had received. Our meeting broke up. I never heard from him again.

2. Lessons from the Hospital

Things don't always run perfectly in the hospital. When something went wrong, and I was upset, I had to remember that the hospital employees did not work for me. I did not pay their salaries. If I was angry about something that was done or something undone, I had to learn to control my temper for at least four reasons:

A. It was my responsibility before God.
B. It was common courtesy. Some of the nurses, or other hospital employees, were more sensitive than others, and I didn't always know which was which. I didn't want to crush anyone's spirit.
C. The nurse was usually the only go-between between me and the patient. For example, if I fussed at the nurse for an *unnecessary* phone call, she might not call me the next time when the situation really was crucial. Also, the nurses were not doctors and did not have the relationship with the patient that I had. I couldn't expect them to have the same grasp of the situation.
D. Going public with my faith caused me to have to watch my words. During my first wife's long illness with breast cancer, I wrote a book about dealing with hard things in life. The emphasis was on what the Bible had to say about dealing with affliction. I couldn't give my book to encourage a nurse one day and be verbally abusive with her the next. My walk had to match my talk.

Nothing would calm me down, however, when talking to a nurse about a misunderstanding over what to do for a patient, than figuring out that ultimately, I was the one responsible for the miscommunication.

3. Lessons from daily life

I don't like to be inconvenienced. It can really irritate me when someone or something wastes my time. I'm a busy person; I have things to do. It bothers me when I go into a store to get something, and the clerk is new and has no idea what I'm talking about. It aggravates me when I'm driving behind a slowpoke, and that person makes it through the yellow light, but I don't. Being caught in a traffic jam because of roadwork or because of an automobile accident can be especially nettlesome.

Over the years, I've discovered that my time is not as important as my timing. For example, in 1974, when I was a Senior Nephrology Fellow, I had the privilege of presenting a paper at the Southeastern Dialysis and Transplantation Association meeting in Charleston, South Carolina. The meeting was all day Saturday and half a day Sunday. My paper was the leadoff paper on Sunday morning. We were to fly back to Memphis via Atlanta on Sunday afternoon. Wanting to be cost-effective, I opted for a shuttle ride to the airport, rather than a taxicab. I believed my reservation time left me plenty of margin to get to the airport. The shuttle was late. I fretted and fumed. I waited and waited and waited. I paced back and forth on the sidewalk. I was sure I would miss my plane. The shuttle finally arrived, and we did make it to the airport. I was so late I had to take the one remaining seat on the airplane. It was in First Class. My seat was next to the Chairman of the Transplant Program at the University of Alabama. He remembered my paper presented that morning. I had a most enjoyable and instructive flight to Atlanta.

In 1996, I went with a team of three other people to Donetsk, Ukraine. Our mission was to take chemotherapy drugs for children with cancer and to exchange ideas. I had prepared several talks on a subject I knew a little something about, the management of patients with kidney disease. I was told that if I needed a slide projector, I had better bring my own. We flew out from Atlanta and were to catch a connecting flight in Frankfurt, Germany. The man at the electronic surveillance station in the Frankfurt Airport became most upset about the slide projector. He did not know what to do about it. He sent me down the hall to have it checked out. By the time I was cleared to take the slide projector on the plane, I had missed the flight to Kiev. The next flight was that evening. I arrived in Kiev too late to catch the overnight train to Donetsk. We caught the overnight train from Kiev to Donetsk the next evening. We arrived in Donetsk 24 hours late, a most upsetting turn of events.

But on that overnight train we met an interesting man who was retired from the Russian Army. He said I could take his picture if I would send him a copy. He gave me his name and address. Later he told our group he was an atheist. After I returned home, I tried to get some resources to send to the man, along with the copies of the pictures. Trans World Radio suggested I contact Slavic Missionary Services in New Jersey. That organization sent me two packets of booklets for atheists in the Russian language and two Russian New Testaments. I sent a copy of each of the resources to the man in Ukraine. I was placed on the mailing list for the mission. I sent them a little money a couple of times a year and stayed on their list. Several years later, the mission's director put out a newsletter that was most upsetting. He listed several bad things that had recently happened. The tone of the letter was very depressing. I thought to myself, "This man needs encouragement." The book I had written about suffering during my first wife's long illness with breast cancer was called *Finding Strength in Weakness*. I sent the man a copy. He wrote me back, "This book needs to be translated into Russian and circulated in the former Soviet Union." I called him up and said, "Tell me what to do." He put me in touch with a man who could have the book translated into Russian and then circulated in the former Soviet Union. The book was translated into Russian and 9000 copies have been circulated. All of this because of a slide projector and a missed flight from Frankfurt to Kiev.

More recently, I arrived one morning at one of our dialysis units to make rounds. In the waiting room there sat an elderly man in a wheelchair, waiting to go back for his dialysis treatment. Two ladies were with him. They were speaking to each other in Spanish. I returned to my car and picked up two Spanish copies of my book. I came back to the waiting room and gave each lady a copy. I went back to the treatment area to see a couple of patients. Later, as I was leaving the unit, I noticed that the waiting room was empty. I realized that if I had been a few minutes earlier, or a few minutes later, I would not have had the opportunity to minister to those two ladies. About a week after our meeting, I saw one of them in the parking lot. She told how she had been reading the book and it was ministering to her. For that "divine appointment", the timing was crucial.

When I was in college, I was curious about a lot of things. I had read science fiction in comic books about two different worlds existing simultaneously in the same location but in different *dimensions*. I had also heard about the fourth dimension. My Sunday school teacher was a Physics Professor at the University of Tennessee. I called him up and asked him to tell me about the fourth dimension. He started out by telling me that he had had seven-dimensional applesauce for breakfast. He used seven different adjectives to describe the applesauce. He said that a dimension is anything by which someone measures something. The three basic dimensions are height, width, and depth. The fourth dimension is time, when the object being measured is in a given location. The universe is not static; it is constantly in motion. When something is at a given location is important. In mathematical equations, time is often represented by the small letter c.

The Bible tells us that God is Sovereign. God determines the times set for us and the exact places we should live (Acts 17:26). "In his heart a man plans his course, but the Lord determines his steps" (Proverbs 16:9). David wrote, "But I trust in you, O Lord; I say, 'You are my God.' My times are in your hands..." (Psalms 31:14, 15a). As human beings, we should realize that we are not in charge of our own destinies. We have a loving God who arranges the events in our lives for His glory and for our benefit.

On our busy city streets, we have stop and go lights. The lights are necessary so that traffic can mesh properly, so that each of us can get where we're going efficiently and safely. I believe God has other kinds of stop and go lights so that His people can mesh efficiently with each other, so that we can interact with those around us in the most profitable way, so that we can carry on God's business in a timely manner. We are told in Philippians 3:20, 21 that everything is under the control of the Lord Jesus Christ. Ephesians 1:11 tells us that God works out everything in conformity with the purpose of His will. That thought should comfort each one of us on the next occasion when someone wastes his time.

4. Lessons from the Ball Park

I didn't grow up on the ball field. I grew up working in my dad's bookstore. We have a granddaughter who plays softball. She has been playing for several years. I have learned many things during those years. One time early on, I was sitting in the bleachers, close to home plate. A man behind me hollered out, "Hey Blue, what's the count?" The umpire turned around and said, "Three and one." I thought, "I know a Mr. Blue. Perhaps they are kin to each other." I asked the man, "Do you know him?" He replied, "No." I said, "Well, you called him Blue." He explained that Blue was another name for the umpires.

I have learned some things about forbearance on the ball field. I've learned that it does no good to become angry about the things I can't do anything about. If the pitcher walks three batters in a row and fills the bases, it does no good for me to be upset. I have no authority to change pitchers. If the umpire makes calls I don't like, it does no good for me to become angry. I can't do anything about it. If the situation becomes bad enough, it's up to the coach to say something. In many situations when we become angry, we have no authority from God to do anything about the situation anyway.

I like some of the players on the team better than others. Some of them seem to have a bad attitude at times. I've found it is hard to maintain a dislike for one of my granddaughter's teammates if I'm rooting for her to get a hit. Also, there are different kinds of teams. There are school teams and then there are travel teams. Frequently, the travel teams are more competitive. Through the years, the girls change teams. It's amazing the familiar faces that pop up at the ball field in different uniforms. It's surprising how someone who was on another team before, that I didn't especially like, becomes more likable when she's on my granddaughter's team, especially when

284

she's up to bat. I can identify with her better. I've discovered that there are good people on all the teams. All these experiences teach me some of the practical aspects of forbearance and forgiveness.

Recently, I was at a ballpark and noticed a couple of the umpires who were on the receiving end of a significant amount of verbal abuse over what was perceived as an erroneous call. I decided that the umpires were feeling some anger toward the hecklers and that initially, they were suppressing it. I spoke with a dad of one of the girls on our softball team; he does some umpiring for girls' softball. He said that when he is umpiring, his first obligation is to the girls who are playing, to call a fair game. In order to do so, he has to diffuse his anger so he can concentrate on the game, so he can make accurate calls. If the heckling is such that he can't shut off his emotional response, he looks for ways to be assertive without being aggressive. Sometimes he speaks to the coach. Speaking to the coach usually works. He does his best not to become confrontational. He says he's done his best job when, after the game, people don't remember much about him.

More recently I talked to another umpire. When I first began speaking with him, he said that he had been umpiring for many years and that the hecklers rarely bothered him; he didn't seem very interested in discussing the subject. Later, he did consent to talk about the issue. He did agree that when hecklers become more nettlesome, it is usually helpful to speak with the coach of the team for which the offensive person is trying to be an advocate. The umpire has the power to eject the heckler and confine the coach to the dugout, something neither the umpire nor the coaches want. The umpire said that everybody's strike zone is different. Each umpire tries to do the best he can. After the game begins, the umpire's only true ally is his partner umpire.

The Greek word for vainglory in Philippians 2:3 is *kenodoxia*, meaning vanity, conceit, or ambition. **(32)** This word refers to the pursuit of personal glory, which is the motivation for selfish ambition. **(33)** Vainglorious coaches and fans do things to be noticed or appreciated. Often they wind up just being obnoxious. It's for sure they are not setting a good example for the players. If they get too carried away defending their cause, they often do more harm than good. When a too-angry coach gets thrown out of the game, he is of no use to those players for whom he has accepted responsibility. It seems to me that the umpires' attitude is usually one of humility, just the opposite of vainglory. They generally do not want to be noticed. They want to make their calls and be men of few words. All these examples from the ballpark are given to demonstrate the futility of an aggressive anger style.

5. Lessons from Creation and the Fall

In the beginning, God created the heavens and the earth (Genesis 1:1). God saw all that He had made, and it was very good (Genesis 1:31). However, in Genesis chapter three, Adam sinned. Both mankind and creation were cursed.

To Adam he said, "Because you listened to your wife and ate from the tree about which I commanded you, 'You must not eat of it.' Cursed is the ground because of you; through painful toil you will eat of it all the days of your life. It will produce thorns and thistles for you, and you will eat the plants of the field. By the sweat of your brow you will eat your food until you return to the ground, since from it you were taken; for dust you are and to dust you will return." (Genesis 3:17–19)

Consider some of the effects of the fall on all mankind.

For all can see that wise men die; the foolish and the senseless alike perish and leave their wealth to others. (Psalm 49:10)

Remember how fleeting is my life. For what futility you have created all men! What man can live and not see death, or save himself from the power of the grave? (Psalm 89:47, 48)

There is a time for everything, and a season for every activity under heaven: a time to be born and a time to die. (Ecclesiastes 3:1, 2a)

It is better to go to a house of mourning than to go to a house of feasting, for death is the destiny of every man; the living should take this to heart. (Ecclesiastes 7:2)

The race is not to the swift or the battle to the strong, nor does food come to the wise or wealth to the brilliant or favor to the learned; but time and chance happen to them all. Moreover, no one knows when his hour will come: As fish are caught

in a cruel net, or birds are taken in a snare, so men are trapped by evil times that fall unexpectedly upon them. (Ecclesiastes 9:11b, 12)

Remember your creator in the days of your youth, before the days of trouble come and the years approach when you will say, 'I find no pleasure in them'—before the sun and the light and the moon and the stars grow dark, and the clouds return after the rain, when the keepers of the house tremble, and the strong men stoop, when the grinders cease because they are few, and those looking through the windows grow dim; when the doors to the street are closed and the sound of grinding fades; when men rise up at the sound of birds, but all their songs grow faint; when men are afraid of heights and of dangers in the streets; when the almond tree blossoms and the grasshopper drags himself along and desire no longer is stirred. Then man goes to his eternal home and mourners go about the streets. Remember him— before the silver cord is severed, or the golden bowl is broken; before the pitcher is shattered at the spring, or the wheel broken at the well, and the dust returns to the ground it came from, and the spirit returns to God who gave it. (Ecclesiastes 12:1–7)

In his *Believer's Bible Commentary Old Testament*, William MacDonald explains Ecclesiastes 12:1-7. He writes that the doleful picture of age and senility is a warning to young people to remember their Creator in the days of their youth. In earlier years, there was a certain amount of rain, i.e. trouble and discouragement. But then the sun would emerge, and the spirit would quickly bounce back. In later life, it often seems that the sunny days are gone, and after each spell of rain, the clouds appear with the promise of more rain. The keepers of the house are the arms and hands. The strong men are the legs and thighs. The grinders are the teeth. Those that look through the windows are the eyes. The doors on the street are the ears. The old man suffers from insomnia, and he rises up bright and early when the first bird begins to chirp. His songs grow faint because the vocal cords are impaired. Men become afraid of heights, and they become fearful of dangers in the streets. They have lost their self-confidence. The blossoming almond tree pictures white hair. The grasshopper caricatures the old man, bent over and twisted, inching forward in jerky, erratic movements. Desire fails in the sense that natural appetites diminish. The snapping of the silver cord probably refers to the breaking of the tender thread of life when the spirit is released from the body. The golden bowl has been understood to mean the cranial cavity. The pitcher and the wheel could be a reference to the circulatory system. **(34)** As we make our decisions about what we are going to do with our lives, we must consider the consequences.

Incidentally, on my first mission trip to Guatemala, the barnyard serenade started about 3:30 AM.

Therefore, just as sin entered the world through one man, and death through sin, and in this way death came to all men. (Romans 5:12a)

Man is destined to die once, and after that to face judgment. (Hebrews 9:27)

For, "All men are like grass, and their glory is like the flowers of the field; the grass withers and the flowers fall, but the word of the Lord stands forever." (1 Peter 1:24, 25a)

If the Lord tarries, each one of us will die. It is not a question of if we will die but of when we will die. When we see others die, it makes us more aware of our own coming departure from this life.

The Bible tells us that the whole of creation was cursed.

The creation waits in eager expectation for the sons of God to be revealed. For the creation was subjected to frustration, not by its own choice, but by the will of the one who subjected it, in hope that the creation itself will be liberated from its bondage to decay and brought into the glorious freedom of the children of God. (Romans 8:19-21)

One consequence of God's judgment was entropy. Let us look at the laws of thermodynamics. Thermodynamics literally means "movement of heat." Consider these quotes from *The World Book Encyclopedia.*

Thermodynamics is based on two laws (principles). These laws are broad conclusions about the nature of energy, drawn from the results of many experiments. The first law of thermodynamics, essentially the law of conservation of energy, can be stated as follows: The energy going into a system, minus the energy coming out of a system, equals the change in the energy stored in the system. **(35)** Another way to state the first law of thermodynamics is that energy can neither be created nor destroyed.

The second law of thermodynamics is as follows: Heat will, of its own accord, flow only from a hot object to a cold object. Scientists conclude from the second law that no heat engine can be completely efficient. A heat engine such as gasoline engine or a turbine, continuously converts heat into work. The second law requires that, even in a perfect engine, only part of the heat supply is converted into work. **(36)**

To operate a machine, or to propel a vehicle or a projectile, heat must be converted to mechanical energy. **(37)** Since any functioning heat engine is warm to the touch, no heat engine is 100% efficient. Another way to state the second law of thermodynamics is that the world is going from order to disorder.

The *American Heritage College Dictionary* defines entropy as follows:

1. For a closed thermodynamic system, a measure of the thermal energy unavailable to do work.
2. A measure of the disorder or randomness in a closed system.
3. A measure of the loss of information in a transmitted message.
4. A hypothetical tendency for all matter and energy in the universe toward a state of inert uniformity.
5. Inevitable and steady deterioration of a system or society. **(38)**

Man is not perfect. He doesn't always do things the way he should. He sins. He makes poor decisions. He is subject to bad behavior. We shouldn't expect perfect treatment from our fellowman.

Creation is not perfect. It has been cursed because of our sin. Creation is going from order to disorder. Entropy is a common cause of traffic delays. If there were no entropy, there would be no potholes to repair. If there were no entropy, there would be no power lines to repair; there would be no utility trucks blocking the roads. If creation were not cursed, men and women would always make good decisions. There would be no mechanical failure in our motor vehicles. There would be no automobile accidents to block our roads.

In summary: there are certain practices or habits that help get us ready to respond correctly to potentially anger-provoking situations. Such practices include accepting things we can't change, dealing with unresolved grief, practicing volitional love, having a forgiving spirit, being able to set boundaries, good money management, and avoiding substance abuse. If we're able to accept things we can't change, there will be fewer triggering events. It is better if we don't become angry in the first place. Then we don't have to make a decision about what to do about our anger. It may be helpful to reason through predictable situations and decide in advance how to respond to a particular triggering event.

Once there is a triggering event, and anger starts to build, we need to allow our reasoning to take over. There are several things that sometimes work for me.

I reflect on the relevant truths in God's word.
I remember similar issues I've resolved in the past.
I remind myself to accept things I can't change.
I resolve to forgive the offenders.
When necessary, I turn my stubborn resentment over to the Lord.
If a confrontation is necessary, I make up my mind to respond assertively rather than aggressively.

Of course, any power to do these things comes from the Holy Spirit.

We are told that reasoning can help control our emotions. For that to happen, we have to be circumspect. It requires us to be attentive both to the world around us and to what is happening inside of us. We must consider the consequences of what we do. We must abide in Christ. Abiding in Christ requires obedience and includes loving God and loving others.

Besides looking within ourselves and to the Lord, the person with anger issues may seek counsel from friends or spiritual leaders. He may feel a need to participate in an anger management course or read a book about the subject. He may seek professional help through a psychologist or psychiatrist. I offer this caveat: he needs to be aware that some of the advice he is given may be unbiblical.

Chapter Twelve
Conclusion

Based on conversations with the people I know, I'm convinced that resentment is a common malady among individuals in our society. In talking with others, I'm convinced the Lord uses different ways to lead us, as individuals, out of the bondage of resentment. What I am most familiar with, however, is how the Lord worked in my life, and what He did for me will be the emphasis of this chapter. My anger was due to my own pride. I identify with Job in his presumption, his sense of entitlement, and his angry reaction to his suffering. Of course, my suffering was nothing compared to that of Job.

After the judgment went against me in the lawsuit, and the trial was over, I continued to be upset about the way I was treated. Certain thoughts or words would ignite rage. I say rage, because at times, my reaction was uncontrollable. I knew it was harmful for me to be this way, but I didn't know how to handle it. I understood Paul's words in Romans 7 as never before.

I do not understand what I do. For what I want to do I do not do, but what I hate I do. And if I do what I do not want to do, I agree that the law is good. As it is, it is no longer I myself who do it, but it is sin living in me. I know that nothing good lives in me, that is, in my sinful nature. For I have the desire to do what is good, but I cannot carry it out. For what I do is not the good I want to do; no, the evil I do not want to do - this I keep on doing. (Romans 7:15-19)

I take great comfort from the fact that even Paul had to learn to be content. It didn't just come automatically.

…I have learned to be content whatever the circumstances. I know what it is to be in need, and I know what it is to have plenty. I have learned the secret of being content in any and every situation, whether well fed or hungry, whether living in plenty or in want. I can do everything through him who gives me strength. (Philippians 4:11b-13)

When I was writing chapter four, I quoted Galatians 5:16-21:

So I say, live by the Spirit, and you will not gratify the desires of the sinful nature. For the sinful nature desires what in contrary to the Spirit, and the Spirit what is contrary to the sinful nature. They are in conflict with each other, so that you do not do what you want. But if you are led by the Spirit, you are not under law. The acts of the sinful nature are obvious: sexual immorality, impurity and debauchery; idolatry and witchcraft; hatred, discord, jealousy, fits or rage, selfish ambition, dissensions, factions and envy; drunkenness, orgies, and the like. I warn you, as I did before, that those who live like this will not inherit the kingdom of God. (Galatians 5:16-21)

As I was typing out this passage in Galatians, it became obvious to me that my reaction to the courtroom experience was my sinful nature expressing itself in fits of rage. It was an example of the conflict between the sinful nature and the Spirit. The world and the devil each contributed their part.

The Bible says that we are a slave to whatever has mastered us (II Peter 2:19).

As a young man, Malcolm Muggeridge was a British newspaperman. During the early 1930s, he was the Moscow correspondent for the *Manchester Guardian*. Muggeridge was the first journalist to tell the world about the hardship, famine, and terror in Russia under Stalin. In the early 1960s, Muggeridge rediscovered Christianity. Afterwards, while working with the BBC, Muggeridge was one of the people responsible for introducing the general public to Mother Teresa. **(1)** He interviewed her for the film *Something Beautiful for God*, and authored a book about her that carried the same title. **(2)** According to Muggeridge, "Any happening, great and small . . . is a parable whereby God speaks to us; and the art of life is to get the message." **(3)**

Recently, the Lord provided me with a resource from Focus on the Family that helped me deal with my resentful feelings. It was a recording of a talk by Frank Peretti which carried the title, *What We Believe*. It was a lecture he had given at a Christian worldview conference. Years ago, after Mr. Peretti wrote his book *This Present Darkness*, people figured he was some kind of expert on spiritual warfare and started relating to him all sorts of stories about terrible things that had happened. It finally got to him in the form of discouragement, depression, and futility. He was spending time with the Lord one day, and it was as if the Lord said to him, "Frank, your problem is you've got your kingdoms mixed up. You're expecting some kind of salvation to come out of an earthly kingdom, such as the United States." Then Peretti said to the audience, "God does not have a covenant with the United States; He did with Israel but not with the United States." Peretti said that God never made promises to the United States, but He did to the Kingdom of God, the Body of Christ, the Church.

My wife and I went to visit an old friend, someone we had not seen in years. The friend told me how she had become upset by some things that were going on in her church. In withdrawing from the church, she had also withdrawn from the Lord. I tried to explain to her that Christians were not perfect, and she should not expect them to be. I wanted her to know that sins committed by imperfect people should not lead her away from God. After I returned home, I sent her a letter and noted some passages from Scripture about people in the church not really acting like Christians.

Jesus told them another parable: "The kingdom of heaven is like a man who sowed good seed in his field. But while everyone was sleeping, his enemy came and sowed weeds among the wheat, and went away. When the wheat sprouted and formed heads, then the weeds also appeared. The owner's servants came to him and said, 'Sir, didn't you sow good seed in your field? Where did the weeds come from?' 'An enemy did this,' he replied. The servants asked him, 'Do you want us to go and pull them up?' 'No,' he answered, 'because while you are pulling the weeds, you may root up the wheat with them. Let them both grow together until the harvest. At that time I will tell the harvesters: First collect the weeds and tie them in bundles to be burned; then gather the wheat and bring it into my barn.'" (Matthew 13:24-30)

In my letter to our friend, I wrote as follows: "The devil has sown weeds among those of the true Christian fellowship. The weeds, referred to in that parable (Matthew 13), are probably darnel. Early on, the young shoots of the wheat and the darnel are so much alike it is hard to tell the difference. At the end of the age, it will be easier to tell the difference between the two, and the weeds will be destroyed." Satan has his people everywhere. I suspect there are false sheep in every Christian assembly. But we are told, by Jesus, that the gates of hell will not prevail against His church (Matthew 16:18).

Paul wrote about the evil that would come into the church.

I [Paul] know that after I leave, savage wolves will come in among you and will not spare the flock. Even from your own number men will arise and distort the truth in order to draw away disciples after them. So be on your guard! Remember that for three years I never stopped warning each of you night and day with tears. (Acts 20:29-31).

Some people in the Church may not really be Christians, while others are Christians but don't act like it. Either way, we should not impugn a holy God because of the failures of some of those who claim to be His followers.

I concluded that if I can't expect perfection in the people who are in the Kingdom of God, the Church, I have no right to expect perfection from the United States government and our justice system. I don't believe God is obligated to meet my unrealistic expectations about other people. I just needed to forgive the offenses and get over them. For me the concept was tremendously liberating. I was able to let go of most of my counterproductive feelings. I was treated unjustly, but so were Jesus and Paul.

Slaves, submit yourselves to your masters with all respect, not only to those who are good and considerate, but also to those who are harsh. For it is commendable if a man bears up under the pain of unjust suffering because he is conscious of God. But how is it to your credit if you receive a beating for doing wrong and endure it? But if you suffer for doing good and you endure it, this is commendable before God. To this you were called, because Christ suffered for you, leaving you an example that you should follow in his steps. (I Peter 2:18-21)

295

From this passage, it is clear to me that in an earthly sense, there is unjust suffering, but in a spiritual sense, there is no unjust suffering.

For men are not cast off by the Lord forever. Though he brings grief, he will show compassion, so great is his unfailing love. For he does not willingly bring affliction or grief to the children of men. (Lamentations 3:31-33)

But even if you should suffer for what is right, you are blessed. (I Peter 3:14a)

There is a reason for our suffering. It's part of the Lord's plan.

Our trials humble us.

Remember how the Lord your God led you [Israelites] all the way in the desert these forty years, to humble you and to test you in order to know what was in your heart, whether or not you would keep his commands. (Deuteronomy 8:2)

Our trials let us know that as individuals, we are not in charge of our own destinies.

Now listen, you who say, "Today or tomorrow we will go to this or that city, spend a year there, carry on business and make money." Why, you do not even know what will happen tomorrow. What is your life? You are a mist that appears for a little while and then vanishes. Instead you ought to say, "If it is the Lord's will, we will live and do this or that." As it is, you boast and brag. All such boasting is evil. (James 4:13-16)

Our trials show us a contrast between what is perishing and what is eternal.

Command those who are rich in this present world not to be arrogant nor to put their hope in wealth, which is so uncertain, but to put their hope in God, who richly provides us with everything for our enjoyment. (I Timothy 6:17)

Our trials test our faith.

I know, my God, that you test the heart and are pleased with integrity. (I Chronicles 29:17a)

The crucible for silver and the furnace for gold, but the Lord tests the heart. (Proverbs 17:3)

When we respond to affliction in a Christ-like manner, it authenticates our faith to ourselves and is a witness to those around us.

Examine yourselves to see whether you are in the faith; test yourselves. Do you not realize that Christ Jesus is in you – unless, of course, you fail the test. Now we pray to God that you will not do anything wrong. (II Corinthians 13:5-7a)

But even if you should suffer for what is right, you are blessed. "Do not fear what they fear; do not be frightened." But in your hearts set apart Christ as Lord. Always be prepared to give an answer to everyone who asks you to give the reason for the hope that you have. But do this with gentleness and respect, keeping a clear conscience, so that those who speak maliciously against your good behavior in Christ may be ashamed of their slander. (I Peter 3:14-16)

God uses our trials to teach us things we need to know. One of the things we need to learn is obedience.

Before I was afflicted, I went astray, but now I obey your [the Lord's] word. You are good, and what you do is good; teach me your decrees. Though the arrogant have smeared me with lies, I keep your precepts with all my heart. Their hearts are callous and unfeeling, but I delight in your law. It was good for me to be afflicted so that I might learn your decrees. The law from your mouth is more precious to me than thousands of pieces of silver and gold. Your hands made me and formed me; give me understanding to learn your commands. May those who fear you rejoice when they see me, for I have put my hope in your word. I know, O Lord, that your laws are righteous, and in faithfulness you have afflicted me. May your unfailing love be my comfort, according to your promise to your servant. (Psalm 119:67-76)

Our fathers disciplined us for a little while as they thought best; but God disciplines us for our good, that we may share in his holiness. No discipline seems pleasant at the time, but painful. Later on, however, it produces a harvest of righteousness and peace for those who have trained by it. (Hebrews 12:10, 11)

We need to learn self-control. One of the words I like, that I see in the media, is *unflappable*.

One time my wife and I went on a trip to Europe that was sponsored by The University of Tennessee Alumni Association. There were four couples from UT. In our larger group, there was good-sized contingent of people from the University of Mississippi. One day one of the ladies from Ole Miss started giving me a hard time about the University of Tennessee and the "Big Orange". I responded to her as follows: "I'll bet if you took a trip to Ole Miss, you would find some good people and some bad people; you would find some people who loved the Lord and some who thought the highest authority in the universe was the human intellect; you would find some people who thought individual initiative should be rewarded, and you would find some people who thought everyone deserved to have the same life style, regardless of his input into society. And if you went to UT, you would find some good people and some bad people; you would find some people who loved the Lord and some who thought the highest authority in the universe was the human intellect; you would find some people who thought individual initiative should be rewarded, and you would find some people who thought everyone deserved to have the same life style, regardless of his input into society." She gave me a strange look and said that she had never thought of it that way. I offer this illustration to affirm the fact that there are good and bad people in different geographical locations, in each of the professions, and in our legal system. There are people who care about the dignity of others and those who don't. I believe it is a fact of life, and we just need to get used to it and not be overcome by it. We need to accept it. When somebody does something we don't like, and it's something we have no power to change, the appropriate response is to submit to the situation and be obedient, do what God tells us to do. As noted previously in chapter eight, "The right attitude in real difficulty in unconditional acceptance and obedience." During our trials, may we all be able to say to the Lord as Mary did to the angel Gabriel when she was told she would be with child by the Holy Spirit, "I am the Lord's servant...May it be to me as you have said" (Luke 1:38). Whatever bad things happen to us, that we did not bring on ourselves, are things the Lord has decreed.

Consider these words in I Peter:

Do not repay evil with evil or insult with insult, but with blessing. (I Peter 3:9a)

298

When we feel we have been wronged by someone else, and it's something we can't change, we need to let go and let God do the judging; we need to turn it over to the Lord and let Him do what we cannot do.

Be still before the Lord and wait patiently for him; do not fret when men succeed in their ways, when they carry out their wicked schemes. Refrain from anger and turn from wrath; do not fret - it leads only to evil. For evil men will be cut off, but those who hope in the Lord will inherit the land. (Psalm 37:7-9)

The faithless will be fully repaid for their ways, and the good man rewarded for his. (Proverbs 14:14)

Be careful to do what is right in the eyes of everybody. If it is possible, as far as it depends on you, live at peace with everyone. Do not take revenge, my friends, but leave room for God's wrath, for it is written: "It is mine to avenge; I will repay," says the Lord. (Romans 17b-19)

One Christmas season, Dr. Mark E. Gaskins, our pastor at Smithwood Baptist Church, in Knoxville, TN, was speaking about the promises of advent. He quoted Isaiah 2:1-5 and said, "More than 2,700 years ago, Isaiah painted a picture of justice and peace among the nations that still resonates with the deepest longings of the human heart…But it's a vision that's far from fulfilled today, no matter how hard we've tried to make it happen…the reality of how things are seems to outweigh the snippets of hope about how things should be…[We have] a longing for that day when justice will prevail." Things are not as they should be, not just yet. The day of justice awaits Christ's second coming. We must wait for it, and while waiting, we must walk in the light of the Lord and walk in obedience to Christ. After Christ's return, He will sit on the throne of His father, David.

"But with righteousness he [the Lord] will judge the needy, with justice he will give decisions for the poor of the earth. He will strike the earth with the rod of his mouth; with the breath of his lips he will slay the wicked. Righteousness will be his belt and faithfulness the sash around his waist. (Isaiah 11:4, 5).

"The days are coming," declares the Lord, "when I will raise up to David a righteous branch, a King who will reign wisely and do what is just and right in the

299

land. In his days Judah will be saved and Israel will live in safety. This is the name by which he will be called: The Lord Our Righteousness. (Jeremiah 23:5, 6)

We need to be patient. The accounts have not been settled yet. God still has many outstanding debts on his balance sheet. We haven't seen the final conclusion of the matter. Eventually we will witness the justice of the Lord, for what is happening now and for what happens in the future.

For the Lord is righteous, he loves justice; upright men will see his face. (Psalm 11:7)

For he [God] has set a day when he will judge the world with justice by the man he has appointed [Jesus]. He has given proof of this to all men by raising him from the dead. (Acts 17:31)

All this [your faith, your love, your perseverance] is evidence that God's judgment is right, and as a result you will be counted worthy of the kingdom of God, for which you are suffering. God is just: He will pay back trouble to those who trouble you and give relief to you who are troubled, and to us as well. This will happen when the Lord Jesus is revealed from heaven in blazing fire with his powerful angels. He will punish those who do not know God and do not obey the gospel of our Lord Jesus. (II Thessalonians 1:5–8)

God's instructions on how to handle offenses and His promise of a payback to the offenders are signs that offenses are going to occur. Becoming angry when someone mistreats us makes about as much sense as living in Michigan and becoming angry when it snows. Offenses are something we should expect to happen. Jesus said,

In this world you will have trouble. But take heart! I have overcome the world. (John 16:33b)

Consider Paul's words in II Corinthians:

So we fix our eyes not on what is seen, but on what is unseen. For what is seen is temporary, but what is unseen is eternal. (II Corinthians 4:18)

We live by faith, not by sight. (II Corinthians 5:7)

When I was with the Army in Viet Nam, I became familiar with the concept of a secondary explosion. When an artillery round lands, the initial explosion is caused by the artillery round. If there is an immediate second explosion, it means the artillery round hit something that itself, also exploded, such as an ammunition cache. Part of the sanctification process is cleaning up our lives, getting rid of all that gunpowder or other explosives sitting around in our lives, waiting to be detonated.

Now I'm happy to say that, by God's grace, the rage about my courtroom experience is gone. I still get a little angry at times, but it is not uncontrollable. When I get angry, my focus is on a person or situation. At the time I feel angry emotions welling up inside of me, I think of Jesus, and those feelings dissipate. I've learned from personal experience that it's hard for me to continue to be angry about something from which I've profited spiritually. I rejoice in what God has taught me through my encounter with the legal system.

> **This book is my attempt to help people deal with anger, to help them prevent or control it. The information ministered to me.**

For those who have read the book and still have serious anger management issues, I would suggest reading an anger management book such as *The Everything Guide to Anger Management*, by Robert Puff and James Seghers **(4)** or taking an anger management course. Anger management protocols would have you sign an intention statement. They would expect you to develop an anger scale, such that you could plot when your anger occurred, how intense it was, what you did about it, and how it worked out for you. These measures may be very helpful, especially for people who already have Christ in their hearts.

In order to keep yourself from all that regimentation you might decide to submit, to forgive, and to accept your situation, to take care of what you need to do yourself, by the power of the Holy Spirit.

Doxology: To him who is able to keep you from falling and to present you before his glorious presence without fault and with great joy — to the only God our Savior be glory, majesty, power, authority, through Jesus Christ our Lord, before all ages, now and forevermore! Amen. (Jude 24, 25)

Appendix

The ways the Israelites Tested God during their Wilderness Wanderings

1. The Israelites did not remember the great things the Lord had already done for them.
2. The Israelites were not satisfied with the Lord's provision.
3. The Israelites lacked faith in God.
4. The Israelites became impatient.
5. The Israelites demanded what they wanted.
6. The Israelites spoke out against God.
7. The Israelites grumbled and were disobedient.
8. The Israelites quarreled with Moses.
9. The Israelites treated God with contempt.
10. The Israelites were stiff-necked.
11. The Israelites rejected the Lord.
12. The Israelites let their behavior get out of control.
13. The Israelites rebelled against the Lord.
14. The Israelites were guilty of idolatry.

Things Believers are to do According to Ephesians 4-6

1. Understand our identity in Christ.
2. Study the Scriptures.
3. Live a life worthy of our calling and be cooperative with God about our sanctification.
4. Love one another.
5. Be humble, gentle, patient, and kind, bearing with and forgiving one another.
6. Live in unity with fellow believers and be at peace with them.
7. Use individual spiritual gifts for service to others and build up one another in the faith.
8. Control our temper and our tongue.
9. In our hearts make music to the Lord, giving thanks for everything.

10. Submit to one another out of reverence for Christ.

11. Husbands love our wives, and wives submit to and respect their husbands.

12. Children obey their parents in the Lord.

13. Fathers bring up our children in the training and instruction of the Lord.

14. Obtain our strength from the Lord and His mighty power.

15. Take our stand against the devil with the weapons of truth, righteousness, and faith.

16. Be ready to defend our faith and to share it with others.

17. Be able to use the truth of God's word to combat error.

18. Be alert.

19. Pray in the Spirit on all occasions, and always keep on praying for all the saints.

20. Be active in sharing our faith.

When we Think we've been Treated Unfairly, there are Things we must not do, and There are Things we must do.

DON'T   Be presumptuous with God.
                 Have a sense of entitlement with God.
                 Charge God with wrongdoing.

DO   Keep the faith.
                 Humble yourself before the Lord.
                 Examine your life and repent of any known sin.
                 Seek the Lord.
                 Remember God's character.
                 Remember what God expects of you and what He has promised.
                 Submit to the reality of the things you cannot change.
                 Ask God for a right understanding of the issues involved.

Spiritual Blindness

1. For people without Christ, a veil covers their minds and hearts, preventing them from perceiving and understanding truth.
2. Willful sin leads to spiritual blindness.
3. For an individual, spiritual blindness may be purposeful.
4. Spiritual blindness may be unintended.
5. Spiritual blindness may be the result of multiple bad decisions and/or acts of carelessness, each one of more or less seriousness, having a cumulative effect over a period of time.
6. God wants to give us light so we can see and understand His truth and then share that truth with others.
7. We must be careful to whom we pay attention and to what we allow to influence us.
8. As we live our lives, and the more we cultivate our relationship with God, the better we understand His ways.

For Successful People in this Life, in some ways their Temptations are Similar to Solomon's.

1. The temptation to worship false idols (e.g. power, prestige, or pleasure).
2. The temptation to accumulate excessive wealth.
3. The temptation to maintain the accouterments or the trappings of the wealthy.
4. The temptation to indulge in sexual sin.
5. The temptation to become over-impressed with ourselves, leading to presumption, and at times, disobedience and willful decision.

Traits of the Believer that Accompany New Life in Christ:

1. Believers confess that Jesus is Lord.
2. Believers have God's Spirit in their hearts.
3. Believers love their brothers.
4. Believers turn from their sinful ways.

5. Believers obey Jesus' commands.
6. Believers persevere during life's difficulties.
7. Believers minister to other people's needs.
8. Believers continue in the faith.

Sanctification

1. God the Father chooses believers for salvation and sanctification.
2. Jesus Christ died on the cross to make provision for our sin debt. That payment was necessary for our justification, regeneration, and sanctification.
3. Sanctification is a work implemented by the Holy Spirit.
4. Believers are to be intentional about their sanctification.
5. God uses believers to provide mutual edification and sanctification for each other.
6. Progressive sanctification requires overcoming the world, the flesh [the sinful nature], and the devil.
7. God uses our difficult situations to discipline us, instruct us, to draw us to Himself.
8. Sanctification requires spending time with the Lord in Bible study and prayer.
9. Holiness is a necessary requirement if God is to hear our prayers.
10. Holiness allows us to know God's will.
11. Our sanctification is for the purpose of glorifying God.

Summary of the New Testament Commandments

1. The Bible commands us to believe in the name of God's Son, Jesus Christ.
2. We are commanded to love God and to love others.
3. God commands people to repent of sin.
4. We are commanded to obey our parents.
5. We are commanded to remember that Jesus is coming again, and we are to live holy and godly lives as we look forward to the day of His coming.
6. A wife must not separate from her husband, but if she does, she

must remain unmarried or be reconciled to her husband. A husband must not divorce his wife.

7. When believers come together for worship and mutual edification, they should be eager to prophesy, speak forth God's truth, but everything should be done in a fitting and orderly way.

8. Believers are commanded to keep away from every brother who is idle [disorderly].

9. We are commanded to not put our hope in wealth and to use what wealth we have to help others.

10. We are commanded to walk in the truth.

11. We are commanded to study the Bible and be able to discern truth from falsehood. We are to sit under pastors who teach accurately the truth of God's word. We are commanded not to teach false doctrine.

12. We are commanded to endure patiently.

13. God commands that the gospel of Jesus Christ be proclaimed to all nations, and we as believers, are commanded to share in that proclamation.

Summary of Reasons to Obey God

1. We are obedient because of guilt and fear of discipline and judgment.

2. We are obedient because we are thankful for our salvation and want to please God.

3. We are obedient because we have a responsibility to live the Christian life as it should be lived, to reflect God's nature in our lives. After making a profession of faith, we are not to profane His holy name by living ungodly lives.

4. We are obedient because God has made each of us a new creation. The Lord guides us, and He gives us the will and power to obey.

5. We are obedient because we desire the joy of the experience.

6. We are obedient because we care about the next generation.

7. We are obedient because we want to be used to bless others.

8. We are obedient in expectation of blessings in this life; they may be in the physical realm, or mental, or spiritual. I have learned that it

is hard for me to approach the throne of grace with confidence, so that I may receive mercy and find grace to help me in my time of need, if I have a guilty conscience. We are obedient so we can experience all that God has for us in this life. We are obedient because obedience gets us ready to do battle with the forces of evil. 9. We are obedient in expectation of rewards in the life hereafter.

A few Observations about God's Sovereignty and some Events during my Formative Years, especially those that Influenced me to Marry Barbara.

1. If I hadn't been so indecisive about a major during my time in college, I would not have been taking that particular first year Physics course and second year Calculus my fourth year in college and would never have met Barbara.

2. If Barbara had not had polio in the third grade and missed a year of school, I would never have met her; we would have had no classes together.

3. If Barbara had not had polio during her childhood and developed the deformity in her arms and hands, I likely would not have paid as much attention to her.

4. If it were not for the comments made by my two friends, I probably would never have dated her.

5. If Barbara had not been sitting in that car studying, there's a good chance I would never have asked her out. Spring quarter had started, and I had no more classes with her.

6. If my medical school classmate had not told me Barbara was in Memphis, we likely would not have gotten back together.

7. If I had not had the research job, I wouldn't have known the couple from the physiology department, and the lady would not have told me how much Barbara cared for me. I doubt my heart would have gone out to Barbara.

8. If Barbara had not been able to get the job in Memphis, we would likely have never married.

9. If we had stayed in Florence, my two sons would have a totally different experience growing up.

10. If it had not been for what I learned during my two previous practice experiences, I likely would not have done so well with starting my own practice.

I believe that before the foundation of the world, it was ordained that I would marry Barbara and be married to her for thirty-five years, that I would be her spousal caregiver for five years until she died of breast cancer, and that I would write a book about our experiences and about tribulation in general called *Finding Strength in Weakness - A Study of Tribulation and our Appropriate Response*. God has used that book to change many lives.

Jesus was Willing to Experience Life and Death on Earth so He could better Understand our Struggles, and so He could Overcome His own Struggles and be our Savior.

Consider some of the abuse Jesus tolerated:

While Jesus was in agony in the Garden of Gethsemane, His closest friends slept. Jesus was betrayed by Judas, a man who was in His inner circle. During the arrest in Gethsemane, Jesus' disciples deserted Him and fled. After making the statement that he would never fall away from Jesus, Peter denied Him three times. While on trial before the Sanhedrin, one of the officials struck Jesus in the face. The men who were guarding Jesus began mocking and beating Him. They spit in His face and struck Him with their fists. They made fun of Him. They blindfolded Him and demanded, "Prophesy! Who hit you?" and they said many other insulting things to Him. The whole assembly led Jesus off to Pilate. When Pilate learned Jesus was a Galilean, he sent Him to Herod Antipas. Herod and his soldiers ridiculed and mocked Jesus. Dressing Him in an elegant robe, they sent Him back to Pilate. The crowd demanded that Jesus be crucified. Pilate took Jesus and had Him flogged. The soldiers twisted together a crown of thorns and put it on his head. They clothed him in a purple robe and put a staff in His right hand. They ridiculed him. They spit on Him and took the staff and struck Him on the head again and again. They crucified Jesus. The crowd hurled insults at Jesus. The soldiers mocked Jesus.

There were times during His ministry when Jesus became angry such as when He cleansed the temple, but He did not become angry about the abuse He received during His arrest, trial, or crucifixion. It is apparent from the text that Jesus was looking at the situation from an eternal perspective.

During the Arrest, Trial and Crucifixion, the Words Jesus Spoke and when He was Silent.

At the time of the arrest:

"Rise, let us go! Here comes my betrayer!" (Matthew 26:46)

To Judas: "Friend, do what you came for…" (Matthew 26:50)

To Judas: "Judas, are you betraying the Son of Man with a kiss?" (Luke 22:48b)

To the detachment of soldiers and some officials from the chief priests and Pharisees: "Jesus, knowing all that was going to happen to him, went out and asked them, 'Who is it you want?' 'Jesus of Nazareth,' they replied." 'I am he,' Jesus said. (And Judas the traitor was standing there with them.) When Jesus said, 'I am he,' they drew back and fell to the ground. Again he asked them, 'Who is it you want?' And they said, 'Jesus of Nazareth.' 'I told you that I am he,' Jesus answered. 'If you are looking for me, then let these men go.' This happened so that the words he had spoken would be fulfilled: 'I have not lost one of those you gave me.'" (John 18:4-9)

To Peter after he cut off the ear of the high priest's servant: "Put your sword back in its place," Jesus said to him, "for all who draw the sword will die by the sword. Do you think I cannot call on my Father, and he will at once put at my disposal more than twelve legions of angels? But how then would the Scriptures be fulfilled that say it must happen in this way?" (Matthew 26:52-54)

Jesus commanded Peter, "Put your sword away! Shall I not drink the cup the Father has given me?" (John 18:11)

To the arresting party: "Am I leading a rebellion," said Jesus, "that you have come out with swords and clubs to capture me? Every day I was with you, teaching in the temple courts, and you did not arrest me. But the Scriptures must be fulfilled." (Mark 14:48, 49)

At the Trial before the Sanhedrin:

Meanwhile, the high priest questioned Jesus about his disciples and his teaching. "I have spoken openly to the world," Jesus replied. "I always taught in synagogues or at the temple, where all the Jews came together. I said nothing in secret. Why question me? Ask those who heard me. Surely they know what I said." When Jesus said this, one of the officials nearby struck him in the face. "Is this the way you answer the high priest?" he demanded. "If I said something wrong," Jesus replied, "testify as to what is wrong. But if I spoke the truth, why did you strike me?" (John 18:19-23)

At daybreak the council of the elders of the people, both the chief priests and the teachers of the law, met together, and Jesus was led before them. "If you are the Christ," they said, "tell us." Jesus answered, "If I tell you, you will not believe me, and if I asked you, you would not answer. But from now on, the Son of Man will be seated at the right hand of the mighty God." They all asked, "Are you then the Son of God?" He replied, "You are right in saying I am." (Luke 22:66-70)

At the Trial before Pilate:

Meanwhile Jesus stood before the governor [Pilate], and the governor asked him, "Are you the king of the Jews?" "Yes, it is as you say," Jesus replied. (Matthew 27:11)

The chief priests accused him of many things. So again Pilate asked him, "Aren't you going to answer? See how many things they are accusing you of." But Jesus still made no reply, and Pilate was amazed. (Mark 15:3-5)

Pilate then went back inside the palace, summoned Jesus and asked him, "Are you the king of the Jews?" "Is this your own idea," Jesus asked, "or did others talk to you about me?" "Am I a Jew?" Pilate replied. "It was your people and your chief priests who handed you over to me. What is it you have done?" Jesus said, "My kingdom is not of this world. If it were my servants would fight to prevent my arrest by the Jews. But now my kingdom is from another place." "You are a king, then!" said Pilate. Jesus answered, "You are right in saying I am a king. In fact, for this reason I was born, and for this I came into the world, to testify to the truth. Everyone on the side of truth listens to me." "What is truth?" Pilate asked. (John 18:33-38a)

The Jews insisted, "We have a law, and according to that law he must die, because he claimed to be the Son of God." When Pilate heard this, he was even more afraid, and he went back inside the palace. "Where do you come from?" he asked Jesus, but Jesus gave him no answer. "Do you refuse to speak to me?" Pilate said. "Don't you realize I have power either to free you or to crucify you?" Jesus answered, "You would have no power over me if it were not given to you from above. Therefore the one who handed me over to you is guilty of a greater sin." (John 19:7-11)

On the Way to Golgotha:

As they led him away, they seized Simon from Cyrene, who was on his way in from the country, and put the cross on him and made him carry it behind Jesus. A large number of women followed him, including women who mourned and wailed for him. Jesus turned and said to them, "Daughters of Jerusalem, do not weep for me; weep for yourselves and for your children. For the time will come when you will say, "Blessed are the barren women, the wombs that never bore and the breasts that never nursed!" Then they will say to the mountains, "Fall on us!" and to the hills, "Cover us!" For if men do these things when the tree is green, what will happen when it is dry? (Luke 23:26-31)

During the Crucifixion:

Jesus said, "Father forgive them, for they do not know what they are doing." (Luke 23:34a)

When we look at life from an eternal perspective, it helps us get our priorities straight.

Patience and Forbearance

1. Our patience and forbearance are powered by the Spirit of God.
2. Our patience and forbearance are evidence that we have a relationship with God.
3. Believers' patience and forbearance with each other promote unity in the Spirit.

4. Our patience and forbearance during times of affliction are part of our ministry.
5. Our patience and forbearance lead to blessings from God.
6. Patience and forbearance are required for us to receive our eternal reward.

Forgiving Others

The New Testament appeals to us to forgive others on several different levels.

1. We are encouraged to forgive on the basis of love. Ideally when we forgive, it should be spontaneous, not forced.
2. The debt that the other person owes us is insignificant compared with the debt we owe God.
3. Jesus said that if we do not forgive others, the Father will not forgive us:
4. If we do not forgive, it gives Satan a foothold in our lives.

The Bible gives us several ways we replace the bad information in our brains (in our hearts). It's all part of the process of learning to live in the Spirit.

1. Bible Study and Meditation.
2. Obedience.
3. Prayer.
4. Crucifying the sinful nature.
5. Keeping our minds and hearts on the things of the Spirit, rather than the things of the sinful nature.
6. Mutual edification in community.
7. Avoidance of alcohol and substance abuse and perhaps other addictive forms of behavior.
8. Living lives of humility and service to others.
   A. Focusing on the needs of others helps us develop humility and teaches us patience. It helps empty us of self.
   B. Focusing on the needs of others helps us learn submission.

God May Speak to us in Several Ways.

1. Through His Word.
2. By the Holy Spirit.
3. By what we hear from others.
4. By what He allows to happen to us.

Reasons to Control Anger

1. We control anger because anger is sin, a manifestation of our sinful nature.
2. We control anger because it leads to multiple physical complaints.
3. We control our anger over adverse circumstances because it shows a lack of trust in the character and justice of God.
4. We control anger because it separates us from God's power in our lives.
5. We control anger because it stunts our spiritual growth.
6. We control anger because it ensnares us and can get us off course; it can dominate our lives.
7. We control our anger because it affects the way we represent God to others. It may cause us to model bad habits for our families. In a professing Christian, an aggressive anger style profanes God's name.
8. We control anger because it affects our ability to think logically; it affects our judgment.
9. We control anger because it divides us from others.
10. We control anger because it may cause us to do things that have harmful effects, i.e. hurtful words, physical abuse, and/or murder. There can be untoward results for the perpetrator as well. The consequences may be long-standing.
11. We control anger because we are commanded to do so.
12. We control anger because it makes good sense to do so.
13. We control anger because anger invites God's judgment.

We control anger because it affects our ability to think logically; it clouds our judgment.

I've experienced times when my anger has spiraled out of control. My mouth got going, and I couldn't stop it. The word *rage* applies to anger that is uncontrolled. I was thinking about my anger one day and the following words came to mind.

1. When I'm angry, I'm less aware; I'm too preoccupied to be in communion with God.

2. When I'm angry, I'm not humble; my sinful nature is in control.

3. When I'm angry, I'm not teachable; my sinful nature is in control.

4. When I'm angry, I'm not submissive to God; my sinful nature is in control.

5. When I'm angry, I'm not obedient to God; my sinful nature is in control.

6. When I'm angry, I'm not trusting God; my sinful nature is in control.

7. When I'm angry, I'm not at peace; my sinful nature is in control.

8. When I exhibit rage, I'm not in control; my sinful nature is in control.

9. When I'm angry, I'm guilty of presuming too much in my own behalf and of rebelling against God.

Causative Factors Related to Anger

1. Our own folly.

2. Unmet emotional needs.

3. Lack of a father at home to provide needed male attention for the daughters and to control the aggressive tendencies of the sons.

4. Poor modeling of anger response by family members, especially parents.

5. Unresolved grief.

6. Emotional fatigue including stress produced by failure to set appropriate boundaries with others.

7. Physical illness or injury.

8. Pride.

9. Economic pressure.

10. Psychiatric Illness, including Personality Disorder, Posttraumatic Stress Disorder, and Paranoid Schizophrenia.

Understanding and Navigating the Anger Response as it Develops and then Subsides

Stage One – A Triggering Event
Stage Two - A Period of Increasing Intensity of Emotion
Stage Three - Responding to the Angry Feelings
Stage Four - A Cooling-down Period
Stage Five – The Aftermath

Some Guidelines for Relationships with Others and for Life's Uncertainties

1. Practice Volitional Love.
2. Learn to Forgive.
3. Live One Day at a Time.
4. Practice acceptance.
   - A. Accept others.
   - B. Accept challenging circumstances.
   - C. Accept the Difficulties of Life.
5. Set boundaries.
6. Avoid alcoholism and/or substance abuse.

Worden's Tasks of Mourning

1. To accept the reality of the loss—Talking about a loss often helps a person accept the reality of that loss. It may also be helpful for the mourner to visit places that remind him of his painful experiences.
2. To work through the pain of grief—Identifying and expressing feelings is therapeutic.
3. To adjust to an environment in which the deceased is missing. To emotionally relocate the deceased and move on with life.
4. To take the emotional energy tied up in what was lost and invest it in existing or new relationships.

Once there is a triggering event, and anger starts to build, we need to allow our reasoning to take over. There are several things that sometimes work for me. Of course, the power comes from the Holy Spirit.

1. I reflect on the relevant truths in God's word.
2. I remember similar issues I've resolved in the past.
3. I remind myself to accept things I can't change.

4. I resolve to forgive the offenders.
5. When necessary, I turn my stubborn resentment over to the Lord.
6. If a confrontation is necessary, I make up my mind to respond assertively rather than aggressively.

There is a Reason for our Suffering. It's Part of the Lord's Plan.

1. Our trials humble us.
2. Our trials let us know that as individuals, we are not in charge of our own destinies.
3. Our trials show us a contrast between what is perishing and what is eternal.
4. Our trials test our faith.
5. When we respond to affliction in a Christ-like manner, it authenticates our faith to ourselves and is a witness to those around us.
6. God uses our trials to teach us things we need to know. One of the things we need to learn is obedience.

Hebrew and Greek Vocabulary Words

The number keyed to *Strong's Exhaustive Concordance* is listed in parentheses.

Hebrew
Galeed – Witness heap; heap of testimony; a memorial cairn East of the Jordan. (1567)

halal – pollute, profane, any action that controverts God's planned order. (2490)

harah - to cause fire to burn; used in reference to anger; emphasizes the kindling of anger like the kindling of a fire; fret. (2734)

harap - casting blame or scorn on someone; imputing blame or guilt to someone in order to harm his character; disgrace, dishonor. (2778)

herpa - a derivative of *harap*, and basically carries the same meaning. (2781)

kabed – honor. (3513)

kapar – forgive, make an atonement, make reconciliation, purge. (3722)

kippur - Atonement. (3725)

leb - heart, mind, the inner part or middle of a thing; the meaning of the word in the individual verses depends on the context; in its abstract meanings, "heart" became the richest biblical term for the totality of man's inner or immaterial nature. (3820)

lebab – a word related to *leb*; can be used of the inner man, as contrasted to the outer man; often compounded with 'soul' for emphasis. (3824)

lun or lin – to stop (usually overnight) or to stay permanently, to be obstinate. (3885)

marah – bitter. (4785)

mashah – applying oil to the body, rubbing a shield with oil, or painting a house; ceremonial application of oil to the tabernacle, altar, or sin offering; pouring of oil from a horn on the head of someone being inducted into a leadership office. (4886)

massah - testing. (4531, 4532)

meribah – quarreling. (4808, 4809)

mizpah (mitzpah)– watchtower. (4707, 4708, 4709)

na' - despise, abhor. (5006)

nasa – to test or try or tempt; having a defiant attitude. (5254)

nasa - to lift up, to bear or carry or support, and to take or take away. (5375)

nepesh - soul, creature, person, appetite, mind; the word connotes the *inner man*, the *life* of an individual. (5315)

orep – stiffness, arrogance, recalcitrance, refractoriness. (6203)

qara - the root qr' denotes primarily the enunciation of a specific message. That message is customarily addressed to a specific recipient and is intended to elicit a specific response. It may refer to God's calling a person or a people to a specific task. It may also be used of people who cry out urgently to God for help; frequently, the context has to do with a critical or chronic need. (7121)

qasha – the subjective effect exerted by an overly heavy yoke or the rebellious resistance of oxen to the yoke; the stubborn (stiff-necked) subjects of the Lord. (7185)

ragaz – agitation growing out of some deeply rooted emotion; the term refers to the agitation itself, and the underlying emotion is to be recognized only from context; tremble, rage. (7264)

salah - forgive; refers to God's offer of pardon and forgiveness to the sinner. (5545)

suk - anointing the body with olive oil, especially for its fragrant effect. (5480)

yasar and musar (a derivative of yasar) - denote correction that results in education. God's corrective discipline seeks the reformation of His people. (3256)

za'am – indignation, intense anger (2194)

zal'apa – indignation, horror, raging heat (2152)

Greek
aganakteo - indignant, aroused, be angry at someone or at something (23)

agapao (a verb) - love (see *agape*). (25)

agape (a noun) – God's love is an exercise of the Divine will in deliberate choice, made without assignable cause save that which lies in the nature of God Himself; *agape* love, whether exercised toward the brethren, or toward men generally, is not an impulse from the feelings; it does not always run with the natural inclinations, nor does it spend itself only upon those for whom some affinity is discovered; *agape* love seeks the welfare of all. (26)

alleelon - one another; used when describing how we are to treat each other. (240)

anecho – put up with, endure, forbear, suffer. (430)

anoche – self-restraint, tolerance, forbearance. (463)

aphieemi – forgive, leave, let go, or send away. (863)

apoluo - set free, release, pardon, let go, send away, dismiss, divorce, forgive. (630)

ascheemoon - shameful, unpresentable, or indecent. (809)

ataktos - not in proper order, undisciplined, disorderly, or insubordinate. (814)

blaspheemeo - injuring the reputation of another, reviling, defaming, using abusive speech, or slandering. (987)

blaspheemia – vilification (especially against God), evil speaking. (988)

charizomai - give freely or graciously as a favor, remit, forgive, pardon. (5483)

chrio - anoint, confined to sacred and symbolic anointing. (5548)

dianoia – mind; a thinking through, or over; a meditation,

reflecting; the faculty of knowing, understanding, or moral reflection. (1271)

diatagma – that which is imposed by decree or law; stresses the concrete character of the commandment; a very authoritative word for command, but the word is only used once in the New Testament, in Hebrews 11:23, and then is used of a command from an earthly ruler. (1297)

diatasso – to set in order, appoint, command; to arrange or prescribe. (1299)

didomi - give, grant, or impose. (1325)

dikaiosunee – uprightness, justice, righteousness, the practice of piety, to do what is right. (1343)

ego – I - first person singular. (1473)

eimi – I am; *Ego eimi* carries more emphasis and is a name for God. *I myself am* is the equivalent of the Hebrew Yahweh. (1510)

eipon – the aorist tense of legoo, to speak, to say and sometimes has the meaning of commanding or bidding; see legoo. (3004)

elegcho - bring to light, expose, set forth, convict or convince someone of something, reprove, correct. (1651)

entalma – a commandment, a commission; used three times in the New Testament, and every time refers to the teachings of men. (1778)

entello - to enjoin upon, to charge with; used in the Middle Voice in the sense of commanding or giving a commandment; an alternate form is entellomai, *to order*; used for true commands including moral commands from God. (1781)

entellomai – see *entello*. (1781)

entolee – an injunction, charge, precept, or commandment; the most frequent term used for moral and religious commands; in line with what we think of when we hear about someone giving true moral commands, including those from God. (1785)

epieikeia – clemency, a disposition to be merciful and especially to moderate the severity of punishment due, gentleness. (1932)

epitagee – command, order, or injunction; word not often used in the New Testament, but is a very strong word, and stresses the authority of the person making the command. (2003)

epitasso – to appoint over, put in charge, to put upon one as a duty; to set or arrange over, to command, enjoin; epitasso seems to be more about following orders in a chain of command or in a hierarchy, rather than a moral command from a Holy God. (2004)

epithymia – passion; in a good sense, eager desire or great longing; in a bad sense, a desire for something forbidden. (1939)

epo - to order, direct, or command; to say, call, or name; probably invented as a present tense of *eipon*. (2036)

erethizo - arouse, provoke, embitter, rouse to anger or rouse to fight; challenge to a boxing match; incite to rivalry; chafe, irritate by rubbing or annoy. (2042)

hagiadzoo - to make holy, consecrate, sanctify, or purify. (37)

hagiasmos - holiness, consecration, or sanctification. (38)

hagios - dedicated to God, holy, or sacred. (40)

hamartanoo [hamartanete] – err, sin, offend, trespass (264)

hupomone – endurance, constancy, waiting, patience with regard to adverse things. (5281)

hupsoma – pretension, height, or exaltation; everything that sets itself up against the knowledge of God. (5313)

kai – and (2532)

kakia – depravity, wickedness, malice, ill-will, malicious behavior. (2549)

kardia - heart, the chief organ of physical life; came to stand for man's entire mental and moral activity [including the mind], both the rational and emotional elements. (2588)

katalalia - evil speech, slander, defamation, backbiting. (2636)

keleuo – to urge, incite, order, command; not used with moral commands. (2753)

kenodoxia – vainglory, vanity, conceit, ambition. (2754)

lambano - denotes either to take or receive. (2983)

legoo - speak, say, sometimes has the meaning of commanding or bidding. (3004)

logizomai - to reckon, calculate, or impute. It can be an accounting word carrying the idea of "place to one's account" or to credit. (3049)

logismos – argument, calculation, reasoning, reflection or thought; sophistry, (subtly deceptive reasoning). It can mean thoughts or sentiments. It can mean the (prejudiced) thoughts that occupy a person's mind or the designs of the heathen. (3053)

makrothumeo - have patience, wait, forbear, suffer long. (3114)

makrothumia – forbearance, longsuffering, steadfastness, endurance, patience with regard to antagonistic persons. (3115)

martyreoo - to bear witness (3140)

martyria – testimony (3141)

martyrion - that which serves as testimony or proof (3142)

martys – witness (3144)

mee – not (3361)

menoo – remain, stay, live, dwell, lodge, or remain in fellowship (3306)

metanoeoo – repent, feel remorse, be converted, change one's mind, make a change for the better; always, except in Luke 17:3, 4, of repentance from sin. (3340)

metanoia - repentance from sin or evil. (3341)

musteerion – refers to the secret thoughts, plans, and dispensations of God, hidden from human reason and from all other comprehension below the divine level; mysteries must be revealed to those for whom they are intended; they are too profound for human ingenuity. (3466)

napesh – breathe; passive, to be breathed upon, refreshed, life, self. (5314)

nepesh - life, soul, creature, person, appetite, mind; denotes the "inner man." (5315)

nous – mind; the seat of reflective consciousness, comprising the faculties of perception and understanding, and those of feeling, judging, and determining; denotes the faculty of knowing, the seat of understanding. (3563)

noeo or noieo – perceive. (3539)

ochuroma – stronghold, fortress, prison. (3794)

orgizesthe [from orgizoo] - be angry at someone because of something; be angry at or with someone. (3710)

paideia - upbringing, training, instruction, as it is attained by discipline or correction. (3809)

paideuo – train or instruct. (3811)

parakaleo - comfort, encourage, cheer up; call to one's side, summon to one's aid, or call upon for help. (3870)

parangellia – charge, commandment. (3852)

parangello – to pass on an announcement, give the word, order, give a charge, command; parangello seems to carry more moral weight than keleuo. (3853)

parazeeloo – provoke, fret; when used in the reflexive thought, provoke yourself. (3863)

parorgizo – irritate, provoke to anger. (3949)

periergazomai –do something unnecessary or useless; have undue anxiety about something; be a busybody; meddle in other people's matters. (4020)

pisteuo - to believe, to be persuaded of, and hence, to place confidence in, to trust – signifies, in this sense of the word, reliance upon, not mere credence. (4100)

prokaleo – provoke; to call forth, as to a contest, hence to stir up what is evil in another. (4292)

pronoeo – consider in advance, think or plan beforehand, provide for; by way of maintenance for others or circumspection for oneself. (4306)

pronoia – provision, foresight; includes the planning for crimes committed with design. (4307)

propheeteuo - proclaim a divine revelation, reveal what is hidden, foretell the future. (4395)

prostasso – to arrange or set in order towards; to prescribe, give command; appears to be a true command of solemn importance, but its uses in the New Testament do not appear to apply to present day believers. (4367)

puroo - set on fire, burn up; be inflamed with sympathy, burn with sexual desire; make red hot, cause to glow, or heat thoroughly - by such heating precious metals are tested and refined. (4448)

sarx – body, flesh, sinful nature (4561)

sophronismos - self-discipline; literally the word means "saving the mind." It is an admonishing or calling to soundness of mind, or to self-control; the word was used in secular Greek to denote the teaching of morality, good judgment, or moderation; advice, improvement. It has to do with prudence. (4995)

stauros – cross; metaphorically used of the renunciation of the world that characterizes the true Christian life; self-denial. (4716)

stauroo - signifies the act of crucifixion and is used metaphorically of the putting off of the flesh with its passions and lusts; to subdue passion or selfishness. (4717)

sustauroo – crucify with; used metaphorically of spiritual identification with Christ in His death. (4957)

Glossary of Terms

acceptance - a state of understanding a difficult situation without becoming agitated or anxious or fretful about it; acceptance does not mean approval or that a person condones what he is accepting; it means that he sees something and knows it for what it is, without feeling the need to take immediate action against it.

accouterment – an ancillary item of equipment or dress; military equipment other than uniforms and weapons; outward forms of recognition.

anger – a strong feeling of displeasure, usually with hostility or antagonism.

antichrist – someone who denies that Jesus is the Christ.

assurance of salvation – certainty that we have a relationship with Jesus Christ and that His power will keep us until the end, based on a present trust in Christ for salvation, evidence of a regenerating work of the Holy Spirit in the heart, and a long-term pattern of growth in the Christian life.

atonement – reconciliation between God and human beings, brought about by the life and death of Jesus.

believe - to be persuaded of, to place confidence in, to trust; reliance upon, not mere credence.

blood urea nitrogen – a laboratory value measured in the blood that rises in the presence of a decline in kidney function. It can be affected by many other factors such as dehydration and malnutrition.

born again – having experienced salvation, born from above, born spiritually as well as physically.

called – used of the Divine call to partake of the blessings of redemption; also used of the summons by God to a particular vocation or destination.

Cardiologist – a physician skilled in the diagnosis and treatment of heart disease.

circumcision – removal of all or part of the foreskin of the penis; a Jewish rite performed on male infants as a sign of inclusion in the Jewish religious community; the procedure was a strict requirement before a young man could have his bar mitzvah.

clemency - disposition to be merciful, to moderate the severity of punishment due; leniency, gentleness.

condemned – being under the judgment of God because of our sin; on our way to hell.

conversion - turning to God; it consists of two elements, repentance and faith.

convict – used of convicting of sin; to make aware of one's sinfulness or guilt, usually with the suggestion of putting the convicted person to shame.

Counselor – one who gives advice; a name for the Holy Spirit.

covenant – God's promise to the human race.

denial - people may deny what they perceive, think or feel in a traumatic situation, either saying something to the effect that it cannot be so, or else trying to invalidate something intolerable by deliberately ignoring its existence.

dialysis-induced arrhythmia – an abnormal heart rhythm that occurs during or at the end of hemodialysis.

discipline – upbringing, training, instruction; God's discipline of believers is primarily for our spiritual growth; correction that results in education.

emotion – a state of feeling; the affective aspect of consciousness.

empathy – the capacity for participation in another's feelings or ideas.

enjoin - direct or impose by authoritative order or with urgent admonition, to forbid or prohibit or to put an injunction on.

entitlement – a person having a sense that he/she should receive certain blessings because he/she deserves them.

entrepreneurial skills – describes a person who has the skills to organize, operate, and assume the risk for a business venture.

faith – being sure of what we hope for and certain of what we do not see; it's living by the principles we've reasoned out as true, even when our emotions would try to convince us otherwise.

flesh – the sinful nature; in Paul's thought especially, the flesh is the willing instrument of sin and is subject to sin to such a degree that wherever flesh is, all forms of sin are likewise present.

forbearance - a refraining from the enforcement of something as a debt, right, or obligation that is due; leniency; tolerance and restraint in the face of provocation.

forgive – to give up resentment or of a claim to requital for an insult; to grant relief from payment of a debt.

fundamental attribution error – the tendency to explain the behavior of people we don't know very well as due to their personality traits while overemphasizing situational factors as determining any aberrant behavior exhibited by ourselves.

glorified – to make glorious by bestowing honor, praise or admiration; to elevate to celestial glory.

grace - unmerited divine assistance given man for his regeneration or sanctification.

hemodialysis – renal replacement therapy by which removal of waste, correction of electrolytes, and adjustment of total body water is brought about by infusing the patient's blood through an artificial kidney.

holiness, holy – the state of being separated or set apart to God with the conduct befitting those so separated; purity.

indignation – anger aroused by something unjust, mean, or unworthy.

judgment – the formation of an opinion after consideration or deliberation; discernment; God's determination of which human beings shall be sent to heaven and which condemned to hell.

justification – the act of freeing a person from the guilt and penalty attached to grievous sin.

longsuffering – self-restraint in the face of provocation which does not hastily retaliate or promptly punish; it is associated with mercy.

malice - depravity or wickedness; ill-will, malignity, trouble, or misfortune; a desire to harm others or see others suffer.

malnutrition – any disorder of nutrition especially due to an insufficient diet or inability to eat.

Nephrologist – a medical physician skilled in the diagnosis and treatment of kidney disease.

Nephrology – a subspecialty of Internal Medicine that deals with the diagnosis and treatment of kidney disease and hypertension.

ordain – to invest officially, as by the laying on of hands, with ministerial or priestly authority; to establish or order by appointment or decree.

paranoid schizophrenia - a subtype of schizophrenia in which the patient has delusions (false beliefs) that a person or some individuals are plotting against them or members of their family; they may also have auditory hallucinations, hearing things that are not real, or delusions of personal grandeur; they may spend a disproportionate amount of time thinking up ways of protecting themselves from their persecutors.

passion – suffering; the emotions as distinguished from reason; intense, driving, or overmastering feeling; an outbreak of anger; ardent affection; a strong liking for or devotion to some activity, object, or concept.

patience – calmness, self-control, the willingness or ability to tolerate delay; the capacity to endure hardship, difficulty, or inconvenience without complaint.

peritoneal dialysis – renal replacement therapy that is brought about by infusing fluid into and out of the peritoneal cavity through a peritoneal catheter. The peritoneal cavity is a potential space between the abdominal wall and the intra-abdominal organs lined by the peritoneal membrane which serves as the dialyzing membrane.

peritonitis – acute inflammation of the peritoneal membrane usually brought about by infection.

perseverance – steadfastness, fortitude, or endurance in a difficult situation; keeping on keeping on in spite of hardship, weariness, or discouragement.

personality disorder - an enduring pattern of inner experience and behavior that deviates markedly from the expectations of the individual's culture, is pervasive and inflexible, has an onset in adolescence or early adulthood, is stable over time, and leads to distress or impairment.

posttraumatic stress disorder – a condition that may develop after a person is exposed to one or more traumatic events, such as major stress, sexual assault, terrorism, or other threats on a person's life. The diagnosis may be given when a group of symptoms, such as disturbing recurring flashbacks, avoidance or numbing of memories of the event, and hyperarousal continue for more than a month after the occurrence of a traumatic event.

Praetermission [pretermission] - to disregard intentionally or allow to pass unnoticed or unmentioned.

predestined – having been chosen by God to be saved.

presumption – a manifestation of pride; present in a person who presumes too much in his own favor; characterized by arrogant or offensive behavior or language.

prevenient grace – antecedent or anticipatory grace; man can of himself neither turn to God, nor repent, nor believe; the only thing prevenient grace enables him to do is to call upon God to turn him.

prima donna – a temperamental, conceited person.

profane – to treat something sacred with abuse, irreverence, or contempt; to debase by wrong, unworthy, or vulgar use.

provision – something provided; think of or plan beforehand; foresight or care.

psychiatrist – a physician who specializes in the branch of medicine which deals with the study, treatment, and prevention of mental illness.
psychologist – a qualified specialist in that branch of science that deals with the mind and mental processes, especially in relation to human and animal behavior.

ransom – the release of property or a person in return for payment of a demanded price; a redemption from sin and its consequences.

rationalization - justification of otherwise unacceptable, ego-alien thought, feeling or action, through the misuse and distortion of facts; a common device in everyday life where people explain away their own defects, failures and misdeeds, as well as those of persons they love and admire; a subconscious mental mechanism when someone does something for one reason but convinces himself he is doing it for another, more socially acceptable reason.

reasoning – using evidence or arguments to form conclusions, inferences, or judgments.

reconciliation – overcoming our separation from God; Jesus provided our reconciliation to bring us back into fellowship with God.

redeem – to buy out, especially of purchasing a slave with a view to his freedom; used metaphorically of delivery by Christ, of believers, from the law and its curse.

redemption – salvation from sin through Jesus' sacrifice; Jesus Christ ransomed us to release us from bondage to sin.

repentance – remorse or contrition for past conduct or sin; to change one's mind or purpose, in the New Testament always involving a change for the better.

regeneration – spiritual or moral revival or rebirth; God the Father and God the Holy Spirit working powerfully in us, to make us alive.

resentment – a feeling of indignant displeasure or persistent ill-will at something regarded as wrong, insult, or injury.

revelation – a dramatic disclosure of something not previously known.

righteous indignation - a form of anger, said to be an emotional reaction to something that is wrongful, unjust, or evil.

righteousness – character or quality of being right or just; *the righteousness of God* means essentially the same as His faithfulness or truthfulness, that which is consistent with His own nature and promises; whatever is right or just in itself; whatever conforms to the revealed will of God.

sacrifice – the act of offering something to a deity in propitiation or homage, especially the ritual slaughter of an animal or a person; a victim offered in this way.

salvation – deliverance from the power or penalty of sin; redemption.

sanctification - the process of being made holy; Scripture mentions three aspects of our sanctification: (1) the initial sanctification occurring at the time of our salvation, (2) the gradual process of sanctification occurring as we live our lives as believers, and (3) the final or complete sanctification, occurring simultaneously with our resurrection; the righteousness we are granted at the time of our salvation is positional; it is an imputed righteousness; the Greek verb for impute means to reckon or calculate. It can be an accounting word carrying the idea of "place to one's account" or to credit; the Lord's gradual process of making us holy, here on earth, is the natural extension of the initial salvation He provides; it is a part of the application of redemption that is a progressive work and continues throughout our earthly lives; it is also a work in which God and man cooperate, each playing distinct roles; the process makes us more and more free from sin and more like Christ in our actual lives; the final sanctification, which will occur at believers' resurrection, will make our sanctification complete.

secondary explosion - when an artillery round lands, the initial explosion is caused by the artillery round. If there is an immediate second explosion, it means the artillery round hit something that itself, also exploded, such as an ammunition cache.

Septuagint – a pre-Christian Greek version of the Jewish Scriptures translated around 200 B. C.

serum albumin – the major protein in the blood. It can be adversely affected by malnutrition or inflammation.

serum phosphorus – a nonmetallic, allotropic element that can be measured in the blood. In patients with kidney disease it is usually elevated due to abnormalities in vitamin D and parathyroid hormone metabolism. When very low, it can be an indicator of malnutrition.

serum potassium – a metallic element that can be measured in the blood. Most of the body's potassium is in the intracellular compartment. When serum potassium is low, it can predispose to cardiac arrhythmias. When serum potassium is high, it can predispose to cardiac standstill.

sin - any failure to conform to the moral law of God in act, attitude, or nature; includes not only individual acts such as stealing or lying or committing murder, but also attitudes that are contrary to the attitudes God requires of us.

slander - injuring the reputation of, reviling, defaming, using abusive speech.

sophistry - a deceptively subtle reasoning or argumentation.

Sovereignty of God – God possesses all power and is the ruler of all things; God rules and works according to His eternal purpose; God rules in human history according to His purpose, from ordinary events in the lives of individuals to the rise, affairs, and fall of nations; God takes the initiative in the provision and application of salvation and in enabling man's willing acceptance.

tabernacle – the portable sanctuary in which the Jews carried the Ark of the Covenant through the desert, a copy of a sanctuary in heaven.

testimony – a declaration by a witness under oath; a public declaration regarding a religious experience.

testing – a putting to proof; God tests the heart with trials in our lives and is pleased when we have a response that demonstrates integrity.

transformation – changed in form, whether an outwardly visible change, such as when Jesus Christ was transfigured, perhaps on Mount Hermon, or when we are changed in a way invisible to the naked eye, for example when God changes our wicked hearts.

tribulation - pressing or pressure; oppression, affliction; distress that is brought about by outward or difficult circumstances; affliction in the spiritual sense embraces the ideas of trouble and anguish of heart.

unregenerate man – unenlightened man; man without God is spiritually blind; his darkened heart has learned ways of living and dealing with life that are ungodly and counterproductive.

unresolved grief – the intensification of grief to the level where the person is overwhelmed, resorts to maladaptive behavior, or remains interminably in the state of grief without progression of the mourning process towards completion.

volitional – doing something because of the act of making a decision to do so.

Endnotes

Introduction

Chapter 1 Testing God

1. William MacDonald, *The Believer's Bible Commentary—Old Testament* (Nashville: Thomas Nelson Publishers, 1992), 183.
2. R. Laird Harris, Gleason L. Archer, Jr., Bruce K. Waltke, *Theological Wordbook of the Old Testament* (Chicago: Moody Press, 1980), 581.
3. James Strong, *The Exhaustive Concordance of the Bible* (Nashville: Abingdon Press, 1890), Hebrew and Chaldee Dictionary Accompanying The Exhaustive Concordance, 59.
4. R. Laird Harris, Gleason L. Archer, Jr., Bruce K. Waltke, *Theological Wordbook of the Old Testament* (Chicago: Moody Press, 1980), 475.
5. Ibid., 818
6. Ibid., 698.

Chapter 2 Satanic Strongholds

1. Walter Bauer, William F. Arndt, F. Wilbur Gingrich, *A Greek—English Lexicon of the New Testament* (Chicago: The University of Chicago Press, 1957), 606.
2. Ibid., 830, 831.
3. Ibid., 477, 478.
4. Ibid., 478.
5. *Webster's New Collegiate Dictionary 150th Anniversary Edition* (Springfield, MA: G. & C. Merriam Company, 1981) 1101.
6. Walter Bauer, William F. Arndt, F. Wilbur Gingrich, *A Greek—English Lexicon of the New Testament* (Chicago: The University of Chicago Press, 1957), 858.

7. *Letters Addressed to Christians in Affliction* (Glasgow: M. Ogle, 1817), 91, 92.

8. R. Laird Harris, Gleason L. Archer, Jr., Bruce K. Waltke, *Theological Wordbook of the Old Testament* (Chicago: Moody Press, 1980), 239.

9. Ibid., 973, 974.

10. Walter Bauer, William F. Arndt, F. Wilbur Gingrich, *A Greek—English Lexicon of the New Testament* (Chicago: The University of Chicago Press, 1957), 854.

Chapter 3 Spiritual Blindness

1. Walter Bauer, William F. Arndt, F. Wilbur Gingrich, *A Greek—English Lexicon of the New Testament* (Chicago: The University of Chicago Press, 1957), 248, 249.

2. John MacArthur, *The MacArthur Study Bible* (Nashville: Thomas Nelson, 1997), 1551.

3. Ibid, 1425.

4. William MacDonald, *The Believer's Bible Commentary—New Testament* (Nashville: Thomas Nelson Publishers, 1990), 254.

Chapter 4 Having a Relationship with God

1. *Webster's New Collegiate Dictionary 150th Anniversary Edition* (Springfield, Massachusetts: G. & C. Merriam Company, 1981) 494.

2. Henry Clarence Thiessen, *Introductory Lectures in Systematic Theology* (Grand Rapids: Wm. B. Eerdmans, 1949) 352.

3. W. E. Vine, *A Comprehensive Dictionary of the Original Greek Words with their Precise Meanings for English Readers* (McLean, Virginia: MacDonald Publishing Company), 118.

4. Wayne Grudem, *Systematic Theology* (Grand Rapids: Zondervan, 1994), 803-806.

5. Barry M. Brenner, Brenner & Rector's *The Kidney* (Philadelphia: Saunders, 1996).

6. Wayne Grudem, *Systematic Theology* (Grand Rapids: Zondervan, 1994), 806.

7. Walter Bauer, William F. Arndt, F. Wilbur Gingrich, *A Greek—English Lexicon of the New Testament* (Chicago: The University of Chicago Press, 1957), 476, 477.

8. Chad Brand, Charles Draper, Archie England, *Holman Illustrated Bible Dictionary* (Nashville: Holman Reference, 2003), 812.

9. Wayne Grudem, *Systematic Theology* (Grand Rapids: Zondervan, 1994), 748.

10. Ibid., 753.

11. Ibid., 756.

12. George V. Wigram, *The Englishman's Greek Concordance of the New Testament* (Peabody, Massachusetts: Hendrickson Publishers, Second Printing - 1998) 6-8.

13. Ibid., 505.

14. Henry George Liddell, Robert Scott, *A Greek-English Lexicon* (Oxford: Clarendon Press, 1996), 1144.

15. Walter Bauer, William F. Arndt, F. Wilbur Gingrich, *A Greek—English Lexicon of the New Testament* (Chicago: The University of Chicago Press, 1957) 529.

16. W. E. Vine, *A Comprehensive Dictionary of the Original Greek Words with their Precise Meanings for English Readers* (McLean, Virginia: MacDonald Publishing Company), 822.

17. *Holman Illustrated Bible Dictionary* (Nashville, TN: Holman Bible Publishers, 2003), 1223.

18. Walter Bauer, William F. Arndt, F. Wilbur Gingrich, *A Greek—English Lexicon of the New Testament* (Chicago: The University of Chicago Press, 1957), 38.

19. Ibid., 608.

20. W. E. Vine, *A Comprehensive Dictionary of the Original Greek Words with their Precise Meanings for English Readers* (McLean, Virginia: MacDonald Publishing Company), 318.

21. Walter Bauer, William F. Arndt, F. Wilbur Gingrich, *A Greek—English Lexicon of the New Testament* (Chicago: The University of Chicago Press, 1957), 809.

22. R. Laird Harris, Gleason L. Archer, Jr., Bruce K. Waltke, *Theological Wordbook of the Old Testament* (Chicago: Moody Press,

1980), 386, 387.

Chapter 5 Things that Disrupt our Relationship with God

1. R. Laird Harris, Gleason L. Archer, Jr., Bruce K. Waltke, *Theological Wordbook of the Old Testament* (Chicago: Moody Press, 1980), 530.
2. W. E. Vine, *A Comprehensive Dictionary of the Original Greek Words with their Precise Meanings for English Readers* (McLean, Virginia: MacDonald Publishing Company), 60, 61.
3. R. Laird Harris, Gleason L. Archer, Jr., Bruce K. Waltke, *Theological Wordbook of the Old Testament* (Chicago: Moody Press, 1980), 619.
4. Walter Bauer, William F. Arndt, F. Wilbur Gingrich, *A Greek—English Lexicon of the New Testament* (Chicago: The University of Chicago Press, 1957), 504, 505.
5. John MacArthur, *The MacArthur Study Bible* (Nashville: Thomas Nelson, 1997), 1044.
6. R. Laird Harris, Gleason L. Archer, Jr., Bruce K. Waltke, *Theological Wordbook of the Old Testament* (Chicago: Moody Press, 1980), 810.
7. John MacArthur, *The MacArthur Study Bible* (Nashville: Thomas Nelson, 1997), 1930.
8. Ibid., 1746.
9. Henry Clarence Thiessen, *Introductory Lectures in Systematic Theology* (Grand Rapids: Wm. B. Eerdmans, 1949) 399.
10. John MacArthur, *The MacArthur Study Bible* (Nashville: Thomas Nelson, 1997), 1527.
11. *The American Heritage College Dictionary* (New York: Houghton Miffin Company, 1993), 1102.
12. R. Laird Harris, Gleason L. Archer, Jr., Bruce K. Waltke, *Theological Wordbook of the Old Testament* (Chicago: Moody Press, 1980), 289.
13. Ibid., 543.
14. Ibid., 325, 326.

15. Ibid.

Chapter 6 The New Testament Commandments

1. David Jeremiah, *The Jeremiah Study Bible* (Brentwood, TN: Worthy Publishing, 2013) 1641.
2. Wayne Grudem, *Systematic Theology* (Grand Rapids: Zondervan, 1994), 700.
3. W. E. Vine, *A Comprehensive Dictionary of the Original Greek Words with their Precise Meanings for English Readers* (McLean, Virginia: MacDonald Publishing Company), 211, 212.
4. Ibid., 211.
5. Ibid., 70.
6. Walter Bauer, William F. Arndt, F. Wilbur Gingrich, *A Greek— English Lexicon of the New Testament* (Chicago: The University of Chicago Press, 1957), 188.
7. John MacArthur, *The MacArthur Study Bible* (Nashville: Thomas Nelson, 1997), 1738.
8. Ibid., 1739.
9. George V. Wigram, *The Englishman's Greek Concordance of the New Testament* (Peabody, Massachusetts: Hendrickson Publishers, Second Printing - 1998) 148.
10. W. E. Vine, *A Comprehensive Dictionary of the Original Greek Words with their Precise Meanings for English Readers* (McLean, Virginia: MacDonald Publishing Company), 211.
11. Henry George Liddell, Robert Scott, *A Greek-English Lexicon* (Oxford: Clarendon Press, 1996), 678.
12. W. E. Vine, *A Comprehensive Dictionary of the Original Greek Words with their Precise Meanings for English Readers* (McLean, Virginia: MacDonald Publishing Company), 127.
13. Walter Bauer, William F. Arndt, F. Wilbur Gingrich, *A Greek— English Lexicon of the New Testament* (Chicago: The University of Chicago Press, 1957), 225.
14. George V. Wigram, *The Englishman's Greek Concordance of the New Testament* (Peabody, Massachusetts: Hendrickson Publishers,

Second Printing - 1998) 291-298.

15. Ibid.

16. W. E. Vine, *A Comprehensive Dictionary of the Original Greek Words with their Precise Meanings for English Readers* (McLean, Virginia: MacDonald Publishing Company), 211.

17. Ibid., 184.

18. *Webster's New Collegiate Dictionary 150th Anniversary Edition* (Springfield, MA: G. & C. Merriam Company, 1981), 375.

19. Ibid.

20. Walter Bauer, William F. Arndt, F. Wilbur Gingrich, *A Greek—English Lexicon of the New Testament* (Chicago: The University of Chicago Press, 1957), 267.

21. George V. Wigram, *The Englishman's Greek Concordance of the New Testament* (Peabody, Massachusetts: Hendrickson Publishers, Second Printing - 1998) 263.

22. W. E. Vine, *A Comprehensive Dictionary of the Original Greek Words with their Precise Meanings for English Readers* (McLean, Virginia: MacDonald Publishing Company), 211.

23. Ibid., 371.

24. *American Heritage College Dictionary* (New York: Houghton Miffin, 1993) 457.

25. Walter Bauer, William F. Arndt, F. Wilbur Gingrich, *A Greek—English Lexicon of the New Testament* (Chicago: The University of Chicago Press, 1957), 302.

26. George V. Wigram, *The Englishman's Greek Concordance of the New Testament* (Peabody, Massachusetts: Hendrickson Publishers, Second Printing - 1998) 288.

27. W. E. Vine, *A Comprehensive Dictionary of the Original Greek Words with their Precise Meanings for English Readers* (McLean, Virginia: MacDonald Publishing Company), 211.

28. Walter Bauer, William F. Arndt, F. Wilbur Gingrich, *A Greek—English Lexicon of the New Testament* (Chicago: The University of Chicago Press, 1957), 428.

29. George V. Wigram, *The Englishman's Greek Concordance of the New Testament* (Peabody, Massachusetts: Hendrickson Publishers,

Second Printing - 1998) 420.

30. W. E. Vine, *A Comprehensive Dictionary of the Original Greek Words with their Precise Meanings for English Readers* (McLean, Virginia: MacDonald Publishing Company), 211.

31. Walter Bauer, William F. Arndt, F. Wilbur Gingrich, *A Greek—English Lexicon of the New Testament* (Chicago: The University of Chicago Press, 1957), 618.

32. George V. Wigram, *The Englishman's Greek Concordance of the New Testament* (Peabody, Massachusetts: Hendrickson Publishers, Second Printing - 1998) 588.

33. W. E. Vine, A *Comprehensive Dictionary of the Original Greek Words with their Precise Meanings for English Readers* (McLean, Virginia: MacDonald Publishing Company), 212.

34. Walter Bauer, William F. Arndt, F. Wilbur Gingrich, *A Greek—English Lexicon of the New Testament* (Chicago: The University of Chicago Press, 1957), 725.

35. John MacArthur, *The MacArthur Study Bible* (Nashville: Thomas Nelson, 1997), 1460.

36. George V. Wigram, *The Englishman's Greek Concordance of the New Testament* (Peabody, Massachusetts: Hendrickson Publishers, Second Printing - 1998) 666.

37. W. E. Vine, *A Comprehensive Dictionary of the Original Greek Words with their Precise Meanings for English Readers* (McLean, Virginia: MacDonald Publishing Company), 212.

38. Walter Bauer, William F. Arndt, F. Wilbur Gingrich, *A Greek—English Lexicon of the New Testament* (Chicago: The University of Chicago Press, 1957), 188.

39. George V. Wigram, *The Englishman's Greek Concordance of the New Testament* (Peabody, Massachusetts: Hendrickson Publishers, Second Printing - 1998) 148.

40. W. E. Vine, *A Comprehensive Dictionary of the Original Greek Words with their Precise Meanings for English Readers* (McLean, Virginia: MacDonald Publishing Company), 212.

41. Walter Bauer, William F. Arndt, F. Wilbur Gingrich, *A Greek—English* Lexicon of the New Testament (Chicago: The University of

Chicago Press, 1957), 268.

42. George V. Wigram, *The Englishman's Greek Concordance of the New Testament* (Peabody, Massachusetts: Hendrickson Publishers, Second Printing - 1998) 263, 264.

43. W. E. Vine, *A Comprehensive Dictionary of the Original Greek Words with their Precise Meanings for English Readers* (McLean, Virginia: MacDonald Publishing Company), 212.

44. Walter Bauer, William F. Arndt, F. Wilbur Gingrich, *A Greek—English Lexicon of the New Testament* (Chicago: The University of Chicago Press, 1957), 267.

45. George V. Wigram, *The Englishman's Greek Concordance of the New Testament* (Peabody, Massachusetts: Hendrickson Publishers, Second Printing - 1998) 263.

46. W. E. Vine, *A Comprehensive Dictionary of the Original Greek Words with their Precise Meanings for English Readers* (McLean, Virginia: MacDonald Publishing Company), 212.

47. Walter Bauer, William F. Arndt, F. Wilbur Gingrich, *A Greek—English Lexicon of the New Testament* (Chicago: The University of Chicago Press, 1957), 302.

48. George V. Wigram, *The Englishman's Greek Concordance of the New Testament* (Peabody, Massachusetts: Hendrickson Publishers, Second Printing - 1998) 288.

49. Walter Bauer, William F. Arndt, F. Wilbur Gingrich, *A Greek—English Lexicon of the New Testament* (Chicago: The University of Chicago Press, 1957), 191, 192.

50. John MacArthur, *The MacArthur Study Bible* (Nashville: Thomas Nelson, 1997), 1957.

51. Ibid., 1965.

52. Walter Bauer, William F. Arndt, F. Wilbur Gingrich, *A Greek—English Lexicon of the New Testament* (Chicago: The University of Chicago Press, 1957), 730.

53. Ibid., 119.

54. Ibid., 652.

55. William MacDonald, *The Believer's Bible Commentary—New Testament* (Nashville: Thomas Nelson Publishers, 1990), 874.

56. W. E. Vine, *A Comprehensive Dictionary of the Original Greek Words with their Precise Meanings for English Readers* (McLean, Virginia: MacDonald Publishing Company), 936.

57. William MacDonald, *The Believer's Bible Commentary—Old Testament* (Nashville: Thomas Nelson Publishers, 1992), 975.

58. John MacArthur, *The MacArthur Study Bible* (Nashville: Thomas Nelson, 1997), 1031.

Chapter 7 Reasons to Obey God

1. Francis Brown, *The New Brown—Driver—Briggs—Gesenius Hebrew and English Lexicon* (Peabody, Massachusetts: Hendrickson Publishers, 1979), 320.

2. R. Laird Harris, Gleason L. Archer, Jr., Bruce K. Waltke, *Theological Wordbook of the Old Testament* (Chicago: Moody Press, 1980), 289.

3. W. E. Vine, *A Comprehensive Dictionary of the Original Greek Words with their Precise Meanings for English Readers* (MacLean, Virginia: MacDonald Publishing Company), 903.

4. Walter Bauer, William F. Arndt, F. Wilbur Gingrich, *A Greek—English Lexicon of the New Testament* (Chicago: The University of Chicago Press, 1957), 531, 532.

Chapter 8 God's Sovereignty

1. William D. Black, *Finding Strength in Weakness - A Study of Tribulation and our Appropriate Response* (Enumclaw, Washington: Winepress Publishing, 2001, 2006, 2009).

2. Walter Bauer, William F. Arndt, F. Wilbur Gingrich, *A Greek—English Lexicon of the New Testament* (Chicago: The University of Chicago Press, 1957), 817.

3. W. E. Vine, *A Comprehensive Dictionary of the Original Greek Words with their Precise Meanings for English Readers* (McLean, Virginia: MacDonald Publishing Company), 1248.

4. Walter Bauer, William F. Arndt, F. Wilbur Gingrich, *A Greek—English Lexicon of the New Testament* (Chicago: The University of

Chicago Press, 1957), 493, 494.

Chapter 9 Recognizing Anger as Sin

1. *The American Heritage College Dictionary* (New York: Houghton Miffin Company, 1993), 51.

2. James Strong, *A Concise Dictionary of the Words in The Hebrew Bible* (New York: Abingdon-Cokesbury, 1890), Strong #7264, 107.

3. R. Laird Harris, Gleason L. Archer, Jr., Bruce K. Waltke, *Theological Wordbook of the Old Testament* (Chicago: Moody Press, 1980), 830, 831.

4. C. H. Spurgeon, *The Treasury of David* (Nashville, TN: Thomas Nelson), 34.

5. Lancelot C. L. Brenton, *The Septuagint with Apocrypha: Greek and English* (Peabody, MA: Hendrickson, 1851), 700.

6. Brooke Foss Westcott, Fenton John Anthony, *The New Testament in the Original Greek* (New York: MacMillan, 1957), 434.

7. Walter Bauer, William F. Arndt, F. Wilbur Gingrich, *A Greek—English Lexicon of the New Testament* (Chicago: The University of Chicago Press, 1957), 583.

8. W. E. Vine, *A Comprehensive Dictionary of the Original Greek Words with their Precise Meanings for English Readers* (McLean, Virginia: MacDonald Publishing Company), 58.

9. H. E. Dana, Julius R. Mantey, *A Manuel Grammar of the Greek New Testament* (Toronto: Macmillan, 1955), 156.

10. Ibid., 157.

11. Ibid.

12. Ibid., 158.

13. Curtis Vaughn, *The Word – The Bible from 26 Translations* (Gulfport, MS: Mathis Publishers, 1993) 2374.

14. R. Laird Harris, Gleason L. Archer, Jr., Bruce K. Waltke, *Theological Wordbook of the Old Testament* (Chicago: Moody Press, 1980), 831.

15. Norman Cameron, *Personality Development & Psychopathology* (Boston: Houghton Miffin, 1963), 239.

16. Ibid., 243.

17. F. LaGard Smith, *The Narrated Bible in Chronological Order* (Eugene, OR: Harvest House, 1984), 1369.

18. Edward Reese, *The Reese Chronological Bible* (Minneapolis: Bethany House, 1977), 1363.

19. Francis Brown, *The New Brown – Driver – Briggs – Gesenius Hebrew and English Lexicon* (Peabody, MA: Hendrickson, 1979), 273.

20. R. Laird Harris, Gleason L. Archer, Jr., Bruce K. Waltke, *Theological Wordbook of the Old Testament* (Chicago: Moody Press, 1980), 247.

21. John MacArthur, *The MacArthur Study Bible* (Nashville: Thomas Nelson, 1997), 1786.

22. Walter Bauer, William F. Arndt, F. Wilbur Gingrich, *A Greek—English Lexicon of the New Testament* (Chicago: The University of Chicago Press, 1957), 4.

23. Ibid., 750-752.

24. Wayne Grudem, *Systematic Theology* (Grand Rapids: Zondervan, 1994), 490.

25. Walter Bauer, William F. Arndt, F. Wilbur Gingrich, *A Greek—English Lexicon of the New Testament* (Chicago: The University of Chicago Press, 1957), 397.

26. *The American Heritage College Dictionary* (New York: Houghton Miffin Company, 1993), 820.

27. Walter Bauer, William F. Arndt, F. Wilbur Gingrich, *A Greek—English Lexicon of the New Testament* (Chicago: The University of Chicago Press, 1957), 142.

28. Ibid., 413.

29. Ibid.

30. Ibid., 489.

31. *Webster's New Collegiate Dictionary 150th Anniversary Edition* (Springfield, Massachusetts: G. & C. Merriam Company, 1981) 444.

32. *The American Heritage College Dictionary* (New York: Houghton Miffin Company, 1993), 531.

33. Walter Bauer, William F. Arndt, F. Wilbur Gingrich, *A Greek—English Lexicon of the New Testament* (Chicago: The University of

Chicago Press, 1957), 489.

34. W. E. Vine, *A Comprehensive Dictionary of the Original Greek Words with their Precise Meanings for English Readers* (McLean, Virginia: MacDonald Publishing Company), 456, 457.

35. R. Laird Harris, Gleason L. Archer, Jr., Bruce K. Waltke, *Theological Wordbook of the Old Testament* (Chicago: Moody Press, 1980), 452, 453.

36. Ibid., 453.

37. Ibid., 600, 601.

38. Ibid., 601.

39. Ibid., 626.

40. Walter Bauer, William F. Arndt, F. Wilbur Gingrich, *A Greek—English Lexicon of the New Testament* (Chicago: The University of Chicago Press, 1957), 125, 126.

41. George V. Wigram, *The Englishman's Greek Concordance of the New Testament* (Peabody, Massachusetts: Hendrickson Publishers, Second Printing - 1998) 97.

42. Ibid.

43. Walter Bauer, William F. Arndt, F. Wilbur Gingrich, *A Greek—English Lexicon of the New Testament* (Chicago: The University of Chicago Press, 1957), 884.

44. Ibid., 95, 96.

45. W. E. Vine, *A Comprehensive Dictionary of the Original Greek Words with their Precise Meanings for English Readers* (MacLean, Virginia: MacDonald Publishing Company), 463.

46. Edward Goodrick, John R. Kohlenberger III, *The NIV Exhaustive Concordance* (Grand Rapids: Zondervan, 1990), 1686.

Chapter 10 Overcoming the Sins of the Flesh

1. C. S. Lewis: *Mere Christianity* (New York: Harper One), 138, 139.

2. Ibid., 140.

3. Ibid., 140, 141.

4. Ibid., 141.

5. Ibid., 142, 146, 147.

6. Ibid., 147, 148.

7. Ibid., 148, 149.

8. Ibid., 149.

9. *Webster's New Collegiate Dictionary 150th Anniversary Edition* (Springfield, Massachusetts: G.&C. Merriam Company, 1981) 831.

10. Ibid.

11. Walter Bauer, William F. Arndt, F. Wilbur Gingrich, *A Greek— English Lexicon of the New Testament* (Chicago: The University of Chicago Press, 1957), 607, 608.

12. Edwin Hatch, Henry A. Redpath, *A Concordance to the Septuagint* (Grand Rapids: Baker Book House, 1987), 1045.

13. Lancelot C. L. Brenton, *The Septuagint With Apocrypha: Greek and English* (Peabody, MA: Hendrickson Publishers, 1992), Preface.

14. Walter Bauer, William F. Arndt, F. Wilbur Gingrich, *A Greek— English Lexicon of the New Testament* (Chicago: The University of Chicago Press, 1957), 738.

15. Ibid., 293.

16. Shad Helmstetter, *What To Say When You Talk To Your Self* (New York: Pocket Books, 1982), 36-40.

17. W. E. Vine, *Vine's Complete Expository Dictionary of Old and New Testament Words* (Nashville: Thomas Nelson, 1996), Old Testament Section, 108.

18. Ibid.

19. Ibid.

20. R. Laird Harris, Gleason L. Archer, Jr., Bruce K. Waltke, *Theological Wordbook of the Old Testament* (Chicago: Moody Press, 1980), 466

21. *Hebrew to English Index – Lexicon of the Old Testament in the NIV Exhaustive Concordance* (Grand Rapids: Zondervan, 1990), 1499, 1500.

22. W. E. Vine, *Vine's Complete Expository Dictionary of Old and New Testament Words* (Nashville: Thomas Nelson, 1996), Old Testament Section, 108.

23. Ibid.

24. R. Laird Harris, Gleason L. Archer, Jr., Bruce K. Waltke,

Theological Wordbook of the Old Testament (Chicago: Moody Press, 1980), 587-591.

25. Walter Bauer, William F. Arndt, F. Wilbur Gingrich, *A Greek—English Lexicon of the New Testament* (Chicago: The University of Chicago Press, 1957), 901.

26. W. E. Vine, *A Comprehensive Dictionary of the Original Greek Words with their Precise Meanings for English Readers* (MacLean, Virginia: MacDonald Publishing Company), 751.

27. Ibid.

28. Ibid., 546, 547.

29. William MacDonald, *The Believer's Bible Commentary—New Testament* (Nashville: Thomas Nelson Publishers, 1990), 516.

30. Bauer, William F. Arndt, F. Wilbur Gingrich, *A Greek—English Lexicon of the New Testament* (Chicago: The University of Chicago Press, 1957), 195.

31. Ibid., 9.

32. Ibid., 513.

33. W. E. Vine, *A Comprehensive Dictionary of the Original Greek Words with their Precise Meanings for English Readers* (MacLean, Virginia: MacDonald Publishing Company), 961, 962.

34. Ibid., 962.

35. Ibid., 963.

36. R. Laird Harris, Gleason L. Archer, Jr., Bruce K. Waltke, *Theological Wordbook of the Old Testament* (Chicago: Moody Press, 1980), 495.

37. Walter Bauer, William F. Arndt, F. Wilbur Gingrich, *A Greek—English Lexicon of the New Testament* (Chicago: The University of Chicago Press, 1957), 504.

38. W. E. Vine, *A Comprehensive Dictionary of the Original Greek Words with their Precise Meanings for English Readers* (MacLean, Virginia: MacDonald Publishing Company), 259.

39. *Webster's New Collegiate Dictionary 150th Anniversary Edition* (Springfield, Massachusetts: G. & C. Merriam Company, 1981) 921.

40. Walter Bauer, William F. Arndt, F. Wilbur Gingrich, *A Greek—English Lexicon of the New Testament* (Chicago: The University of

Chicago Press, 1957), 715.

41. Henry George Liddell, Robert Scott, *A Greek-English Lexicon* (Oxford: Clarendon Press, 1996), 1491.

42. Ibid., 1490.

43. Walter Bauer, William F. Arndt, F. Wilbur Gingrich, *A Greek—English Lexicon of the New Testament* (Chicago: The University of Chicago Press, 1957), 622.

44. J. William Worden, *Grief Counseling and Grief Therapy* (New York: Springer Publishing, 1991) 42-47.

45. *Holman Illustrated Bible Dictionary* (Nashville, TN: Holman Bible Publishers, 2003), 1094.

46. John MacArthur, *The MacArthur Study Bible* (Nashville: Thomas Nelson Bibles, 1997) 994.

47. David Jeremiah, *The Jeremiah Study Bible*, NKJV (Franklin, TN: Worthy Publishing, 2013) 830.

48. *Alcohol Alert*, National Institute on Alcohol Abuse and Alcoholism. U.S. Department of Health and Human Services, No. 38, October 1997, Updated October 2000.

49. Ibid.,

50. Vernon E. Johnson, *I'll Quit Tomorrow – A Practical Guide to Alcoholism Treatment* (New York: Harper-Collins Publishers, 1980), 19.

51. Ibid., 35.

52. Ibid., 44.

53. Timothy Keller, with Kathy Keller, *The Meaning of Marriage* (New York: Riverhead Books, 2011), 47.

54. W. E. Vine, *A Comprehensive Dictionary of the Original Greek Words with their Precise Meanings for English Readers* (MacLean, Virginia: MacDonald Publishing Company), 903.

55. Billy Graham, *The Holy Spirit* (Dallas: Word Publishing, 1988), 157.

56. Ibid., 158.

57. Ibid., 159.

58. Ibid., 162.

59. Ibid., 163.

60. John MacArthur, *The MacArthur Study Bible* (Nashville: Thomas Nelson Bibles, 1997) 898.

61. Ibid., 1768.

62. W. E. Vine, *A Comprehensive Dictionary of the Original Greek Words with their Precise Meanings for English Readers* (MacLean, Virginia: MacDonald Publishing Company), 1171.

63. John MacArthur, *The MacArthur Study Bible* (Nashville: Thomas Nelson Bibles, 1997) 1768.

64. Ibid.

65. Walter Bauer, William F. Arndt, F. Wilbur Gingrich, *A Greek— English Lexicon of the New Testament*) Chicago: The University of Chicago Press, 1957), 513

66. John MacArthur, *The MacArthur Study Bible* (Nashville: Thomas Nelson Bibles, 1997) 1769.

Chapter 11 Anger Management

1. Joseph Mercola, *Risk for Heart Attack or Stroke Increases After Anger Outburst* (Meercola.com, March 20, 2014).

2. W. B. Stevens, Arr. By J. R. Baxter, Jr. *New Songs of Inspiration* Volume Twelve compiled by W. Elmo Mercer (Grand Rapids: Stamps – Baxter Music of the Zondervan Corporation, 1965), Hymn #167.

3. William MacDonald, *The Believer's Bible Commentary—New Testament* (Nashville: Thomas Nelson Publishers, 1990), 1039.

4. John MacArthur, *The MacArthur Study Bible* (Nashville: Thomas Nelson Bibles, 1997) 681, 682.

5. William MacDonald, *The Believer's Bible Commentary—Old Testament* (Nashville: Thomas Nelson Publishers, 1992), 188.

6. W. E. Vine, *A Comprehensive Dictionary of the Original Greek Words with their Precise Meanings for English Readers* (MacLean, Virginia: MacDonald Publishing Company), 910.

7. R. Laird Harris, Gleason L. Archer, Jr., Bruce K. Waltke, *Theological Wordbook of the Old Testament* (Chicago: Moody Press, 1980), 509, 510.

8. John MacArthur, *The MacArthur Study Bible* (Nashville: Thomas Nelson Bibles, 1997) 1814.

9. Tony Dungy, *Uncommon* (Carol Stream, IL: Tyndale House, 2009), 52.

10. James Dobson, *Bringing up Boys* (Carol Stream, IL: Tyndale House, 2001), 55, 56, 60.

11. Walter Bauer, William F. Arndt, F. Wilbur Gingrich, *A Greek-English Lexicon of the New Testament* (Chicago: The University of Chicago Press, 1957), 635.

12. Henry George Liddell, Robert Scott, *A Greek-English Lexicon* (Oxford: Clarendon Press, 1996), 1343.

13. Walter Bauer, William F. Arndt, F. Wilbur Gingrich, *A Greek-English Lexicon of the New Testament* (Chicago: The University of Chicago Press, 1957), 308.

14. Henry George Liddell, Robert Scott, *A Greek-English Lexicon* (Oxford: Clarendon Press, 1996), 684.

15. J. William Worden, *Grief Counseling and Grief Therapy* (New York: Springer Publishing Company, 1991), 21.

16. Ibid., 70.

17. Ibid., 1.

18. Ibid., 10-18.

19. *Diagnostic and Statistical Manual of Mental Disorders* – DSM – 5 (Washington, D.C.: American Psychiatric Publishing, 2013), 670.

20. Ibid., 645.

21. Ibid., 646.

22. Ibid., 649.

23. R. Laird Harris, Gleason L. Archer, Jr., Bruce K. Waltke, *Theological Wordbook of the Old Testament* (Chicago: Moody Press, 1980), 322.

24. Lancelot C. L. Brenton, *The Septuagint with Apocrypha: Greek and English* (Peabody, MA: Hendrickson Publishers, 1851), 719.

25. George V. Wigram, *The Englishman's Greek Concordance of the New Testament* (Peabody, MA: Hendrickson Publishers, 1998), 590.

26. R. Laird Harris, Gleason L. Archer, Jr., Bruce K. Waltke, *Theological Wordbook of the Old Testament* (Chicago: Moody Press, 1980), 845.

27. Robert Puff, James Seghers, *The Everything Guide to Anger Management* (Avon MA: Adams Media, 2014), 38, 39.

28. W. E. Vine, *A Comprehensive Dictionary of the Original Greek Words with their Precise Meanings for English Readers* (MacLean, Virginia: MacDonald Publishing Company), 702, 703.

29. James D. Mallory, Jr., *The Kink & I* (Wheaton, Victor Books, 1965).

30. John MacArthur, *The MacArthur Study Bible* (Nashville: Thomas Nelson Bibles, 1997) 1949.

31. R. Laird Harris, Gleason L. Archer, Jr., Bruce K. Waltke, *Theological Wordbook of the Old Testament* (Chicago: Moody Press, 1980), 479.

32. Walter Bauer, William F. Arndt, F. Wilbur Gingrich, *A Greek-English Lexicon of the New Testament* (Chicago: The University of Chicago Press, 1957), 428.

33. John MacArthur, *The MacArthur Study Bible* (Nashville: Thomas Nelson Bibles, 1997), 1822.

34. William MacDonald, *The Believer's Bible Commentary—Old Testament* (Nashville: Thomas Nelson Publishers, 1992), 912-914.

35. *The World Book Encyclopedia* (Chicago: World Book, Inc., 1983) T volume 19, 191.

36. Ibid., 192.

37. Francis Weston Sears, Mark W. Zemansky, *University Physics* (Reading, MA: Addison Wesley Publishing Company, 1955) 341.

38. *The American Heritage College Dictionary* (New York: Houghton Mifflin Company, 1993), 460.

Chapter 12 Conclusion

1. Richard Ingrams, *Muggeridge—The Biography* (New York: Harper Collins Publishers, 1995).

2. Malcolm Muggeridge, *Something Beautiful for God—Mother*

Teresa of Calcutta (New York: Walker and Company, 1971).

3. Harold J. Sala, *Joyfully Single in a Couple's World* (Camp Hill, Pennsylvania, 1998), 24.

4. Robert Puff, James Seghers, *The Everything Guide to Anger Management* (Avon, MA: Adams Media, 2014).

Personal Contact and Book Information

Dr. Black may be reached by email at: **ckwdblack@att.net**

Dr. Black's book may be purchased online at several various sites, e.g. Amazon.com, BarnesandNobel.com, Buybooks.com and others.